Marine Mammals and Fisheries

Marine Mammals and Fisheries

Edited by
J. R. BEDDINGTON
R. J. H. BEVERTON
and D. M. LAVIGNE

London
GEORGE ALLEN & UNWIN
Boston   Sydney

George Allen & Unwin (Publishers) Ltd,
40 Museum Street, London WC1A 1LU, UK

George Allen & Unwin (Publishers) Ltd,
Park Lane, Hemel Hempstead, Herts HP2 4TE, UK

Allen & Unwin Inc.,
8 Winchester Place, Winchester, Mass. 01890, USA

George Allen & Unwin Australia Pty Ltd,
8 Napier Street, North Sydney, NSW 2060, Australia

First published in 1985

British Library Cataloguing in Publication Data

Marine mammals and fisheries.
1. Fisheries   2. Marine mammals—Food
I. Beddington, J.   II. Beverton, R. J. H.
III. Lavigne, D. M.
639.2   SH331
ISBN 0–04–639003–0

Library of Congress Cataloging in Publication Data

Main entry under title:
Marine mammals and fisheries.
Bibliography: p.
Includes index.
1. Marine mammals.   2. Fisheries—Environmental
aspects.   3. Fishery management.   I. Beddington, J. R.
II. Beverton, R. J. H.   III. Lavigne, D. M.
QL713.2.M35   1985   333.95′9   85-6008
ISBN 0-04-639003-0

Set in 9 on 11 point Times by
Mathematical Composition Setters Ltd, Salisbury, UK
and printed in Great Britain by Mackays of Chatham

Foreword

This book had its origins in the Marine Mammals Project launched in 1973 by the Food and Agriculture Organization of the United Nations (FAO) and the newly formed United Nations Development Programme (UNEP). This project had as its focus a Scientific Consultation on Conservation and Management of Marine Mammals, held in Bergen, Norway, in 1976. (The proceedings of the Consultation have been published by the FAO in four volumes under the title *Mammals in the seas.*)

The International Union for the Conservation of Nature and Natural Resources (IUCN) was involved in the FAO/UNEP project from an early stage. It followed up some of the recommendations from Bergen, establishing a Committee on Marine Mammals which brought together competence from its Specialist Groups on whales and dolphins, on seals, on sirenians (manatees and the dugong) and on otters.

In this period the IUCN Species Survival Commission (SSC), under whose wing the Committee on Marine Mammals nestled, was grappling with another set of problems closely related to those presented by interactions between various types of marine mammals and fisheries operations and resources. These problems arose from the effects of locally abundant mammals – mainly terrestrial species – on their habitats and on human activities in and around those habitats. Such problems were becoming particularly sharp in places where wild habitat was being restricted in extent and where previously depleted mammals were increasing under protection. Thus it happened that the SSC, led at that time by its founder, Sir Peter Scott, undertook two parallel investigations. So this book is in a sense complementary to the one that resulted from the study of locally abundant mammals (*Problems in management of locally abundant wild mammals*, Ed. P. A. Jewell and S. J. Holt, London, Academic Press, 1981). A theme common to these is the scientific examination of increasingly frequent proposals for the 'culling' of mammals in – supposedly – their own interests, or to ameliorate or avoid their perceived interference with human interests.

A Workshop on Marine Mammal/Fishery Interactions was convened in La Jolla, California, from 30 March to 2 April, 1981 (report available from IUCN, Avenue du Mont Blanc, 1196-Gland, Switzerland).

Revised versions of several of the scientific papers considered by the workshop are included in this book. Other chapters are papers written since the workshop in response to issues that were identified at it. Neither the workshop nor the book deal with problems involving all the groups of marine mammals. In particular, the special problems associated with the herbivorous sirenians and with the polar bear are excluded; they have been examined elsewhere. Similarly, the workshop was not concerned with the 'local nuisance' aspect of interactions of marine mammals with fishing, for example by damage to nets. And, lastly, little attention was given to what has since become a matter of growing and worldwide concern. This is the entanglement and massive incidental kill of marine mammals, as well as other vulnerable – and in many cases threatened – species, such as marine turtles and seabirds, in operational and abandoned fishing nets constructed from tough, non-biodegradable fibres.

These exclusions left, nevertheless, a hard core of difficult ecological problems centred on the relations between the populations of marine mammals and their food resources, some of which are of direct interest to humans, as fishery resources. The workshop did not 'solve' those problems, nor was it expected to do so. But the report from it, together with this book, do provide an up-to-date review of what, in a few cases, we think we now know about these ecological problems, and of what we do not yet know. Thus they give some general guidance to those whose responsibility it is to take practical steps in response to public concern – from many sides and points of view – about perceived or presumed interactions, and they point the way to the kinds of scientific research that are now needed.

It is worth quoting remarks with which the report of the La Jolla workshop ends. The first was a question: Is the concern of IUCN and other bodies, about the seriousness of the conflict, actual and potential, between marine mammals and fisheries, justified? The answer given was 'yes, despite the frequent lack of conclusive evidence'. But instances that have caused the greatest public uproar so far may not be the most important ones. And this is true not only of possible harmful effects of the animals on fisheries, but equally of the threat to the mammals posed by actions taken with the aim of stabilizing or reducing their numbers.

The final remark in the report is this: 'The juxtaposition between a perceived threat, on the one hand to a food resource and dependent livelihoods, and on the other to the protection of a highly prized wildlife population and perhaps other dependent livelihoods, is a conflict of interest which science cannot resolve. Some form of compromise will be needed, based on a mutual recognition and understanding of respective positions'. The task of scientists, as such, is to offer the best impartial guidance to the interested parties that is possible on the basis of existing knowledge. Perhaps more often than not, in the present state of affairs, existing knowledge will be far from adequate for this task. And scientists, being human, will sometimes take sides in particular controversies. They may have, too, a tendency to bolster their advice with barely concealed guesses and assumptions, and thus conceal the full extent of their ignorance. Experience has shown that the public needs to be vigilant in this respect, as with all authoritative pronouncements. Those who find themselves directly responsible for decisions that affect marine mammals and fisheries will have to decide how they are going to take uncertainties into account. Scientific advice could, if they seek it, also contribute to that decision, by elaborating the possible consequences, in both long and short term, of various available options. That is possibly the topic of a further investigation. For the moment this book marks where we now are. The contributors and editors are to be congratulated on having sucessfully focused much experience and great skill on a matter of worldwide concern.

Sidney Holt

Preface and acknowledgements

Interaction between marine mammals and fisheries is becoming an increasingly significant factor in the formulation of policy on the conservation and management of both kinds of resources. It is also proving of particular interest to those concerned with the scientific problems of predator–prey dynamics.

This book brings together accounts of some of the best studied of marine mammal/fisheries interactions. It may be regarded as a sequel to the scientific workshop on this subject held at La Jolla, California in 1981, under the auspices of the International Union for the Conservation of Nature (IUCN). Some of the chapters are more substantive accounts of findings which were submitted in shorter or provisional forms to that workshop; others have been specially written for this book. The coverage of the subject does not aim to be comprehensive but is fairly representative of the range of problems that arise in this complex but fascinating topic, and of the extent and limitation of our present knowledge about them.

The editors would like to acknowledge the financial support for preparing and convening the Marine Mammal/Fishery Interactions Workshop. This came from the World Wildlife Fund and UNEP (via IUCN), from the People's Trust for Endangered Species (PTES) and from the International Fund for Animal Welfare (IFAW). It is appropriate to express here appreciation not only of the generosity of those organisations but also of their recognition that their diverse interests would be served by an as far as possible dispassionate scientific review of issues which currently arouse strong emotions in those persons who are in one way or another directly involved.

In the production of the book a number of individuals were particularly helpful and we would like to acknowledge here the assistance of Sue Mitchinson, Simon Northridge and Jhansi Steel.

J. R. Beddington
R. J. H. Beverton
D. M. Lavigne

Contents

Tables

Contributors

Allen, Robin, L., Fisheries Research Division, MAF, Wellington, New Zealand

Beddington, J. R., Marine Resource Assessment Group, Centre for Environmental Technology, Imperial College, 48 Prince's Gardens, LONDON SW7, UK

Beverton, R. J. H., Dept Applied Biology, UWIST, King Edward VII Avenue, CARDIFF, CFI 3XF, UK

Bigg, Michael A., Department of Fisheries and Oceans, Fisheries Research Branch, Pacific Biological Station, Nanaimo, British Columbia V9R 5K6, Canada

Bowen, W. D., Marine Fish Division, Department of Fisheries and Oceans, P. O. Box 1006, Dartmouth, N. S. Canada B2Y 4A2

Clark, Colin W., Department of Mathematics, University of British Columbia, 2075 Westbrook Mall, Vancouver B.C., Canada

Coe, J. M., National Marine Fisheries Service, North West and Alaska Fisheries Centre, 7600 Sand Point Way NE, Seattle, Washington 98115, USA

de la Mare, W. K., Department of Biology, University of York, Heslington, York, YO1 5DD, UK

DeMaster, D., National Marine Fisheries Service, South West Fisheries Center, P.O. Box 271, La Jolla CA 92038, USA

Estes, James A., US Fish and Wildlife Service, Center for Marine Studies, University of California, Santa Cruz, California 95064, USA

Fawcett, Ian, Department of Fisheries and Oceans, Fisheries Research Branch, Pacific Biological Station, Nanaimo, British Columbia V9R 5K6, Canada

Frost, Kathryn J., Alaska Department of Fish and Game, Fairbanks, Alaska 99701, USA

Greenwood, J. J. D., Department of Biological Sciences, The University, Dundee DD1 4HN, UK

Haar, Robert T., Center for Quantitative Science, University of Washington, Seattle, Washington 98195, USA

Harwood, John, Natural Environment Research Council, Sea Mammal Research Unit, c/o British Antarctic Survey, Madingley Road, Cambridge, UK

Henderson, J. R., National Marine Fisheries Service, Honolulu Laboratory, P.O. Box 3830, Honolulu, HI 96812, USA

Hiby, A. R., Natural Environment Research Council, Sea Mammal Research Unit, c/o British Antarctic Survey, Madingley Road, Cambridge, UK

Innes, S., Department of Zoology, University of Guelph, Guelph, Ontario N1G 2W1, Canada

Kajimura, Hiroshi, National Marine Mammal Laboratory, Northwest and Alaska Fisheries Center, National Marine Fisheries Service, National Oceanic and Atmospheric Administration, 7600 Sand Point Way NE, Seattle, Washington 98115, USA

Kasuya, T., Far Seas Fisheries Research Laboratory, 5-7-1 Orido, Shimizu, Shizuoka, Japan

Lavigne, D. M., Department of Zoology, University of Guelph, Guelph, Ontario N1G 2W1, Canada

Lowry, Lloyd F., Alaska Department of Fish and Game, Fairbanks, Alaska 99701, USA

Miller, D., California Department of Fish and Game, 2201 Garden Road, Monterey, CA 93940, USA

Murie, D. J., Department of Biology, University of Victoria, Victoria, B. C. Canada V8W 2Y2

Pascal, M., Laboratoire de Faune Sauvage et Cynegetique, INRA CNRZ, 78 350 Jouy en Josas, France

Perez, Michael A., National Marine Mammal Laboratory, Northwest and Alaska Fisheries Center, National Marine Fisheries Service, National Oceanic and Atmospheric Administration, 7600 Sand Point Way NE, Seattle, Washington 98115, USA

Shaughnessy, P. D., CSIRO, P.O. Box 225, Dickson, ACT 2602, Australia

Stewart, R. E. A., Department of Fisheries and Oceans, Western Region, Freshwater Institute, 501 University Crescent, Winnipeg, Manitoba R3T 2N5, Canada

Swartzman, Gordon L., Center for Quantitative Science, University of Washington, Seattle, Washington 98195, USA

VanBlaricom, Glenn R., US Fish and Wildlife Service, P.O. Box 67, San Simeon, California 95234, USA

Worthy, G. A. J., Department of Zoology, University of Guelph, Guelph, Ontario N1G 2W1, Canada

Yablokov, Alexey, Institute of Developmental Biology, USSR

Management problems

1 Analysis of marine mammal-fisheries interaction

R. J. H. Beverton

The nature and origin of the problem

The term 'marine mammal' as used in this book refers to those mammals that spend all or the greater part of their life cycle in the marine environment. The two main groups comprise the cetaceans (whales, dolphins and porpoises, typically inhabitants of the open ocean) and pinnipeds (seals, sea-lions and walruses, typically with littoral or coastal habitats). Certain other mammals also qualify as 'marine' by the above definition, but only one – the sea-otter – is of major significance in the present context.

As a group, marine mammals are remarkably ubiquitous. Although most successful in the higher latitudes, they have colonised virtually every marine habitat that offers the essentials of food and breeding facilities. Although a few are specialised feeders – baleen whales and crab-eater seals on krill, walruses on clams, and sea-otters on a variety of invertebrates – marine mammals are typically large, powerful, intelligent carnivores feeding opportunistically on those marine organisms large and plentiful enough for the purpose – fish and squid.

Marine mammals therefore constitute an integral part of the marine ecosystem (See Ch. 6), usually as top predators. It is to be expected that as fisheries science grapples with the problems of the interaction between fish species, it would also begin to ask whether the role of marine mammals should not be taken into account as well. This approach is extending also to management policy: most notable is the 1981 Convention on the Conservation of Antarctic Marine Living Resources (CCAMLR), which requires the Southern Ocean to be managed on an ecosystem basis. In practice, this means taking account of whatever significant interaction exists between the main components of the ecosystem – whales, seals, birds, squid, fish and krill. The interaction between dolphins and the yellowfin tuna fishery in the Pacific is recognised by the International Tropical Tuna Commission and by domestic US legislation (see Ch. 13).

In general, however, it is not easy for either the scientist or the legislator to embrace marine mammals within the conventional fisheries scene. As mammals, their biology, behaviour and population dynamics are far removed from those of the typical commercial fish species. Where marine mammals are still exploited as a resource, the associated industry, methods and markets are usually quite distinct from those of fisheries and are not interchangeable with them. More important still is that the conservation significance of marine mammals as rare or endangered species and the ethics of killing them for any purposes, have no parallel in fish.

The conflict of interests arising from the interactions (real or supposed) between marine mammals and fisheries has, indeed, become something of a *cause célèbre* in recent years. Action and re-action have taken various forms, sometimes at a level and with an intensity that to the uncommitted observer may have seemed incommensurate with the issues at stake. In fact, the problems created by the interactions between marine mammals and fisheries, both for the decision-makers and the scientists, are among the most challenging yet fascinating that have arisen so far in the management of natural resources. Several independent but interlocking developments can be traced which together have given rise to this situation.

The first concerns what has been happening to the marine mammal populations themselves. Hunting of cetaceans and pinnipeds for skins, meat and blubber, primarily for subsistence, has of course gone on from the earliest recorded times. At various periods during the last century and the early decades of the present century, as trade intensified and the more remote areas frequented by some of the largest and previously hardly touched populations of marine mammals became accessible, the hunting of them intensified to the point at which it caused serious depletion. Although accurate records are not available, there is little doubt that many marine mammal populations were reduced to a small fraction (perhaps no more than a tenth or so) of their former levels. Some, like the sea-otter, disappeared from parts of their range (see Ch. 12); in at least one case (the Steller sea-cow, *Hydrodamalis gigas*), the species became truly extinct (see Ch. 3).

This hunting pressure could not, of course, be maintained as the populations declined, if only for economic reasons; but additionally, in many cases, legislation was introduced to give partial or complete protection to the marine mammal. As a result, many of these populations started to increase, but their recovery is slow because of their long life-span and low relative reproductive capacity. So, many are still in the growing phase, with the prospect of considerable further expansion in size or range, or both, before natural checks come into play. The extreme case, and one of the best documented, is that of the Antarctic blue whales, the present numbers of which are still only a fraction of their peak abundance in the early years of the century.

But the world into which these mammal populations are recovering is not the same as it was when they were at their height decades ago. In some instances major new commercial fisheries have been established in the more remote regions favoured by marine mammals where before fishing was either slight or non-existent; the Bering Sea is the classic example. In other regions fisheries have expanded, or are planned to do so, in response to the world demand for fish. More intensive fishing is not, of course, the only change, nor is the story always one of recovery. The numbers of the common seal (*Phoca vitulina*) on the Dutch North Sea coast have declined substantially, while neither that species nor the monk seal (*Monachus monachus*) now breeds on the French coast; the latter species has, in fact, become rare throughout the Mediterranean. Reijnders (1983) points out that although in some cases the decline of a pinniped population has coincided with an elevation in the concentration of certain pollutants in the animals' tissues, no cause-and-effect relationship has yet been established between pollutants and altered physiological processes. He concludes that the general disturbance resulting from greatly increased use of coastal regions in recent decades may prove to be an important controlling factor. The inhibiting effect on pup production in the Orkney grey seals following the disturbance caused in the abortive cull of 1978 is documented in Chapter 10.

Nevertheless, fishing is perceived to be – and probably is – the most significant factor affecting marine mammals generally, apart from direct hunting. Fishermen in many parts of the world have, of course, long been aware of the damage that seals and whales can do to their gear and to their catch. In the UK, for example, legislation to regulate and legalise action by fishermen to protect the means of their livelihood against marauding seals dates back to the early years of the century. The trends described above in both marine mammal populations and in commercial fisheries are such as to intensify the previous degree of interaction between them.

The potential for conflict is further accentuated by developments of a different kind, in concept and attitude. On the one hand, increasing sophistication in the aims and methods of fishery management (especially the move towards multispecies assessments) focuses attention on the possible competitive effect of marine mammals in a way that it used not to be. Conversely, public awareness of and concern for wildlife conservation, articulated through the conservation bodies, have greatly increased in the last two decades. So the reciprocal issue of the possible harm to the marine mammal caused by the fishery – by accidental or incidental death during fishing operations, by depletion of its food supply, or through the application of crude or excessively severe measures for controlling its numbers – is now argued with a competence and eloquence previously lacking. This has introduced new dimensions into the debate; raising questions concerning, for example, the criteria on which to judge whether a species is truly 'endangered' (Holt & Lavigne 1982) and how to establish reliably and economically whether control measures are having the desired effect.

The above factors, varied and often controversial though they may be, are at least in principle capable of being analysed objectively and, if enough data are available, quantitatively. In other words, science can offer an impartial assessment of these factors and of the consequences of following, or not following, various courses of action. The problem is perhaps more straightforward (or at least more homogeneous) if the marine mammal is itself exploited as a natural resource for skins, meat or blubber. It then becomes more a question of balancing the relative rates of exploitation so that each resource is harvested as desired but on a sustainable basis.

But typically these days, even if the marine mammal is commercially exploited, the decision-maker has to take other considerations into account on which science can say little or nothing to help. Notable among these is pressure from the animal welfare lobby, which may nowadays extend beyond the prevention of suffering to the abhorrence on ethical grounds of killing a marine mammal in any circumstances. The options facing the unfortunate decision-maker are therefore strongly loaded with emotional and political overtones. Furthermore, he is likely to find that the issues are a strong attraction to the media, for whom conservation, especially if it is laced with controversy and the prospect of authority being challenged, is a popular theme. When he turns for help to the scientist he has not, it must be admitted, had the response he might have expected (although there are some good reasons, as we shall see later in this chapter and elsewhere in this book, why this should have been).

It was the realisation by the international conservation bodies of the growing seriousness of these problems – created partly by the success of their own policy for the protection of marine mammals – that caused them to set in motion enquiries to establish the facts of what soon proved to be a particularly intractable and poorly documented web of problems. The International Union for the Conservation of Nature (IUCN) has been the prime mover, supported by the United Nations Environment Programme (UNEP) and with the active help of the International Whaling Commission (IWC) and the Food and Agriculture Organisation of the UN (FAO). These initiatives culminated in the 1981 Workshop referred to in the Preface, the preparations for which were undertaken by a Steering Committee under the auspices of the new Standing Committee on Marine Mammals (CMM) established by the IUCN Species Survival Commission. The Workshop was chaired by Dr Sidney J. Holt with the author of the present chapter as Rapporteur.

The central question for the scientists to try to answer was simple enough: what is the true nature and extent of interactions between various species of marine mammals and fisheries? Put in more popular terms, do marine mammals really harm commercial fisheries, or might they do so in the future if no action is taken now? Conversely, is the recovery of marine mammal populations, or even in some cases their continued existence, being threatened by modern fishing activities?

The report of the conclusions of the Workshop represented at the time the best available consensus view of expert scientists concerned with both marine mammals and fisheries on the extent and nature of the problem. Paragraph 8.2 of the report summarises their conclusions in the following way:

> The first is whether the concern of the IUCN and other bodies about the seriousness of the conflict, actual and potential, between marine mammals and fisheries is justified. By and large the answer is yes, despite the frequent lack of conclusive evidence. Some of the instances which have generated the most public controversy so far may prove eventually to be of less significance than has been thought. This is true both as regards the adverse effect of the marine mammal on the fishery and of the threat to the marine mammal of action to stabilise or reduce its numbers. But there are instances where it is at least necessary to reserve judgement, and yet others where the probability is that the interaction between the marine mammal and the fishery is already substantial, or is soon likely to become so.

That conclusion remains essentially unchanged by the four years that have elapsed since the La Jolla Workshop, although the conflicts have, if anything, tended to intensify rather than lessen. The case for or against remedial action therefore remains very much a live issue, but a number of supplementary questions need to be answered before it can be satisfactorily resolved in any particular situation. For instance, if the 'harm' to the marine mammals or to the fishery is 'significant' – which, for the present purposes, we can define as sufficient to generate (though not necessarily to justify) a demand for action – what in practice can be done? If the problem is to lessen the effect of the marine mammal on the fishery, is it feasible to control the size of the marine mammal population without hazarding its viability, what scientific data would be needed, and how could the resultant benefits be assessed? If the aim is to benefit the marine mammal, what kind of evidence would be required to justify what may be a substantial restriction of fishing activity, with consequent loss of production and adverse effect on the livelihood of these engaged in it?

For the most part, data, theory and, indeed, our general understanding of marine mammal–fishery systems, are insufficient to answer those and other related questions satisfactorily. The subject is still at a stage when much is to be gained from a comparative review of what has been learnt and what is still obscure. The main purpose of this book (in Chs. 3–14) is therefore to bring together accounts by the scientists responsible for substantial investigations into various examples of interaction between marine mammals and fisheries. The last six chapters are devoted to the problem which is central to the estimation of the effect of predation, namely that of estimating the kind and quantity of prey eaten by the marine mammal population.

Following the approach adopted by the La Jolla Workshop, a useful primary distinction can be made between *operational* and *biological* (*ecological*) interaction. In the former, the marine mammal becomes involved in (often, literally entangled with) fishing operations to the detriment, usually, of both; this form of interaction is typically local and immediate in its manifestation. Biological interaction arises mainly through the marine mammal being a predator on fish or invertebrate marine organisms which are also exploited commercially, or which are the food of other commercially important species. The predatory role of the mammal when it is foraging near where fishing is in progress may also be local and have an obvious immediate effect; but biological interaction is typically more remote, happening at a distance and on timescales which may be very long term.

A quite different form of biological interaction arises from the fact that certain marine mammals are the intermediate hosts for nematode parasites of fish, the presence of which can certainly adversely affect the latter's market value and possibly their viability. Infestation of cod by the codworm parasite (*Phocanema decipiens*) can be a serious problem in coastal fisheries in Britain, Canada and Norway, the grey seal (*Halichoerus grypus*) being the main intermediate host among the marine mammals.

Little is known, however, about the dynamics of the interaction between the parasite and the fish stocks or, in quantitative terms, of the rôle of the marine mammal: *Phoconema*, for example, has a complex life cycle with a number of alternative hosts. Thus, Rae (1972) found that the level of codworm infestation in fish in Scottish coastal waters was highest near the major breeding colonies of grey seals. Similarly, Bjørge *et al.* (1981) reported the highest incidence of *Phocanema* (up to 90 per cent of the cod examined) near to colonies of grey and common seals (*Phoca vitulina*) on the Norwegian coast. The dynamics of infestation are, however, obscure. Rae (1972) reported that both codworm infestation and local grey seal populations increased during the 1960s, but although the seals have continued to increase up to the present time, the level of infestation apparently has not (Parrish & Shearer 1977). It is clear that considerably more research is needed before the rôle of parasites in the interaction between marine mammals and fisheries can be properly evaluated.

Operational interaction

Marine mammals are among the more intelligent and inquisitive of their phylum. It is not surprising, therefore, that pursuance of their normal way of life – and especially hunting for their food – should bring them into contact with man when he is similarly engaged. The results are often sufficiently disruptive and damaging as to cause anger and protest on the part of the fishermen: not infrequently, the marine mammal is also at risk.

Later chapters of this book describe this 'operational' interaction at some length. The diversity of the mechanisms are such that generalisations are not easy. Coastal-living seals and sea-lions seem to be the most often involved, and set gear (nets, lines and traps) the most vulnerable. Anadromous fish, migrating regularly through confined channels, and the associated gill-net and trap fisheries, are particularly susceptible to the attentions of a marauding marine mammal. The reader will recognise the grey seal–salmon interaction as fitting this prognosis particularly well. The interaction of harp seals with coastal cod and capelin fisheries also creates serious operational problems. This is true not only in the much publicised harp seal hunt in Labrador;

Bjørge *et al.* (1981) report harp seal damage to cod gill-nets in the fjord fisheries of northern Norway of up to a million Norwegian krone in 1980.

It is not, in principle, difficult to obtain a fair idea of the extent of gear damage. Published data (e.g. IUCN Workshop Report, Table 2) mostly give figures in the range of 2–10% of gear damaged on an annual basis, but whether this is a representative rate is less clear. In any event, it is the loss of fishing time and opportunity due to having to replace damaged and tangled gear, which is often the most serious manifestation of the unwelcome attentions of the marine mammal (Bjørge *et al.* 1981). Shaughnessy's reference to the confusion caused when a more than usually adventurous Cape fur seal (*Arctocephalus pusillus*), having been brought aboard accidentally in a trawl, pursued its prey even into the fish holds of the trawler, is amusing for the reader but probably not for the crew!

Although cetaceans, because of their open ocean distribution, are typically much less involved in fishing operations than pinnipeds, those that make inshore sorties can cause serious problems, if only because of their size. Humpback whales straying close inshore on the Eastern Canadian seaboard damage cod and herring traps and can tear loose long lengths of a set net if they happen to strike it. Not only is this costly to the fishermen, the whale itself (an endangered species) is also at risk of becoming entangled with synthetic nets which have broken free. This is one of many reported instances of reciprocal interaction. In the Norwegian gill-net fishery referred to above, the authors report that more than 10 000 harp seals were drowned in gill-nets in each of the years between 1979 and 1981. However, disturbingly large though this figure is, it is only of the order of 1 per cent of the harp seal population in the Barents Sea and there are no indications that the population as a whole is being significantly affected.

The same cannot be said about the population of the northern fur seal (*Callorhinus ursinus*) of the Pribilof Islands, which has failed to recover to the levels of the 1950s despite cessation of harvesting of females after 1968, and seems now to be declining. While some form of biological interaction arising from greatly increased fishing activity in the Bering Sea during the last two decades cannot be ruled out, the available evidence does not support this explanation. However, Fowler (1982) has shown that entanglement in fragments of trawl netting (some weighing many kilograms) could account for something in the region of a 5% mortality rate of seals a year, i.e. the death of 50 000 individuals annually. Despite the circumstantial nature of the link between frequency of entanglement and resultant death, there seems little doubt that this, and perhaps other kinds of operational interaction arising from the increased trawling, is a major factor in determining the otherwise inexplicable decline of the Pribilof fur seal population.

The best documented and most dramatic of the operational interactions is that of the incidental capture of dolphins in the purse-seine fishery for yellowfin tuna in the open Pacific, described by Allen (see Ch. 13). In the early years of the changeover from line fishing (which did not harm the dolphins) to purse-seines (in which they became entangled and drowned), it is reliably estimated that of the order of half a million dolphins were killed annually. The irony – tragedy is hardly too strong a word – of this situation is that the tendency for dolphins and tuna to be found together in the open ocean, apparently without any antagonism or even significant competition between them, is actually advantageous to the fishermen, tuna fishing being significantly more successful when dolphins are present than when they are absent.

This is one of the simplest possible cases to assess, because time and money spent by the fishermen in protecting the marine mammal – for example by modifying the construction and use of their gear — are of direct and tangible benefit to them. It is encouraging that considerable progress has been made in this direction, so that the dolphin is no longer in danger. Typically, however, there is no such trade-off for the fisherman, who views the marauding mammal which has damaged his gear and his catch (and is suspected, possibly with some reason, to have frightened other fish away) as an unmitigated nuisance.

Even so, the fact that some forms of operational harm to fisheries by marine mammals can be reduced (if not eliminated) by ingenious technology, and that others can be assessed in financial terms fairly reliably (see Ch. 7), opens the way to remedial action. It may be that the costs of such action are simply added to the price of fish, so that the market ultimately pays; or the official authorities may pay compensation, as in Norway. Provided the marine mammal population is not put at risk by over-zealous action by the fishermen to protect their catch and gear, there is the basis for a workable compromise on fairly objective and quantifiable grounds. As we shall see, no such solution is usually available in the case of biological interaction.

Predatory interaction

Types of interactive systems

The diversity of species and habitats within the group we are calling 'marine mammals' brings with it a corresponding variety among the animals, (fish or invertebrates) with which they interact, and hence of the structure of the resulting food chain. To help explore some theoretical ideas in the next section of this chapter, and to locate some of the examples which are discussed in detail in later chapters, it is useful to classify schematically the main types of systems which are encountered.

The simplest possible situation is that of a marine mammal feeding on one fish or other prey species which is also exploited commercially. This is shown in Figure 1.1. Here (and in Figs. 1.2–1.6), the broken lines represent the direction of predatory force, and the solid lines represent the resultant flow of material as prey caught in the fishery or consumed by the predator.

In practice, it is rare for a marine mammal, but not unusual for a fishery, to be dependent on a single 'prey' species, and even rarer for such specialisation to coincide. Nevertheless, competitive predation between fishing and a marine mammal is the central mechanism of biological interaction, and the system illustrated in Figure 1.1 is a useful starting point. Thus, the more usual situation in which both the commercial catch and the food of the marine mammal are made up of several prey species can, to a first approximation, be analysed species by species and the results combined, with weighting to reflect their relative market and dietary importance respectively. One complication is that the predatory interest shown by the fishery and the marine mammal is likely to vary with changes in the abundance of the common prey in ways which may not be easy to predict — neither market forces nor the gastronomic preferences of marine mammals being altogether predictable.

Almost invariably, the prey species will have other predators (non-mammalian) than man and the marine mammal in question. Birds are one important class of such predators which are rarely hunted by the marine mammal or fished commercially, and therefore the system that applies to them is that illustrated in Figure 1.2. In practice, this is a reminder that when attempting to formulate the dynamics of the prey species, explicit account may have to be taken of the rôle of the predators such as birds, even though they are not directly involved in the marine mammal–fishery interaction (see Ch. 5).

Rather different considerations apply if the second predator is a fish. In the fully symmetrical case (shown in Fig. 1.3), the fish predator is itself eaten by the marine mammal and fished commercially.

Several examples of such a system have been reported. In the Gulf of St Lawrence, cod feed on capelin and both are eaten by harp seals and fished commercially (see Ch. 9). Shaughnessy (see Ch. 8) records that snoek (barracuda, *Sphyraena* spp.), which is of commercial importance, is at times eaten by the Cape fur seal, both being predators on smaller fish species (e.g. anchovy) which support the main commercial fishery. In such cases, a change in the intensity of fishing or in the abundance of the marine mammal might be expected to affect the abundance of both the predator and prey fish

Figures 1.1–1.6 Schematic representation of possible interactive systems for marine mamals and fish.

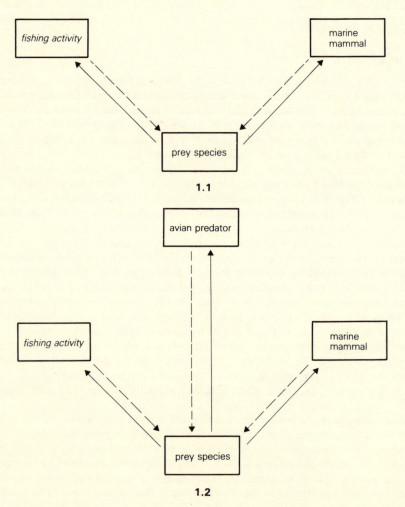

populations, thus altering the intensity of their interaction. However, provided both are fished, at least the direction of the resultant effect on the fishery yield or on the food to the marine mammal should be assessed correctly, even if the resulting balance between the two fish species cannot be anticipated.

These somewhat conservative conclusions may no longer apply if asymmetry is introduced into the system. Suppose that the commercial fishery is exploiting only the prey species but the marine mammal is feeding on both that and the fish predator, as

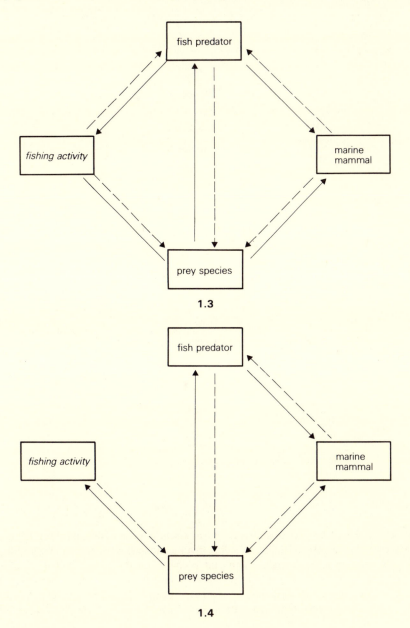

1.3

1.4

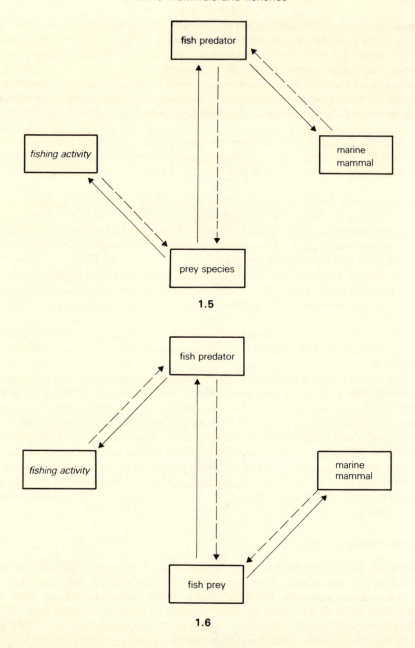

1.5

1.6

illustrated in Figure 1.4. An elegant example of essentially this system has been reported by Mate (1981): namely, of sea-lion feeding in a Pacific west coast river on both salmon and lamprey, the latter being a significant predator on the former but itself of no commercial value. In this case, attempting to reduce the impact of predation by the marine mammal on the commercially valuable prey will also benefit the valueless predator, and so probably increase predation from this source. Without a detailed understanding of the interaction between the fish predator and the prey population, there is no way of knowing whether control of the marine mammal in such a case would benefit or harm the fishery. On the other hand, relaxation of fishing would be expected to increase the abundance not only of the common prey species but perhaps also, in the longer term, that of the fish predator, so that the food supply to the marine mammal would stand to be increased on both counts. Thus interaction between the marine mammal and the fishery is no longer reciprocal.

The limiting form of asymmetry is shown in Figure 1.5, with the marine mammal feeding only on the fish predator and the fishery exploiting only the prey. In this case the commercially fished prey is two trophic levels below the marine mammal and would be expected to be small and abundant. The best of the documented examples is to be found in the Antarctic, where krill are both exploited commercially and consumed by an intermediate predator – squid, which is itself eaten by the top predator, sperm whales (May *et al.* 1979). The same system may also apply where a fishery specialises on a small species (e.g. sprat or sandeel for processing), with a marine mammal feeding on its intermediate predator (e.g. dogfish) which is not itself exploited, but no properly documented case has yet been reported.

The dynamics of this form of interaction are clearly no longer reciprocal, even in direction. Thus it is conceivable, though speculative in practice, that the food supply to the marine mammal (i.e. the predatory fish) could be improved indirectly by relaxation of fishing on the prey fish. In contrast, management of the marine mammal to benefit the fishery would aim to increase its abundance, not decrease it, in the hope that the influence of the fish predator on the abundance of the prey fish would thereby be decreased.

The inverse of the asymmetry of Figure 1.5 may also arise, i.e. where the marine mammal feeds only on the prey and the fishery exploits only the predator (as in Fig. 1.6). In this case, any beneficial effect that control of the marine mammal might have on the commercial fishery could only be indirect, through causing the abundance of the prey species and in turn the fish predator, to increase. Again, improving the food supply to the marine mammal would presumably be best achieved by increasing the fishing activity, not relaxing it, thereby depleting the fish predator and so lessening its competition with the mammal. In practice, interaction dependent on a two-stage linkage, as illustrated in Figures 1.5 and 1.6, is likely to be correspondingly unpredictable.

Some theoretical ideas

Important advances in the theoretical formation of predator–prey systems have been made in the last decade. Most have taken as their starting point the classical Lotka–Volterra equations (Maynard Smith 1974), superimposing on them the additional effect of harvesting of either the prey or predator, or both (May 1976). Shirakihara and Tanaka (1978), May *et al.* (1979), Beddington and May (1980) and Beddington and Cooke (1982) have examined the general properties of such systems, with particular reference to stability, extinction and conditions for obtaining the maximum sustainable yield from one or more of the component populations.

These theoretical investigations have provided a valuable insight into the kinds of dynamic responses that may be expected from complex systems which are also exploited. The particular kinds of questions posed by the interaction between marine mammals and fisheries fall within this general framework, but will usually call for a closer analysis of certain of the processes and responses of the system in question. There are four aspects that need particular consideration.

(a) The effect of a given predation rate on the prey population. Most mathematical formulations mediate effects of this kind through the essentially logistic growth dynamics of the prey, but in practice they may need to be explicitly identified and incorporated into the conventional fishery assessment methodology.

(b) The relationship between abundance of predator and the predation mortality rate it generates in the prey. Most of the above authors have explored the consequences of introducing a non-linear term for the predatory effect, but usually it is assumed that the predation mortality coefficient is a constant proportion of the size of the predator population and, in particular, is independent of the abundance of prey. In practice, hunger and satiation require this assumption to be modified, at least at extremes of predator–prey ratios; while the opportunistic feeding habits typical of the fish-eating marine mammals are likely to introduce marked discontinuities in the predatory process.

(c) Factors limiting the abundance of the predator. Most of the above treatments assume that, in the absence of harvesting, the abundance of the predator population would be limited only by that of its prey. This will no doubt be true in many cases, but the size of certain marine mammal populations (e.g. seals) may be limited by habitat restrictions unrelated to food, such as availability of suitable breeding sites. This question has obvious implications for management.

(d) Size and age – specificity of interaction. The above-mentioned formulations usually deal only with total numbers (or biomass) of the component populations. In contrast, nearly all interactions between marine mammals and fish populations are size and age specific, often very sharply so, with important practical consequences.

To incorporate these and other practical complications in a general theory of predator–prey interaction would probably be impracticable. We must now see how far they can be usefully explored in the more limited context of marine mammal–fishery interactions and their management implications. (see also Ch. 2).

The effect of marine mammal predation on a fish population

Suppose we are dealing with the simplest case of one marine mammal feeding on a single prey species which is also fished commercially, as in Figure 1.1. In the first instance, the mortality rate in the fish population caused by marine mammal predation can be regarded as a subset of what would normally be the 'natural mortality rate', i.e. total deaths due to all causes other than fishing. If the mortality rate in the fish population due to predation, in terms of instantaneous coefficients, is designated as M^*, and that due to all other natural causes as M^1, then, with the usual notation, the total mortality rate in the fish population can be written as:

$$Z = F + M^* + M^1 \qquad (1.1)$$

Let us further suppose that the marine mammal and the fishery operate on effectively the same size range of the prey population, and that the coefficients of Equation 1.1 do not vary with the size or age of prey (or are weighted mean values with respect to those parameters). Then, if the mean biomass of the prey is $\bar{P}$, the annual amount of it caught by the commerical fleet is Y, and the amount of it consumed annually by the predatory marine mammal is C^*:

$$Y = \frac{F\bar{P}}{F + M^* + M^1} \tag{1.2}$$

and

$$C^* = \frac{M^*\bar{P}}{F + M^* + M^1} \tag{1.3}$$

Hence the ratio of the amount caught by the fleet to the amount consumed by the marine mammal population is:

$$Y/C^* = F/M^* \tag{1.4}$$

The quantity Y/C^* is therefore of immediate interest in establishing the relative impact, in terms of mortality, of fishing and predation on the prey species (see p. 25). From the point of view of management, however, a more direct question might be: given that the fishery is at present producing an average Y_1 in the presence of a marine mammal predator generating a predation mortality M_1^*, how different would the yield be expected to be if the size of the predator population changed so as to generate a predation mortality rate M_2^*, other things being equal? Calling this latter yield Y_2, this amounts to calculating the ratio $Y_2 : Y_1$. From Equation 1.2 and putting $\bar{P} = R\bar{W}$, where R = average recruitment and $\bar{W}$ = the mean weight of fish in the catch:

$$Y_1 = \frac{FR\bar{W}_1}{F + M^1 + M_1^*} \tag{1.5}$$

from which

$$Y_2 = \frac{FR\bar{W}_2}{F + M^1 + M_2^*} \tag{1.6}$$

from which

$$\frac{Y_2}{Y_1} = \frac{\bar{W}_2}{\bar{W}_1} \cdot \frac{F + M^1 + M^*}{F + M^1 + M_2^*} \tag{1.7}$$

So far, this is no more than a formalised description of the response of the fish part of the system represented in Figure 1.1 to a change in one of the components of its mortality, using the simplest possible conventional mathematics. To judge the predictive value of Equation 1.7, for example for estimating the gain to fishery yield if the marine mammal population was smaller or absent, or how the marine mammal would be effected by a change in the intensity of fishing on its prey population, it is necessary to examine the simplifications on which it is based.

One simplifying assumption in using the above forumulation is that the parameters are not density-dependent – at least not over the span of age and range of population density likely to be involved. However, a change in M^* will, in theory, affect the density of that section of the fish population to which it applies, just as would an equivalent change in the fishing mortality coefficient F. If that caused the residual natural mortality coefficient M^1 to change in the opposite direction, it would tend to diminish the value of attempts to benefit the fishery by control of the predator or the mammalian predator by restriction of the fishery. It is therefore necessary to consider briefly the evidence on this question. (It is important to note that it is the instantaneous coefficients of mortality, not the mortality itself, to which the term 'density dependent' is applied. Thus, if the abundance of the fish population increased, more would die from the totality of causes represented by the coefficient M^1, simply because there would be more individuals there to die. This is automatically taken into account in Equations 1.1–1.5 by the use of instantaneous coefficients (instead of percentages).)

The near impossibility of detecting small changes in a natural mortality rate in the presence of a larger fishing mortality rate, even in the best sampled of fish populations, means that direct evidence of subtle changes in M^1 over the exploited phase due to density-dependent factors just does not exist. On the other hand, during the last two decades there have been dramatic changes, natural and man-made, in the abundance of several of the best documented of the world's major fish stocks – changes which, in their magnitude and speed, far exceeded anything that could normally result from even the total disappearance of a marine mammal predator. In none of these instances has a change in natural mortality been actually measured, even although the stock size has varied manyfold.

The main evidence for density-dependent control of numbers in fish populations is indirect. It derives from the fact that where a relationship between parent stock and subsequent recruitment to the fishery (or to the parent population) can be established, recruitment varies much less than parent stock over a wide range of stock size. This means that the main density-dependent controls are operating in the pre-recruit phase, and possibly in the early part of that. Thus, one of the few positive clues is due to Lockwood (1981), who has shown that the natural mortality rate of North Sea plaice is density dependent during their first summer when, as very small newly metamorphosed fish, they first reach their shallow-water nursery grounds. In species with pelagic larvae which form sufficiently dense aggregations, it may well be that density-dependent controls operate here too, though possibly only for short periods.

The possibility of compensatory changes in M^* and M^1 due to density-dependent effects therefore remains, strictly speaking, an open question. My own view is that such mechanisms will usually be confined to early stages of the life history when the fish may be too small to constitute a major food supply to a marine mammal. However, if the species is itself 'small', as, for example, capelin, which are a major prey for harp seals, density dependence of mortality coefficients may extend to older fish. In such a case, for the residual natural mortality coefficient M^1 to increase with density as M^* decreases, it would be necessary for the local or general abundance of other predators, such as birds or large fish, or possibly parasites, to increase, so that they took a larger proportion of the more abundant prey population than before. It would be reasonable to expect to have tangible evidence of this kind before introducing explicit compensatory changes in M^* and M^1 in assessments.

Another possible complication to which the IUCN Workshop Report draws attention (Para 5.6) is that of the marine mammal being more easily able to catch fish that are already moribund, and whose prospects of survival are therefore lower than those of 'normal' individuals. No evidence of this appears to have been published for marine mammals, but the phenomenon is well known in some terrestrial predators, which hunt and 'run-down' their prey.

To the extent that the marine mammal predator is taking prey which are of below average 'health' and vigour, a decrease in predator mortality (M^*) would tend to increase the average susceptibility of the rest of the prey population to death from other natural causes; in other words, M^1 would tend to increase and the abundance of the prey population would not therefore increase by as much as predicted from Equation 1.7.

On the other hand, in those fisheries where the gear is itself behaving like an active predator (as in trawls and seines), the evidence of underwater photography suggests that the less active and more easily tired individuals would be more likely to be caught. In that event, decreasing predation by the marine mammal would allow fish to survive that are, on average, more readily caught than those of the rest of the population, thus tending to offset the selectivity of the marine mammal's predation. In the absence of any positive information, however, it is impossible to assess whether differential susceptibility of the prey to predation and/or capture is likely to be a significant factor.

A basic assumption in the above formulation is, of course, that the impacts of fishing and predation are both distributed in the same way over the size and age range of the prey population. While this will rarely be exactly true, the result is not sensitive unless the discrepancies are marked. It is also possible to anticipate the direction of the resulting bias. The older the fish consumed by the marine mammals compared with those comprising the commercial catch, the less the effect on the fishery – at least, in the short to medium term. In the extreme, if predation by the marine mammal is wholly confined to fish older than those that appear in the commercial catch, then its effect can operate only in the long term, through whatever kind of stock-recruitment relationship applies to the prey species, with all the variability and uncertainty thereby involved. Situations like this seem to be uncommon; if they do arise, it is likely to be in species in which the adults do not become vulnerable to predation until after they have matured, but which are exploited commercially as immatures.

The converse arises when predation by the marine mammal is mainly or wholly on fish smaller than commercial size, which will then affect directly the recruitment to the fishery; this can, potentially, have an important effect. Let us suppose that fish recruit to the fishery at age t_r but that predation on them begins at a lower age (t_p) and lasts until they recruit. Then, designating the predation mortality rate by M^* as before, the proportional reduction in numbers of the year-class due to predation by the time it is recruited to the fishery is:

$$\exp - M^*(t_r - t_p) \tag{1.8}$$

Whether the effect of 'pre-recruit' predation could be more severe than 'post-recruit', (as suggested in the IUCN Workshop Report, p. 34), depends on the circumstances. For example, suppose that the marine mammal population in question needs to consume prey at a given rate, by weight, irrespective of whether the prey individuals are small or large. If prey are consumed as small pre-recruits while the total biomass of the prey cohort is also still small, then greater subsequent depletion of the adult prey population may be expected than if the same weight of prey had been taken later in life.

How frequently this 'pre-recruit predation' happens in practice is not clear. If the prey individuals are too small, the marine mammal (unless it is a filtering cetacean) would either be unable to catch them or would be obliged to exert a disproportionate amount of time and effort trying to; being intelligent animals, they would probably turn to other more rewarding prey. The most potentially damaging situation is that in which the prey species has a low intrinsic natural mortality (i.e. M^1) and a considerable growth span, leaving a substantial pre-recruit population of individuals large enough to constitute an efficient food supply to the marine mammal and old enough to have passed through the compensatory density-dependent phase. The larger gadoid species fit this specification rather well; for example, Swartzman and Haar (see Ch. 4) record that pollock (*Theragra chalcogramma*) eaten by the northern fur seal (*Callorhinus ursinus*) in the Bering Sea are of a size range 6–20 cm, whereas the commercial fishery takes pollock of 35 cm upwards, equivalent to a difference of thirtyfold or so in the average weight of individual fish.

The predatory response of the marine mammal

We have so far designated the two 'predation' components of mortality in the common prey population by the instantaneous coefficients F and M^*, operating on each side of the predator–prey system shown in Figures 1.1–1.6. The relationship between F and fishing activity is a well-investigated field of fisheries dynamics. The corresponding relationship, that between M^* and the abundance of the marine mammal generating it, is less well-charted territory, but is obviously fundamental to modelling the predatory–prey system as well as to the practical question of predator control. It is necessary to consider, in particular, how far it is safe to assume that a given change in the size of the marine mammal will be reflected in a corresponding change in M^* – if, indeed, such an assumption can be made at all.

   The fishery analogy provides a useful start. Experience has shown that for many types of fisheries and over a considerable range of stock size, the catchability coefficient (q) relating the fishing mortality coefficient (F) to the fishing effort (f) generating it can be regarded as effectively constant, i.e.

$$F = qf \qquad (1.9)$$

There are, however, certain circumstances in which this simple formulation breaks down, and these are vitally important in determining the ultimate stability of the system. One arises in purse-seine fisheries for shoaling fish which can easily be detected (e.g. by sonar or aircraft). In these circumstances the fleet can aggregate on the few remaining shoals with little extra searching time; and so, at low stock densities, q tends to increase, sometimes dramatically (Ulltang 1980). This increase of q at low densities is conventionally represented by putting $q = kN^{-b}$ in Equation (1.9) where N is the fish stock abundance, giving:

$$F = fkN^{-b} \qquad (1.10)$$

where k and b are constants.

   Conversely, other kinds of gear, e.g. set-lines and gill-nets, can become 'saturated' when fish are plentiful, thus reducing their effective fishing power and causing q to decrease. Economic forces, manifest in the short term by the capacity of the market to accommodate unusually large landings, can also limit the effective catching power of the fleet when fish are abundant; whereas if a particular species becomes very scarce, the fishermen may well decide (if they have the choice and can break with tradition) to leave it altogether and fish elsewhere on other, albeit less preferred, species.

It is likely that all these considerations apply in analogous ways to the predatory activity of a marine mammal, a conclusion which follows also from the analysis and classification of functional responses of a predator to its prey developed by Holling (1965). Several of the contributors to this book emphasise the opportunistic feeding habits of the more omnivorous fish-eating marine mammals, so that when the initially preferred prey species falls below a certain level of availability, they switch to another rather than continue hunting for the first. Bailey and Ainley (1982) have developed a model representing the switching of predation by California sea-lion (*Zalophus californianus*) between hake and rockfish. The possibility that marine mammals with this feeding strategy could reduce the prey species to extinction is remote. On the other hand, the account by Estes and VanBlaricom (see Ch. 12) of the depletion that sea-otters can create in certain of their invertebrate prey (notably sea-urchins and some molluscs) shows that the more persistent feeders on slow-moving or sessile prey can completely eliminate a prey species locally before turning their attention to the next-best alternative available. The concern that killer whales (*Orcinus orca*) may be impeding the recovery of the drastically depleted Norwegian spring herring stock derives from the anticipation of enhanced predatory efficiency at extremely low prey–predator ratios, although there is as yet no positive evidence of this.

At the other end of the scale, the analogy to 'saturation' will certainly apply, since there is a finite limit to the rate at which a marine mammal can eat, however abundant its food. This limiting effect on M^* will be more marked if the size of the marine mammal population is constrained by factors other than food supply, such as breeding facilities. Those considerations suggest that at high levels of prey, or, strictly, when the prey–predator ratio is high, the coefficient M^* would decline in the short and medium term with the size of the marine mammal population by a factor such as $(r_{max} - r)/r_{max'}$, where r is the actual daily ration and r_{max} the largest possible daily ration if food were in excess supply. If the marine mammal population were not restricted by other factors, it would presumably increase in the longer term in response to a sustained abundance of food, in which case M^* would not decline and might even increase. The dynamics of most marine mammals are, however, such that if this response occurred, it would be manifest on a timescale of decades rather than years.

To sum up, it seems that the relationship between the abundance of a marine mammal predator (P^*) and the mortality coefficient it generates in its prey (M^*) would exhibit a similar range of characteristics to those found in other predators and in the analogous relationship between fishing effort and fishing mortality coefficient (f). In the short to medium term and over a moderate range of a relative abundance, the ratio $q^* = M^*/P^*$ can probably be treated as effectively constant; but in the longer term and over wider ranges of relative abundance, the following departures from constancy would be expected, namely:

(a) at low levels of prey, or of the prey–predator ratio, two alternative responses may appear: specialised feeders, becoming hungry, may intensify their hunting, whereas opportunistic feeders may abandon their preferred food and turn to a more abundant alternative;

(b) at high levels of prey, or of the prey–predator ratio, all marine mammals are likely to exhibit food satiation, probably to a more marked degree than do most fisheries exhibit 'saturation'. Whether the resulting decline in M^* would persist in the long term would depend on whether the marine mammal is ultimately limited by food or space.

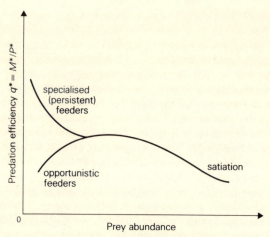

Figure 1.7 Possible form of relationship between predation efficiency factor q^* (= ratio of predation mortality coefficient M^* to size of predator population P^*) and prey abundance.

These considerations are illustrated schematically in Figure 1.7.

Even though the precise form of such a relationship will be difficult to establish, one conclusion of practical significance seems to emerge. This is that if, by suitable control measures, the abundance of the predator is reduced to a lower level and maintained there, and the prey–predator ratio thereby increases as intended, then the efficiency of predation (q^*) is likely, if anything, to decrease in the short and medium term. In other words, assessments of such an effect made by assuming M^* to decrease no more than in proportion to the abundance of the marine mammal population, are likely in this respect to be on the conservative side.

Attempting to anticipate the predatory response of a marine mammal simply by applying what seem to be rational criteria based on the need for food is, however, hardly an exact science. Two examples illustrate this point. Not infrequently, grey seals are known to kill a salmon by taking one bite and then leaving it, presumably because they were not hungry. Again, predators can sometimes take a liking to a particular kind of prey and feed almost exclusively on it for a time, even though alternatives are available which would be eaten in other circumstances. The possibility of such gastronomic eccentricities has always to be borne in mind.

Effect on the marine mammal population

According to the systems we are considering here, the only biological (as distinct from operational) mechanism whereby a fishery can affect a marine mammal population is by altering, in the first instance, the supply of food available to the individuals comprising it. The less straightforward problem is to anticipate the demographic consequences of a given change in food supply.

The fishery analogy developed above is still a useful starting point. Catch per unit of effort (CPUE) suitably transformed into monetary equivalents of value and cost, is a fundamental determinant of the economic viability of a fishery. The amount of prey that an individual marine mammal can capture, or needs to capture, per unit expenditure of time and energy is of corresponding significance in establishing the trophic viability of the population. In both cases there is an upper limit to the catch rate (or consumption rate) at which the individual units can operate effectively.

If the food species is already in ample supply, so that the predator can easily catch prey as fast as it can eat and assimilate it, any further increase in the abundance of the prey species will have no demographic effect on the predator population. In practice, this means that the predator population is below the maximum size that the food supply of the habitat could support – either because it is depleted by harvesting or natural causes of death, or because its size is limited by factors other than food supply.

Suppose now that the abundance of the prey decreases. The amount of food an individual predator can catch per unit of expenditure of time and effort averaged over the population (which, by analogy with CPUE, can be termed the rate of food intake per unit foraging effort, FUFE), will also decrease. Judging by the results of experimental work on growth and feeding, moderate decreases in FUFE may have little adverse effect on the health of the individual predator or its reproductive capacity, possibly even the reverse. Sooner or late, however, the FUFE will fall to the level at which the animal cannot maintain its normal functions without drawing upon its metabolic energy reserves (i.e. body fat in the first instance). This is clearly no more than a temporary expedient, which may itself bring other difficulties, especially for marine mammals living in cold climates where body fat is needed for buoyancy and insulation as well as a reserve of energy. In other words, the animal begins to suffer from starvation.

It is at this point that one would expect to see signs of the demographic changes typically associated with density-dependent effects involving (or presumed to involve) a shortage of food intake per capita. Hanks (1981), following Eberhardt (1977), suggests that the sequence of events might then be:

(1) juvenile mortality rate increases
(2) age at first reproduction increases
(3) age-specific fecundity declines
(4) adult mortality rate increases

but it is likely that a decrease in growth rate will be the precursor to all these changes. The precise mechanisms, and the most susceptible phase of the life history, are bound to vary according to the species. This is particularly the case with the mortality in early life, which could occur during lactation, soon after weening, or later in the immature phase of the life history.

It is only in recent years, and in a small number of marine mammal populations, that convincing evidence of such density-dependent changes have come to light. These have been summarised by Fowler (1981). For practical reasons, most information is available on maturation and reproduction. Fowler *et al.* (1980) set out the best of this evidence for cetaceans and pinnipeds, which suggests that enough is known at least to begin to introduce, with due care, density dependence of particular parameters into population models for management purposes. The need for caution is well illustrated by the analysis by Bowen *et al.* (1981) of the 'by no means unqualified' evidence for relationships between maturation age, ovulation rate and fertility rate, and population size in the North-west Atlantic harp seal (*Phoca groenlandica*), which is one of the best-studied pinniped populations.

Because most research has been done on marine mammal populations which have been depleted by hunting, the observed responses are mostly in the opposite directions

to those listed above. The assumption of reversibility is, of course, implicit and probably sound. Rather less satisfactory is that in no case are accurate direct measurements
of the food supply or intake available. It is therefore also necessary to make the
assumption that the density-dependent response is a manifestation of a change in the
food supply per capita to the marine mammal population, which may not always be
true.

Long-term dynamics

The mechanics of interaction considered above have been primarily those that might
be expected in the short to medium term, i.e. within the generation time of the marine
mammal. In the absence of fishing, and judging by such historical records as are
available, the marine mammal would presumably reach some form of equilibrium in
whatever constitutes the ecological or habitat unit of which it would be the top
predator. The interaction between it and its prey populations would then be largely
determined by whether food or space was the ultimate factor limiting its population
size. If food, then in theory the predation mortality rate in the prey population (M^*)
could become very high; the prey might in fact be 'overgrazed' by the predator until
the effect of a reduced food supply worked through to the predator (in the way outlined
above) to cause its population size to fall. If space were the limiting factor, then it could
be that generally, if not locally, predation by the marine mammal was only one of a
number of causes of mortality in the prey and possibly quite a minor one, in which case
the two populations would be effectively de-coupled.

   In practice, apart from this very important question of food or space limiting the
marine mammal, two other interrelated factors would probably emerge as of overriding
importance.

(a)   One is the widely differing timescales of the dynamics of the marine mammal
      predator and its prey. The immature phase of northern seals, for example, is of
      a similar duration (5–7 years) to the whole life span of capelin, which is one of
      their most important prey species (see also Ch. 5).
(b)   The other is that the incidence of extraneous factors causing variability in popula-
      tion size also differs widely. It is nothing unusual for fluctuating recruitment to
      cause changes in size of fish populations of several fold within a few years, in the
      shorter-lived species. In contrast, the evidence from marine mammal populations
      is that they are remarkably steady from year to year, as would be expected from
      their reproductive pattern. Even those that are recovering from severe depletion
      by hunting and are clearly not in equilibrium, typically change by no more than
      10% or so annually (Chapman 1981).

   Differential time responses of whales, seals and krill in an interacting system following the start or cessation of harvesting have been examined using deterministic models
by May *et al.* (1979). When the fluctuating characteristics of a fish prey population are
also taken into account, the long-term picture is best visualised as that of stable or very
slowly changing marine mammal populations subsisting on a complex of much more
variable food populations. Some of the latter would be very much 'held down' by the
mammalian predator, and others hardly affected, with the opportunistic marine
mammal taking advantage of temporary and local prey abundances and not wasting
time and effort hunting scarce species. If so, that might not be a bad example of how

to conduct a multispecies fishery, but it makes the development of a generalised marine mammal fishery model for purposes of prediction rather difficult!

Assessment and control

The limitations of the factual record

The La Jolla Workshop, on the evidence available to it, concluded that there were as yet no instances in which predation by fish-eating marine mammals could be shown, unambiguously, to have affected the abundance of a commercial fish stock. Conversely, the Workshop was unable to find a case in which a fish-eating marine mammal had been adversely affected at the population level by biological interaction with a fishery. This is still true, as will appear from the accounts in this volume of some of the best-documented marine mammal–fishery interactions. In view of the obvious policy significance, it is important to be clear as to why this should be.

The situations where demographic evidence of biological interaction would be expected, *a priori*, to be most visible are confined water basins supporting large populations of marine mammals feeding on fish species which are also at least moderately heavily fished. It is also necessary that the mammal or fish populations, or both, should have changed substantially in size over a fairly long period, during which the necessary statistics and research data have been collected. The marine mammals and fish communities of the Bering Sea and the Gulf of St Lawrence come closest to meeting these criteria, but clear evidence of biological interaction between them has not yet been obtained.

Studies on the predation of fish by southern elephant seal (*Mirounga leonina*) and Antarctic fur seal (*Arctocephalus gazella*) at South Georgia have shown that the annual amounts consumed exceed the commercial catches and are between 30% (in the case of *Notothenia rossi*) and 60% (in the case of *Champsocephalus gunnari*) of the standing stock. (McCann 1980, Croxall *et al.* in press). Indeed, so high are these consumption : stock ratios that the authors raise the possibility that either the fish stocks have been underestimated or the marine mammals obtain a significant part of their food by foraging outside the fished area of the shelf.

The only really convincing case of which I am aware of seals depleting fish populations is that reported by Power and Gregoire (1978) for Lower Seal Lake, Quebec. This is a freshwater lake which, unlike others in the vicinity, has been frequented by a freshwater-living colony of harbour seals (*Phoca vitulina*). Not only is the fish fauna of Lower Seal Lake very sparse compared with that of its neighbours, but the most vulnerable of the prey species (lake trout, *Salvelinus namaycush*) shows all the signs of sustained severe depletion, i.e. high mortality, reduced age at maturity, fast growth rate and high specific fecundity.

As we have earlier observed, for clear evidence of depletion of prey populations in marine habitats it is necessary to turn to the sea-otter on the Pacific West Coast of North America and the walrus of the North Pacific, feeding on localised sessile invertebrates. Even here, it is interesting that Estes and VanBlaricom (ch. 12) reject several of the supposed depletions by sea-otter, because a thorough analysis shows that the observed changes in the invertebrate populations have more probably been caused by fishing or other 'natural' causes; while Fay and Lowry (1981) conclude that the proven influence of walruses is on local clam populations only.

To the fisheries scientist – who has difficulty enough in measuring changes in total mortality rate in well-sampled fish stocks which have been subjected to substantial and relatively well-documented changes in fishing effort – the inconclusive nature of the evidence for marine mammal–fishery interaction comes as no surprise. It must be remembered in this connection that despite imperfections in the statistical record, the total catch taken by the fishery is usually fairly well known. In contrast, the total amount of a prey species consumed annually by a marine mammal population is an elusive quantity which at best can only be estimated indirectly by methods such as stomach contents or metabolic requirements, which are themselves imprecise measures.

It is perhaps rather more surprising that the high variability typical of fish populations should not have caused easily detectable changes in at least the biological precursors of demographic change in marine mammal predators. Yet the cases where density-dependent effects can be established (noted in the previous section) do not seem to be associated with any obvious change in the expected directions in the food species – see, for example, Lowry and Frost for the northern fur seal (Ch. 3) and Bowen for harp seal (Ch. 9).

It might be thought that the depletion of the great whales in the Southern Ocean (which for nearly 30 years have been at a small fraction of their earlier abundance) would have furnished one of the clearest examples of this interaction, and to an extent this is true. Thus Laws (1977) has drawn attention to changes in the biology of various species of Antarctic marine mammals which could be interpreted as a response to an increase in their main supply of food (krill) resulting from the decrease in their main predator (whales). On the other hand, Horwood (1970) has pointed out that not all the evidence is consistent with this hypothesis, and further, that allowance must also be made for the warming of the Antarctic since 1960 (Raper *et al.* 1983), which is likely to have increased the productivity of the Antarctic ecosystem and perhaps caused changes in the predators similar to those that would have been expected from the disappearance at about the same time of the great whales.

Nevertheless, the baleen whales (*B. musculus, physalus* and *borealis*) provide three of the seven cases listed by Fowler (1981) of statistically established evidence of density dependence in marine mammal populations. The difficulty remains of linking this with any direct measures of changes not only in the abundance but also in the distribution of krill. As Chapman (1981) puts it:

> While the rôle of krill in the (Antarctic) ecosystem is of major importance, the partitioning of krill between its users now and in the past is very uncertain. Nor can it be predicted with any certainty what will happen if there is a direct harvest of krill by man.

This matter is discussed further by Beddington and de la Mare in Chapter 5.

Practical assessment and monitoring

In the light of this indeterminate picture, it is tempting to conclude that predatory interaction between marine mammals and fisheries, except locally and temporally in certain circumstances, is a non-problem. The inadequacy of the factual record and the intrinsic variability of the system are a warning, however, that such a conclusion is premature. Both conservationists and fishermen may reasonably expect to be given some idea of what the underlying interaction might amount to if the signal were more clearly visible.

However, even put in this simple way, it is hardly possible, as we have seen, to say anything about the benefit to the marine mammal of relaxing fishing on its food species unless there is tangible evidence that the mammal is in some way being adversely affected by a shortage of food. It may, however, be possible to gain some idea of the converse effect, i.e. on the yield from the fishery through control of the marine mammal, from the simple theory developed above despite its imperfections, provided the predator–prey system is not of the kinds shown in Figures 1.4, 1.5 and 1.6.

To establish the possible range of the interactive effect, the simplest question to ask is: how much larger would the yield be from the fishery in question in the absence of the marine mammal, other things being equal? Taking first the case in which predation is confined to the pre-recruit phase, then with the previous notation and assumptions (see Eqn 1.9), this amounts to estimating the quantity:

$$\exp\left[M^*(t_r - t_p)\right] - 1 = \frac{Y_2 - Y_1}{Y_1}$$

The three quantities which, given appropriate sampling, it might be possible to estimate directly are:

(a)   the duration of pre-recruit predation, $t_r - t_p = \Delta t^*$, from the size and growth of the prey species;
(b)   the number of pre-recruit prey consumed annually by the marine mammal = C^*;
(c)   the mean annual recruitment to the fished population = R_r, by cohort analysis etc.

These alone do not provide a unique estimate of $(Y_2 - Y_1)/Y_1$ but if they are known approximately, the possible range within which $(Y_2 - Y_1)/Y_1$ lies can be narrowed. Thus, if R_p is the size of the year-class when it becomes susceptible to predation, we have:

$$R_p = R_r \exp(M^* + M^1)\Delta t^*$$

and hence the number of fish consumed annually by the predator per fish surviving to recruitment to the fishery is:

$$C^*/R_r = \frac{M^* \exp(M^* + M^1)\Delta t^*}{M^* + M^1}\left[1 - \exp - (M^* + M^1)\Delta t^*\right] \qquad (1.11)$$

from which

$$\exp(M^*\Delta t^*) - 1 = \frac{Y_2 - Y_1}{Y_1} = C^*/R_r \cdot \frac{(M^* + M^1)\exp - (M^1\Delta t^*)}{M^*[1 - \exp - (M^* + M^1)\Delta t^*]} - 1 \quad (1.12)$$

The relationship between $\exp(M^*\Delta t^*) - 1$ and C^*/R_r calculated from Equation 1.12 for values of $M^1\Delta t^*$ from zero to 2.4 is nearly proportional. It is exactly so when $M^1\Delta t^* =$ zero, at which, from Equation 1.12,

$$C^*/R_r = \exp(M^*\Delta t^*) - 1 = \frac{Y_2 - Y_1}{Y_1} \qquad (1.13)$$

The departure from strict proportionality increases with $M^1 \Delta t^*$ and with C^*/R_r, the true relationship being slightly concave downwards. However, a straight 'best-fitting' line does not depart by more than $\pm 5\%$ at most, for values of C^*/R_r up to 3 and $M^1 \Delta t^*$ up to 2.5. Figure 1.8 shows this approximately proportional relationship between $\exp(M^* \Delta t^*) - 1$ and C^*/R_r, which is sufficiently accurate to indicate the order of magnitude of the predation effect.

As an example, suppose that C^*/R_r has been estimated (as described above) to be about unity. The relative enhancement of yield in the absence of marine mammal predation must therefore lie somewhere in Figure 1.8 on the vertical line at $C^*/R_r = 1.0$, with a maximum possible value of 100% (i.e. a doubling of the present level) if there were no other causes of natural mortality, i.e. if $M^1 = $ zero. In practice, M^1 will not, of course, be zero, and if Δt^* can be estimated (which should be relatively easy), it may be possible to gain some idea from the biology and ecology of the prey species how much less the actual enhancement could be expected to be.

To take this line of reasoning a little further, suppose that Δt^* has been found to be 1.2 years, which is what might be expected in a relatively fast-growing fish which is exposed to this source of predation while still in the pre-recruit phase. If M^1 were 0.5, $M^1 \Delta t^*$ would be 0.6 and, from Figure 1.8, a better idea of the relative enhancement of yield to be expected in the absence of predation would be about 70%.

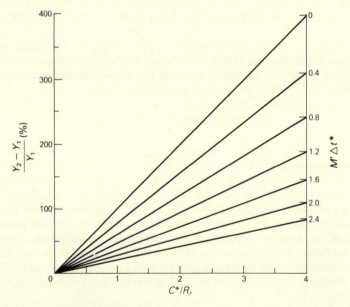

Figure 1.8 Potential enhancement of yield

$$\left(\frac{Y_2 - Y_1}{Y_1} \% \right)$$

in the absence of pre-recruit predation (duration Δt^*), as a function of numbers of prey consumed (C^*) per recruit surviving to enter the fishery (R_r). The other causes of mortality in the pre-recruit phases are denoted by M^1.

Some indication of whether a value of M^1 of 0.5 is realistic might be gauged after calculating the corresponding value of M^* which it implies. Thus, from Equation 1.13, with $\Delta t^* = 1.2$:

$$\exp(M^* \Delta t^*) - 1 = 0.7$$

so that

$$M^* = \frac{\log 1.7}{1.2} = \frac{0.53}{1.2} = 0.44$$

i.e. similar to M^1 but a little lower. This is what might be expected if there were other predators (e.g. birds) having an effect comparable to that of the marine mammal. In the absence of any such obvious additional predation, a lower value of M^1 might be considered, say 0.1. With $\Delta t^* = 1.2$ and $C^*/R_r = 1.0$ as before, the yield enhancement for $M^1 \Delta t^* = 0.12$, in the absence of marine mammal predation, would then be about 95% (Fig. 1.8) and the corresponding value of M^* would be 0.55.

If predation operates over the exploited phase of the prey species, as does the commercial fishery, the theory developed earlier is directly applicable. Thus if the suffix 2 denotes the regime in the absence of predation, i.e. $M_2^* = $ zero, then the relative enhancement in yield, from Equation 1.7, is:

$$\frac{Y_2 - Y_1}{Y_1} = \frac{\overline{W}_2}{\overline{W}_1} \cdot \frac{F + M^1 + M^*}{F + M^1} - 1 \qquad (1.13)$$

To establish the general pattern, it is sufficient to disregard the increase in average weight of fish in regime 2 compared with regime 1 and simply compare the two yields in numbers. Thus, putting $\overline{W}_2 = \overline{W}_1$ in Equation 1.14 gives:

$$\frac{Y_2 - Y_1}{Y_1} = \frac{F + M^1 + M^*}{F + M^1} - 1 = \frac{M^*}{F + M^1} \qquad (1.14)$$

Figure 1.9 shows how the ratio $Y_2 - Y_1/Y_1$ calculated from Equation 1.14 changes with $F + M^1$, for different values of M^*. The curves are, of course, simple hyperbolas; more interesting is their application to actual situations. Thus, the fact that M^1 must have a positive value, even though F may be zero, sets the left-hand limit to the range over which these curves would apply in practice. For example, it would be reasonable to regard M^1 as being at least 0.1, which is the vertical broken line delineating 'zone A'. It could further be anticipated that M^1 would be larger in small, short-lived species, which would also be more vulnerable to other sources of predation and have a higher intrinsic mortality; for these, even the region marked 'zone B' might in practice be rarely occupied.

It is self-evident that the enhancement of yield in the absence of predation would be relatively greater if predation were previously heavy (M^* large) than if it were light (M^* small). Figure 1.9 and Equations 1.13 and 1.14 also show that while the economic effect of losses by predation would probably be felt most acutely in a heavily fished stock, the actual amount consumed by a given predator population, both absolutely and relative to the commercial yield, increases as the fishing intensity is decreased. From that standpoint it could therefore be legitimately argued that the case for control of the

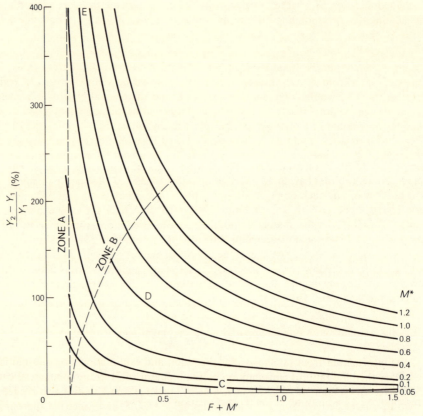

Figure 1.9 Potential enhancement of yield

$$\left(\frac{Y_2 - Y_1}{Y_1}\%\right)$$

in the absence of predation in the exploited phase (M^*), as a function of the coefficient of total mortality from all causes other than marine mammal predation ($F + M^1$).

directly competing predator is strengthened as a previously overfished state is being successfully remedied by decreasing the fishing intensity. Indeed, if the resulting greater abundance of the prey species should cause the marine mammal also to increase in the longer term, its predatory influence would increase still further. This contrasts with pre-recruit predation where the effect is confined to recruitment to the fished stock and is therefore independent of whether fishing is light or heavy.

It need hardly be emphasised that Figures 1.8 and 1.9 as they stand are intended to show only the order of magnitude of the potential effect of a predator on a commercial fishery and the pattern of response. For one thing, Figure 1.9 is calculated on numbers, and so to this extent underestimates the enhancement of yield in weight that might be expected from appreciable reductions of predation in a highly fished stock, possibly by a considerable margin. This particular cause of underestimating does not, of course, apply to the pre-recruit predation illustrated in Figure 1.8, which, however, for the reason discussed earlier, is more likely to be affected by compensatory changes in other causes of natural mortality.

Nevertheless, it is possible to locate the general area on Figure 1.9 where some of the cases described later in this book might lie. Thus, a relatively small marine mammal population, consuming annually an amount of prey that is a small fraction of the commercial catch from a fairly heavily fished stock, would be somewhere in the region marked C. This would correspond to grey seals and the general North Sea demersal fisheries. On the other hand, the case where a large marine mammal population is consuming an amount of a prey species equivalent to the annual catch from a moderately heavily fished stock would lie in the region marked D, with a correspondingly greater potential for enhancement. The extreme depletion by predation of a potentially long-lived prey species, as exemplified by the harbour seals–lake trout interaction in Quebec Province (see p. 55), would be located at the top left-hand of the diagram in the vicinity of E.

Criteria for predator control and monitoring

It is clear from the foregoing that to establish whether there is even an *a priori* case for predator control, it is necessary to know enough about:

(a) the kind and size of prey consumed by the marine mammal compared to the composition of the catches of the commercial fishery;
(b) the amounts consumed compared with the magnitude of those catches.

If the information from (a) shows that predation and exploitation sizes substantially overlap, then the ratio of consumption by the predator (C^*) to the commercial catch (Y) gives an estimate of M^*/F. This is a help, but an estimate of F is also needed so that M^* can be derived from the relationship $M^* = FC^*/Y$, and hence the appropriate curve of Figure 1.9 located. It may also be noted that the ratio of prey consumed by the predator to the amount caught in the commercial fishery ($C^*:Y$) is itself a fair approximation to the potential enhancement of yield if the residual natural mortality (M^1) is small compared with the fishing mortality. Thus, substituting for M^* in Equation 1.14 gives:

$$\frac{Y_2 - Y_1}{Y_1} = \frac{M^*}{F + M^1} = \frac{C^*}{Y} \cdot \frac{F}{F + M^1} \tag{1.15}$$

Therefore, if $F \gg M^1$,

$$\frac{F}{F + M^1} \simeq 1; \text{ and } \frac{Y_2 - Y_1}{Y_1} \simeq \frac{C^*}{Y}$$

If predation is found to be confined to the pre-recruit phase, the contemporary level of recruitment to the fishery (R_r) has to be estimated in absolute numbers by the usual techniques so that assessment of predation can proceed as outlined above.

In all cases, therefore, the status of the prey fishery needs to be known before it is possible to assess the potential gain from predator control – together, of course, with any special features of its biology and ecology that might invalidate a simple predator–prey analysis. The variety and variability in diet of opportunistic-feeding marine mammals put a heavy demand on sampling programmes, as is emphasised in some of the contributions in this book. No less difficult is to estimate the amount of food consumed by a marine mammal, partly because of regurgitation and digestion; but this quantity is so important that it seems essential to attempt to refine measurements of food consumption or requirements by every possible means, under experimental as well as field conditions.

Let us suppose, however, that these and other requirements have been fulfilled in a particular case and it is decided that the prospects of achieving a significant gain to a fishery are strong enough to justify a degree of predator control. To do this without endangering the marine mammal requires a sufficient knowledge of its population dynamics – particularly whether it is in a steady state or increasing, and, if the latter, by what rate. To go much further into this aspect of the subject is beyond the scope of this chapter, but it may be observed that nowadays proper monitoring of a predator control programme, to check whether the measures are having the desired effect on the size and replenishment rate of the marine mammal population, would usually be insisted on. In view of the difficulties normally to be expected in making population assessments of marine mammals, together with the effect on pup production of disturbance caused by culling (see Ch. 10), a considerable research and monitoring effort may be required, the costs of which must be set against the expected improvements in the fishery.

There is, however, one situation that avoids some of these risks and difficulties, namely that in which the marine mammal population is recovering from earlier depletion and has already reached the size at which assessments point to its competitive effect on the fishery being significant, and it is still growing. Several of the larger marine mammal populations discussed in later chapters meet this description. In these circumstances a properly organised and monitored culling programme, which removes just the surplus growth and so maintains the marine mammal population steady, would at least prevent what would otherwise have been an increasing loss to the fishery, without hazarding the marine mammal.

Whatever form of control programme is adopted, there will undoubtedly be the need to establish that the effect, not just on the marine mammal population, but also on the prey population and the fishery, is proving to be what was expected. The foregoing analysis shows how difficult it is to do this in a way that would be immediately and unambiguously evident to the non-technical (and possibly sceptical) observer without recourse to indirect evidence, deductive scientific reasoning and, in the end, 'best scientific judgement'.

For example, to bring about an increase in prey abundance of some 20–30% by predator control might well be feasible where predation is initially heavy in a lightly or moderately fished stock. An abrupt change in the prey population size of this magnitude is technically detectable in most well-sampled fish stocks, but when it is spread over a period of several years – perhaps even a decade – as would be the case in practice, it is likely to be swamped by changes due to other factors. Of these, fluctuations in year-class strength would usually be most pronounced, but changes in growth rate and fishing intensity must also be reckoned with. In principle, given good enough sampling and ancillary data (e.g. on fishery statistics), these various causes can be diagnosed and allowed for, but the simplicity of the signal is lost. Direct demonstration at the population level becomes even more difficult if the purpose of the control measure is not to lessen the impact of the present observed level of predation but to prevent it increasing in the future – even though this is, as we have noted above, the safest situation to deal with in other respects.

This dilemma is not, however, unique to the sphere of predator control in fisheries. It is essentially the same as that of trying to prove that a reduction in the amount of fishing or an increase in the gear selectivity in an overfished stock is having the effect for which the regulatory measure was justified in the first place. In each case the scientist is not necessarily predicting what the actual catches will be in the future; he is saying that whatever the future productivity of the stock, it will be that much enhanced and better utilised with the regulatory measure than without it. Because the 'improvement' is relative rather than absolute does not necessarily diminish its real value, even though its perceived value in terms of stock enhancement may be questioned.

Nevertheless, everything possible should, of course, be done to follow what is happening, not only for purposes of demonstration but also to check on whether the circumstances in which the original decision was made have changed. The most crucial information concerns the feeding habits of the marine mammal, in view of the gastronomic capriciousness of the more generalised opportunistic feeders. Indeed, if this means that the marine mammal's predatory impact varies appreciably from year to year, even without a change in its total population size, it might be possible to turn this to good effect if a rough estimate of this variation can be made and compared with the contemporary value of the total natural mortality coefficient ($M^1 + M^*$) in the prey population. This is something of a long shot, but the case for predator control is strongest where the predation mortality (M^*) is a high proportion of total mortality, and it is these circumstances that offer the best chance of estimating the value of M^* by the above approach.

The detection of stress in a marine mammal (except where it is acute and sustained) presents its own problems of a different kind. Hanks (1981) has reviewed the various kinds of physiological and other characteristics of individual animals that have been used for diagnosis. He concludes that there is none that is fully satisfactory, but that deposited fat reserves (either kidney fat index, KFI, or bone marrow fat, BMF) are the best. However, in the absence of the nutritional history of the animal and other evidence, it is difficult to know whether an abnormally low value of fat is due directly to a shortage of food which could conceivably be remedied by restriction of fishing on the prey population, or to the side-effects of illness or disease causing loss of appetite. Hanks goes on to point out that social and behavioural changes will usually be manifest before shortage of food reaches starvation levels, and that these may prove to be the best diagnostic characteristics to monitor.

Demographic indicators must also be treated with care. A population that is growing steadily, especially if historically it has been larger, is unlikely to be in difficulties. However, as it approaches its asymptotic size, the usual density-dependent constraints – increase in juvenile mortality rate and in age at first maturity, and a decrease in specific fecundity thereafter – must come into play, otherwise equilibrium will not be reached. If the appearance of these symptoms is interpreted as requiring 'remedial' action, such as increasing the food supply to the mammal population by restricting fishing on its prey, the population may be enabled to reach a higher asymptotic level than would otherwise have been the case, but the same symptoms would then reappear. The appearance of demographic symptoms of what would conventionally be regarded as 'stress' must therefore be interpreted with care and in the context of the overall ecological status of the marine mammal population, and is not necessarily indicative of the need for action.

Conclusion

It will be evident from the foregoing that if the policy objective is to maximise the benefit either to the fishery by control of the marine mammal, or to the marine mammal by control of the fishery, there is no logical end-point short of elimination of the marine mammal or closure of the fishery, respectively. (If, however, the marine mammal is also harvested as a resource in its own right, then various intermediate stable solutions for management of the system as a whole are possible – see, for example, May *et al.* 1979.) There may be circumstances when one or other of these extremes is the accepted or imposed solution; but usually the policy will be either to do nothing or to try to achieve some form of intermediate solution which offers a reasonable, if not wholly acceptable, compromise between the opposing interests. The concluding paragraph of the La Jolla Report puts it in the following way:

> The juxtaposition between a perceived threat, on the one hand to a food resource and dependent livelihoods, and on the other to the protection of a highly-prized wildlife population and perhaps other dependent livelihoods, is a conflict of interest which science cannot resolve. Some form of compromise will be needed, based on a mutual recognition and understanding of respective positions. It is for the scientists to attempt to establish the true substance of the perceived threat to each side, distinguishing fact from guesswork, and so to offer the best impartial guidance that is possible on existing knowledge to those with whom the ultimate decision will lie.

To meet this challenge in the emotionally charged adversarial situation created by the opposing interests, places a special burden on the scientists. They must endeavour to preserve a strictly objective and dispassionate approach if their advice and assessments are to be taken notice of by the many on both sides who start from preconceived ideas as to what should or should not be done. Of fundamental importance in this connection is the building up of a sound base of rigorously tested scientific facts and theory, to which objective it is hoped that this book will make a worthwhile contribution.

References

Bailey, K. M. and D. G. Ainley 1982. The dynamics of California sea-lion predation on Pacific hake. *Fish. Res.* **1**, 163–76.

Beddington, J. R. and J. G. Cooke 1982. Harvesting from a prey–predator complex. *Ecol. Modelling* **14**, 155–77.

Beddington, J. R. and R. M. May 1980. Maximum sustainable yields in systems subject to harvesting at more than one trophic level. *Math. Biol. Sci.* **51**, 261–81.

Bjørge, A., I. Christensen and T. Øritsland 1981. *Current problems and research related to interactions between marine mammals and fisheries in Norwegeian coastal and adjacent waters.* ICES, C.M. 1981/N, 18 (mimeo).

Bowen, W. D., P. K. Capstick and D. E. Sergeant 1981. Temporal changes in the reproductive potential of female harp seals (*Pagophilus groenlandicus*). *Can. J. Fish. Aquat. Sci.* **38**, 495–503.

Chapman, D. G. 1981. Evaluation of marine mammal population models. In *Dynamics of large mammal populations*, C. W. Fowler and T. D. Smith (eds), 277–96. New York: Wiley.

Croxall, J. P., P. A. Prince and C. Ricketts. Relationships between prey life-cycles and the extent, nature and timing of seal and seabird predation in the Scotia Sea. In *Nutrient cycling and food webs in the Antarctic*, W. R. Siegfried, P. Condy and R. M. Laws (eds). Proceedings of the Fourth SCAR Symposium on Antarctic Biology. Berlin: Springer-Verlag.

Eberhardt, L. L. 1977. Optimal policies for conservation of large mammals, with special reference to marine ecosystems. *Environ. Conserv.* 4, 81–6.

Fay, F. H. and L. F. Lowry 1981. *Seasonal use and feeding habits of walruses in the proposed Bristol Bay clam fishery area.* Unpubl. final report contract No. 80-3, North Pacific Fish. Man. Council, Anchorage, AK.

Fowler, C. W. 1981. Comparative population dynamics in large mammals. In *Dynamics of large mammal populations*, C. W. Fowler and T. D. Smith (eds), 437–55. New York: Wiley.

Fowler, C. W. 1982. Interactions of Northern fur seals and commercial fisheries. *Trans. 47th N. Am. Wildl. and Nat. Res. Conf.*, 278–92.

Fowler, C. W., W. T. Bunderso, R. J. Ryel and B. B. Steele 1980. A preliminary review of density-dependent reproduction and survival in large mammals. In *Comparative population dynamics of large mammals: a search for management criteria*, 330. Washington DC: US Department of Commerce.

Hanks, J. 1981. Characterization of population condition. In *Dynamics of large mammal populations,* C. W. Fowler and T. D. Smith (eds), 47–76. New York: Wiley.

Holling, C. S. 1965. The functional response of predators to prey density and its role in mimicry and population regulation. *Mem. Ent. Soc. Can.* 45, 3–60.

Holt, S. J. and D. M. Lavigne 1982. Seals slaughtered – science abused. *New Sci.* 11 March, 636–9.

Horwood, J. W. 1980. Competition in the Antarctic? *Rep. Int. Whal. Comm.* 30, 513–17.

Laws, R. M. 1977. Seals and whales of the southern seas. *Phil. Trans. R. Soc.* B, 81–96.

Lockwood, S. J. 1981. Density-dependent mortality in O-group plaice (*Plemonectes platessa* L.) populations. *J. Cons. Int. Explor. Mer.* 39(2), 148–53.

McCann, T. S. 1980. Size, status and demography of Southern elephant seal (*Mirounga leonina*) populations. In *Sea mammals of Southern latitudes,* J. K. Ling and M. M. Bryden (eds), 133–50. Adelaide: South Australia Museum.

Mate, B. R. 1981. Verbal communication to La Jolla Workshop.

May, R. M. (ed.) 1976. *Theoretical ecology: principles and applications.* Oxford: Blackwell Scientific.

May, R. M., J. R. Beddington, C. W. Clark, S. J. Holt and R. M. Laws 1979. Management of multi-species fisheries. *Sci.* 205, 267–77.

Maynard Smith, J. 1974. *Models in ecology.* Cambridge: Cambridge University Press.

Parrish, B. B. and W. M. Shearer 1977. *Effects of seals on fisheries.* ICES C.M. 1977/M, 14.

Power, G. and J. Gregoire 1978. Predation by freshwater seals on the fish community of Lower Seal Lake, Quebec. *J. Fish. Res. Bd Can.* 35, 844–50.

Rae, B. B. (1972). A review of the cod-worm problem in the North Sea and in western Scottish waters, 1958–1970. *Mar. Res.* 1972, No. 2, Edinburgh: HMSO.

Raper, S. C. B., T. M. L. Wigley, P. D. Jones, P. M. Kelly, P. R. Mayes and D. W. S. Limbert 1983. Recent temperature changes in the Arctic and Antarctic. *Nature* 306, 458–9.

Reijnders, P. J. H. 1983. *Man-induced environmental factors in relation to fertility changes in pinnipeds.* ICES, C.M. 1983/N, 11.

Shirakihara, K. and S. Tanaka 1978. Two fish species competition model with non-linear interactions and equilibrium catches. *Res. Pop. Ecol.* 20, 123–40.

Ulltang, Ø. 1980. Factors affecting the reaction of pelagic fish stocks to exploitation and requiring a new approach to assessment and management. *Rapp. P-v. Reun. Cons. Int. Explor. Mer.* 177, 489–504.

2 Economic aspects of marine mammal-fishery interactions

Colin W. Clark

Introduction

Marine mammal–fishery interactions differ in a number of important respects from fishery–fishery interactions, not the least of which is political. The numerous 'protect the whale/seal...' movements do not appear to have many 'protect the cod/hake...' counterparts. Both situations, however, are often characterised by *conflicts of interest*, in the sense that biologically interdependent populations are exploited by, or are of interest to, distinct groups of people.

In such cases, any notion of a uniquely 'optimal' management policy becomes largely irrelevant, although some sense might be made of the general notion of Pareto optimality (Vincent 1980). (A management policy would be termed 'Pareto' if no change in the policy would be considered beneficial, or at least non-detrimental, to each interest group.)

It therefore seems appropriate to search for alternative principles of management that get away from the traditional notions of optimality (maximum sustainable yield MSY, optimum economic yield OEY, etc.), which in any case were largely devised for application to single-species fisheries. It is unlikely that any single principle will suffice to cover all situations. Certainly reduction of conflicts and maintenance of ecosystem integrity are two criteria which any good management policy should achieve. On these scores, most simple economic optimisation models would fail miserably, since in most cases such models call for some form of exclusion, either of one group of exploiters or of one component of the interacting populations.

As an obvious example, if a mammal population preys on a commercial fish stock, a simple economic analysis would probably call either for elimination of the mammalian predators, or for exclusive harvesting of the mammals, depending on whether fish were more valuable for human consumption or as a food supply for the mammals.

Marine mammal–fishery interactions

The predator–prey relationship is probably the most common form of interaction between fish and mammals. The fish, mammals, or both, may be of direct commercial importance. To a first approximation, it appears that appropriate management of such a system would involve the selection of a target population (or target yield) for the mammals, plus an allocation of an appropriate portion of fish production to maintain this target mammal population. This follows the accepted principle of quota allocations in multinational fisheries (Munro 1979); determination of quota allocations will involve political, historical, and economic considerations. The question of efficient harvesting of the corresponding quotas can then be addressed separately, if desired (Clark 1980).

But even apart from the usual (and severe) biological difficulties associated with population and yield estimates, certain special problems, primarily of an economic nature, may arise. For example, different timescales may apply to the dynamics of predator and prey populations (May *et al.* 1979), and this may be economically significant. Also, the concentration ('patchiness') of prey populations may influence both the population dynamics of predator and prey as well as the costs of fishing (May *et al.* 1979, Clark 1981). These questions are discussed further below.

Other trophic relationships between mammal and fish populations are conceivable, if less prevalent. But while estimation of these relationships may be even more difficult than for a predator–prey relationship, the general principles of management are probably the same.

A different situation arises when mammals have a direct influence on fishing operations, whether beneficial (e.g. porpoise–tuna) or deleterious (seals in fishing gear). The porpoise–tuna interaction is interesting, in that it implies common-property externalities not only for tuna, but also for porpoises, so that even purely economic considerations (ignoring porpoise protection motives *per se*) would involve regulation of both tuna and porpoise catches. As far as the US is concerned, however, it is obviously the Marine Mammal Act (and not economics) that sets the porpoise quota.

Concentration effects

It is clear that as exploitation of a given fishery increases in intensity, more detailed biological information is required. The spatial distribution characteristics of a lightly exploited stock, for example, may be more or less irrelevant, but extrapolation of catch–effort curves to more intense levels of exploitation may be quite misleading, and has proven so especially for pelagic schooling species with so-called Type IV concentration profiles (Fig. 2.1, Clark 1981).

The concentration profile for an exploited fish population represents the marginal concentration ρ of fish, as a function of stock abundance X; here, 'marginal' means the maximum concentration (density) of the population, the idea being that fishermen will be motivated to deplete high concentrations first. Type I profiles pertain to sedentary species, Type II to diffusive species, and Type III and IV to agglomerative (e.g. schooling) species of fish. Catch per unit effort (CPUE) in the fishery should be proportional to $\rho(X)$, so that the catchability coefficient q would be proportional to $\rho(X)/X$.

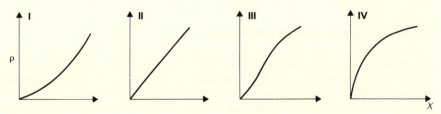

Figure 2.1 Concentration profiles: X = stock abundance, ρ = marginal concentration (from Clark 1981).

Thus catchability declines as stock abundance decreases, for Type I species, but q increases as X decreases for Type IV species. (See Clark (1981) for further discussion.)

Consider now a marine mammal population relying exclusively on a single prey species – whales and krill provide an obvious example. The following krill–whale model has been described at some length by May *et al.* (1979):

$$\dot{N}_1 = \gamma_1 N_1 [1 - N_1/K - aN_2 - F_1] \tag{2.1}$$

$$\dot{N}_2 = \gamma_2 N_2 [1 - N_2 /(\alpha N_1) - F_2] \tag{2.2}$$

where N_1 and N_2 represent krill and whale population sizes, respectively. On the right side of Equation 2.1, K represents krill carrying capacity, the term $a\gamma_1 N_1 N_2$ represents whale predation rate, and $\gamma_1 N_1 F_1$ is the harvest rate of krill. In Equation 2.2, it is assumed that $K_2 = \alpha N_1$, i.e. the whale carrying capacity, is completely determined by (and is proportional to) the size of the krill stock.

Note that the above model ignores any concentration effects, and assumes in effect that both krill and whale stocks retain uniform densities over the entire range of exploitation rates F_1, F_2. The model can be modified in various ways so as to eliminate this rather extreme assumption, for example:

$$\dot{N}_1 = \gamma_1 N_1 [1 - N_1/K_1 - a\bar{\rho}(N_1)N_2 - F_1] \tag{2.3}$$

$$\dot{N}_2 = \gamma_2 N_2 [\varrho(N_1) - b - N_2/K_2 - F_2] \tag{2.4}$$

where $\bar{\rho}(N_1) = \rho(N_1)/N_1$.

The predation term $a\gamma_1\varrho(N_1)N_2$ in Equation 2.3 reflects an assumption that whales 'target' on high krill concentrations; this is a simple generalisation of the model of May *et al.* The density-dependent term $\varrho(N_1) - b - N_2/K_2$ in Equation 2.4, however, is of a different form from that in Equation 2.2. The term $\varrho(N_1) - b$ is derived from energetic considerations. The intrinsic growth rate of the whale population depends upon the availability (density) of krill; if this falls below a critical level b, whale metabolism cannot be maintained, and the population suffers a positive mortality rate independent of N_2. The addition term N_2/K_2 reflects an additional density-dependent mortality rate; this term could be omitted without seriously affecting the qualitative behaviour of the model. We will assume that krill, being relatively immobile, have a Type I concentration profile $\rho(N_1)$.

In the revised model, as in the original, catch rates are represented by the terms $\gamma_i N_i F_i$, so that (in the usual terminology), $\gamma_i F_i$ represents fishing *mortality* for species i. If E_i denotes fishing *effort* as usually defined (e.g. number of standardised fishing days per year), then the fact that krill (and probably also whales) exhibit a non-linear concentration profile implies that E_i will be a biased index of F_i. Roughly, one expects (if whales and krill fishermen both target on the same highest krill concentrations) that $F_1 \sim \rho(N_1)E_1$, and also $F_2 \sim \rho_2(N_2)E_2$.

Figure 2.2 is the phase-plane portrait of Equations 2.3 and 2.4. It is easy to see that any combination of F_1, F_2 (= constant) such that

$$K_1(1 - F_1) < \rho^{-1}(b + F_2)$$

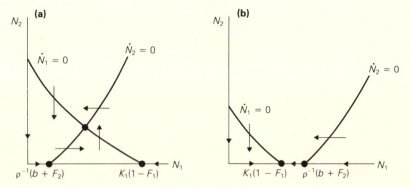

Figure 2.2 Phase portraits for Equations 2.3 and 2.4: (a) subcritical exploitation rates; (b) supercritical rates. Both isoclines shift downwards as F_1 or F_2 increases.

results in the extinction of the whales at equilibrium. In particular, sufficiently high krill exploitation rates result in whale extinction even for zero exploitation of whales. This is in sharp contrast with the original model, for which the $\dot{N}_2 = 0$ isocline always passes through the origin, so that the constant F_i -equilibrium ($F_i < 1$) always has $\dot{N}_1 > 0$ for both species.

The implications of this analysis are quite obvious. Where concentration of prey is important to predators, the mere setting of total catch quotas for the prey species (allowing even for predator consumption) may not achieve the desired effect of maintaining the predator stocks. Instead, prey catch quotas would have to be made area specific, with special limitations or prohibition of catches from the most highly concentrated areas. Since these are the areas most likely to be preferred by the prey harvesting fishery, the need for protection is exaggerated.

Another aspect of concentration that may have economic significance in some fisheries (e.g. Pacific salmon, herring) is the tendency for marine mammals to inflict severe losses on spawning or migrating stocks of fish. In such cases, the economic cost of protection of marine mammal stocks could rise sharply as these stocks build up. A similar situation could arise if mammals compete for prey with some commercially valuable fish species, although I am not aware of such a case.

Time discounting

Marine mammal populations typically possess low intrinsic rates of growth, e.g. as low as 1 per cent per annum estimated for some species of fur seals (Shaughnessy & Butterworth 1980). This renders such populations liable to severe overexploitation, and also reduces the incentive for conservation as a consequence of normal discounting of future resources (e.g. Clark & Lamberson 1982).

The effect of discounting on multispecies systems has not been modelled in detail, but the effect is discussed briefly, in the krill–whale setting, by May *et al* (1979). In general, for the case of a mammalian predator and fish prey, the choice may be between harvesting the prey for an immediate return, and instead harvesting the predator at some time in the future. This choice is particularly evident in cases, such as in the Antarctic, where the mammal population is currently in a depleted state. Even though the ultimate long-term yield from whales may far exceed krill in value, the fishing industry may be motivated to harvest krill and forego whales. The conflict between present and future extends down the trophic chain. Ecosystem-orientated management objectives may thus conflict with economic objectives in a variety of ways.

Interference

Marine mammals interfere with fishing operations both negatively (raiding netted fish) and positively (aiding in the capture of tuna). Economic motives would call for the reduction of populations that interfere negatively, to a degree depending on the commercial value of fish versus the mammals. As elsewhere, however, it would generally be hopeless to try to use some concept of MEY (maximum economic yield) as an operational objective. Instead, some simplistic compromise, at least recognising the interference problem, would seem best.

Somewhat more interesting economically is the apparently perverse killing of large numbers of porpoises by tuna fishermen, to whom the porpoises provide a valuable service in helping to locate and capture tuna. Economic theory recognises this phenomenon as a standard common-property externality. The costs of minimising the kill of porpoises are borne by the individual vessel, but the benefits are shared (later!) by the entire industry. This seems to imply that yellowfin tuna catches *and* porpoise quotas should both be managed by the tuna commission. However, there are so many other complications – legalistic, international, etc. – that a really satisfactory solution seems remote.

References

Clark, C. W. 1980. Towards a predictive model for the economic regulation of commercial fisheries. *Can. J. Fish. Aquat. Sci.* **37**(7), 1111–29.

Clark, C. W. 1981. *Concentration profiles and the production and management of marine fisheries*. Univ. of B.C. Inst. Appl. Math. Stat. Tech. Report 80–1.

Clark, C. W. and R. H. Lamberson 1982. Pelagic whaling: an economic history and analysis. *Marine Policy*. April 1982, 103–20.

May, R. M., J. R. Beddington, C. W. Clark, S. J. Holt and R. M. Laws 1979. Management of multispecies fisheries. *Sci.* 205, 267–77.

Munro, G. R. 1979. The optimal management of transboundary renewable resources. *Can. J. Econ.* **12**, 354–76.

Shaughnessy, P. D. and D. S. Butterworth 1980. Historical trends in the population size of the Cape fur seal *Arctocephalus pussillus*. In *Worldwide furbearer conference proceedings*, Vol. II, J. A. Chapman and D. Pursley (eds), 1305–27. Falls Church, Virginia: R. R. Donnelley.

Vincent, T. L. 1980. Vulnerability of a prey–predator model under harvesting. In *Renewable resource management*, T. L. Vincent and J. M. Skowronski (eds), 112–32. Proceedings of a Workshop on control theory applied to renewable resource management and ecology held in Christchurch, New Zealand, 7–11 January 1980.

Case studies of interactions

3 Biological interactions between marine mammals and commercial fisheries in the Bering Sea

Lloyd F. Lowry and Kathryn J. Frost

Introduction

Exploitation of marine mammal and fish populations has been a major factor in the exploration, colonisation, and development of the Bering Sea region. Although these resources have been utilised by indigenous peoples for several thousand years, it was not until the 17th and 18th centuries that the abundance of seals, sea otters, walruses, and whales was 'discovered' by Europeans (Fay 1981). Over the next two centuries, populations of several species were depleted to the point of commercial extinction, while one, the Steller sea cow (*Hydrodamalis gigas*), became biologically extinct. Through a series of domestic and international laws and treaties, a framework for the conservation and management of marine mammal populations was slowly developed. Most recently, the Marine Mammal Protection Act (MMPA) of 1972 (PL-92-522) has attempted to provide guidelines for the protection and management of marine mammals in the United States, with the stated primary objective of maintaining the 'health and stability of the marine ecosystem'.

Commercial exploitation of Bering Sea fish stocks did not begin until after the peak of marine mammal harvests. Small catches of Pacific cod (*Gadus macrocephalus*) and halibut (*Hippoglossus stenolepis*) were made in the late 1800s, but substantial harvests did not occur until early in the 20th century (Pruter 1973). These two species, along with salmon (*Oncorhynchus* spp.), were the principal target species prior to 1940. After World War II, a major diversification occurred in the fisheries, resulting in exploitation of many additional species, including yellowfin sole (*Limanda aspera*), walleye pollock (*Theragra chalcogramma*), Pacific ocean perch (*Sebastes alutus*), Atka mackerel (*Pleurogrammus monopterygius*), herring (*Clupea harengus*), sablefish (*Anoplopoma fimbria*), shrimps (*Pandalus* spp.), king crabs (*Paralithodes* spp.), and tanner crabs (*Chionoecetes* spp.). Domestic fishing has been regulated primarily by the federal government; after 1960 the State of Alaska developed management programmes for salmon, herring, shrimp, and crab fisheries. Foreign fisheries were in some instances regulated by domestic legislation and international agreements which were generally not adequate to prevent overexploitation and decline of stocks (Pruter 1973). The Magnuson Fishery Conservation and Management Act (FCMA) of 1976 (PL-94-265) established a 200-mile Fishery Conservation Zone (FCZ) in seas adjacent to the United

States and provided a framework for management of existing commercial fisheries and development of fisheries for species not presently utilised commercially.

Natural history studies of Bering Sea marine mammals have documented the importance of commercially harvested fish and shellfish species in marine mammal diets (e.g. Scheffer 1950, Lowry *et al*. 1979). Preliminary estimates indicated that the annual consumption of commercially important fishes by marine mammals exceeded the amount harvested by the fisheries (McAlister & Perez 1976). Considering the magnitude of the trophic interaction between marine mammals and commercially important fishes in the Bering Sea, an ecosystem-based approach to management of fish and shellfish populations is obviously desirable. Since ecosystem-based management is encouraged by provisions of both the MMPA and the FCMA (Hammon 1980), an attempt was made to consider marine mammal food requirements in the development of the Bering Sea/Aleutian Islands groundfish fishery management plan. This attempt was only partially successful due to the lack of adequate data and models with which to analyse and simulate the possible interactions. We have recently reviewed and evaluated the available data on foods and population status of Bering Sea marine mammals (Lowry *et al*. 1982). In this chapter we will summarise the results of that effort and present an assessment of present and potential interactions between marine mammals and fisheries in the Bering Sea.

Description of Bering Sea/Aleutian Islands area

The Bering Sea is the northernmost peripheral sea of the North Pacific Ocean. The coastline includes three major embayments: Bristol Bay and Norton Sound on the east and the Gulf of Anadyr in the north-west. Its surface area of approximately 2.3 million km^2 makes the Bering Sea the third largest semi-enclosed sea in the world. This area comprises 44% continental shelf, 43% abyssal depths, and 13% continental slope (Hood & Kelley 1974). The shelf, covering an area of 1.2 million km^2, is most extensive in the northeastern Bering.

Oceanographic studies indicate distinguishable water masses (Ingraham 1981) and a complex flow pattern, including several major gyres (Takenouti & Ohtani 1974). Although seasonal fluctuations in flow rate and directions have been recently documented, net annual transport of water through Bering Strait is to the north (Coachman & Aagaard 1981). The majority of the water entering the Bering Sea is of North Pacific origin and flows through passes in the Aleutian Islands. Oceanographic features important to productivity include vertical transport (upwelling) near passes in the Aleutians (Hood 1981) and hydrographic structures (fronts) which occur along the continental slope and shelf (Kinder & Schumacher 1981).

The climate of the Bering Sea fosters the development of seasonal sea ice in a large portion of the region, which in turn has a major effect on weather (Konishi & Saito 1974). Ice formation in the northern Bering begins in November, with pack ice coverage progressing southward during winter and early spring. The maximum southward extent, which usually reaches the continental shelf break, occurs in late March. Considerable annual variations in ice coverage occur and are correlated with fluctuations in sea surface temperature, air temperature, and wind direction (Niebauer 1981).

The Bering Sea is an area of high biological productivity, as indicated by abundant fish, bird and mammal populations. Upwelling near passes in the Aleutian Islands and the presence of fronts on the shelf and shelf break provide nutrient regimes and water column characteristics that may favour high primary production. In addition, the presence of sea ice may enhance annual primary production both through the contribution of epontic (ice-associated) algae (McRoy & Goering 1974) and an enhancement of water column stability (Niebauer *et al*. 1981).

The benthic invertebrate fauna of the Bering Sea shelf is well described, with recent summaries available for both infauna (Haflinger 1981, Stoker 1981) and epifauna (Jewett & Feder 1981). The fauna is dominated by boreal Pacific forms with high-arctic species common only in northern regions. Clams, polychaetes, and amphipods dominate the infauna; echinoderms, crabs, and snails are major components of the epifauna. Of particular importance to marine mammals and fisheries are the abundant populations of crabs (Jewett & Feder 1981), clams (Hughes & Bourne 1981), and snails (MacIntosh & Somerton 1981).

The fish fauna of the Bering Sea includes approximately 300 species, which can be divided into two major groups: a cold-region fauna consisting primarily of arctic species and associated with negative bottom temperatures found north and west of St Matthew Island, and a boreal Pacific fauna found in the remainder of the area (Wilimovsky 1974). The three dominant families, Cottidae (sculpins), Liparidae (snailfishes), and Stichaeidae (pricklebacks), contain 45% of the known species, but are of no commercial value. Species of commercial interest are primarily of the families Gadidae (cods), Pleuronectidae (flatfishes), Clupeidae (herring), and Salmonidae (salmon).

Seabirds, shorebirds and waterfowl are all major components of the Bering Sea avifauna (Hunt *et al*. 1981b, 1981c, Gill & Handel 1981, King & Dau 1981). Seabirds are of primary concern in considerations of the Bering Sea marine ecosystem and possible interactions with fisheries. Many species form large breeding colonies on island and mainland coasts. Major colonies occur on Nunivak, St Matthew, St Lawrence, Diomede, King, and the Pribilof islands, and at Cape Newenham. Up to 20.5 million seabirds have been estimated to breed in the eastern Bering Sea (Hunt *et al*. 1981b). An additional 20 million non-breeding visitors and immatures of breeding species are also estimated to occur there (Hunt *et al*. 1981c). Feeding ecology of major species has been described in detail by Hunt *et al*. (1981d).

Bering Sea marine mammal fauna

The marine mammal fauna selected for study includes 26 species which occur or can occur in the Bering Sea/Aleutian Islands region. Included are eight species of baleen whales, eight toothed whales, eight pinnipeds, and two carnivores (Table 3.1).

The presence of sea ice in the Bering Sea has a major effect on marine mammal distribution and ecology. Fay (1974) has discussed in detail the importance of ice in the ecology of Bering Sea marine mammals. For all species it forms a barrier which they must penetrate in order to have access to air to breathe and to water where they can feed and escape inclement weather or predators. For pagophilic (ice-loving) species which are adapted to living on and among the ice, this habitat provides protection, transportation, and a substrate on which to rest, socialise, and bear and nurture young. The pagophilic fauna includes eight species: bowhead and belukha whales, walruses, polar bears, and spotted, ribbon, ringed, and bearded seals. The remaining species contact ice only occasionally or virtually never. Within the sea ice habitat, the pagophilic species show associations with ice of particular characteristics (Burns 1970, Burns

Table 3.1 Taxonomic listing of marine mammal species known to occur in the Bering Sea and Aleutian Islands regions.

Phylum Chordata	Subphylum Vertebrata	Class Mammalia

Order Cetacea — whales, dolphins, and porpoises
  Suborder Mysticeti — baleen or whalebone whales
    Family Eschrichtidae
      grey whale — *Eschrichtius robustus*
    Family Balaenopteridae — rorquals
      fin or finback whale — *Balaenoptera physalus*
      minke whale — *Balaenoptera acutorostrata*
      blue whale — *Balaenoptera musculus*
      sei whale — *Balaenoptera borealis*
      humpback whale — *Megaptera novaengliae*
    Family Balaenidae — right whales
      right whale — *Balaena glacialis*
      bowhead whale — *Balaena mysticetus*

  Suborder Odontoceti — toothed whales
    Family Physeteridae
      sperm whale — *Physeter macrocephalus*
    Family Monodontidae
      belukha, beluga, or white whale — *Delphinapterus leucas*
    Family Ziphidae
      Cuvier's beaked whale — *Ziphius cavirostris*
      Baird's beaked whale — *Berardius bairdi*
      Stejneger's beaked whale — *Mesoplodon stejnegeri*
    Family Delphinidae
      killer whale — *Orcinus orca*
    Family Phocoenidae
      Dall's porpoise — *Phocoenoides dalli*
      harbour porpoise — *Phocoena phocoena*
Order Carnivora — carnivores
  Suborder fissipedia
    Family Ursidae
      polar bear — *Ursus maritimus*
    Family Mustelidae
      sea otter — *Enhydra lutris*
  Suborder Pinnipedia — seals, sea-lions, and walruses
    Family Otariidae — eared Seals
      northern fur seal — *Callorhinus ursinus*
      Steller or northern sea-lion — *Eumetopias jubata*
    Family Odobenidae
      pacific walrus — *Odobenus rosmarus*
    Family Phocidae — true seals
      harbour seal — *Phoca vitulina richardsi*
      spotted or large seal — *Phoca largha*
      ribbon seal — *Phoca (Histriophoca) fasciata*
      ringed seal — *Phoca (Pusa) hispida*
      bearded seal — *Erignathus barbatus*

et al. 1980). Distribution and characteristics of sea ice therefore influence access to resources by marine mammals. For example, the northern limit of sea otters is probably determined by the regular occurrence of ice; grey whales are excluded from their feeding grounds in the northern Bering Sea until the ice pack loosens sufficiently in spring; and shorefast ice excludes all species except ringed seals and polar bears from the coastal zone during winter months. Several of the pagophilic species (bowhead whales, polar bears, and ringed and bearded seals) virtually disappear from the Bering Sea during the open-water season.

Table 3.2 Categorisation of maximum numerical abundances and biomass of marine mammals in the Bering Sea.

Species	Maximum numerical abundance			Population biomass (tonnes)		
	<10 000	10 000– 100 000	>100 000	<10 000	10 000– 100 000	>100 000
Baleen whales						
grey whale		×				×
fin whale[a]	×				×	
minke whale	×				×	
blue whale[a]	×			×		
sei whale[a]	×			×		
humpback whale [a]	×			×		
right whale[a]	×			×		
bowhead whale	×				×	
Toothed whales						
sperm whale		×				×
belukha		×		×		
Cuvier's beaked whale[a]	×			×		
Baird's beaked whale[a]	×			×		
Stejneger's beaked whale[a]	×			×		
killer whale[a]	×			×		
Dall's porpoise		×		×		
harbour porpoise[a]	×			×		
Pinnipeds						
northern fur seal			×		×	
Steller sea-lion		×			×	
walrus			×			×
harbour seal		×		×		
spotted seal			×		×	
ribbon seal		×		×		
ringed seal			×		×	
bearded seal			×		×	
Carnivores						
polar bear	×			×		
sea otter		×		×		

[a] Indicates population estimated at 1000 or less.

The total number of marine mammals inhabiting the Bering Sea and Aleutian Islands region is not accurately known, but is probably between 2 and 3 million. The number and species composition vary seasonally, in large part due to summer replacement of the pagophillic species by those such as the fur seal and grey, humpback, and fin whales which come into the Bering Sea to feed during ice-free seasons.

In Table 3.2 we have categorised the numerical and biomass abundance of the Bering Sea marine mammal species based primarily on estimates available in the literature (see Lowry *et al*. 1982). The population size of most cetacean species is small in comparison to the pinnipeds: 12 of the 16 cetacean species occurring in the Bering Sea number less than 10 000, and 10 of those probably number 1000 or less. The most numerous cetacean species is the Dall's porpoise, with a population of nearly 100 000 (Bouchet 1981). In contrast, all pinniped populations are estimated to exceed 10 000 individuals, with five of the eight species numbering in excess of 100 000. Due to the large individual size of some whales, population size estimated in terms of biomass shows a more equal distribution among taxonomic groups. Species with population biomasses in excess of 100 000 tonnes include one baleen whale (grey whale), one toothed whale (sperm whale), and one pinniped (walrus). It is obvious that the species contributing the most to marine mammal biomass in the Bering Sea are both abundant and large.

The economic significance of Bering Sea marine mammals is indicated by their past and present contribution to commercial and subsistence harvesting. Virtually all species except polar bears and some of the small toothed whales have at some time been commercially harvested. Commercial harvesting of all pinnipeds and two cetacean species continues at present, primarily by the Soviet Union and Japan. All pinnipeds, both carnivores, and several species of cetaceans have in the past supported subsistence harvests.

The ecological rôle of marine mammals in the Bering Sea is a complex topic. Their effect on the distribution and abundance of prey stocks and related species is likely to be of great importance. In one well-documented instance (Simenstad *et al*. 1978), the foraging activities of sea otters have been shown to have a dramatic effect on the dynamics and composition of the nearshore biotic community. Grey whales and walruses disturb the bottom during feeding, and their foraging activities may regulate the composition of the benthic community in certain areas (Nerini 1981, Oliver *et al*. in prep.). Ingestion and defecation by walruses result in a substantial redistribution of sediment (Fay *et al*. 1977). Recycling and redistribution of nutrients in the faeces of marine mammals may be of importance to the ecosystem (FAO 1978), as may the breakdown products of carcasses of dead animals.

Documentation of marine mammal-fishery interactions in the Bering Sea

As one would expect, the earliest observations of stomach contents of marine mammals showed that marine fishes and shellfishes were major items in their diets. However, prior to 1950, few studies of marine mammals documented their foods in any quantitative fashion. In the Bering Sea and North Pacific, Soviet commercial harvests of ice seals provided some data on foods of those species (e.g. Arseniev 1941, Fedoseev 1965, Shustov 1965, Gol'tsev 1971, Kosygin 1971). Other experimental and opportunistic observations added data on foods of fur seals, sea-lions, and harbour seals (e.g. Scheffer & Sperry 1931, Imler & Sarber 1947, Scheffer 1950). Interestingly, although several samples were collected at areas and times when salmon were present, fishes of the cod, herring and smelt families were usually the major prey. Nonetheless, due to acknowledged direct interactions with salmon fisheries and a perceived competition for resources, harbour seals and sea-lions in particular were subject to bounties and control programmes with the aim of reducing their effects on fisheries (see Mate 1980). Such control programmes were terminated by 1970. Further studies of foods of pinnipeds generally confirmed the dietary importance of herring, smelts, and cods (see summary by Lowry & Frost 1981a).

General information on foods of cetaceans became available with the examination of animals taken in commercial harvests (e.g. Tomilin 1957, Zimushko & Lenskaya 1970). This has been supplemented by examination of animals, particularly small cetaceans, which were taken by subsistence hunters (e.g. Seaman *et al*. 1982), caught in fishing gear or washed up dead on shore (Scheffer 1953). In general, zooplankton, squids, and small schooling fishes have been found to be the major prey of cetaceans, and, given the offshore distribution of most species and their observed foods, interactions with fisheries have appeared slight. A notable exception involves belukha whales in Bristol Bay. There, a systematic study (summarised in Lensink1961) documented the consumption of adult and smolt salmon by belukhas in the Kvichak and Nushagak River estuaries. Calculations indicated that belukhas consumed 2.7% of the sockeye (*Oncorhynchus nerka*) runs in 1954 and 1.0% in 1955, which was considered significant, especially in light of the depleted status of stocks. This led to the development of a non-lethal acoustic system which was used to displace the whales from the rivers at critical times (Fish & Vania 1971). With improved management and recovery of sockeye stocks, use of this system has been discontinued.

Major changes in the pattern of exploitation of Bering Sea fish stocks occurred during the period following the end of World War II (see Bakkala *et al*. 1981), of which the development of the groundfish fishery is probably most significant. The aggregate catch of groundfish by all nations increased from 12 500 tonnes in 1954 to over 2.2 million tonnes in 1972 an increase of 176 times. In addition, due at least in part to depletion of stocks of other target species (Pruter 1973), the percentage of pollock in the catches increased from 0 to 83% during that period (Bakkala *et al*. 1981). This increase in finfish catches from the Bering Sea can be partly attributed to human population increases and reductions in the catch of whales, which have been used as a source of protein and other products, particularly by Japan and the Soviet Union. The percentage (by weight) of whales in the world marine resource harvest decreased from 10.2% in 1949–50 to about 1% in 1973–74 (FAO 1978). This decrease is due both to decreased whale catches and to increased catches of other marine resources.

The increased yield from the Bering Sea groundfish fisheries, particularly of pollock, and better information on the food of marine mammals in the area, suggested the possibility of major competition between them (McAlister & Perez 1976, Lowry *et al*. 1979). Frost and Lowry (1981b) documented the presence of pollock in the diet of 11 species of marine mammals and 13 species of seabirds. Calculations by McAlister and Perez (1976) indicated that 2 853 000 mt of finfish were consumed annually by pinnipeds in the Bering Sea, an amount considerably in excess of the commercial fish catch. Two questions could then be formulated, each of which could be applied either specifically to pollock and their predators or to the entire suite of Bering Sea marine mammals and fisheries. First, is predation by marine mammals affecting the yields that can be taken by commercial fisheries? Second, is the commercial yield affecting the availability of food to marine mammals and therefore their population status?

The amount of commercial fish consumed by Bering Sea marine mammals is without doubt substantial (McAlister & Perez 1976, McAlister 1981). In fact, food consumption by marine mammals has been judged to be significant enough that levels of apex predator consumption (including marine mammals, birds, and elasmobranchs) have been used as primary inputs for a dynamic numerical ecosystem model (DYNUMES) of the Bering Sea (Laevastu & Favorite 1977). However, the effects of predation by marine mammals on Bering Sea fish stocks are poorly understood and have not been documented. Fluctuations of those stocks have instead been considered as regulated by the fishing activities, environmental factors, and lower trophic level interactions. Observations of sea-otters in California (Lowry & Pearse 1973) and walruses in the Bering Sea (Fay & Lowry 1981) demonstrate, however, the ability of marine mammals to deplete at least local stock of fishable resources. Calculations by Winters and Carscadden (1978) for North Atlantic capelin have assumed that potential yields to fisheries are a direct function of marine mammal abundance.

The question of the reciprocal effect, of fisheries on marine mammals, is more complex and there is a less well-developed array of observations, data, and theory to support it. To establish conclusively that a commercial fishery affects populations of marine mammals, it could be argued that four criteria must be met. First, stocks of the forage species must be significantly depleted over and above the predatory effect of the marine mammals. Second, changes in the abundance of the species must affect the actual amount of them consumed by marine mammals. Third, such a change in food intake must result in a change in one or more of the vital parameters (e.g. growth, survival, reproduction) of the marine mammals. Fourth, changes in these parameters must in turn affect the major population characteristics of the marine mammal, such as its abundance and productivity.

Evidence of interaction satisfying these four criteria has not been demonstrated between marine mammals and fisheries in the Bering Sea. Instead, however, attempts have been made to correlate observed population characteristics of marine mammals with observed changes in fisheries or presumed changes in fish stocks. Such studies dealing with fur seals (Swartzman & Haar 1980) and sea-lions (Braham *et al.* 1980) have not succeeded in conclusively documenting causal relationships.

Despite the lack of adequate documentation for the Bering Sea, information from other areas suggests that marine mammals may respond to changes in their food supply. The evidence is based on the assumption that a reduction in population size of the principal or competing species makes more food available to the marine mammal population. The marine mammal should then respond by increased productivity and/or survival, and, provided harvesting does not prevent it, its population size should increase. In the North Atlantic, a reduction of the harp seal (*Phoca groenlandica*) population during 1952 to 1972 was accompanied by a significant increase in fertility rate – from 85 to 94 per cent – and decrease in mean age at maturity – from 6.5 to 4.5 years – (Bowen *et al.* 1981). These responses should have caused the harp seal population to increase and indeed there is some evidence to indicate that it has done so (e.g. Bowen & Sergeant 1983). A second example involves the Antarctic ecosystem, where a single species of krill (*Euphausia superba*) is the principal food of many species of birds and marine mammals. Recent increases in populations of several krill predators, including penguins (*Aptenodytes patagonica Pygoscelis* spp.), minke whales, crabeater seals (*Lobodon carcinophagus*), and fur seals (*Arctocephalus* spp.), are thought to be the result of an increase in availability of krill brought about by the reduction of large whale populations which had formerly consumed great quantities of that species (Laws 1977). The evidence is not, however, entirely unambiguous (e.g. Horwood 1980).

Thus, the available information suggests that populations of some marine mammal species are probably limited by food availability and that individual and population parameters will respond to changes in levels of available food. It must be noted that the important factor is the relative abundance of predator and prey populations rather than the absolute size of either, i.e. the *per capita* food availability. That is, a reduction in a marine mammal population while abundance of prey remains constant would have a similar effect to an enhanced prey abundance with a constant mammal population.

Conceptual assessment of marine mammal-fishery interactions in the Bering Sea

It is comparatively easy to document which species of marine mammals consume commercial fish species. Analysis of opportunistically obtained specimens (e.g. stomachs) and observations of distribution and behaviour of animals in fishing areas are usually adequate to detect which target species are eaten by marine mammals. For most species, a careful evaluation of all available data of food habits can provide a semi-quantitative assessment of the dietary importance of commercially exploited prey, as has been done by Fiscus (1979, 1980), Frost and Lowry (1981a), and Lowry and Frost (1981). An evaluation of this kind for Bering Sea marine mammals and fisheries is given in Table 3.3, based on the data summarised in Lowry *et al.* (1982). However, such an evaluation must be accepted with caution, since reasonably adequate descriptions of diet for mammals of the Bering Sea, including at least seasonal and geographical resolution, are available only for fur seals and perhaps ringed seals, bearded seals, and walruses.

In considering the likelihood that a particular species of marine mammal may be affected by Bering Sea commercial fisheries, three factors other than diet composition appear to be of major importance.

(a) Feeding strategy, i.e. degree of specialisation on one or a few food species.
(b) Overall importance of the feeding which occurs in the Bering Sea in the annual nutrition of individuals and the population.
(c) Relationship of the present population to carrying capacity, i.e. is per capita food availability presently limiting population size?

A general assessment of these factors can be made, given the presently available data base. For example, although many types of prey are eaten by both walruses and bearded seals, walruses obviously specialise in clams, while bearded seals can and do eat large amounts not only of clams, but also of shrimps, crabs, snails, and fishes. Minke, fin, and humpback whales are generalised feeders, while right and bowhead whales are much more specialised.

Although distinctions are not completely clear cut, residency of Bering Sea marine mammal species can be largely classified into three categories: (a) year-round residents (harbour seal, ribbon seal, sea-lion, and some belukha whales, Dall's porpoise, and harbour porpoise); (b) summer seasonals (fur seals, sperm whales, and all baleen whales except bowheads); and (c) winter seasonals (ringed seals, bearded seals, most walruses, and bowhead whales). Generally speaking, feeding in the Bering Sea is most important for resident species and summer seasonals, although winter feeding in the Bering is considered important for ice seals and walruses. Summer feeding in the Bering

Table 3.3 Importance of present and potential commercial fish and shellfish in the diets of Bering Sea marine mammals.

| | Commercial fish species/group | | | | | | | | | | | |
| | Present | | | | | | | | Potential | | | |
	Ground-fish	Herring	Salmon	Halibut	Squid	King crab	Tanner crab	Snails	Capelin	Saffron cod	Shrimp	Clams
Mysticete cetaceans												
grey whale	0	1	0	0	0	1	1	1	1	0	1	1
fin whale	3	3	1	0	3	0	0	0	3	2	0	0
minke whale	3	2	0	0	2	0	0	0	2	1	0	0
blue whale	0	1	0	0	1	0	0	0	1	0	0	0
sei whale	1	1	0	0	1	0	0	0	1	1	0	0
humpback whale	3	3	1	0	1	0	0	0	3	3	1	0
bowhead whale	0	0	0	0	0	0	0	0	0	0	0	0
right whale	0	0	0	0	0	0	0	0	0	0	0	0
Odontocete cetaceans												
sperm whale	2	1	1	1	3	1	1	0	1	0	0	0
belukha	2	3	3	1	1	0	1	1	2	3	2	0
beaked whales	1	0	1	0	3	0	0	0	0	1	0	0
killer whale	2	2	2	1	1	1	0	0	1	1	1	0

	1	2	3	4	5	6	7	8	9	10	11
Dall's porpoise	2	2	1	0	3	0	0	3	0	1	0
harbour porpoise	2	2	1	0	1	0	0	2	3	1	0
Pinnipeds											
northern fur seal	3	2	1	1	3	0	0	3	0	1	0
steller sea-lion	3	2	1	1	1	0	0	2	1	1	0
pacific walrus	0	0	0	0	0	1	2	0	0	1	3
harbour seal	3	3	1	1	1	0	0	3	0	2	0
spotted seal	3	3	1	0	1	0	0	3	3	2	0
ribbon seal	3	1	0	1	2	0	0	2	2	3	0
ringed seal	1	1	0	0	1	1	0	1	3	3	0
bearded seal	1	0	0	0	0	3	2	0	1	3	3
Carnivores											
polar bear	0	0	0	0	0	2	2	0	0	0	0
sea-otter	1	0	0	0	0	2	2	0	0	0	2

3 = known major.
2 = potentially major.
1 = known or potentially minor.
0 = probably not eaten.

Sea may be somewhat optional for most baleen whales since their relative summer distributions in the Bering and North Pacific appear to fluctuate in different years, presumably based on where optimum feeding conditions exist (Bryant *et al*. 1981).

We have considered two factors as indicative of the relationships of populations to carrying capacity: (a) the present abundance compared to historical levels as indicated by direct estimates of population sizes or by harvest records, and (b) the recent trend in abundance. Obviously, it is unlikely that a population that is increasing in numbers or is at a low level compared to previous abundance will presently be limited by food availability. Where no data on abundance are available, we have considered populations to be stable and at abundance levels comparable to earlier periods.

We have assigned ranked values to feeding characteristics, based on whether they suggest a probable interaction with fisheries, and to population size and trends, based on whether they indicate probable food limitation (Table 3.4). A species which is stenophagous on commercially exploited prey, uses the Bering Sea as a major feeding area, and is near carrying capacity would receive high rankings (maximum total of 15). Conversely, a mobile and omnivorous species which consumes prey not exploited by fisheries, feeds only briefly in the Bering Sea, and is below carrying capacity would receive low rankings (minimum total of 5).

Results of this analysis, considering all factors combined, are given in Table 3.5. Total rank values range from 13 (highest probability of significant interaction) to 8 (lowest probability of interaction). Characteristics of species in each of the rank values will be briefly discussed as categories 1 (ranked value of 13) through 6 (ranked value of 8).

Table 3.4 Criteria for assigning ranked values of the likelihood of marine mammal–fishery interactions in the Bering Sea. Low values indicate that the decribed characteristics suggest a low probability of significant interactions.

Rank value	Composition of the diet	Feeding strategy	Importance of Bering Sea as feeding area	Relative population size	Population trend
		Feeding		Relation to carrying capacity	
1	feed principally on non-commercial species	omnivorous with high mobility of predators and prey	important only for a small fraction of annual nutrition or feeding available elsewhere	greatly reduced	increasing
2	feed moderately on commercial species	moderately diverse diet (opportunistic)	moderately important	slightly reduced	stable
3	feed heavily on commercial species and use size classes similar to those targeted on	stenophagous or with low mobility of predators and prey	major feeding area without other regular or optional feeding grounds	comparable to historic	declining

Table 3.5 Ranked values of the likelihood of marine mammal–fishery interactions in the Bering Sea, based on characteristics of feeding and population status.

Species/group	Diet composition	Feeding Feeding strategy	Bering Sea importance	Status Relative size	Population trend	Total
mysticete cetaceans						
grey whale	1	3	3	3	1	11
fin whale	2	1	2	1	2	8
minke whale	2	1	2	2	2	9
blue whale	1	3	1	1	2	8
sei whale	1	3	1	1	2	8
humpback whale	2	1	2	1	2	8
bowhead whale	1	3	1	1	2	8
right whale	1	3	1	1	2	8
odontocete cetaceans						
sperm whale	1	1	2	2	2	8
belukha	3	2	2	3	2	12
beaked whales	1	1	2	3	2	9
killer whale	2	1	1	3	2	9
Dall's porpoise	2	2	2	2	2	10
harbour porpoise	3	1	3	3	2	12
pinnipeds						
northern fur seal	3	2	3	2	3	13
Steller sea-lion	3	2	3	2	3	13
pacific walrus	1	3	3	3	1	11
harbour seal	3	2	3	3	2	13
spotted seal	2	2	3	3	2	12
ribbon seal	2	2	3	2	1	10
ringed seal	1	1	2	3	2	9
bearded seal	2	1	2	3	2	10
carnivores						
polar bear	1	2	1	3	2	9
sea-otter	2	2	3	3	2	12

Category 1 (rank 13)

Based on this assessment, the species for which there is greatest potential for interaction are the northern fur seal, Steller sea-lion, and harbour seal. For all three species the Bering Sea is a major feeding area, and commercially exploited fishes (principally pollock, herring and salmon) comprise substantial proportions of the diet. In addition, although they are somewhat opportunistic, much of their intensive feeding may be limited by the proximity of terrestrial hauling-out areas. Based on available data, populations are probably at levels close to carrying capacity, and reductions in prey abundance would be likely to affect ingestion rates and hence population productivity.

Category 2 (rank 12)

Species in this category also rely on the Bering Sea as an important feeding area and are thought currently to be near carrying capacity. In the case of the sea-otter the probability of interactions with fisheries is somewhat lessened because a moderate proportion only of species in the diet are of commercial importance. Although belukha and harbour porpoise forage extensively on commercial species, their mobility may reduce the probability of significant interactions. We have considered that commercial species comprise only a moderate portion of the diet of spotted seals, since much of their feeding occurs in the northern Bering Sea and is concentrated on species that are not presently fished commercially.

Category 3 (rank 11)

The grey whale and walrus share a number of common characteristics. Population sizes of both are at, if not above, historical levels and may still be increasing. The Bering Sea is a major feeding area for both, and they show little feeding plasticity, specialising in comparatively sedentary invertebrates which are of no present commercial importance. Nonetheless, if commercial fishing were to develop which either directly or indirectly affected their prey, it could have major effects on the status of walrus and grey whale populations.

Category 4 (rank 10)

Species in this category exhibit a variety of characteristics. Placement of Dall's porpoise in this category rather than the previous one is based on the judgement that the Bering Sea is of only moderate importance for feeding, since animals in this region comprise only a small proportion of the North Pacific population. In any event, the population is probably somewhat reduced due to mortality caused by entanglements in nets and is less likely to be food limited. The Bering Sea is an important feeding area for ribbon seals, and a substantial portion of their known diet consists of commercially harvested species. However, their population size, although increasing, may still be somewhat below historical levels. Bearded seals are highly omnivorous and include only a moderate proportion of commercial species in their diet.

Category 5 (rank 9)

The species in this category – killer whale, minke whale, beaked whales, ringed seal, and polar bear – do not depend extensively on commercially important species, depend only in part on the Bering Sea for their annual nutrition, and are relatively mobile and opportunistic in their feeding.

Category 6 (rank 8)

This category includes the sperm whale and all species of baleen whales except the minke and grey whale. Populations of the included baleen whales are all greatly reduced, which suggests that they are presently far below the point of food limitation. Species that eat commercially exploited fishes (fin and humpback whales) are highly mobile and opportunistic, while the prey of more stenophagous species (blue, sei, bowhead, and right whales) are not commercially harvested. Based on available information, the sperm whale is relatively euryphagous and concentrates its feeding on non-commercial species.

Conclusions

There is no question that competition occurs when fisheries exploit species that are significant components of the diets of marine mammals. Other, more complex interactions are possible, but they cannot appropriately be termed competition, which refers only to mutual attempts to gain a common object or goal. Even in the simplest cases, it has proven extremely difficult to measure the magnitude of competition or to assess the likely effects on fishery harvests and marine mammal populations. This is due largely to lack of information about the fishery and the biology of target species and their predators.

Also, available theory and models are deficient in at least two respects. First, insufficient is known as to how marine mammals obtain their foods, (especially in relation to changing prey abundances) and how the energy obtained from feeding relates to growth, maturation, reproductive output, and survival. Second, ecosystem models, which are needed to integrate environmental and biological factors and simulate effects of changes in various factors on system components, are at a primitive stage of development. Although ecosystem simulations are beginning to appear, they generally are difficult to understand, costly to develop and use, involve untested assumptions, and have not been verified with respect to how accurately the simulation corresponds to the actual ecosystem. Their present utility for management purposes is therefore open to question.

In some particular instances, the interaction between the marine mammal and the fishery has been observed or can be inferred with some reliability. Fay and Lowry (1981) present information which suggest that, although a potentially commercial surf clam resource exists in southern Bristol Bay, successful development of a fishery is unlikely in view of the already severe depletion caused by walruses. Since a commercial fishery would be size selective and limited to harvesting at or below the MSY level, it would probably have a less drastic impact on the clam resources (*Spisula polynyma*) than walruses, which consume all size-classes of clams and which are at present exerting a mortality rate in the clam stocks substantially greater than that required to produce the maximum sustainable yield. Similarly, it has been abundantly demonstrated that sea-otters in California have a dramatic impact on commercial yields of some shellfishes, and, in fact, the presence of otters simply prevents significant human utilisation of some species such as abalone, *Haliotis* spp. (FAO 1978). These examples deal, however, with species that prey on sessile and weakly motile organisms, and may not be relevant to interactions involving more motile prey such as finfishes, squids, and shrimps. The investigations required to detect the latter type of interaction is far more difficult.

Power and Gregoire (1978) have published a very significant study of the impact of freshwater seals on the fish community of Lower Seal Lake, Quebec. By comparisons with neighbouring lakes, they established that harbour seal (*Phoca vitulina mellonae*) predation has greatly modified the fish community by selecting 'against species that are lake spawners and whose reproductive behaviour results in aggregations of large mature fish at specific times and places in the lake'. The population of lake trout

(*Salvelinus namaycush*) has been most affected and, 'displays an almost classic response to overexploitation'. They consider that the seal population consumes the potential fish yield annually, and observe that fishing in Lower Seal Lake is notoriously poor.

It therefore appears quite likely that marine mammals will affect fisheries, at least in certain situations. Direct competition will occur when humans attempt to harvest the same species and sizes of organisms that are consumed by marine mammals. This competition is likely to be most intense if a commercial fishery attempts to exploit a species which is the principal prey of a marine mammal population already at the limit of its carrying capacity. Baleen whales in particular prey on organisms which are major foods of commercially important fishes and may therefore affect exploitable stocks.

However, it is important to recognise that some marine mammals may enhance fishery yields if they prey on predators or competitors of commercially desirable species. For example, sea-otters consume invertebrates which feed on kelp (*Macrocystis* spp.), thereby enhancing development of kelp plants, which are harvested and used for various products. Although seals in Lower Seal Lake reduced the lake trout population, they apparently had little, if any, impact on brook trout (*Salvelinus fontinalis*), whose spawning sites are dispersed in tributary streams (Power & Gregoire 1978). In the Bering Sea, marine mammals consume considerable amounts of capelin and sand lance, which are probably trophic competitors of herring and pollock. Harbour seals and other marine mammals prey on cod which are commercially valuable but which are also predators on juvenile king and tanner crabs.

Although fisheries often cause substantial depletion of target species stocks, we have located no conclusive evidence of instances where fisheries have affected marine mammal populations through depleting their food supply. Schaeffer (1970), working in a relatively simple sysem with direct trophic linkages, has documented an impact of the Peruvian anchovetta (*Engraulis ringens*) fishery on the population of guano birds. The lack of detectable impact of fisheries on marine mammals may be due in part to plasticity in the diet and feeding strategy of many mammals and to the complexity of trophic connections in most ecosystems.

There is no question that the sea-otter – a species with a diverse and adaptable diet – has been able to expand into areas where some of its prey were being fished commercially. However, it has been suggested that the pollock fishery has prevented expansion of the Pribilof fur seal population. Obviously (as discussed above), direct competition is most likely when mammals and fisheries exploit the same species and size-classes. Other possible effects of fisheries on the food resources of marine mammals are more difficult to conceptualise and evaluate. Fisheries may reduce the availability of food for one marine mammal species while enhancing prey abundance for one or several others. Depletion by fishing of the total stocks of pelagic and semidemersal finfishes may enhance the availability of copepods and euphausiids for baleen whales; the juvenation (shift in biomass from older to younger age-classes) of pollock stocks caused by fishing may be beneficial to pinnipeds which prey on small pollock.

Where major commercial fisheries have developed in areas where mammal populations have previously been reduced, as for example in the Antarctic, exploitation of the presumed available surpluses resulting from such reductions is presently a major consideration. It is quite possible that the large pollock population in the Bering Sea has benefited from reduced competition for food from large whales, and perhaps reduced predation by fur seals and ribbon seals. Whether or not populations of other zooplankton and fish predators (e.g. seabirds, belukha whales, harbour porpoises, sea-lions, and harbour seals) might have experienced and responded to increased prey availability is not known. Obviously, the Bering Sea is not a pristine ecosystem, and the carrying capacity for each species, as well as the interactions among species, may not be what they were 50 or 100 years ago. These factors have undoubtedly changed many times, for example with the periodic exposure and flooding of the Beringian platform.

Agencies and persons concerned with maintaining healthy and stable marine ecosystems must optimise the allocation of resources between humans (= fisheries) and marine mammals. Although choices may sometimes be fairly clear (as in the case of the sea-otter) this is far from true in the Bering Sea as a whole, where one must be concerned with optimising populations of 26 species of marine mammals and fisheries for nearly that number of other marine organisms. A comparison of past and present mechanisms and policies for fishery management suggests that the present situation overall is unlikely to affect marine mammals adversely. Provisions of the FCMA allow for the rebuilding of depleted stocks and harvests to achieve sustained optimum yields. Indeed, present harvests include mostly traditionally exploited species, and overall harvest levels are below those of the recent past. Similarly, proximate plans for development of Bering Sea fisheries, i.e. a transfer of the allowable harvests from foreign to domestic fishermen, are unlikely to have major impacts on mammal populations, although relevant economic and political factors may change.

Management philosophies and options for marine mammals are much less clear cut. Population status is generally considered in relation to carrying capacity, which is a dynamic, variable, and scarcely understood parameter and appears in some ways to be a poor choice for a benchmark. Other indicators, such as the maintenance of marine mammals as significant functional elements of ecosystems, defy quantification. Considerations of ecology, economics, and risk will have to be blended when attempting to manage fisheries and marine mammal populations in the optimum manner.

Acknowledgements

The compilation, review, and evaluation of available data on feeding and status of Bering Sea marine mammals were supported by the North Pacific Fishery Management Council and the US Marine Mammal Commission (Contract No. 81-4). Susan Hills was largely responsible for the collection and compilation of the data. Much of the data collecting and background research was supported by the Alaska Department of Fish and Game, the National Oceanic and Atmospheric Administration through the Outer Continental Shelf Environmental Assessment Program, and by the Federal Aid in Wildlife Restoration Program. John J. Burns has had substantial and valuable input into the data and concepts presented in this paper. The manuscript was typed and edited by Kathleen Pearse.

References

Arseniev, V. A. 1941. Feeding of the ribbon seal. *Izv. TINRO* **20**, 121–7. (Trans. from Russian by J. J. Burns, Alaska Dep. Fish and Game, Fairbanks, AK.

Bakkala, R., K. King and W. Hirschberger 1981. Commercial use and management of demersal fish. In *The eastern Bering Sea shelf: oceanography and resources*, Vol. 2, D. W. Hood and J. A. Calder (eds), 1015–36. Seattle, WA: Univ. Washington Press.

Bouchet, G. C. 1981. *Estimation of abundance of Dall's porpoise* (Phocoenoides dalli) *in the*

North Pacific Ocean and Bering Sea. Northwest and Alaska Fish. Cent. Processed Rep. 81-1, Natl. Mar. Fish. Serv., Nat. Oceanic Atmos. Adm., Seattle, WA.

Bowen, W. D. and D. E. Sergeant 1983. Mark–recapture estimates of harp seal pup. *Phoca groenlandica* production in the Northwest Atlantic. *Can. J. Fish. Aquat. Sci.* **40**, 728–42.

Bowen, W. D., C. K. Capstick and D. E. Sergeant 1981. Temporal changes in the potential of female harp seals (*Pagophilus groenlandicus*). *Can. J. Fish. Aquat. Sci.* **38**, 495–503.

Braham, H. W., R. D. Everitt and D. J. Rugh 1980. Northern sea lion population decline in the eastern Aleutian Islands. *J. Wild. Man.* **44**, 25–33.

Bryant, P. J., G. Nichols, T. B. Bryant and K. Miller 1981. Krill availability and the distribution of humpback whales in south eastern Alaska. *J. Mammal.* **62**, 427–30.

Burns, J. J. 1970. Remarks on the distribution and natural history of pagophilic pinnipeds in the Bering and Chukchi seas. *J. Mammal.* **51**, 445–54.

Burns, J. J., L. H. Shapiro and F. H. Fay 1980. Relationship of marine mammal distribution, densities, and activities to sea ice conditions. In *Environmental assessment of the Alaskan continental shelf, final reports of principal investigators,* Vol. 11, 489–670. Outer Continental Shelf Environmental Assessment Program, Boulder, CO.

Coachman, L. K. and K. Aagaard 1981. Reevaluation of water transports in the vicinity of Bering Strait. In *The eastern Bering Sea shelf: oceanography and resources,* Vol. 1, D. W. Hood and J. A. Calder (eds), 95–110. Seattle, WA: Univ. Washington Press.

FAO 1978. Mammals in the seas. Report of the FAO advisory committee on marine resources research, working party on marine mammals. *FAO Fish. Ser.* **5** (1), 1–275.

Fay, F. H. 1974. The role of ice in the ecology of marine mammals of the Bering Sea. In *Oceanography of the Bering Sea with emphasis on renewable resources,* D. W. Hood and E. J. Kelley (eds), 383–99. Occ. Publn. No. 2, Inst. Mar. Sci., Univ. Alaska, Fairbanks, AK.

Fay, F. H. 1981. Marine mammals of the eastern Bering Sea shelf: an overview. In *The eastern Bering Sea shelf: oceanography and resources.* Vol. 2, D. W. Hood and J. A. Calder (eds), 807–11. Seattle, WA: Univ. Washington Press.

Fay, F. H. and L. F. Lowry 1981. *Seasonal use and feeding habits of walruses in the proposed Bristol Bay clam fishery area.* Unpubl. final rep. Contract No. 80-3, North Pacific Fish. Man. Council, Anchorage, AK.

Fay, F. H., H. M. Feder and S. W. Stoker 1977. *An estimation of the impact of the Pacific walrus population on its food resources in the Bering Sea.* Final. Rep. Contracts MM4AC006 and MM5AC-024, U.S. Mar. Mammal Comm., Washington, D.C. NTIS Publ. PB-273 505.

Fedoseev, G. A. 1965. Food of the ringed seal. *Izv. TINRO* **59**, 216–23. (Transl. from Russian by M. Poppino, Defense Languages Inst., Monterey, CA.

Fiscus, C. H. 1979. Interactions of marine mammals and Pacific hake. *Mar. Fish. Rev.* October 1979.

Fiscus, C. H. 1980. Marine mammal-salmonid interactions: a review. In *Salmonid ecosystems of the North Pacific.* W. J. McNeil and D. C. Himsworth (eds) 121–32. Corvallis, OR: Oregon State Univ. Press.

Fish, J. F. and J. S. Vania 1971. Killer whale, *Orcinus orca,* sounds repel white whales, *Delphinapterus leucas. Fish. Bull.* **69**, 531–5.

Frost, K. J. and L. F. Lowry 1981a. Foods and trophic relationships of cetaceans in the Bering Sea. In *The eastern Bering Sea shelf: oceanography and resources.* Vol. 2, D. W. Hood and J. A. Calder (eds), 825–36. Seattle, WA: Univ. Washington Press.

Frost, K. J. and L. F. Lowry 1981b. Trophic importance of some marine gadids in northern Alaska and their body-otolith size relationships. *Fish. Bull.* **79**, 187–92.

Gill, R. E. Jr and C. M. Handel 1981. Shorebirds of the eastern Bering Sea. In *The eastern Bering Sea shelf: oceanography and resources,* Vol. 2, D. W. Hood and J. A. Calder (eds), 719–38. Seattle, WA: Univ. Washington Press.

Gol'tsev, V. N. 1971. Feeding of the common seal. *Ekologiya* **2**(2), 62–70. In Russian.

Haflinger, K. 1981. A survey of benthic infaunal communities of the southeastern Bering Sea shelf. In *The eastern Bering Sea shelf: oceanography and resources,* Vol. 2, D. W. Hood and J. A. Calder (eds), 1091–103. Seattle, WA: Univ. Washington Press.

Hammond, K. A. G. 1980. *Fisheries management under the Fishery Conservation and Management Act, the Marine Mammal Protection Act and the Endangered Species Act.* Final Rep. Contract No. MM1300885-3, U.S. Mar. Mammal Comm., Washington, D.C.

Hood, D. W. 1981. Preliminary observation of the carbon budget of the eastern Bering Sea shelf. In *The eastern Bering Sea shelf: oceanography and resources,* Vol. 1, D. W. Hood and J. A. Calder (eds), 347–58. Seattle, WA: Univ. Washington Press.

Hood, D. W. and E. J. Kelley (eds) 1974. *Oceanography of the Bering Sea with emphasis on renewable resources.* Occ. Publ. No. 2., Inst. Mar. Sci., Univ. Alaska, Fairbanks, AK.

Horwood, J. W. 1980. Competition in the Antarctic? *Rep. Int. Whal. Comm.* **30**, 513–17.

Hughes, S. E. and N. Bourne 1981. Stock assessment and life history of a newly discovered Alaska surf clam resource in the southeastern Bering Sea. In *The eastern Bering Sea shelf: oceanography and resources*, Vol. 2, D. W. Hood and J. A. Calder (eds), 1205–14. Seattle, WA: Univ. Washington Press.

Hunt, G. L. Jr, B. Burgeson and G. A. Sanger 1981a. Feeding ecology of seabirds of the eastern Bering Sea. In *The eastern Bering Sea shelf: oceanography and resources,* Vol. 2, D. W. Hood and J. A. Calder (eds), 629–47. Seattle, WA: Univ. Washington Press.

Hunt, G. L. Jr, Z. Eppley and W. H. Drury 1981b. Breeding distribution and reproductive biology of marine birds in the eastern Bering Sea. In *The eastern Bering Sea shelf: oceanography and resources,* Vol. 2, D. W. Hood and J. A. Calder (eds), 649–87. Seattle, WA: Univ. Washington Press.

Hunt, G. L. Jr, P. J. Gould, D. J. Forsell and E. Peterson Jr 1981c. Pelagic distribution of marine birds in the eastern Bering Sea. In *The eastern Bering Sea shelf: oceanography and resources,* Vol. 2, D. W. Hood and J. A. Calder (eds), 689–718. Seattle, WA: Univ. Washington Press.

Imler, R. H. and H. R. Sarber 1947. *Harbor seals and sea lions in Alaska.* U.S. Fish Wild. Serv. Spec. Sci. Rep. No. 28.

Ingraham, W. J. Jr 1981. Shelf environment. In *The eastern Bering Sea shelf: oceanography and resources*, Vol. 1, D. W. Hood and J. A. Calder (eds), 455–69. Seattle, WA: Univ. Washington Press.

Jewett, S. C. and H. M. Feder 1981. Epifaunal invertebrates of the continental shelf of the eastern Bering and Chukchi seas. In *The eastern Bering Sea shelf: oceanography and resources*, Vol. 2, D. W. Hood and J. A. Calder (eds), 1131–53. Seattle, WA: Univ. Washington Press.

Kinder, T. H. and J. D. Schumacher 1981. Hydrocarbon structure over the continental shelf of the southeastern Bering Sea. In *The eastern Bering Sea shelf: oceanography and resources*, Vol. 1, D. W. Hood and J. A. Calder (eds), 31–52. Seattle, WA: Univ. Washington Press.

King, J. G. and C. P. Dau 1981. Waterfowl and their habitats in the eastern Bering Sea. In *The eastern Bering Sea shelf: oceanography and resources*, Vol. 2, D. W. Hood and J. A. Calder (eds), 739–53. Seattle, WA: Univ. Washington Press.

Konishi, R. and M. Saito 1974. The relationship between ice and weather conditions in the eastern Bering Sea. In *Oceanography of the Bering Sea with emphasis on renewable resources*, D. W. Hood and E. J. Kelley (eds), 425–50. Occ. Publ. No. 2, Inst. Mar. Sci., Univ. Alaska, Fairbanks, AK.

Kosygin, G. M. 1971. Food of the bearded seal, *Erignathus barbatus nauticus* (Pallas), of the Bering Sea in the spring-summer period. *Izv. TINRO* **75**, 144–51. (Transl. from Russian by Transl. Bur., Dep. Sec. State, Ottawa, Ont., Canada, Fish. Mar. Serv. Transl. Ser. No. 3747.)

Laevastu, T. and F. Favorite 1977. *Preliminary report on dynamical numerical marine ecosystem model (DYNUMES II) for eastern Bering Sea.* Processed rep., Northwest and Alaska Fish. Cent., Natl. Mar. Fish. Serv., Nat. Oceanic Atmos. Adm., Seattle, WA.

Laws, R. M. 1977. Seals and whales of the southern ocean. *Phil. Trans R. Soc. London Ser. B* **279**, 81–96.

Lensink, C. J. 1961. *Status report: beluga studies.* Unpubl. rep., Div. Biol. Res., Alaska Dep. Fish and Game, Juneau, AK.

Lowry, L. F. and K. J. Frost 1981. Feeding and trophic relationships of phocid seals and walruses in the eastern Bering Sea. In *The eastern Bering Sea shelf: oceanography and resources,* Vol. 2, D. W. Hood and J. A. Calder (eds), 813–24. Seattle, WA: Univ. Washington Press.

Lowry, L. F. and J. S. Pearse 1973. Abalones and sea urchins in an area inhabited by sea otters. *Mar. Biol.* **23**, 213–19.

Lowry, L. F., K. J. Frost and J. J. Burns 1979. Potential resource competition in the southeastern Bering Sea: fisheries and phocid seals. In *Proc. 29th Alaska Sci. Conf.,* Fairbanks, 15–17 August 1978. B. R. Melteff (ed), 287–96. Univ. Alaska Sea Grant Rep. No. 79-6.

Lowry, L. F., K. J. Frost, D. G. Calkins, G. L. Swartzman and S. Hills 1982. *Feeding habits, food requirements, and status of Bering Sea marine mammals.* Draft Rep. Contract No. 81-4, submitted to North Pac. Fish. Manage. Counc., Anchorage, AK.

McAlister, W. B. 1981. *Estimates of fish consumption by marine mammals in the eastern Bering Sea and Aleutian Island area.* Draft rep., Natl. Mar. Mammal Lab., Northwest and Alaska Fish. Cent., Nat. Mar. Fish. Serv., Nat. Oceanic Atmos. Adm., Seattle, WA.

McAlister, W. B. and M. A. Perez 1976. *Ecosystem dynamics birds and marine mammals.* Processed rep., Northwest and Alaska Fish. Cent., Nat. Mar. Fish. Serv., Nat. Oceanic. Atmos. Adm., Seattle, WA.

MacIntosh, R. A. and D. A. Somerton 1981. Large marine gastropods of the eastern Bering Sea. In *The eastern Bering Sea shelf: oceanography and resources*, Vol. 2, D. W. Hood and J. A. Calder (eds), 1215–28. Seattle, WA: Univ. Washington Press.

McRoy, C. P. and J. J. Goering 1974. The influence of ice on the primary productivity of the Bering Sea. In *Oceanography of the Bering Sea with emphasis on renewable resources,* D. W. Hood and E. J. Kelley (eds), 403–21. Occ. Publ. No. 2, Inst. Mar. Sci., Univ. Alaska, Fairbanks, AK.

Mate, B. R. 1980. *Workshop report for marine mammal-fisheries interactions in the eastern Pacific.* Final Rep. Contract No. MM8AC-003, U.S. Mar. Mammal Comm., Washington, D.C.

Nerini, M. 1981. Grey whales and the structure of the Bering Sea community. In *Abstr. 4th Biennial Conf. Biol. Mar. Mammals*, 14–18 December 1981, San Francisco, CA, 84.

Niebauer, H. J. 1981. Recent fluctuations in sea ice distribution in the eastern Bering Sea. In *The eastern Bering Sea shelf: oceanography and resources*, Vol. 1, D. W. Hood and J. A. Calder (eds), 133–40. Seattle, WA: Univ. Washington Press.

Niebauer, H. J., V. Alexander and R. T. Cooney 1981. Primary production at the eastern Bering Sea ice edge: the physical and biological regimes. In *The eastern Bering Sea shelf: oceanography and resources,* Vol. 2, D. W. Hood and J. A. Calder (eds), 763–72. Seattle, WA: Univ. Washington Press.

Power, G. and J. Gregoire 1978. Predation by freshwater seals on the fish communities of Lower Seal Lake, Quebec. *J. Fish. Res. Bd. Can.* **35**, 844–50.

Pruter, A. T. 1973. Development and present status of bottomfish resources in the Bering Sea. *J. Fish. Res. Board Can.* **30**, 2373–85.

Schaeffer, M. B. 1970. Men, birds and anchovies in the Peru Current – dynamic interactions. *Trans Am. Fish. Soc.* **99**, 461–7.

Scheffer, T. H. and C. C. Sperry 1931. Food habits of the Pacific harbor seal, *Phoca richardii.* *J. Mammal.* **12**, 214–26.

Scheffer, V. B. 1950. The food of the Alaska fur seal. U.S. Fish. Wild. Serv. Wild. Leafl. **329**.

Scheffer, V. B. 1953. Measurements and stomach contents of 11 delphinids from the northeast Pacific. *Murrelet* **34**, 27–30.

Seaman, G. A., L. F. Lowry and K. J. Frost 1982. Foods of belukha whales (*Delphinapterus leucas*) in western Alaska. *Cetology* **44**, 1–19.

Shustov, A. P. 1965. The food of ribbon seals in the Bering Sea. *Izv. TINRO* **59**, 178–83. (Transl. from Russian by F. Essapian, Miami, FL, 1968.)

Simenstad, C. A., J. A. Estes and K. W. Kenyon 1978. Aleuts, sea otters, and alternate stable-state communities. *Science* **200**, 403–11.

Stoker, S. 1981. Benthic invertebrate macrofauna of the eastern Bering/Chukchi continental shelf. In *The eastern Bering Sea shelf: oceanography and resources,* Vol. 2, D. W. Hood and J. A. Calder (eds), 1069–90. Seattle, WA: Univ. Washington Press.

Swartzman, G. and R. Haar 1980. *Exploring interactions between fur seal populations and fisheries in the Bering Sea.* Final Rep. Contract No. MM1800969-5, U.S. Mar. Mammal Comm., NTIS.

Takenouti, A. Y. and K. Ohtani 1974. Currents and water masses in the Bering Sea: a review of Japanese work. In *Oceanography of the Bering Sea with emphasis on renewable resources.* D. W. Hood and E. J. Kelley (eds), 39–57. Occ. Publ. No. 2, Inst. Mar. Sci., Univ. Alaska, Fairbanks, AK.

Tomilin, A. G. 1957. Cetacea. In *Mammals of the USSR and adjacent countries*, V. G. Heptner (ed.). (Transl. from Russian by Israel Program Sci. Transl., 1967. NTIS No. TT 65-50086).

Wilimovsky, N. J. 1974. Fishes of the Bering Sea: the state of existing knowledge and requirements for future effective effort. In *Oceanography of the Bering Sea with emphasis on renewable resources.* D. W. Hood and E. J. Kelley (eds), 243–56. Occ. Publ. No. 2, Inst. Mar. Sci., Univ. Alaska, Fairbanks, AK.

Winters, G. H. and J. E. Carscadden 1978. Review of capelin ecology and estimation of surplus yield from predator dynamics. *Int. Comm. Northwest Atl. Fish. Res. Bull.* 13, 21–30.

Zimushko, V. V. and S. A. Lenskaya 1970. Feeding of the grey whale (*Eschrichtius gibbosus* Erx.) at foraging grounds. *Ekologiya* 1, 26–35. In Russian.

4 Interactions between fur seal populations and fisheries in the Bering Sea

Gordon L. Swartzman and Robert T. Haar

Introduction

In this chapter we assess and clarify possible relationships between fur seals and fisheries in the Bering Sea. The event most prominent in focusing concern on fur seal–fisheries interactions was the failure of the Pribilof Island fur seal herd to recover as predicted from large female harvests in the years 1956 to 1968. While the present herd appears to have stabilised, it has done so at a population 30% below the maximum sustained productivity estimates made in 1955 (York & Hartley 1981). A number of possible explanations for this have been presented, including reduced fur seal carrying capacity.

Ecological simulation models can be used to examine species interactions and therefore they have potential for (a) increasing our understanding of the interactions between fish stock abundance and marine mammal populations, (b) indicating possible changes in abundance of non-target fish species resulting from changes in harvest intensity, and (c) suggesting how long undesirable changes will take to be detected and corrected.

This chapter briefly summarises and highlights the available fur seal and fish data, including studies of cases of other known marine mammal–fish interactions, and briefly discusses and evaluates the usefulness of present-generation ecological simulation models for studying fur seal populations and fish–seal interactions. The evidence relating to fur seal population dynamics and seal–fish interactions is considered, and further modelling approaches, field sampling, and analysis of existing data needed to clarify the effect of the Bering Sea fishery on fur seal populations are suggested.

Available data

The relevant data may be divided into fur seal data, Bering Sea fish stock and fishery data, and anecdotal marine mammal–fish interaction data. The fur seal data consist of: (a) annual fur seal collections at sea during the period 1958–74 in the eastern north Pacific Ocean and the eastern Bering Sea, conducted jointly by the United States and Canada under terms of the fur seal Interim Convention (Kajimura *et al*. 1979, 1980); (b) harvests from 1950 to 1978 on the Pribilof Islands of subadult males (Lander 1981), and counts of harem and non-harem bulls from 1905 to 1978 on other island rookeries; (c) estimates of pup production on the Pribilof Islands from 1912 to 1924, and 1951 to 1979 (Johnson 1975, Lander 1981), and counts of dead pups from 1950 to 1979

(Lander 1981); and (d) studies of fur seal rookery behaviour (Batholomew & Hoel 1953, Gentry 1980), food habits (May 1937, Wilke & Kenyon 1957, Spalding 1964, Fiscus 1979, Perez 1979, Perez & Bigg 1980), and fertility (Abegglen & Roppel 1959).

Bering Sea groundfish and pelagic fisheries data, which give estimates of relative abundance, life-history parameters, and migratory patterns of important fish stocks, are contained in a number of Northwest and Alaska Fisheries Center reports (Pruter 1973, Pereyra *et al.* 1976, Bakkala *et al.* 1979, Favorite *et al.* 1979). These data cover the period of development of the large foreign groundfish fishery in the eastern Bering Sea (1954–78) and include catch, catch per unit effort (CPUE), mortality, seasonal migration patterns and diets for a number of commercially important fish, including walleye pollock and herring – important food sources for the fur seal in the eastern Bering Sea.

Fur seal data synopsis

Seal data collected at sea
Seal migration patterns were deduced from seals sampled at sea from 1958 to 1974. Adult males remain throughout the year in the Bering Sea and Gulf of Alaska, whereas females migrate south in winter, with smaller (younger) females tending to migrate the farthest south. Many subadult males also migrate south, but not nearly so far as the females. Females begin returning to the Pribilof Island rookeries in June, and the rookeries are almost completely established by the end of July.

The pelagic data were also used to construct a seal life table (Lander 1981) which, together with a pup production estimate, gave an overall fur seal biomass estimate for the Pribilof Islands stock of 29 000 tonnes or 1.25 million animals. Seasonal patterns of growth were also computed from the pelagic survey data (Lander 1981). Stomach content data were pooled over years by region and by month and were presented as the frequency of occurrence (proportion of stomachs containing a particular food item), the volume and the per cent of total food volume comprised by each prey type and the number of specimens of each prey type and their per cent of the total diet. Diet composition of seal stomachs by per cent volume (which we consider to be the most reliable measure of prey abundance in predator stomachs) in the eastern Bering Sea is given in Table 4.1 (modified from Perez & Bigg 1980), pooled by month over all years of data collection.

Fur seals are pelagic feeders and are highly opportunistic (Kajimura 1981), feeding on a wide variety of species. Of their major prey, only pollock and herring are target

Table 4.1 Major species in fur seal diets in the eastern Bering Sea (per cent volume). (From Perez & Bigg 1980.)

Species	June	July	August	September
herring	—	0.2	13.2	0.2
capelin	69.6	16.4	17.0	15.2
pollock	4.1	50.9	26.1	38.3
deep-sea smelt	—	4.0	3.5	8.6
atka mackerel	19.4	1.5	1.7	1.8
squid	4.9	22.0	29.4	17.5
other	2.0	5.0	9.1	18.4

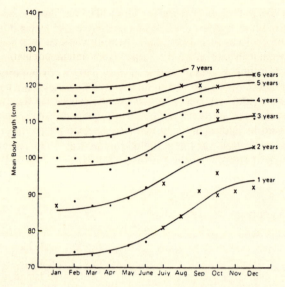

Figure 4.1 Seasonal pattern of growth in mean length (cm) of non-pregnant female fur seals of ages 1–7 years. Curves are drawn by inspection with the restriction of no downward curvature. An x designates fewer than 10 seals (From Lander 1981.)

species for a fishery. Data on fur seal diets outside the eastern Bering Sea corroborate the pattern of fur seals feeding primarily on schooling fish. South of British Columbia, hake replaces pollock in seal stomachs, and herring and sandlance are increasingly important, whereas capelin decreases in importance. Anchovy is the most important seal food source off California. Since fur seals and fisheries both tend to exploit schooling species, a possible competitive relationship may exist between fur seals and fisheries. Most fur seal feeding in the Bering Sea is done by lactating females during the summer pupping period, so the importance of food during this period cannot be overemphasised. Since this is the period of rapid pup growth and is also the period of maximum growth for non-pregnant females and subadult males (Fig. 4.1), food limitation during this period could have drastic consequences to pup survival, especially after they leave the rookeries.

Sampling on the seal rookeries
The herds on the Pribilof Islands (St Paul and St George Islands and Sea Lion Rock) are estimated to comprise 80 per cent of the total world fur seal population. Every year from 1912 to 1924 and since 1950, some census of pup births has been made. Dead pup counts have also been made. Harvests of subadult males on the island hauling grounds have yielded information on weights, lengths and age composition of these animals as well as limited food data from stomach samples. An estimate has also been made annually of the number of harem bulls.

From 1956 to 1968, almost 300 000 females were harvested from St Paul and St George Islands. The herd subsequently failed to achieve the higher sustained productivity that had been anticipated from higher pregnancy and survival rates predicted from population projections (Abegglen *et al.* 1956).

From 1912 to 1924, pup populations were estimated from direct counts. Seal populations increased steadily over this period at an 8% annual rate as they recovered from heavy losses due to pelagic sealing in the late 19th and early 20th centuries. Direct counts were discontinued from 1924 to 1948, but an 8% annual population increase was assumed. However, estimates of pups in 1948 showed that the 8% increase had not continued. In 1947, tagging studies were set up to estimate the numbers of pups, and these were continued until 1961. In 1960 a procedure involving pup shearing and direct counts was initiated to replace the tagging method. Estimates of the number of pups born were computed by adding live pup estimates to dead pup counts.

The 1951–61 tagging studies are now thought to have greatly overestimated actual pup abundance due to procedural difficulties and lost tags (Chapman 1973). The pup shearing procedure, although shown to be unbiased by comparison of the number of pups estimated in this way with direct counts on small rookeries (Chapman & Johnson 1968), may be biased for large rookeries in such a way as to underestimate actual pup numbers (Fowler 1980a).

Age specific survival and weight at age were estimated from the weighing and ageing of the pre-adult males harvested annually on the rookeries. Male harvest was discontinued on St George Island in 1972 to study the effect of the male population density on seal population dynamics. Recent pup survival on St George Island appeared lower than on St Paul Island (Lander 1981), and this has been linked to the increased abundance of idle males on the rookeries (Fowler 1980a).

Bering Sea fish data

Species data on commercially important Bering Sea fish stocks by species has been compiled by the Northwest and Alaska Fisheries Centre (NWAFC). Catch data from Japanese, Russian, Korean, Polish, US, and Canadian fishing operations have been included. The major species (in order of magnitude of catch) are walleye pollock (*Theragra chalcogrammus*), yellowfin sole (*Limanda aspera*), herring (*Clupea harengus*), Pacific salmon (*Onchorynchus* spp), Pacific cod (*Gadus macrocephalus*), sablefish (*Anoplopoma fimbria*), Pacific halibut (*Hippoglossus stenolepis*), other flatfish (rock sole, flathead sole, Alaska plaice, Greenland turbot and arrowtooth flounder), and Pacific ocean perch (*Sebastodes alutus*). Herring and pollock are the most important of these species in the diet of fur seals in the Bering Sea, and have been heavily fished (as have yellowfin sole, halibut and Pacific ocean perch). The intensity of fishing on herring and pollock suggests the possibility of fur seal stock depletion due to decreased food abundance, although stock depletions can also have other causes.

Figure 4.2 (adapted from Pereyra *et al*. 1976, and Favorite *et al*. 1979) gives the total catch for pollock and herring as well as an index of relative abundance (CPUE) based on research trawl surveys conducted by the International Pacific Halibut Commission (IPHC), NMFS and the Japanese Fishery Agency (JFA).

Pollock stocks have been heavily fished since 1964, with peak yields coming in the early 1970s. A steady increase in CPUE between 1964 and 1968 may have been due in part to improvements in fishing gear and tactics, but must also have been due to higher levels of recruitment of young fish (Pruter 1973), possibly as a result of reduced cannibalism. Pruter (1973) pointed out that, since only a few age groups of pollock are utilised in any given year, poor recruitment could have a disastrous effect on the fishery.

Herring fishing in the Bering Sea before 1968 usually occurred west of 170° longitude.

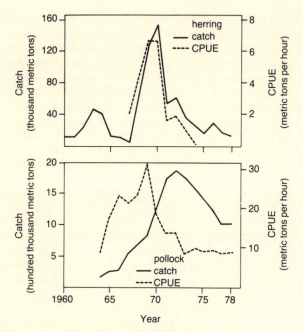

Figure 4.2 Catch and relative abundance of pollock and herring in the eastern Bering Sea. (Adapted from Pereyra *et al.* 1976, and Favorite *et al.* 1979.)

However, when stocks there declined, effort was shifted to the eastern Bering Sea, where the stock was heavily exploited for three years before abundance levels fell.

Relating stock abundances to fur seal food availability requires examination of the overlap between Pribilof rookery feeding grounds and the area of the fishery. Since both seals and fishermen concentrate on areas of high fish density, we might expect competition for those fish species they both pursue.

Herring is a preferred food of fur seals, and evidence for heavy feeding on herring by fur seals in the Bering Sea was obtained from stomach samples taken in 1964 (Perez 1980). Since no large herring fishery exists in the eastern Bering Sea, we cannot be sure whether 1964 was a year of herring abundance or the high diet incidence of herring that year was just a local effect. Fur seals heavily exploit herring off Washington (Perez & Bigg 1980) where they are usually abundant. Heavy seal feeding on herring has also been observed near Sitka, Alaska (Wilke & Kenyon 1957).

Schooling species, such as herring, pollock and squid, provide a spatially heterogeneous (patchy) feeding environment, making it difficult to interpret feeding patterns by average stomach content data. Pollock populations are patchy and mobile (Pereyra *et al.* 1976). The distribution of pollock between 1965 and 1970 (generally warmer years) was more concentrated on the inner shelf than in the relatively colder years 1971 to 1975 (Pereyra *et al.* 1976). However, the region of the lower shelf between the Pribilof Islands and Unimak Island has consistently provided a large proportion of the Japanese catch of pollock throughout the history of the fishery in all months of the year (Pereyra *et al.* 1976). Thus, it may be that the fishery and the fur seal are most closely in competition for the pollock on the outer shelf. While fur seals are capable of taking relatively large prey, most pollock taken seem to be in the 6–20 cm range, while the fishery takes fish averaging 35–40 cm (Salveson & Alton 1976).

Since there were no stomach content data for fur seals near the Pribilofs from 1968 to 1970 – the years of the major herring fishery in the eastern Bering Sea – it was not possible to estimate how much interaction there was between fur seals and the herring fishery. Although herring is an important food of fur seals, the reason for it being uncommon in nursing female seal stomachs may be because in summer the herring are not common in fur seal feeding areas, mostly remaining in coastal waters (Wespestad 1978).

Studies on related systems

Marine mammals are integrally tied to their environment. They can respond to reduction in competition by increases in abundance, which implies that many marine mammal populations are existing at or near their carrying capacities. Many are opportunistic and voracious predators and can strongly affect the trophic dynamics of lower trophic levels (Simenstad *et al.* 1978). Marine mammals are also frequently in food competition with each other. This is demonstrated (a) by the reduction in age of maturity of minke whales in the Antarctic Ocean after drastic reduction of sei and blue whales through harvesting (Hofman 1980), (b) by the increase in ringed seal populations after depletion of bowhead whales in the Beaufort Sea (Lowry 1981), (c) in the fairly heavy predation of sea-lions on fur seal pups – 3.5–5.5 per cent annually on St George Island, according to Gentry (1980), and (d) in the feeding overlap on hake by a large number of marine mammals (Fiscus 1979).

Work by Fowler (1981), showing that k-selected (low fecundity) animals demonstrate density dependence when near their carrying capacities, and the above arguments, suggest that it seems probable that most marine mammals exhibit density dependence in at least some of their population or growth parameters. Also, temporary reductions of a marine mammal population might provide an opportunity for a food competitor to reduce the carrying capacity of that marine mammal population. An important question in this case is whether the density-dependent effects experienced by a population at or near its carrying capacity are primarily a behavioural or a physiological phenomenon. The term 'density dependent' generally means that a population variable varies non-linearly with changing population density. This does not, in itself, imply a direct cause or mechanism for this response. However, it may occur through increased mortality, reduced fecundity, reduced weight gains, or changes in animal condition. Each of these population parameters may be affected by a variety of density-related factors.

In the case of the fur seal, it has been hypothesised that reduction in their populations due to female harvest gave the competing fishery an opportunity to increase harvest rates and thereby reduced the fur seal's carrying capacity. If this hypothesis is true, we should see a change in one or several of the population parameters discussed earlier.

Review of models applicable to fur seal investigations

Relevant models

There are a number of simulation models in the literature which consider multispecies interactions. These include: (a) a group of models being developed at NWAFC for eastern Bering Sea fisheries management and fish stock assessment called BIODIS (BIOmass DIStribution model), BBM (Bulk Biomass Model), PROBUB (PROgnostic BUlk Biomass model) and DYNUMES (DYnamic NUMerical Ecosystem Simulation) (Laevastu & Larkins 1981); (b) a North Sea multispecies multitrophic level model (Andersen & Ursin 1977); (c) GEMBASE (General Ecosystem Model of the Bristol channel and Severn Estuary) – Radford (1979); and (d) a number of other multispecies models including a general fish growth model by Parrish (1975), Havbiomodeller – a Norwegian fjord model by Balchen (1980) – a tuna–porpoise model by Innis *et al.* (1978) and a larval anchovy feeding model by Vlymen (1977).

Model classification

Figure 4.3 shows the types of aquatic system simulation models that can be used to investigate fur seal–fisheries interactions. The figure is constructed as a dendrogram in which each model class of interest is depicted as a combination of various assumptions that are distinguished by the direction in which they branch at each decision point. For example, all models that are environmentally coupled (have environmental conditions explicitly included in model equations) branch downwards (note the arrow pointing down next to 'environmentally coupled'), whereas all those that are not environmentally coupled (no explicit consideration of environmental conditions) branch upwards. The same directional branching occurs for each of eight other factors used in Figure 4.3 to distinguish between the types of models. The branches of the tree correspond to particular model types distinguished by their directions (slanting up, slanting down, or horizontal).

As much of the terminology in Figure 4.3 may be unfamiliar to non-modellers, we explain it here. An age or size-structured model is one that separates populations into age (or size) classes, whereas a pooled model lumps age (or size) classes together. A third alternative, the cohort model, organises populations into classes of individuals of the same age, sex, average weight, breeding status or any other attribute of interest. Whereas numbers/weight-based models represent populations by both the population density and the average weight of the individuals, biomass-based models consider only their biomass densities. Spatially heterogeneous models divide the area of interest into a grid of separate segments and consider the migration or other transfer of animals or biomass between the segments; spatially homogeneous models do not recognise spatial aspects of a system, but instead assume spatially averaged conditions for the entire area. A distinction is made between linear models, where all parameters are constants, and density-dependent models, where some parameters in the model (for example pup survival or survival of young-of-the-year fish) depend on population density. The harvest rate factor in Figure 4.3 distinguishes between models that treat harvest rate as a constant and models which have time-varying harvest involving changes in harvest policy through time.

Examples are given in Figure 4.3 for each of the types of models considered by our classification scheme. There are some possible branch combinations which are not included in this figure – for example, environmentally coupled, age-structured, single-species models (e.g. Sissenwine 1977). These are omitted because they do not seem as applicable to fur seal problems as the ones included. For example, the Sissenwine (1977) type model was not included because no relationship has as yet been demonstrated between environmental conditions and fur seal parameters that might simply and directly be included in a model, while with fish such environmental conditions as temperature have been linked to year-class strength.

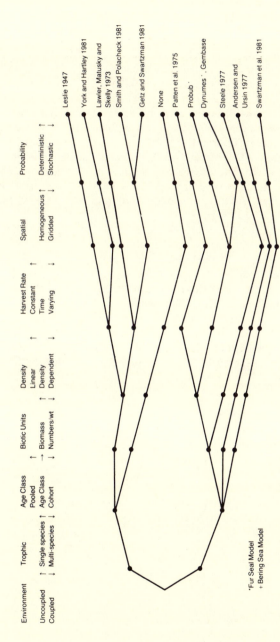

Figure 4.3 Hierarchical tree showing relationships between simulation models.

Fur seal and multi-species fish model comparison

York and Hartley (1981), used a Leslie matrix model to investigate the effect of the female fur seal harvest in the Pribilofs from 1956 to 1968 and of pelagic collections from 1958 to 1970 on subsequent pup production. They took the data on harvested females and, using survival and fecundity estimates similar to those provided by Lander (1981), calculated, using matrix multiplication, the number of female pups that would have been born over time as descendants of these harvested females. These were added to sample estimates of actual pup births in the Pribilofs to compare actual births with potential births (Fig. 4.4). It was noted that pre-1956 rates of pup survival were significantly lower than post-1956 rates, implying increased survival presumably due to lower pup, female, or adult densities. If this increase in pup survival was density dependent, then using the post-1956 survival schedule would bias the potential female pup births upward. To obtain a lower bound on the potential female pup births, pre-1956 survival rates were also used. The difference between the two bounds on pup births was only 15 000 after 22 years. The two curves probably represent reasonable bounds on the loss of female recruits if the major compensatory response of the herd to harvest is a change in survival of yearlings.

Figure 4.4 indicates the difference between potential female pup births and observed female pup births. The results show that the female harvest can account for about 70% of the decline in pups born on St Paul Island. The cause of the remaining discrepancy is not clear, although it could be due to possible sampling bias as a result of change in sampling methods. One unusual feature of this model is that it projects future progeny from harvested, rather than surviving, individuals.

The models PROBUB and DYNUMES were developed by Dr Taivo Laevastu and associates (Laevastu & Larkins 1981) to estimate fish stock abundance in a number of marine ecosystems in the north Pacific Ocean and in the Bering Sea. The models were also designed to examine the effect of temperature changes and food limitation on

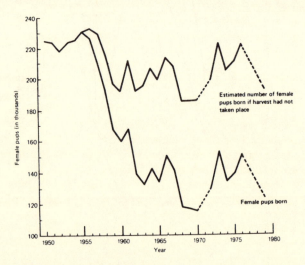

Figure 4.4 Numbers of female northern fur seal pups born, and estimated numbers of female pups born had the harvest not taken place (St. Paul Island, Alaska). Dotted lines indicate no data were available for those years. (From York 1981.)

migration patterns and subsequent stock abundance in the Bering Sea, and to predict the effect of changing the intensity and spatial distribution of fishing effort on fish yields and adult fish stocks.

The PROBUB and DYNUMES models are biomass-based models, with age distribution of biomass in each fish stock determined by a model called BIODIS. Growth rates of the population may be altered by such factors as fishing in such a way as to reflect shifts in biomass–age distribution. PROBUB and DYNUMES differ mainly in that DYNUMES is a spatially gridded model (population abundances are divided into spatial segments with migration allowed between segments) whereas PROBUB is assumed spatially homogeneous over relatively large management areas. Marine mammals are considered as driving variables in these models, i.e. their abundance is unaltered by fish stocks and predation, and food selection by marine mammals is used to estimate fish stock abundances in a top-down approach (from the top of the food chain down to lower trophic levels).

Procedurally, the BIODIS model is run initially for each species separately to determine its age distribution of biomass, and these are used as initial conditions for the PROBUB model. BIODIS requires data on weight at age and numbers of individuals in each age class (taken from catch data). 'Age-specific numerical increase factors' are used to calculate the distribution of numbers for pre-recruited age classes (those too young to be recruited into the fishery) from the numbers distribution in the catch. The turnover rate – the ratio of total annual mortality to average standing crop – is also required. The turnover rate and age-specific increase factors are not easily obtained from available data. Thus, the numerical increase factors are not necessarily kept constant during a run of BIODIS. Also the BIODIS model is run with several turnover rates representing a range of plausible values to indicate the sensitivity of model behaviour to changes in this unmeasurable parameter. BIODIS produces the following outputs for each species:

(a)   the biomass distribution with age,
(b)   annual and monthly growth rates by age-class,
(c)   the average growth rate for the whole population, for juveniles, and for the part of the population that dies during the year.

The PROBUB model is run next in 'diagnostic' mode. The following inputs are required:

(a)   monthly growth rates from the BIODIS model,
(b)   initial guesses for biomass of each species,
(c)   monthly fishing mortality rates (assumed constant from year to year),
(d)   marine mammal and bird monthly biomasses,
(e)   'target' diet fractions (preliminary or average diet composition estimates) for all fish, birds, and mammals,
(f)   monthly biomasses of plankton and
(g)   the maximum allowable fraction of each fish species that can be taken by fish predations (mammal predations targets are always met in PROBUB).

The outputs from PROBUB are equilibrium biomass estimates for all fish species. This model is run with a monthly time step, keeping mammal and bird biomasses constant, until equilibria are reached for biomasses of all fish groups.

The fish, crustacean, benthos and plankton groups used in PROBUB and DYNUMES are given in Table 4.2 (from Laevastu & Larkins 1981). Table 4.3 gives estimates of equilibrium fish stocks, used as initial conditions for DYNUMES and computed from the PROBUB model run in diagnostic mode. Catch, spatial distribution and migration information for each species is also given in Table 4.3. Marine mammal data used in DYNUMES and PROBUB are given in Table 4.4 (adapted from Laevastu & Larkins 1981).

Table 4.2 Species, ecological groups, and numerical relations within some groups in the Bering Sea and Gulf of Alaska. (From Laevastu & Larkins 1981.)

1–4   Species under special study (by age groups), 4 Hake (in West Coast model)

demersal (L-'largemouth', S-'smallmouth')
  5   Greenland halibut (turbot), Pacific halibut (L) (ca 3.5 : 1 in Bering Sea)
  6   Flathead sole, arrowtooth flounder (L) (ca 4 : 1 in Bering Sea; 1 : 2 in Gulf of Alaska)
  7   Yellowfin sole (until Vancouver Island), rock sole, Alaska plaice (S) (9 : 1.5 : 1 in Bering Sea; 2 : 8 : 0.5 in Gulf of Alaska). (Petrale sole, starry flounder, and English sole in West Coast model.)
  8   Other flatfishes (S) (longhead dab, Dover sole, rex sole – last two in Gulf of Alaska). (Sand dab in West Coast model.)
  9   Cottids and others (e.g. elasmobranchs, etc.)

semi-demersal
 10   Pacific cod, saffron cod (saffron cod, polar cod in northern part of Bering Sea)
 11   Sablefish
 12   Pollock
 13   Pacific ocean perch (and other *Sebastes* spp.)

Pelagic
 14   Herring
 15   Capelin, other smelts, sand lance (sauri, myctophids, lanternfishes in West Coast model)
 16   Atka mackeral (mackerels in West Coast model)
 17   Salmon (5 species, temporary presence). (Tunas in West Coast model.)
 18   Squids (mainly gonatids). (*Loligo* sp. in West Coast model.)

Crustaceans
 19   Crabs (king and tanner crabs)
 20   Shrimp

Benthos
 21   Predatory benthos
 22   Infauna
 23   Epifauna

Plankton
 24   Phytoplankton
 25   Copepods
 26   Euphausids
 27   Ichthyoplankton

The DYNUMES model requires the following input data.

(a) Equilibrium biomasses for each fish population obtained from the PROBUB model (see Table 4.3).
(b) Mean growth rate for each fish population obtained from the BIODIS model.
(c) Target diet fractions (fractions of various fish and other food in their diet under normal conditions) for all fish, bird, shark and marine mammal groups.
(d) Daily food requirements as a fraction of body weight for sharks, marine mammals, and birds.
(e) Marine mammal, bird, and shark biomasses for each grid segment (these are not influenced by the behaviour of the model and as such are driving variables).
(f) Monthly biomass of plankton for each grid segment.
(g) Initial biomass of each fish group for each grid segment.
(h) Monthly midwater and bottom temperatures for each grid segment.
(i) Benthos growth and mortality rates.
(j) Grid length and locations, depth, bottom type and distance from the coast for each grid segment.
(k) Migration speed components for each species for each grid segment.
(l) Fishing mortality rates for each grid segment for each month.

With these data, and with a number of additional parameters involving acclimation temperatures, assimilation efficiency, starvation, the effect of fishing rate on growth, and migration in search of food, the DYNUMES model then computes fish biomasses and fishery yield for each grid segment each month. Biomass updating at each time step depends upon the combined affect of growth, mortality, consumption and migration. The average growth rate for each species is modified according to temperature, food limitation, fishing mortality, and recruitment. Growth rate is assumed to increase with increasing fishing rate, since fishing tends to 'juvenate' the population (make juveniles a higher proportion of the total population). This then leads to a higher mean growth rate, since juveniles tend to grow faster than adults. The population density effect on recruitment is included in DYNUMES as another modification in growth rate. Here Cushing's (1973) observation that large stocks of fish lead to low recruitment and that small stocks lead to large recruitment is cited to increase fish growth rates in the model when fish population densities are low (since reduced population densities are assumed to lead to high recruitment, which increases the average growth rate). We are interested in the sensitivity of model output to the recruitment and fishing mortality effects on growth equations in DYNUMES. Generally speaking, there is a large variance in recruitment coming from a given sized stock (Cushing 1973), with variance often increasing with stock size. This feature of fish population dynamics presents a problem for deterministic models such as DYNUMES which tend to be unrealistic in their representation of recruitment.

Growth rate in DYNUMES is assumed to increase with increasing temperature and is arbitrarily reduced when food availability decreases below a certain threshold. Not only the fish growth rate, but also the prey species composition in fish diets may be affected by fish abundance. Diet fractions are reduced from target fractions for less abundant prey and increased for more abundant prey.

Fish mortality in DYNUMES consists of fishing mortality, spawning stress or senescent mortality, cold shock mortality and starvation mortality. Spawning stress mortality, which is assumed to influence the older adult age classes, is implemented in

Table 4.3 Notes on abundant and commercial fish in the Bering Sea and Gulf of Alaska. (From Laevastu & Livingston 1980.)

Species	Equil. biomass 10³ t	Earlier estimates of exploited stocks 10³ t	Maximum annual catches 10³ t	Estimated maximum catch (exp.)	Distribution and other notes	Migrations
turbot (Greenland turbot)	410	140	90		continental slope; winter 600–1000 m, summer 200–700 m; juveniles on the shelf	seasonal depth and North–South migrations
halibut		42(BS)	2(BS)	60	occurs as far N. as St Lawrence Island; winter 300–600 m; summer 150–450 m; juveniles over continental shelf in south and central Bering Sea; optimal temp. 3–8°C	seasonal depth and North–South migrations; exchange between Bering Sea and Gulf of Alaska
flathead sole	700	132	50		on slope, deeper than yellowfin sole; feeds little in winter, spawns in April	
Arrowtooth flounder (turbot)		33	25	70	from Northern California to Gulf of Anadyr; distribution to 1000 m; major concentrations 200 m; dominant flounder in Gulf of Alaska	seasonal depth migration; immatures in 100–200 m in summer
yellowfin sole	130	1–2 million	610		from Vancouver Island to Bering Strait; winter 120–200 m; spawns in autumn and early winter	migrates towards NE in May and June
rock sole		200	67	300	from Mexican border to Gulf of Anadyr; in shallower water than yellowfin; second important in Gulf of Alaska	seasonal depth migration
Alaska plaice		150	7		over continental shelf in Bering Strait; feeds little in winter	seasonal depth migration; winter 100–150 m; summer 30–100 m

Species					Distribution	
other flatfishes, Longhead dab	880				(starry flounder, lemon sole, sand dab, and petrale sole off west coast of America)	
Dover sole		(48)		50	from S. California to Gulf of Alaska	
rex sole					in Gulf of Alaska	
Cottids, elasmobranchs and other demersal species	4,120					
pacific cod	5% of pollock	59			Shelf and slope from S. Oregon to Gulf of Anadyr; spawns in deep water 300 m in spring and early summer	Insufficient data available – *Eds*
saffron cod	1,030	30		70	central and northern part of Bering Sea	
sablefish	130	20	26(BS)	20	from Mexican border to Kamchitka. Off Calif. 800–1500 m; Bering Sea 150–1200 m. Spawns in winter in deep water; juveniles over shelf	Insufficient data available – *Eds*
pollock	9,210	1–2 mil.	1.8 mil	1.2 mil	from Vancouver Is. northward; upper shelf slope and deep water; spawns Feb. to June	Insufficient data available – *Eds*
Pacific Ocean perch	1,630	110(BS)	74(BS) 110(Aleut) 344(GA)	150	from Mexican border to Gulf of Anadyr; Along the slope and deep 150–1000 m; most catch 250 m	Insufficient data available – *Eds*

Table 4.3 *continued*

Species	Equil. biomass 10³ t	Earlier estimates of exploited stocks 10³ t	Maximum annual catches 10³ t	Estimated maximum catch (exp.)	Distribution and other notes	Migrations
Herring	1.970		132	60		
Capelin, sandlance, other smelts, myctophids (in deep water) and other pelagic	3,500					
Atka mackerel	1,160		28	25	Gulf of Alaska and Eastern Bering Sea	
salmon				35	six highly migratory anadromous species	
squid	1,270		(10)	20		
crab	850	122 mil in Bering Sea	9 mil	20	southern Bering Sea and around Pribilof and St. Lawrence Islands	
shrimp	930			3		
hake		1.8 mil	170	170	Gulf of California to British Columbia; spawns off southern California, January–April	

the age-pooled DYNUMES model by increasing fishing mortality. We think the approach of using an age-pooled model (a model having juveniles and adults lumped into one group) while postulating how changes in age structure will affect parameters for the entire population, is ingenious, although potentially inaccurate, especially when the age distribution changes rapidly in a population. Predation mortality for each fish population is computed by summing the consumption by all predators on that population.

Migration is computed according to known migration patterns by an advection formula commonly used in hydrodynamics (Laevastu & Larkins 1981). Input data on migration velocities are used to determine the direction and speed of migration, but these may be modified by fish density differences (gradients) between adjacent grid points if food is limited for a particular fish species at a grid point. The time step for migration may be smaller than a month (the time step for all other model computations) and depends upon the criterion that the migration time step must be less than the ratio of the grid length to the maximum migration speed.

To place the DYNUMES model (Laevastu & Larkins 1981) in perspective, we compared it to another large multispecies fish model – a model for the North Sea by Andersen and Ursin (1977) (hereafter designated A&U). In the A&U model the fish are divided into age classes, and weights and numbers are separately computed. The North Sea model is extremely complex, and a complete description will not be attempted here. However, several salient features will be described and compared with DYNUMES. To compute feeding rates, the A&U model computes growth using a maximum growth rate, which is a power function of body weight, multiplied by a Michaelis–Menten function of available prey to represent food limitation effects on growth. Prey selection, instead of being computed from a target diet matrix as in DYNUMES, is computed by a size-selective feeding equation. Food preference is assumed to depend on the relative weight of predator to prey with each species having as model parameters a preferred weight ratio to their prey and a measure of the weight range they are willing to accept around this preferendum. Prey availability for each predator is the sum of the biomass of each prey species multiplied by both the preference factor computed for that predator on each prey type and by the prey's (constant) vulnerability factor. Thus, whereas the DYNUMES model alters target diets for a predator population due to limited availability of some prey types, the A&U model computes a target diet vector for each predator based on the relative average weights of that predator population and their prey and on prey abundance. Each predator's ration is then modified, based on the total available prey calculated as a sum of the prey biomasses weighted by the predator's preference factors for various prey and the prey species' vulnerability factors.

Unlike DYNUMES, the A&U model computes recruitment explicitly and calculates larval mortality as inversely proportional to the ratio of the larvae's weight to their density. Species with high egg production have a small weight-to-density ratio and therefore a high larval mortality rate. A starvation factor is included in the A&U model by increasing larval mortality if weights are low relative to the maximum (starvation free) weight at a given age. This factor is completely ignored in DYNUMES, and possibly well so, since little is known about the relative importance of various sources of larval mortality. A target recruitment level for each species is included as a parameter in the A&U model and reduces the year-to-year variability in recruitment.

Andersen and Ursin reported a great deal of difficulty with calibrating their larval weight and numbers model. Given the results of a model by Vlymen (1977) that

Table 4.4 Marine mammals in the eastern Bering Sea, Gulf of Alaska and west coast of North America. From Laevastu & Larkins (1981).

Rank no.	Name	Latin name	Grp wt	Avg wt	Est. no. in N. Pacific	Maximum and minimum numbers and months	
						Areas 1 to 9	Area 11 to 16
Baleen whales							
1	grey whale	*Eschrichtius robustus*	31	30t	11 000(E)	8 000(7)–	4 100(1)– 1 150(7)
	right whale	*Balaena glacialis*		50	(200)?	50(8)–	50(12)– —
2	fin whale	*Balaenoptera physalus*	36	50	17 000	4 000(8)–	1 300(12)– 1 000(7)
	minke whale	*Balaenoptera acutoratrata*		9	?	3 000(8)–	800(12)– —
3	bowhead whale	*Balaena mysticetus*		35	3 000	2 500(3)– 200(8)	—
4	blue whale	*Balaenoptera musculus*	45	75	1 700	Aleut. 500	800(12)– 200(7)
	sei whale	*Balaenoptera borealis*		30	28 000	Alaska 1 500(8)	1 500
5	Bryde's whale	*Balaenoptera edeni (brydei)*		30	25 000	—	500(7)– 100(2)**
'Sperm whales'****							
6	giant bottlenose whale	*Berardius bairdi*	8	10	10 000?	2 000(8)–	1 000(2)– 500(8)
	Bering Sea beaked whale	*Mesoplodon steinegeri*		2.5	?	600(8)–	200(2)– 100(8)
7	sperm whale	*Physeter catodon*		32	200 000	20 000(8)–	10 000(11)– 6 000(8)
'Toothed whales'***							
8	humpback whale****	*Meg_ptera novaengliae*		25	1 400	200(6)–	200(2)– 50(6)
9	beluga (white) whale	*Delphinapterus leucas*		2.0	60 000	10 000	—
10	killer whale	*Orcinus orca*	8	10	3 000?	900	600
	goosebeak (or Cuvier's) whale	*Ziphius cavirostris*		3	500?	200	200
Porpoises and Dolphins							
11	Pacific white-sided dolphin	*Legenorhynchus obliquidens*	120	60 kg	10 000?	3 000(8)–	4 000
	Dall's porpoise	*Phocoenoides dalli*		140	500 000	30 000(8)– 10 000(3)	10 000

No.	Common name	Scientific name				
12	harbour porpoise	*Phocoena phocoena (vomerina)*	80	20 000	5 000(8)– 4 000(3)	500
13	northern right whale dolphin	*Lissodelphis borealis*	70	40 000	—	20 000
	Risso's dolphin	*Grampus griseus*	100	?	—	2 000
	common dolphin	*Delphinus delphinus*	55	?	—	4 000
	bottlenose dolphin	*Tursiops truncatus*	100	?	—	2 000
	pilot whale	*Globicephala macrorhyncha (scammoni)*	200	500?	—	1 000
14	sea-otter	*Enhydra lutris*	35	120 000	100 000	18 000
Pinnipeds, group 1						
15	northern fur seal	*Callorhinus ursinus*	45	1 400 000	1 100 000(7)– 200 000(3)	500 000(1)– 15 000(17)
16	steller (northern) sea-lion	*Eumetopias jubatus*	350	275 000	100 000(8)– 55 000(3)	60 000(3)– 15 000(17)
17	California sea lion	*Zalophus californianus*	100	110 000	—	50 000(7)– 35 000(2)
18	northern elephant seal	*Mirounga angustirostris*	900	35 000	—	20 000
19	harbour seal	*Phoca vitulina (Richardi)*	50	750 000?	270 000	19 000
Pinnipeds, group 2 ('ice seals')						
20	walrus	*Odobenus rosmarus*	800	175 000	175 000(3)– 20 000(8)	—
21	bearded seal	*Erignathus barbatus*	200	300 000	250 000(3)– 5 000(8)	—
22	ribbon seal	*Phoca fasciata*	70	100 000	100 000(3)– 60 000(8)	—
	large (spotted) seal	*Phoca vitulina largha*	55	250 000	220 000(3)– 30 000(8)	—
	ringed seal	*Phoca hispida*	60	up to 1 mil	200 000(3)– 20 000(8)	—
23	sharks		100	?	50 000(8)– 10 000(3)	40 000

* Estimated Arctic population.

** Rare occurrence north of 35°N

*** The groups 'sperm whales' and 'toothed whales' signify groupings by feeding habits.

**** Humpback whale, although a baleen whale, has been included in the 'toothed whale' group.

anchovy larvae depend on prey patchiness to satisfy their food needs and would starve if they had to subsist at average prey concentrations, it is not surprising that the A&U model, with its spatially homogeneous populations and its omission of patch considerations, was difficult to calibrate to known growth patterns. The explicit inclusion of larvae in the model also made the A&U model very expensive to run. This is because the model time step changed depending on the maximum rate for all processes. During times of larval abundance, this maximum rate was the larval mortality rate, which was several orders of magnitude higher than any other rate in the model.

In the A&U model, fish growth depends explicitly on production at lower levels in the food chain, unlike DYNUMES. However, the A&U model parameters were adjusted to fit 1960–70 fishery yield data for the 11 fish species included in the model, which linked model behaviour to the fish rather than lower trophic levels. Migration is included in the A&U model only as migration in or out of the North Sea, whereas in the DYNUMES migration patterns are computed over the Bering Sea. Marine mammals were not considered in the A&U model. This may be due both to the relative scarcity of marine mammals in the North Sea and to the greater importance of the fishery there, allowing the fishery (rather than marine mammals) to be used to estimate fish stock abundances in the North Sea. (See Ch. 3 for a discussion of the relative importance, as fish harvesters, of marine mammals and the fishery in the Bering Sea.)

Both models (DYNUMES and A&U) have, in addition to the complex 'full' models, simple versions. These were necessary because of the costs of the full versions – about $500 per run in both cases. The choice was between having a spatially gridded or an age-structured model, both of which increased run cost by two orders of magnitude. No model currently known to us has both spatial gridding and explicit age classes.

Evidence of changes in fur seal carrying capacity

Fur seal population trends

The fur seal population appears at present to be dropping. After the female harvests between 1956 and 1968, an increase in pregnancy rate and survival was expected. However, this did not materialise, and population numbers are reduced over model population projections.

The following hypotheses attempt to explain the reduction since 1956 (Fowler 1980a).

(a) The discrepancy is mainly due to over-estimates of pup abundance during the tagging studies (1951–61) and under-estimates in the subsequent pup shearing studies.

(b) There has been a reduction in carrying capacity due to reduced available food in the Bering Sea, resulting from overfishing of major food sources for the fur seal (pollock and herring) in the feeding areas of the rookery seals.

(c) The reduced pup abundance may be a transient effect of the female harvest. This is in spite of the observation that the direct effect of the animals removed has by now largely passed through the population (Lander 1981).

(d) Increased abundance of non-harem adult males and an increase in ratio of these males to harem bull on St Paul Island may have reduced land survival of pups. In pinniped populations on other islands (fur seals on the Commander Islands, Robben Island and St George Island, and elephant and grey seal populations on other islands), total adult populations are increasing and pup survival is decreasing. Thus, although pup production is increasing due to increased numbers of adult females, pup survival is reduced.

(e) There may be reductions in survival and birth rates due to pollutants and entrapment in fishing gear.

Among the most serious alternatives (from the standpoint of its implications to man) is that increased fishing intensity in the Bering Sea during the female harvest period has reduced the carrying capacity of the Bering Sea for fur seals. In our discussion of the Bering Sea fishery data, we noted that the most probable link, if any, is in depletion by the fishery of pollock and herring in the feeding area of nursing females. Demonstration or corroboration of this hypothesis relies on showing that pollock and herring stocks have been reduced in rookery fur seal feeding areas, and that this has resulted in reductions of these foods in female fur seal diets, and reductions in lactating fur seal feeding rates and, consequently, in pup growth and survival. Present data available on fur seals, while substantial, are not sufficient to provide a conclusive a test of this hypothesis. For example, no fish surveys were made in conjunction with pelagic seal surveys, so we do not know how selective seals are in their feeding or how dependent the seal's feeding rates are on prey density and relative prey abundance. Also, we do not have direct estimates of the abundance of non-commercial species such as capelin and squid, which comprise large portions of the seal's diet and may be abundant in the absence of pollock and herring.

We suggest, and others have suggested before (Eberhardt & Siniff 1977, Fowler 1980b), examining changes in a number of behavioural and physiological indices of seal populations that might have presaged or reflected reduced carrying capacity. Measures that we considered are: (a) the age females attain sexual maturity, (b) the weight at age of harvested pre-adult males, (c) the number of pup deaths on land compared with total pup births, (d) the average time spent at sea by lactating females (or some composite index of the time at sea plus the time suckling pups), (e) the survival rate of pups to age 3 computed from harvest of 3-year old males and pup counts three years earlier, and (f) changes in diet composition after the development of the pollock fishery. We also used estimates of seal abundance, fish stock, and daily food intake to see how great an impact the seal actually made on this stock and whether estimated fishery reductions in the stock were sufficient to have an impact on the fur seals.

Fur seal population indices

Age at sexual maturity

York (1980) used a method modified from Lett and Benjaminsen (1977) to compute an average age of maturity for year classes from 1954 to 1964 from the 1958–74 pelagic cruises. Graphs of these results are shown in Figure 4.5 (from York 1980). The average age at maturity increased sharply for the 1956 year-class – the first year females were harvested. The age at maturity subsequently dropped and remained stable, though at a higher average age than before 1956. The graph in Figure 4.5, as well as the results of other studies done before 1956 on age at maturity, suggest that post-1956 age at maturity was greater than pre-1956 averages.

There are a number of alternative explanations for the apparent increase in age of maturity in addition to the reduction of carrying capacity of seals. First, the increase may also have been due to the female harvest on the Pribilofs selecting a higher fraction

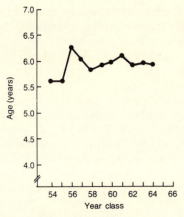

Figure 4.5 Estimated average age at first reproduction of female northern fur seals based on females pregnant at least once for the 1954–64 year-classes. (From York 1980.)

of mature females at a given age than actually existed in the population. Since the Pribilofs are a rookery, the presence of mature females in higher proportion than in the entire population would leave the non-rookery population with a higher proportion of immatures, which would then affect the samples taken at sea. Another difficulty is that only 2 years of pre-1956 age-class data were available from pelagic cruises, and the other pre-1956 data (reported by York 1980) may not have involved the same index of maturity as that used by York. Other possible sources of bias in the age at maturity estimate were the tendency of the pelagic seal samples to contain a higher number of older individuals than expected, and the underlying assumption that survival rates of pregnant and non-pregnant females are the same (York 1980).

Growth with age
Preliminary analysis by the NMML (Fowler 1980a) of data from 3-year-old males harvested on the Pribilof Islands indicated a statistically significant increase in weight over time from 1964 to 1970, in contrast to growth rate reductions which would be expected under a reduced fur seal carrying capacity.

Bigg (1979) plotted the average length of pregnant females against age for the time periods 1958–62, 1963–8 and 1969–74. His results (Fig. 4.6, from Bigg 1979) indicate that growth rates were greater from 1963 to 1974 than from 1958 to 1962. These results raise the possibility that the fur seal might actually have experienced an increase in carrying capacity since 1963. However, Berdine (1980) noted that if fur seal population density and carrying capacity both decline, growth rate could still show an increase. As mentioned earlier, changes in carrying capacity can result from a variety of causes, and until stronger links are established between fur seal populations and their controlling processes, arguments that carrying capacity changes are reflected by certain changes in population parameters will remain unsubstantiated.

Pup deaths on the rookery
Counts of dead pups on the Pribilof Islands rookery are an indication of the survival rate of pups when these are used in conjunction with total pup birth estimates. Gentry

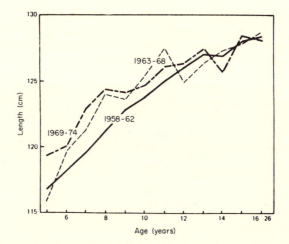

Figure 4.6 Comparison of average lengths of pregnant females aged 5 to 16–26 years for combined months of January to April, combined years 1958–62, 1963–8 and 1969–74. Sample size > or = 10 seals (From Bigg 1979.)

(1980) estimated that dead pup counts include around 95% of the actual dead pups on the islands. From 1970 to 1979, pup death estimates on the Pribilof Islands, varied between 4500 and 54 000, averaging about 25 000 – about 7% of the average pup population (Lander 1981). Earlier pup count data indicated extremely high pup mortality in the years 1954, 1956, 1960 and 1961, three of which were also years of large female harvests, which may account for the high pup mortalities.

Facts about the dead pup counts are: (a) that large pup losses appeared more frequently before 1956 than after, although this needs further corroboration, (b) that the year-to-year variability in pup mortality was large, and (c) that pup mortality on St Paul Island did not appear to be correlated with that on St George Island, whereas temporal patterns of pup mortality from one rookery to the next on either island were more closely correlated with each other. The last fact seems to argue against food limitation as the controlling factor for pup survival through the rookery period, and suggests instead some more local effects on the populations.

Average time at sea for mother seals
Bartholomew and Hoel (1953) recorded time at sea and nursing for 12 nursing seals in 1952 on St Paul Island. Gentry (1980) made similar observations on nursing seals in the late 1970s, and his data concerning time at sea were not significantly different from those of Bartholomew and Hoel.

Pup survival to age two
Lander (1981) calculated early survival rates to age 2 for male fur seals from the 1950 to 1970 year classes, and York and Hartley (1981), analysing these estimates using Mann–Whitney and Student's t tests, found pre-1956 rates to be significantly lower than post-1956 rates (0.32 versus 0.40 average). This does not appear to support the hypothesis of reduced carrying capacity.

Time trends in fur seal diets

Seal stomach contents taken on cruises in 1960, 1962–4, 1968, and 1973–4 were used to investigate trends in fur seal diets to see whether these might have changed after development of the pollock fishery. These data were summarised by month.

Figure 4.7 indicates that the age composition in catch in the pollock fishery shifted from a mode of 4 years in 1964 to three years in 1974, with the 2-year-old catch also being strongly represented. Kajimura (who was present on the cruises) suggested that the size of pollock in fur seal stomach samples decreased from 1964 to 1974. Examination of average volume per pollock specimen in fur seal stomachs (NMML unpublished data in Table 4.5) corroborates this observation, with average specimen size decreasing significantly between 1968 and 1973–4. We also note that the percentage volume of the total stomach content comprised of pollock was consistently high in 1973–4 (above 48%) whereas earlier (especially before 1968) pollock comprised a variable and usually low percentage of the diet (less than 20% in 8 of the 11 months sampled).

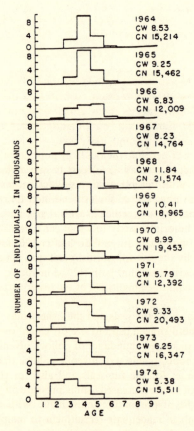

Figure 4.7 Age composition in catch per unit effort (CPUE) of pollock from the Japanese trawl fishery in the eastern Bering Sea. Japanese trawl fishery includes the mother ship fishery and the North Pacific trawl fishery, but not land-based dragnet fishery. (From Salveson & Alton 1976.) CW: CPUE in weight in tons; CN: CPUE in number.

Table 4.5 Fur seal diet of pollock from pelagic samples in the eastern Bering Sea. NMML unpublished data obtained by permission of NMML (1980).

Date	Number of stomachs with food	Volume pollock in diet (cm³)	%	Number of pollock in diet	% of total numbers	Pollock (cm³)
June 1960	4	385	12.3	19	5.2	20.26
July 1960	152	39807	61	403	9.8	98.7
Aug. 1960	61	37124	75	148	10	251
June 1962	53	295	2.4	2	0.16	147.5
July 1962	137	4343	12.6	45	1.1	96.5
Aug. 1962	277	17266	18.3	323	3.1	53.45
Sept. 1962	111	10342	28	235	5.4	44.0
July 1963	256	11188	14.16	62	0.56	180.45
Aug. 1963	536	9758	5	163	0.59	59.9
Sept. 1963	17	700	11.06	1	0.11	700
July 1964	97	2354	9.5	7	0.27	336
Aug. 1964	213	29296	15.4	792	9.8	37
July 1968	78	31901	76.9	384	14.3	83
Aug. 1968	53	11206	37.4	30	1.21	373.5
July 1973	148	72427	90.7	1418	33.0	51.07
Aug. 1973	191	36564	60.7	1305	15.1	43.34
Sept. 1973	178	32511	48.5	2172	23.7	14.9
July 1974	52	13658	87.4	244	58.6	36.0
Aug.1974	110	15198	63.2	390	20.2	38.9

These data indicate that there may have been an interaction between fur seal diets and the pollock fishery. As fishing pressure on pollock increased, fishing out of older age-classes reduced the average size of the fish and increased the average growth rate of the pollock. Furthermore, young pollock survival may have been increased through reduced cannibalism. These increased stocks of smaller fish were reflected by the increase in abundance of pollock in fur seal diets after 1968 and by a marked decrease in the size of fish taken by the fur seals. This increase in total stock biomass, mostly in the younger age-classes, can account both for the increased fur seal diets on (mostly smaller) pollock and the continued high yield of the fishery after over 10 years of heavy fishing pressure.

Table 4.5 indicates that both fur seals and the fishery may have exploited the same pollock resource, since both show a drop in size of 'catch' over time. We suspect that the trend toward greatly increased abundance of pollock juveniles in the Bering Sea has also resulted in larger schools (patches) of juvenile pollock than previously, which has made them an easier target for the fur seals and also for the fishery. One possible dangerous consequence of future increased fishing pressure on pollock, however, is that most of the catch will be of pre-mature individuals. With continued heavy fishing pressure, this might result in inadequate recruitment to maintain the stock.

A possible alternative explanation for why pollock were so consistently taken by fur seals in 1973–4 is that these were relatively cold years, with pollock aggregating more on the outer shelf than in warmer years (Pereyra *et al.* 1976). Another possible explanation is that the Pribilof area, where the bulk of the 1973 and 1974 stomach samples were taken (unlike the earlier samples which did not focus as heavily on this area), is a nursery area for young-of-the-year pollock, which may account for the reduced average size and increased abundance of pollock in fur seal stomachs during 1973 and 1974. Despite these possible alternatives, the most plausible hypothesis is that pollock has increased in importance in fur seal diets since the initiation of the pollock fishery.

Energetics approach to fur seal food consumption

The total amount of food consumed by fur seals (and other marine mammals as well) in the eastern Bering Sea has been estimated by a number of individuals (McAlister & Perez 1976, Anonymous 1979, Laevastu & Larkins 1981). McAlister and Perez (1976) estimated that fur seals eat 378 000 mt of fish and squid every year. They used an estimated feeding rate of 7.5% body weight daily (BWD), whereas Miller (1978) suggested that 14% BWD may be more appropriate to support seals at 7°C – the average summer temperature in the Bering Sea. Miller based his arguments on metabolic studies in which he recorded oxygen consumption at different temperatures in the laboratory for a number of juvenile seals, and also conducted feeding studies using food most commonly found in the diet of fur seals in the Bering Sea. Using Miller's estimate for consumption would give a figure of 705 000 tonnes eaten annually by fur seals. Laevastu and Larkins (1981) gave an estimate of 513 000 tonnes taken by fur seals annually in the eastern Bering Sea, with an additional 368 000 tonnes taken in the Aleutian region. Miller's figures were based on runs of the PROBUB model. Estimates of Bering Sea and Aleutian Island fur seal populations and their mean consumption rates (given in Table 4.6 – Anonymous 1979) were used to compute a total fur seal consumption of 219 000 tonnes.

These estimates can be compared with annual fish catches in the eastern Bering Sea and Aleutian Islands (North Pacific Fishery Management Council). Between 1968 and 1976, annual fish catches varied between 750 000 and 2 100 000 tonnes in the eastern Bering Sea and between 40 000 and 80 000 tonnes near the Aleutian Islands. These figures indicate that fish harvests by marine mammals and man in the Bering Sea are comparable, and that those of the marine mammals exceed man's in the Aleutian Island area. It is important to note, however, that fur seals prey on a larger number of species than does man, and thus a part of their harvest is not in direct competition with man's. As a consequence of the fur seals greater ability to switch prey when abundances of preferred prey species are low, total consumption by fur seal is probably fairly steady from year to year, whereas man's is highly variable.

It has been estimated (Anonymous 1979, Table 12) that 9.8% of fish standing stock in the eastern Bering Sea and Aleutians is consumed annually by marine mammals, 5% by man and 1.8% by birds (1.9% by fur seals). Laevastu and Larkins (1981) estimated a total commercial fish standing stock of 24 880 000 tonnes in the Bering Sea and Gulf of Alaska, which implies that 3.5% of all commercial fish stocks are taken by fur seals annually, and 10.7% by all marine mammals. The fur seal figures are deceptive, since fur seal impact on fish stocks is relatively localised. Thus, fur seals near the Pribilof Islands are probably consuming considerably more fish than man, though man may be harvesting some different species. This energetics computation is inconclusive with respect to fur seal–fishery interaction except to show that competition between the two is possible.

Table 4.6 Fur seal population estimates at sea (June–November) in the eastern Bering Sea and Aleutian area. (Anonymous 1979.)

Age class	Population[1] total	June–Nov. eastern Bering Sea and Aleutian	Estimated percent of time at sea (June–Nov.)	Estimated population at sea (June–Nov.)	Mean[2] weight (kg)	Mean[3] daily consumption rate (%)
Pups	349 000	321 000[7]	10	32 100	10.00	14.00
M + F, age 1	174 000	67 000	90[4]	78 300	9.54	13.76
M + F, age 2	122 000	61 000	75[4]	45 750	16.69	12.32
F, age 3	55 000	23 000	80[4]	22 400	18.80	12.53
F, >age 4	582 000	46 000	79[5]	368 140	35.64	11.76
M, age 3–7	101 000	71 000	10[6]	7 100	32.60	7.60
M, >age 7	11 000	9 000	10[6]	900	105.25	7.00
Total	1 394 000	1 043 000 (754 100)[8]		554 690	29.92	11.71

[1] Average 1969 to 1974.

[2] Based on MMN, NMFS pelagic research data, 1958–74, $n = 13772$, except average weight for pups (10 kg) based on observations in the Pribilof Islands during September; total mean weight based on an effective fishery population 754 000 based on time spent on land and at sea for each class during June and September.

[3] Weighted by mean animal weight of estimated body weight for animals weighing < 10 kg or < 45 kg in waters colder than 15°C; 7% for > 10 kg on land or > 45 kg at sea.

[4] 8% mortality, pups estimated to feed at sea only 18 days (10% of time) during September–November.

[5] These percentages represent proportions of the total population of the respective age class not on the rookeries during the breeding season.

[6] Based on percent of time out of 130 days not on rookery.

[7] Based on the ratio of males to females (0.085) in the Eastern Bering Sea during June–November from NNM, NMFS pelagic research data, 1958–74 ($n = 4451$).

[8] Effective fishery population (June–November).

Usefulness of models for fur seal studies

Models may be useful for fur seal investigations in the following general ways.

(a) To investigate the plausibility of various explanations for observed phenomena.
(b) To suggest hypotheses to explain observed phenomena.
(c) To establish priorities for future research needs.
(d) To explore the effects of alternative management options.
(e) To organise available data and information.

Figure 4.8 shows six general types of models and describes (in the left column) the data needed to run each of them, and (in the right column) the results that can be obtained from them and what questions they can answer concerning fur seals and their relationship to the fishery. The data source is prefixed by an 'H' if it is available and relatively accurate, an 'M' if it is difficult to obtain or less accurate, or an 'L' if it is

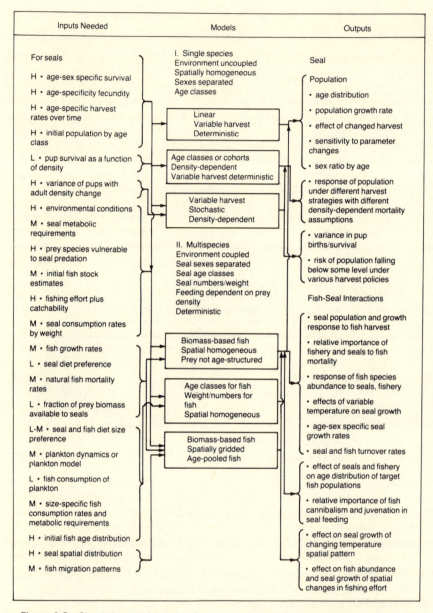

Figure 4.8 Simulation models related to their necessary inputs and potential outputs.

unavailable, very difficult to obtain, or based on scanty evidence. The models in Figure 4.8 are divided into two groups, each of which contains three types. For example, the three model types in group I are all single-species models without environmental driving variables, assume spatial homogeneity, and have populations separated by age and sex. Examples of existing models like those considered in Figure 4.8 are given in Figure 4.3.

It can be seen from Figure 4.8 that the weakest links in the data base are: (a) inferring pup survival as a function of density, (b) obtaining seal diet preferences (this is not the same as actual seal stomach contents, which are easier to measure, stomach contents depend both on predator preference and prey abundance), and (c) determining the fraction of the total fish stock actually available to seals (which depends both on the spatial and size distributions of the prey). Figure 4.8 clarifies why Leslie matrix models are so prevalent: all data needed to run them are usually available. The multispecies models all suffer from weak data support, primarily in describing mammal feeding, since so little is known about feeding in the sea. Notice that all the model types included in Figure 4.8 are separated by sex for seals (though not for fish in the models in group II) since harvest, growth, and survival parameters differ markedly between the sexes in this species. Sex-separated models differ from ordinary Leslie matrix models which consider females only and are impractical for including density-dependent assumptions involving male populations (non-harem males or harem bulls). It is necessary to keep track of male and female populations separately in order to include the effects of male abundance on birthing success and density-dependent pup survival. Several model outputs (e.g. seal population age distribution) can be obtained from all the model types, whereas others are specific to a single type of model (e.g. consideration of risk is specific to a stochastic model).

To investigate our earlier proposed fur seal–pollock fishery relationship, which postulated a shift in both pollock abundance and pollock size in seal diets following the development of the pollock fishery, would require a model which has size or age classes of fish (e.g. pollock), as well as age and sex classes for the fur seals.

Discussion of future work

Future work can be divided into: (a) suggested analysis of existing data, (b) suggested simulation model development, and (c) further necessary field research.

Suggested analysis of existing data

Population indices
Following Eberhardt and Siniff's (1977) suggestion that a population's response to impact may be reflected by various indices, we suggest that the available data from which these indices are computed should also be studied for trends. Indices that are most easily obtained for the fur seal are pup birth estimates, dead pup counts, male survival to age 3 (from male harvest data), and length at age for pre-adult males (from harvested males).

Fur seal diet trend
We have suggested a relationship between fur seals and the fishery via greatly increased abundance of juvenile pollock (see Table 4.5). The data used, however, were already combined in such a way that we were unable to separate them according to the region in which they were collected and the degree of digestion of the prey. We suggest that the original data be used to conduct a complete statistical analysis with corrections made for the area in which the sample was taken, and, if possible, the time of day the samples were taken (assuming that the correlations found between the proportion of the stomachs empty and the time of day at which the samples were taken also apply

to the percentage of food digested). Variance estimates can also be computed and used to make statistical tests for time trends, both in the average size of pollock in seal stomachs and in the percentage of the total diet comprised of pollock.

The role of patchiness in seal feeding   Although we suspect, from survey data on pollock (Smith 1979), that pollock are quite patchily distributed in the eastern Bering Sea, the survey data need to be re-examined for an indication of the size of patches or degree of aggregation. An attempt should be made to represent this patchiness stochastically (in terms of probability). One important question to be considered with these data is whether or not there has been a trend in pollock school size from 1963 to 1974 in the eastern Bering Sea. Another approach to considering patchiness is to use the abundance of pollock in fur seal stomachs collected at different locations as an index to the spatial separation and size of pollock schools.

The suggested future rôle for models

Single-species models are useful to investigate population changes with different harvesting strategies and to explore the importance of density dependence in the response of a population to harvesting, given that the form of the density-dependent relationship is known. However, substantiation of this relationship is at present not available. Other relevant questions which could possibly be explored with single-species simulation models are (Fowler 1980a):

(a)   What is the influence of fur seal harvest on their maximum sustainable yield?
(b)   How might the fur seal population respond to a cessation of harvest?
(c)   What mortality level can be expected from pollution and entanglement in fishing gear and how does it effect fur seal population dynamics?

Due to the variability in year-to-year pup production and survival, deterministic models may not produce realistic predictions. Alternatively, a stochastic modelling approach, such as that followed by Getz and Swartzman (1981), may be useful. Here, a deterministic density-dependent stock–recruit relationship is replaced by a matrix of probabilities of transfer from various stock densities to surviving pup densities. This model can generate as output the variance in population densities and also the risk (probability) that the population will fall below a given level under different harvest strategies.

Multispecies models consider interactions between species through predation and feeding competition, and are useful for exploring such questions as the effect of harvest of a particular species on its predator's species composition. The DYNUMES model, however (which uses marine mammals as a driving variable), cannot be used to explore fur seal–fishery interactions; the use of age-structured, spatially homogeneous models for these investigations is recommended – specifically to test the hypothesis that reduction of older pollock, resulting in increased survivorship of younger pollock, has had a positive effect on fur seal food availability. Since our preliminary perusal of these data indicates a reduction in pollock size but an increase in relative abundance, a model having pollock size classes is mandatory. Mechanisms of prey choice by fur seals, as well as the energetics of nursing mothers, should be included in this model. The model should be confined to the Pribilof Islands area (or the feeding area of nursing fur seals) during the rookery period. With a model of this limited spatial and temporal scale we would: (a) have a good chance to obtain the data necessary for model development and corroboration, and (b) address the most probable area and time of intensive fur seal–fishery competition. It might also be desirable to consider the effect of pollock school size and school abundance on fur seal feeding, if pollock schooling data can be obtained. Vlymen (1977) demonstrated the importance of considering patch distribution in explaining the feeding rates of larval anchovy by using a stochastic patch feeding model.

Suggested future data collection

We suggest that a fish trawl survey targeting on pollock be conducted between the Pribilof Islands and Unimak Pass from June to September, with the study designed to focus on areas of high pollock density to determine the size distribution of pollock, the size of the schools, and, if possible, to observe seal feeding intensity around the schools. The pollock and seals might be tracked using multibeam sonar techniques. Additional stomach samples of fur seal taken in conjunction with the trawl survey would give a useful insight into fur seal food selectivity.

Conclusions

In summary, we see rookery fur seal behaviour and multispecies, age-classed, patch feeding models as directions for future study. Before proceeding in this direction, we recommend: (a) the use of deterministic single-species models (with behavioural observations to improve abundance estimates) to attempt to replicate recent known abundance patterns of fur seals and to examine intra-specific sources of population control, and of stochastic single-species models to examine variability of fur seal populations; (b) further detailed analysis of fur seal stomach content data to explore more fully the interaction between the fur seal and the pollock fishery suggested by Table 4.5, and to elucidate other interactions with fisheries of which we may be unaware at this time; and (c) development of an eastern Bering Sea marine mammal–fish interaction model to organise available data and to explore the plausibility of the hypothesis that the fishery is affecting fur seals through reducing their food base and hence their carrying capacity.

The available fur seal and fishery data, while limited, appear to be the best mammal–fishery data in the world, and as such deserve to be fully archived and fully utilised.

Acknowledgements

The authors wish to acknowledge the help of Anne York, Jerry Hornof, Mike Perez, Hiro Kajimura, Bruce McAlister, Ron Ryel, Jim Berdine and Mike Tillman in conducting the work leading to this report. We are especially grateful to Chuck Fowler for his ideas and support, and for his making data and other resources openly available to us.

Others whose help in reviewing the manuscript and/or providing suggestions on our work we appreciate include Gary Smith, Robert Francis and Taivo Laevastu at NWAFC, Nigel Bonner of Cambridge, England, Douglas Chapman at the University of Washington, Robert Hofman and Peter Major of the Marine Mammal Commission and Lee Eberhardt at Battelle Pacific Northwest Laboratory. In our office, Ed Small and Stan Clark supplied computer support and Pat Sullivan editorial and clerical assistance.

This work was funded in part by the Marine Mammal Commission.

References

Abegglen, C. F. and A. Y. Roppel 1959. Fertility in the northern fur seal, 1956–57. *J. Wildl. Manag.* **23**, 75–81.

Abegglen, C. F., A. Y. Roppel and F. Wilke 1956. *Alaska fur seal investigations, Pribilof Island, Alaska.* Ms. report NWAFC.

Andersen, K. P. and E. Ursin 1977. A multispecies extension to the Beverton and Holt theory of fishing, with accounts of phosphorus circulation and primary production. *Medd. Dan. Fisk Havund.* **7**, 319–435.

Anonymous, 1979. *Draft environmental impact statement of the Interim Convention on Conservation of North Pacific Fur Seals.* Seattle, Washington: US Department of Commerce, National Marine Fisheries Service.

Bakkala, R., L. Low and V. Wespestad 1979. *Condition of groundfish resources in the Bering Sea and Aleutian area.* NMFS Northwest and Alaska Fisheries Center report submitted to the International North Pacific Fisheries Commission.

Balchen, J. G. 1980. Modeling and identification of marine ecological systems with applications in management of fish resources and planning of fisheries operations. *Model. Ident. & Control* **1**, 67–8.

Bartholomew, G. and P. Hoel 1953. Reproductive behaviour of the Alaskan fur seal, *Callorhinus ursinus. J. Mammal.* **34**, 417–36.

Berdine, J. 1980. Personal communication.

Chapman, D. G. 1973. Spawner-recruit models and estimation of the level of maximum sustainable catch. *Int. Coun. Exp. Sea. Rapp. Proc. Verb.* **164**, 325–32.

Chapman, D. G. and A. M. Johnson 1968. Estimation of fur seal pup populations by randomized sampling. *Trans. Am. Fish. Soc.* **97**, 264–70.

Cushing, D. H. 1973. *Recruitment and parent stocks in fisheries.* Wash. Sea Grant Publn 73–1. Div. Mar. Res. Univ. Washington.

Eberhardt, L. L. and D. B. Siniff 1977. Population dynamics and marine mammal management policies. *J. Fish. Res. Bd Can.* **34**, 183–90.

Favorite, F., W. J. Ingraham, K. D. Waldron, E. A. Best, V. G. Wespestad, L. H. Barton, G. B. Smith, R. G. Bakkala, R. R. Straty and T. Laevastu 1979. *Fisheries oceanography – Eastern Bering sea shelf.* NWAFC Processed Report 79–20.

Fiscus, C. 1979. Interactions of marine mammals and Pacific hake. *Mar. Fish. Rev.* Oct. 1–9.

Fowler, C. W. 1980a. Personal communication.

Fowler, C. 1980b. Appendix G: Indices of population status. In *Comparative population dynamics in large mammals. A Search for management criteria.* C. W. Fowler, M. B. Cherry, W. T. Bunderson, R. J. Ryel and B. B. Steel (eds), NTIS PB80-178627. Washington DC: US Department of Commerce.

Fowler, C. 1981. Density dependence as related to life history strategy. *Ecol.* **62** (3), 602–10.

Gentry, R. 1980. Personal communication.

Getz, W. and G. Swartzman 1981. A probability transition matrix model for yield estimation in fisheries with highly variable recruitment. *Can. Fish. & Aquat. Sci.* **38** (7), 847–55.

Hofman, R. 1980. Personal communication.

Innis, G. S., J. W. Haefner, G. L. Worthen and C. W. Fowler 1978. Eastern tropical pacific modeling study – final report. Report to Southwest Fisheries Center (NMFS), La Jolla, Calif.

Johnson, A. M. 1975. The status of northern fur seal populations. *Rapp. P. -V. Reun., Cons. Int. Explor. Mer.* **169**, 263–6.

Kajimura, H. 1981. The opportunistic feeding of northern fur seals off California. Unpublished manuscript. Seattle, Washington: National Marine Mammal Laboratory.

Kajimura, H., R. H. Lander, M. A. Perez and A. E. York 1979. *Preliminary analysis of pelagic fur seal data collected by the United States and Canada during 1958–74.* Report submitted to the 22nd Annual Meeting of the Standing Scientific Committee, North Pacific Fur Seal Commission.

Kajimura, H., R. H. Lander, M. A. Perez and A. E. York 1980. *Further analysis of pelagic fur seal data collected by the United States and Canada during 1958–74.* Part 1. Report submitted to the 23rd Annual Meeting of the Standing Scientific Committee, North Pacific Fur Seal Commission.

Laevastu, T. and H. A. Larkins 1981. *Marine fisheries ecosystem: its quantitative evaluation and management.* Farnham, England: Fishing News Books.

Laevastu, T. and P. Livingston 1980. Basic inputs to PROBUB model for the eastern Bering Sea and western Gulf of Alaska. NWAFC Processed Report 80–3.

Lander, R. H. 1981. A life table and biomass estimate for Alaskan fur seals. *Fish. Res.* 1 (1981/1982), 55–70.

Lett, P. F. and T. Benjaminsen 1977. A stochastic model for the management of the northwestern Atlantic harp seal (*Pagophilus groenlandicus*) population. *J. Fish. Res. Bd. Can.* 34, 1155–87.

Lowry, L. 1981. Personal communication.

McAlister, W. B. and M. A. Perez 1976. Preliminary estimates of pinniped–fin fish relationship in the Bering Sea. Background paper for the 19th meeting of the North Pacific Fur Seal Commission.

May, G. H. 1937. The food of the fur seal. *J. Mamm.* 18, 99–100.

Miller, L. K. 1978. *Energetics of the northern fur seal in relation to climate and food resources in the Bering Sea.* NTIS PB-275296. Washington DC: US Department of Commerce.

Parrish, J. D. 1975. Marine trophic interactions by dynamic simulation of fish species. *Fish. Bull. US* 73, 695–716.

Patten, B. C., D. A. Egloff and T. H. Richardson 1975. Total ecosystem model for a cove in Lake Texoma. In *Systems analysis in ecology*, Vol. III, B. C. Patten (ed.), 206–423. New York: Academic Press.

Pereyra, W., J. Reeves and R. Bakkala 1976. Demersal fish and shellfish resources of the eastern Bering Sea in the baseline year 1975. NWAFC Processed Report.

Perez, M. A. 1979. Preliminary analysis of feeding habits of the northern fur seal in the eastern North Pacific and Bering Sea. In Kajimura *et al.* 1979, above.

Perez, M. A. and M. A. Bigg 1980. Interim report on the feeding habits of the northern fur seal in the eastern North Pacific and eastern Bering Sea. In Kajimura *et al.* 1980, above.

Pruter, A. 1973. Development and present status of bottomfish resources in the Bering Sea. *J. Fish. Res. Bd. Can.* 30, 2373–85.

Radford, P. J. 1979. Some aspects of an estuarine ecosystem model-Gembase. In *State of the art in ecological modelling*, Vol. 7, 301–22. Amsterdam: Elsevier.

Sissenwine, M. P. 1977. A compartmentalized simulation model of the southern New England yellowtail flounder (*Limanda ferruginea*) fishery. *Fish. Bull. US* 75, 465–82.

Smith, T. D. and T. Polacheck 1981. Reexamination of the life table for northern fur seals with implications about population regulatory mechanisms, In *Dynamics of large mammal populations*, C. Fowler and T. Smith (eds). New York: Wiley.

Spalding, D. J. 1964. Comparative feeding habits of the fur seal, sea lion and harbor seal on the British Columbia coast. *Fish. Res. Bd Can. Bull.* 146.

Steele, J. H. 1977. The structure of plankton communities. *Phil. Trans. Soc. London*, Series B. 280 (976), 485–534.

Swartzman, G. L., R. T. Haar, D. H. McKenzie and T. Zaret 1981. Evaluation of the usefulness of ecological simulation models in power plant cooling systems. In: *Energy and ecological modelling, developments in environmental modelling* 1, 173–184. W. J. Mitsch, R. W. Bosserman, and J. M. Klopatek (eds), Amsterdam: Elsevier.

Vlymen, W. J. 1977. A mathematical model of the relationship between larval anchovy (*Engraulis mordax*) growth, prey microdistribution and larval behaviour. *Env. Biol. Fish.* 2, 211–33.

Westpestad, D. G. 1978. *Exploitation, distribution and life history features of Pacific herring in the Bering Sea.* NWAFC Processed Report.

Wilke, F. and K. Kenyon 1957. The food of fur seals in the eastern Bering Sea. *J. Wildl. Manag.* 21, 237.

York, A. E. and J. R. Hartley 1981. Pup production following harvest of female northern fur seals, (*Callorhinus ursinus*). Can. Fish. & Aquat. Sci. 38 (1), 84–90.

5 Marine mammal–fishery interactions: modelling and the Southern Ocean

J. R. Beddington and W. K. de la Mare

Background

The exploitation of marine mammals played a fundamental rôle in attracting attention to the Antarctic in the 19th century. In the light of the decimation of the stocks of whales in this century, it is often overlooked that some species of marine mammals in the Southern Ocean were virtually extirpated in the 19th century. Fur seals, elephant seals and right whales fall into this category, although in terms of ecological effects, these are more likely to have been of local rather than global significance.

The more significant impact on the Antarctic ecosystems will have come from the depletion of the stocks of great whales, and this story is by now so familiar that it requires no more than the briefest recapitulation here.

The era of modern whaling began in the Antarctic in 1904. In the early period, whaling was from land-based stations in the South Atlantic, and the main target was humpback whales, though some blue and fin whales were also taken. Some Antarctic stocks of humpback whales were also exploited in their wintering grounds in lower latitudes.

In 1925 the first Discovery expedition marked the beginning of serious marine research in relation to whales and krill in the Antarctic. However, more significantly, 1925 also saw the introduction of the first factory ship with a stern slipway, and by 1930 the industry was in the main pelagic, with the blue whale as the most important target species. By 1940 it was already apparent that significant inroads were being made into the stocks of blue whales (Mackintosh 1942), and by the time protection was given by the International Whaling Commission (IWC) in 1964, the stock – thought to have numbered originally around 200 000 animals – had been reduced to no more than a few thousand.

When whaling resumed after World War II, fin whales formed an increasing proportion of the catch and became the mainstay of the industry throughout the 1950s and 1960s, when catches often exceeded 25 000 fin whales per year. Eventually these stocks were reduced to the point where they were no longer commercially significant and sei whales became the chief target of the industry. These, however, were very quickly depleted, and today only a remnant of the pelagic whaling industry operates on the smallest of the rorquals, the minke whale.

In all, the biomass of baleen whales was reduced from around 40–50 million tonnes before 1930 (Laws 1977) to less than 5 million tonnes today. However, it should be mentioned that these figures may not reflect the true change in biomass because most estimates of initial and current population sizes are based on catch per unit effort (CPUE) methods, which are problematic. For example, recent research (Beddington

1979, Fowler 1980, Cooke 1984) has shown that these methods will underestimate population declines when using with typical whaling CPUE data.

Nonetheless, taking these figures at face value suggests that the biomass of baleen whales in the Antarctic is now around 40 million tonnes less than it was in the pristine state, and Laws (1977), from considerations of the food requirements of whales, calculates that the amount of food (mainly krill, *Euphausia superba*) eaten by baleen whales will have declined by around 150 million tonnes per year.

However, sperm whales have also been heavily exploited in the Southern Hemisphere and a disproportionate share of the catch has come from large males which migrate to high latitudes. Although it is much more difficult to obtain estimates of the degree of depletion of sperm whales in the Southern Hemisphere, it is apparent that in some areas the declines are considerable (Cooke *et al.* 1983).

Sperm whale depletion, though smaller than that of the baleen whales in terms of biomass, may be comparable in the magnitude (but not direction) of its effect on the ecosystem because of the higher trophic level of sperm whales. We return to this theme later.

Predator–prey interactions

There are a number of possible ways in which the interaction between krill and its marine mammal predators can be viewed. Such views will determine the goals for management and ultimately the practice of management. Accordingly, a brief review of the three main possibilities is appropriate.

One possibility is to consider the marine mammals as pests which, by their predation on krill, reduce its potential for producing a sustainable harvest. A second possibility is that both marine mammals and krill are potentially harvestable resources and that a final choice of harvesting levels will be determined by an intermix of social and economic factors. Finally, the marine mammals may be considered as species requiring conservation in their own right and the krill fishery may be thought of as a particular type of habitat deterioration.

Whatever the views of the interaction, a decision to manage in this instance is in part based on the belief that marine mammals can affect the yield of fisheries on their food and that fisheries can in turn affect the dynamics of marine mammals. This problem has been explored in more detail in Chapter 1 but it is pertinent to consider it in the context of the Southern Ocean system here. The main management instrument in the Southern Ocean is the Convention for the Conservation of Antarctic Marine Living Resources (CCAMLR), whose relevant articles are as follows.

1 The objective of this Convention is the conservation of Antarctic marine living resources.
2 For the purpose of this Convention, the term 'conservation' includes rational use.
3 Any harvesting and associated activities in the area to which this Convention applies shall be conducted in accordance with the provisions of this Convention and with the following principles of conservation:
   (a) prevention of decrease in the size of any harvested population to levels below those which ensure its stable recruitment. For this purpose its size should not be allowed to fall below a level close to that which ensures the greatest net annual increment;

(b) maintenance of the ecological relationships between harvested, dependent and related populations of Antarctic marine living resources and the restoration of depleted populations to the levels defined in sub-paragraph (a) above; and

(c) prevention of changes or minimization of the risk of changes in the marine ecosystem which are not potentially reversible over two or three decades, taking into account the state of available knowledge of the direct and indirect impact of harvesting, the effect of the introduction of alien species, the effects of associated activities on the marine ecosystem and of the effects of environmental changes, with the aim of making possible the sustained conservation of Antarctic marine living resources.

Clearly, there are a number of problems in interpreting the precise scientific meaning of certain portions of the text. In particular it is hard to interpret unless, following Edwards and Heap (1981), distinction is made between:

(a) species in the low trophic levels which form the food base for species in high trophic levels (e.g. zooplankton, particularly krill);

(b) species at intermediate trophic levels which prey on the species of the low trophic level but are themselves subject to significant predation by the top trophic level (e.g. squid and fish);

(c) species at the top trophic level which prey on levels (a) and (b) but are not themselves subject to significant natural predation (e.g. whales, seals and birds).

With this distinction, it is possible to recognise that top predators may only be adequately treated by the articles if levels of 'greatest net annual increment' are interpreted as those occurring when some specific amount of krill is harvested. To put the problem in simple terms, in the absence of exploitation of their food supply, top predators will have some population level at which their net annual increment is at a maximum. If their food supply is exploited, there will be a new and lower population level at which their net annual increment will be maximised. Hence there is a range of possible protection levels for top predators and the precise level will be determined by the level of krill harvesting: the higher the level of krill harvesting, the lower the protection level. This would appear to be against the spirit of the Convention and hence some interpretation which avoids this ambiguity is necessary. An obvious choice is the level that is defined when no krill are harvested. It has proved to be very difficult in the case of marine mammals to determine where such levels might be, and in practice it is more likely that an arbitrary percentage of pristine abundance will be more useful.

There are a number of other scientific problems of interpretation of this text, which are really only illuminated by the use of a model of the system. Indeed, the problem discussed above has been addressed with a particularly simple model of the interaction between the trophic levels in mind.

Scientific questions posed by the Convention

The text of the Convention raises a variety of complex scientific problems. One whole set of problems is concerned with the interpretation and likely behaviour of the system under different types of perturbation. It is in this context that simple theoretical models can play a useful rôle. In some of the other problems, and in particular in any practical area where precise quantitative answers are required, models of a different type are needed. In this section we consider the likely behaviour of the system in the light of simple theoretical models. In the following sections we consider the way in which the quantitative estimates necessary for practical management can be obtained.

Theoretical models
In a series of papers (May *et al.* 1979, Beddington & May 1980, Beddington & Cooke 1982) various authors have reviewed simple models of components of the Southern Ocean system. In essence the models employ simple predator–prey interactions framed in differential equations based on density-dependent processes and assume that the unexploited system is in equilibrium. It is inappropriate to review these here and readers interested in the technical detail of the models are referred to the original work. In this chapter we describe the conceptual background of the models and then go on to consider the changes that might be expected in the system on the basis of these models.

In the discussion that follows we will frequently refer to maximum sustainable yield (MSY), not because it is likely to be a practically achievable objective, but because its familiarity makes it a useful concept around which to develop discussion. In addition, for all practical purposes, the MSY level can be equated with the level of 'greatest net annual increment' referred to in the Convention.

Krill–whales This simple model assumes that the population growth rate of the predator species is determined by the abundance of prey relative to the abundance of predators. The level of predation by whales on krill is proportional to the abundance of each. Such a model is general in the sense that a whole variety of similar models will produce predictions similar to the following.

(a)   There is no unique solution to the level of MSY for either predator or prey when both are harvested. The sustainable yield for one depends on the harvesting rate of the other.
(b)   Population growth rates of the predators should increase following their depletion, for example in the case of the baleen whales following commercial whaling.
(c)   Krill abundance should increase when predator abundance is reduced, and predator abundance decline when krill abundance is reduced.
(d)   Harvesting the prey at a level close to the 'surplus' (the difference between the amount eaten before predator depletion and that after predator depletion) could produce overexploitation of the prey.

Krill–whales–seals A variant of the krill–whale model allows there to be more than one species of predator at the same trophic level. This model implies the following.

(a)   Calculation of the MSY level for any one species involves specifying the harvest level for both of the other species. Hence, there is further ambiguity in the interpretation of the convention text which requires clarification.
(b)   Following depletion of one predator, both the prey and the other predator should increase in abundance. This parallels the situation in the Southern Ocean with respect to the guild of baleen whales and to other predators such as seals, birds, squid and fish.

Krill–cephalopods–sperm whales   This model extends the prey–predator model to predators at more than one trophic level. In the context of the Southern Ocean, predation by the cephalopod community (presumed to be on krill) is offset by predation by sperm whales on cephalopods. This model implies the following:

(a)   Following depletion of the top predator, the intermediate predator increases in abundance and hence increases its predation on the prey, and prey abundance decreases.
(b)   Recovery of the top predator or harvesting of the intermediate predator will increase prey abundance.

One of the key parameters in all of these models is the extent to which the various species actually compete for the same food source. In general, one would expect that competition is limited in the pristine system, though in a severely perturbed system this may no longer be so.

This brief review of the implications of the simple models poses interesting questions about the Southern Ocean ecosystem. Following depletion of both baleen whales and sperm whales, we may expect some increase in the cephalopod community, which benefits from reduced competition and predation. It is possible that the balancing effect of increased predation from the various competitors of the exploited baleen whales could have resulted in any outcome in the range of no change in krill abundance over time to a net increase in abundance. For example, increases in other animals such as fish, cephalopods or birds could take up part or all of the krill no longer consumed by the baleen whales.

How the various components in the system react to a change depends critically on the timescale of the response of the various predators on krill. There is little direct evidence to indicate what the response rates might be for marine mammals in the Southern Ocean. Typically, changes in large mammal populations may be expected to occur at a few per cent a year, though the Antarctic fur seal has shown a capacity for increase somewhat greater than this (Payne 1977). In contrast, the cephalopod could be expected to have short generation times and relatively high fecundity and hence could change markedly in abundance in a rather short time. Accordingly, the response of the community may be difficult to detect.

It is thus possible that the community of cephalopods could be playing a central rôle in the behaviour of the ecosystem. Unfortunately, there is considerable ignorance about even the natural history of these species. The numbers of marine mammals and birds which feed on squid imply that they are quite abundant, yet they are rarely taken in net hauls and hence the possibility of directly investigating these species poses a formidable problem.

In this situation, simple conceptual models have a rôle to demonstrate the possible behaviours and their effects on the rest of the system. However, it is clear that if progress is to be made in answering quantitative questions, it is necessary to move to the alternative sources of information. These could be via the indirect effects of major changes on the krill and on the marine mammal predators of krill.

Practical considerations
The implementation of the Convention raises a number of scientific problems of a more practical nature. Leaving aside questions of how to estimate the abundance of krill and where to set catch limits, Article II of the Convention implies that we have to determine

some procedures for ensuring that the marine mammals are not being adversely affected by fisheries. Some insight into the nature of these problems can be gained from considering some present difficulties in interpreting the current status of marine mammals in the Antarctic from existing data collected from both research activities and commercial whaling operations.

The idea that the depletion of the larger species of baleen whales has led to a competitive release of other marine mammals (and birds) has been around for some time (for example Sladen 1964, Gambell 1973). This is one of the types of effects predicted by the simple theoretical models discussed above. However, there is a paucity of data which will admit any reliable quantification of such effects. What was once regarded as strong evidence for a super-abundance of krill available to marine mammals came from observed trends in the demographic rates of baleen whales and crab-eater seals.

There are considerable quantities of data on pregnancy rates for the major exploited whale species. However, these data were collected from commercial whaling operations and have not been clarified by statistical analysis; it has therefore not been possible to arrive at an unambiguous interpretation of the trends indicated by them. A number of factors affect apparent pregnancy rates, such as time of season of capture, and latitude of capture (Gambell 1973, IWC 1979). Indeed, even the nationalities of the inspectors collecting the data seem to reflect different reporting efficiencies (Grenfell 1981, Mizroch & York 1983). Viewed simply as a time series by pooling the data across time of season, latitudinal zone, country taking the catch etc., these data do show an increase in pregnancy rate, which is what would be expected from the reduction in intraspecific competition due to exploitation. Taking into consideration the effects of different factors which may account for some of the observed features of the data can produce different interpretations. For example, Grenfell (1981) fitted a linear model to the data for blue, fin and sei whales which corrected for a number of factors including month of capture, latitudinal zone, and country. This analysis showed qualitatively the same increasing trends as the simple pooling procedures in pregnancy rate, and this was statistically significant. In another analysis of the data for fin whales, Mizroch and York (1983) fitted a model which corrected for a change in length structure of the catches as well, and this generally did not show statistically significant trends.

It is not helpful in this discussion to debate the minutiae of the interpretation of confounded statistics; it is more important to note the lesson that such problems can arise from data collected incidentally to a commercial fishery. Left to themselves, commercial fisheries seek to optimise their catch rates, for example, by moving from one area to another or changing the time of the fishing season. Thus, the data they collect may be of diminished scientific value, particularly if important trends are to be recognised at an early stage. Although whale biomass data may therefore be unreliable, the important point is that pregnancy rates may have the potential to indicate deleterious effects of fisheries on marine mammal populations.

A much more significant type of evidence for competitive release in the Antarctic was thought to be found in data on changes in demographic parameters of some species of marine mammals which occurred even though they were not subject to any significant exploitation in the period when these changes were apparently taking place. The most striking examples of such changes come from the analysis of earplugs in whales and teeth in seals. These materials, when sectioned, show a number of laminae which in young animals are diffuse and irregular and in older animals become well defined and regularly spaced (Laws 1953, Hewer 1964, Lockyer 1972). The total number of laminae is related to the age of the animal, and the point where the laminae become well defined is termed the transition layer. The age at which this transition occurs is thought to be associated with the attaining of sexual maturity. Thus, in principle, each animal has a record of its age and the age at which it reached sexual maturity. Hence, by plotting year of birth against the ages at maturity for a large sample of animals, any trend in ages of attaining sexual maturity would be shown. However, recent studies have shown that this method of analysis may not give a reliable indication, and in fact may be fundamentally flawed (Cooke & de la Mare 1983, 1984). Some evidence that this is the case has been found for minke whales (IWC 1984a), and even more strongly so in crab-eater seals (Bengtsen & Laws 1983). There are a number of mechanisms which could cause spurious declines to be deduced from this method of analysis and these are discussed in Cooke and de la Mare (1983, 1984), but are too complex to review here.

The more important consideration is the evidence which demonstrates the unreliability of the method. In 1983 a workshop on the reliability of age determination in minke whales was held under the auspices of the International Whaling Commission. Particular attention was paid to determination of trends in the age at sexual maturity from the transition layer analysis. A number of different workers read a sample of ear plugs for age and transition layer and quite good agreement was obtained between readers for the total age of the animals, but the overall agreement on transition layers was poor. At the extreme, the correlation between transition layer readings for some readers was negligible, but the declining trend in age at transition layer from these different readings were virtually identical. This means that the trend is not dependent on the signal perceived from the ear plugs by the different readers, indicating that there are mechanisms in the reading process which are not as yet understood. However, this result supports the possibility that the observed trends in the age of sexual maturity of minke whales are an artifact of the method.

The most convincing evidence that the transition layer method is flawed comes from Bengtsen and Laws (1983). The analysis of transition layers from crab-eater seals sampled in the early part of the 1960s showed a decline in the age at sexual maturity. However, an analysis of samples collected in 1980 showed exactly the same pattern of decline but shifted in time by an amount equal to the time between the samples. Since the apparent trend depends on the year in which the samples are collected, it can be concluded that the trends in age at maturity deduced from transition layers in crab-eater seals are also an artifact of the method.

The important point is that the available information does not give clear indications of the nature and extent of competition between krill predators in the Antarctic. This does not constitute evidence that such competition does not occur but it does mean that we are unable to estimate the strength of competition between species. Lacking such data, it is unlikely that models which would give reliable predictions about the actual effects of the depletion of the great whales could be proposed and tested.

These problems also indicate some of the difficulties that may be faced in the future in determining trends in demographic parameters. This would not be so serious if we could reliably detect small changes in abundance of a given species. Unfortunately, this also is now being seen to be an area with considerable practical difficulties. The major problem is that the inherent variability in typical indices of abundance can mask trends until a very large change has taken place or a very long time series of data has been collected (de la Mare 1984). This will still apply even for properly designed surveys because animals have patchy distributions and this results in high sampling variability.

This is exacerbated by the well-known problem that simple indices of abundance may not be linearly related to total population size. Moreover, recent studies have shown that even very detailed indices of abundance based on recorded searching time may still not be linearly related to stock size (Zahl 1982, Cooke 1984). This is another manifestation of the patchy distribution of animals. These problems are particularly marked in the estimation of whale population sizes from catch data, and this is why we are now rather uncertain as to the magnitude of the decline in whale populations in the Southern Ocean.

The estimation of trends in whale population size from catch rates depends on commercial whaling, the future of which is in doubt. Moreover, there have not been any catches of blue, humpback, fin or sei whales for a number of years, and it is unlikely that these populations will recover to exploitable levels for some considerable time.

In principle, sightings surveys such as those carried out under the International Decade of Cetacean Research (IDCR) programme can give the requisite information. However, some methodological problems remain to be solved (de la Mare & Cooke 1984, IWC 1984b) and also, more problematically, the indications are that the inherent variability in the results (IWC 1984b) is such that the same problem arises in reliably detecting trends in abundance. Thus we find ourselves in the situation where the system to be managed has been significantly perturbed and our information about the effects of the perturbation is not sufficient to give quantitative insight into the effects of various management actions. It follows that our future management procedures must be designed in such a way that we will acquire the required information while avoiding significant risks that some component of the system will be adversely affected to an extent not reversible over a timescale of two or three decades, as required by the Convention.

Information needs for assessing marine mammal–fishery interactions

The theoretical models discussed above give us some insight into the management principles which will have to be developed if the impact of a krill fishery is not to have a deleterious effect on the population levels of marine mammals. Clearly, the Convention implies that a krill fishery is not to prevent the recovery of the severely depleted baleen whale populations to their level of 'greatest net annual increment'. However, converting these principles into a scientifically based management system requires the identification of objective scientific measures of the state of the system and the setting of criteria on which management decisions will be taken. The preceding discussion on our uncertainty about the current state of the system indicates some of the practical difficulties in detecting changes in the system, particularly if management advice is to be timely and thus avoid the need for dramatic changes in catch levels. The design of such a management system presents formidable but not necessarily insuperable scientific problems. The necessary first step in this process must be to gain a better understanding of the interaction between the marine mammals and their prey.

A number of the chapters in this book raise the problem of identifying the diet of marine mammals, many species of which are polyphagous. In the Southern Ocean the system is *prima facie* simpler because of the predominance of krill as the major prey species. However, as we have indicated, there are a number of problems in assessing any effects of interaction in spite of this natural simplification.

Although rare in normal fisheries practice, the appropriate way to acquire the requisite information is by statistically designed experiments. Unfortunately, in a system as large and as perturbed as the Southern Ocean, the scale of the experiments is rather daunting. However, as mentioned above, the history of exploitation in the Southern Ocean shows that the reliance on data collected incidentally during commercial operations is unwise. Such data alone may only yield ambiguous statistical relationships, which are often open to a number of alternative interpretations.

A possibility that might be considered is the regulation of the commercial fisheries by the management body in such a way that it implements a designed experiment. Ideally, specification of areas, and catch levels from those areas, give the possibility of applying different experimental treatments to different areas, and the effects of these can be monitored. Such an approach implies that one of the treatments is for there to be no exploitation in some areas to provide suitable experimental 'control'. Conceptually, specifying different levels of exploitation around different land-based breeding colonies of a gregarious species and monitoring breeding success would constitute such an experiment. This approach obviously requires very considerable cooperation between the management body and the fisheries, and the degree of regulation implied in the type of experiment above may not support a commercially viable fishery. In such a case, the minimum objective must be to have some substantial reference areas closed to fishing.

The land-based marine mammals, at least in principle, offer the opportunity for monitoring their demographic rates and, in some cases, abundance. However, the problems of obtaining similar information for oceanic species such as the great whales are clearly more difficult. As there is no longer commercial whaling on the blue, humpback, fin and sei whales (and this could be the case for minke whales if the moratorium on commercial whaling becomes effective in 1986), it is probable that there will be no information available on whale demographic rates. As discussed earlier, the direct monitoring of whale abundance is not likely to give the requisite information over a short timescale, and thus monitoring responses to krill fishing in the great whales will be practically very difficult.

One suggestion that has been made to overcome these problems is that there are some species which can serve as indicators (the idea is reviewed in Green-Hammond *et al.* 1983). To be of practical use, such a species would have to be land based and thus relatively easily monitored, and to respond to a depletion of a shared food supply in a way similar to the oceanic predator. There are a number of reasons for doubting that such a paradigm would provide an indefinitely long-term solution to the problem. For example, land-based predators have a limited foraging range, particularly during the breeding season. The patchy distribution of krill implies that the amount available to the different species will vary widely within the same general area. Even within the feeding range of the indicator species, a fundamental problem remains with this concept: that of detecting and calibrating the relationship between the species. This approach could, however, give grounds for some optimism in establishing an interim procedure that will meet the objectives of the Convention. It is likely that the initial impact of krill harvesting on the marine mammal community will be most noticeable in those species that are restricted in their range. This is because such species cannot compensate for changes in local abundance of their food supply by movement. Accordingly, detectable changes in the health of the populations of land-based predators may foreshadow changes in the whales. It seems unlikely that the oceanic species will respond as immediately to a decrease in food supply when they have the opportunity to range widely in their search for food. One possibility, therefore, is for the management regime to ensure that some fishing occurs in experimental reference areas and that the fishing intensity outside these areas is not more than that inside.

The rôle of models

It should be clear from the preceding that there are several classes of models, each of which has its particular uses and shortcomings. The value of theoretical models is that they give insight into the system, they make predictions into the kinds of phenomena that might be observed, and, finally, they provide a framework for reconciling the observations and thus give a starting point for refined models. In general, such models do not give useful quantitative predictions about specific aspects of the system, for example catch limits. In fact, they may not even give correct qualitative predictions; in one sense their rôle is to generate the hypotheses to be tested by observation.

The second class of models defined here is that of estimation models which are fitted to data to produce estimates of parameters. The aim of such models and their associated parameters is to encapsulate some aspect of the system under consideration and, in particular, to produce quantitative estimates about the system, such as yields or demographic parameters of particular species. The rôle of this class of models in the management of resources is obvious. There is a very wide range of such models, for example surplus production models, growth models, and population estimators based on catch per effort. Such models are designed to incorporate few parameters and as such may not always be applicable in a particular set of circumstances, nor give a good fit to the data. The practical problem, however, is a well-known one: the generality of a model can be increased and thus give a better fit to the data by adding more parameters, but at the expense of being less certain about the individual values of the resultant parameter estimates.

The third class of models is categorised as strategic simulation models, which we see as forming a link between theoretical system models and estimation models. The most important rôle of such models is to evaluate strategies for the acquisition of information about a system, and hence management decisions. This is an aspect of resource management which has been rather neglected, but this does not detract from its importance, particularly in the emergence of the approach to management adopted for the Southern Ocean.

The management required in the Antarctic seeks (amongst other aims) to limit the impact of a krill fishery on marine mammals; thus the rôle of strategic simulation models is fundamental to the way in which this objective is effected. In essence, there are three sources of information about the ecosystem relevant to the problem, namely, historical information, commercial catch statistics, and data from scientific surveys. Of course, nothing can be done about the 'experimental design' of historical information, but this cannot be said of the planning of data gathering in the future. Scientific surveys are expensive and the amount of resources available for such work will inevitably be limited. In this context, the crucial rôle of strategic simulation modelling is as an aid in planning experimental programmes in a way which optimises the information gained about the system for the amount of scientific resources available. It is particularly important to estimate how much research effort is required, given a range of models (hypotheses) of the system, to determine whether some effect is occurring, to some specified level of precision. A related consideration is how commercial operations can be integrated into the management system to maximise the scientific utility of commercial catch statistics and thus avoid some of the problems of statistical confounding mentioned earlier.

Thus, in the context of marine mammal-fisheries interactions in the Antarctic, the theoretical models give guidance as to what sort of phenomena to look for; the strategic simulation models indicate how to look for them; and the estimation models are the tools which summarise the observations for practical purposes. Such a process can be recursive. One thing should be clear from this discussion: modelling cannot substitute for experimentally rigorous observation. Conversely, unguided observation provides only data, not insight.

References

Beddington, J. R. 1979. On some problems of estimating population abundance from catch data. *Rep. Int. Whal. Commission* **29**, 149–54.

Beddington, J. R. and J. G. Cooke 1982. Harvesting from a predator–prey complex. *Ecol. Mod.* **14**, 155–77.

Beddington, J. R. and R. M. May 1980. Maximum sustainable yields in systems subject to harvesting at more than one trophic level. *Math. Biosci.* **51**, 261–81.

Bengtsen, J. L. and R. M. Laws 1983. *Trends in crabeater seal age at maturity: an insight into Antarctic marine interaction.* Paper presented to the Fourth Symposium in Antarctic Biology, Wilderness, South Africa, 12–16 September, 1983.

Cooke, J. G. 1985. On the relationship between CPUE and stock size. *Rep. Int. Whal. Commission* **34**, (in press)

Cooke, J. G. and W. K. de la Mare 1983. The effects of variability in age data on the estimation of biological parameters of minke whales (*Baleanoptera acutorostrata*). *Rep. Int. Whal. Commission* **33**, 333–8.

Cooke, J. G. and W. K. de la Mare 1984. Some notes on the estimation of time trends in the age at sexual maturity in baleen whales using transition layer data. *Rep. Int. Whal. Commission* **34**, 701–10.

Cooke, J. G., W. K. de la Mare and J. R. Beddington 1983. Stock estimates for Southern Hemisphere sperm whales using the Beddington–Cooke length-specific technique. *Rep. Int. Whal. Commission* **33**, 725–9.

de la Mare, W. K. 1984. On the power of catch per unit effort series to detect declines in whale stocks. *Rep. Int. Whal. Commission* **34**, 655–62.

de la Mare, W. K. and J. G. Cooke 1984. A review of the stratification of sightings data used in the estimation of populations of Southern Hemisphere minke whales (*Baleanoptera acutorostrata*). *Rep. Int. Whal. Commission* **34**, 315–22.

Edwards, D. M. and J. A. Heap 1981. Convention on the Conservation of Antarctic Marine Living Resources: a commentary. *Polar Record* **20** (127), 353–62.

Fowler, C. W. 1980. A rationale for modifying effort by catch, using the sperm whale in the North Pacific as an example. *Rep. Int. Whal. Commission* Special issue **2**, 99–102.

Gambell, R. 1973. Some aspects of exploitation on reproduction in whales. *J. Reprod. Fert.* Suppl. **19**, 533–53.

Green-Hammond, K. A., D. G. Ainley, D. B. Sinnif and N. S. Urquhart 1983. *Selection criteria and monitoring requirements for indirect indicators of changes in availability of Antarctic krill applied to some pinniped and seabird information.* Rep. US Marine Mammal Commission, Contract No. MM2324753-6.

Grenfell, B. T. 1981. Population dynamics of baleen whales and krill in the Southern Ocean. D Phil. thesis, University of York, UK.

Hewer, H. R. 1964. The determination of age, sexual maturity, longevity and a life table for the grey seal (*Halichoerus grypus*). *J. Zoo. Proc. Zool Soc. Lond.* **142**, 593–624.

IWC 1979. Report of the special meeting on Southern Hemisphere sei whales, Cambridge 18–21 June 1979. *Rep. Int. Whal. Commission* **30**, 493–503.

IWC 1984a. Report of the Workshop on minke whale ageing techniques. *Rep. Int. Whal. Commission* **34**, 675–700.

IWC 1984b. Report of the Sub-Committee on minke whales. *Rep. Int. Whal. Commission* **34**, 77–101.

Laws, R. M. 1953. A new method for age determination for mammals with special reference to the elephant seal, *Miroungu Leonina*, Linn. *Sci. Rep. Falkland Is. Dep. Surv.* **2**, 1–11.

Laws, R. M. 1977. The significance of vertebrates in the Antarctic marine ecosystem. In *Adaptions within Antarctic ecosystems*, G. A. Llano (ed.), 411–38, Washington: Smithsonian.

Lockyer, C. 1972. The age at sexual maturity of Southern Hemisphere fin whales (*Baleanoptera physalus*) using annual layer counts in the ear plug. *J. Cons. Explor. Mer.* **34** (2), 276–94.

Mackintosh, N. A. 1942. The Southern stocks of whalebone whales. *Discovery Reports* **22**, 197–300.

May, R. M., J. R. Beddington, C. W. Clarke, S. J. Holt and R. M. Laws 1979. Management of multi-species fisheries. *Science* **205**, 267–77.

Mizroch S. A. and A. E. York 1983. Have baleen whale pregnancy rates increased? *Rep. Int. Whal. Commission* **33**, 769 (abstract).

Payne, M. R. 1977. Growth of a fur seal population. *Phil Trans R. Soc. Lond.*, Series B **279**, 67–79.

Sladen, W. J. L. 1964. The distribution of Adelie and chinstrap penguins. In *Biology Antarctique*, R. Carrick, M. W. Holdgate and J. Prevost (eds), 359–65. Paris: Hermann.

Zahl, S. 1982. Bias of the CPUE using search time as effort measure. *Rep. Int. Whal. Commission* **32**, 809–13.

6 Marine mammal–fishery interactions in the Baikal and Ladoga Lakes and in the Caspian and White Seas

Alexey Yablokov

Some problems of marine mammals and fisheries interactions may be clarified by analysis of the history of seals and fish fisheries in closed basins (such as the Baikal Lake, the Caspian Sea, and the Ladoga Lake) and partially closed basins (the Baltic Sea and the White Sea). The analysis is difficult because of: (i) the scarcity of statistical data concerning catches of seals and, even more so, catches of fishes; and (ii) the lack of data on catch per unit effort (to provide a measure of changes in population size, catches alone being unreliable because they may be due to changes in the amount of fishing).

Fishermen usually complain that seals eat quantities of fish which could be used by man. If the fishermen are right, pronounced decreases in seal population numbers should lead to equally pronounced, or at least noticeable, increases in fish population numbers and hence, other things being equal, in the catches.

We now consider the situation in different water basins.

Ladoga Lake

Among the main food components of the Ladoga seal (*Phoca lispida*) are cisco (*Coregonus albula*) and smelt (*Osmerus eperlanus*); representatives of *Salmo* genus are less important in the seal's diet. The Ladoga seal population has been reduced during this century from 15 000 to 9 000–11 000 individuals (Fig. 6.1). The population is currently thought to be stable. The catch of salmon was reduced to zero after the decrease of the seal population and there was no increase in salmon population numbers.

The catches of cisco and smelt fluctuate a great deal, showing a tendency to increase. An increase in catches during the period from 1960 is undoubtedly connected with an increase in the fishing intensity. The initial increase of fish catches (in the 1940s) coincided with the decrease in seal population numbers, and was followed in the 1950s by a steep fall. The scale and pattern of fluctuations in the fish catches (several fold) bear no relation to the slow decline of seal population numbers during the period (no more than 50%).

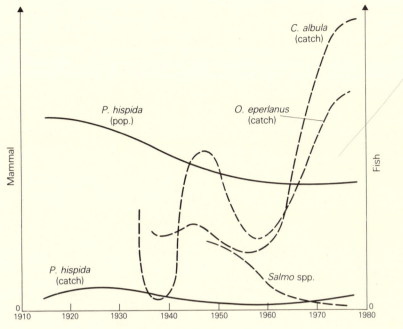

Figure 6.1 Ladoga Lake.

Baikal Lake

Among the main food components of the Baikal seal (*P. sibirico*) are gobies, for which there is no regular fishery. The most valuable Baikal fish − omul (*Coregonus autumnalis migratorius*) − constitutes less than 1% of the seal's diet. In the period 1950–70, the take of Baikal seals was reduced to half or less of the previous level of the 1930s and 1940s (Fig. 6.2). The population increased, and the numbers of Baikal seals is now estimated as more than 60 000. Indeed, some indications of overpopulation have been observed (e.g. retarded growth, decrease in weight of some individuals), and, starting in 1975, it was decided to reduce the Baikal seal population to about 50 000.

The omul catches increased markedly in the period from 1930 to 1960; this caused the stock to be depleted to such an extent that the fishery had to be stopped. Beginning in the early 1970s, a steady increase in the omul population has been observed. The catches of goby increased in parallel with the increase in seal population numbers.

White Sea and Barents Sea

The situation here is more complicated because the basins are not closed and are inhabited by two seal species: the Greenland harp seal (*Phoca groenlandica*) and the ringed seal (*Phoca hispida*), the latter being scarce and only occasionally caught.

The Greenland seal population numbers were as high as 3 million in the 1930s and more than 1 million in the 1950s (Fig. 6.3). As a result of overcropping by the USSR and Norway (the annual take reached 300 000 in 1928–30), some severe restrictions were introduced in 1955. The population is now slowly recovering and in the last 10 to 15 years has increased from around 250 000 to 500 000 or 600 000. Among the main

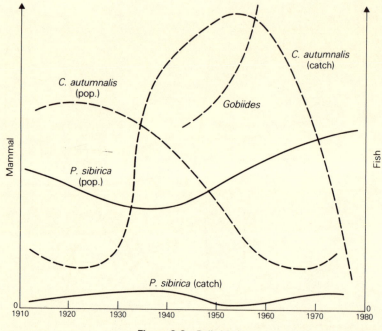

Figure 6.2   Baikal Lake.

components of the food of these seals are capelin (*Mallotus villosus*) and Polar cod (*Boreogadus saida*); among the less important are herring (*Clupea harengus*) and cod (*Gadus morhua*). The abundance of herring has declined in parallel with the decrease of the seal population. Catches of *Boreogadus saida* in the White Sea have fluctuated widely due to the intensification of the fishery, and a rapid decline has taken place in recent years. Over the last 15 years, catches of *Boreogadus* in the Barents Sea grew quickly and then rapidly decreased due to overfishing. The capelin fishery in the Barents Sea has begun only recently and is still at a comparatively high level. Catches of cod and redfish are decreasing quickly due to overfishing.

Caspian Sea

Among the main components of the food of the Caspian seal (*Pusa caspica*) are several representatives of the clupeidae (mainly shad, *Alosa* spp.), cyprinids, gobies and small crustaceans.

   The population of the Caspian seal has been reduced by one-half during this century and is now stabilised at a level of 500 000 animals (Fig. 6.4). There is no obvious connection between shad catches and the seal population numbers, and fluctuations of the cyprinid catches are also out of phase with the dynamics of the seal population. The position is complicated by the fact that exploitation of the fish stocks has been intensified to the point at which serious depletion of the resources has occurred.

Baltic Sea

The analysis here is difficult because three seal species live in the Baltic Sea and the intensity of the fishery fluctuates greatly. Seal hunting has been carried on for a long

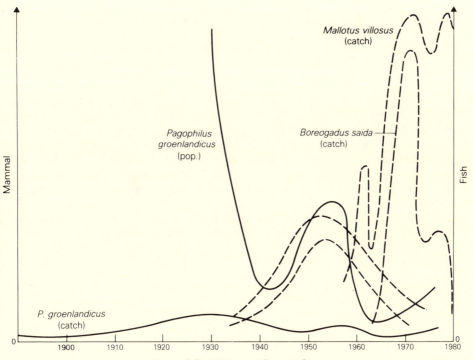

Figure 6.3 White and Barents Sea.

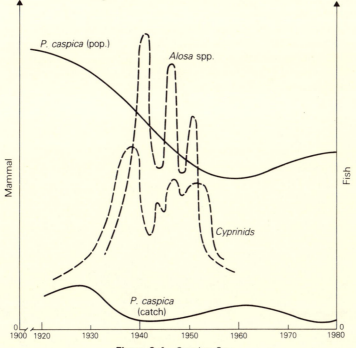

Figure 6.4 Caspian Sea.

time, the seals being considered harmful to the fishery, and the seal populations are now several times less numerous than at the beginning of the century. Catches of fish (sprat, herring, cod) increased quickly up to the middle of the 1960s, due undoubtedly to the intensification of the fishery.

An analysis of the situation in different regions of the Baltic Sea would be desirable.

The above review of the long-term trends in fisheries in closed and semi-closed basins inhabited by marine mammals reveals no convincing evidence that seals have depressed the level of the fish populations. In some instances, simultaneous increases and decreases in numbers of fish and seal populations have occurred. The above analysis could be improved if more complete information on the dynamics of the fish stocks were available. It is difficult, however, to avoid the conclusion that the rôle of marine mammals as stabilisers of ecosystems is more important than the harm they do to fisheries.

The example of the Baikal seal shows the possibility of self-regulation in seal populations and indicates that the fears of overgrowth of seal populations may be unfounded.

7. Conflicts between marine mammals and fisheries off the coast of California

D. DeMaster, D. Miller, J. R. Henderson and J. M. Coe

Introduction

Marine mammal–fishery interactions can result in both revenue losses to fishermen and mortality of marine mammals. These interactions can involve damage to captured fish, damage to nets and gear, reduced catch rates due to scaring of target species, reduced availability of target species, and incidental entanglement. The purpose of this chapter is to describe two research projects that have been supported by the National Marine Fisheries Service to document the nature and extent of marine mammal–fishery interactions in California. The first project was contracted out to the California Department of Fish and Game, and was directed by Dan Miller (California Fish & Game, Monterey office). The second project is part of the research programme of the Coastal Marine Mammal Project (Southwest Fisheries Center, La Jolla, California). This study, the cooperative Marine Mammal Salvage Program, was originally headed by John Hendersen, and is currently directed by Larry Hansen.

Marine mammal–fisheries interaction study

Beginning in July 1979, the Southwest Fisheries Center and the Southwest Regional Office of the National Marine Fisheries Service jointly sponsored a contract with the California Department of Fish and Game to determine the nature and extent of interactions between marine mammals and all commercial and recreational fisheries in California. The results of the first year of this study are summarised in an annual report (Miller 1981), and a summary of its first two years is given Miller *et al.* (1982) and Herder (1982).

In this contract, an effort was made to determine the loss of fish and damage to gear due to marine mammals by questioning fishermen who had recently completed trips and by sending out observers on fishing trips when possible. In addition, an effort was made to monitor the incidental take of marine mammals in various fisheries. Miller (1981) reported that there was considerable concern on the part of the gill-net and trammel-net fishermen and salmon trollers that information on incidental take of marine mammals may eventually curtail their operations. Estimates of fish loss and gear damage were generally available for all fisheries, whereas estimates of marine mammal take were not available for most fisheries.

Seven fisheries were identified in which a consistent loss of fish and/or damage to gear was occurring (Table 7.1): the commercial salmon trolling fishery, the California

Table 7.1 The value of fish and gear depredated by marine mammals annually (data from Miller *et al.* 1982).

Fishery	Fish lost ($)	Gear lost ($)	Total ($)
Salmon fisheries			
commercial troll	274 000	12 220	286 220
commercial sport boat	6 000	360	6 360
skiff	2 300	0	2 300
Klamath River − subsistence	74 000	10 000	84 000
Total salmon	365 300	22 580	378 880
sport boat non-salmon	27 000	10 730	37 730
Pacific herring	57 100	4 550	61 650
Gill-net	63 360	57 070	120 430
Total fisheries	503 760	94 930	598 690

halibut gill-net fishery, the Native American gill-net fishery in the Klamath River, the commercial sport-boat fishery out of San Diego, the Pacific herring fishery, the partyboat and skiff salmon fisheries, and the round-haul fisheries for anchovy and mackerel. In addition interactions between the southern California squid fishery and California sea-lions and short-finned pilot whales were described (Miller *et al.* 1982), but financial losses were not quantified. Significant interactions with marine mammals were not observed in the following fisheries: the pier fishery, the shoreline hook-and-line sport fishery, the bottomfish skiff fishery, the partyboat bottom-fish fishery north of Morro Bay, the lamprey fishery of the Eel and Klamath rivers, the night and surf smelt fisheries, the bottom-trawl fishery, the lobster fishery, and the swordfish spearing fishery.

The largest financial loss due to interactions with marine mammals was reported from the commercial salmon trolling fishery. A minimum loss of $130 000 during the month of May 1980 was estimated. This estimate does not include losses due to gear damage. The total value of salmon landed in California during May was about $5 000 000. Miller *et al.* (1982) reported that roughly two-thirds of the total value of fish and gear lost due to marine mammals occurred in this fishery (Table 7.1).

The marine mammal species primarily involved in the salmon fishery interactions is the California sea-lion (*Zalophus californianus*). During the 113 observed trips made in 1979–80, only one sea-lion was shot at. Miller (1981) reported that more animals were probably taken in 1979 than are indicated by this one observation. The annual loss of salmon from the recreational catch and from the skiff fishery was much less than for the ocean salmon fishery (Table 7.1).

Miller (1981) reported that the Klamath River Native American (subsistence) gill-net fishery was the most difficult fishery to monitor. He also reported that this is the fishery that is thought to be most affected by marine mammal predation. Harbour seals (*Phoca vitulina*) have been observed to remove netted salmon quickly from the nets (Miller 1981). Entanglement of harbour seals in nets was observed, as well as harbour seals and California sea-lions being shot near the nets (Miller 1981). Herder (1982) reported that roughly 926 salmonids were damaged out of a total harvest of 6800

(14%). If fishermen were to replace these with market fish, this would represent a total loss of roughly $84 000, or $2400 per fisherman.

Losses to marine mammals from the commercial sport-boat fishery were negligible in central California, roughly 2.5% of the total catch in southern California, and over 6% in Baja California (Miller 1981). This loss was primarily due to predation by California sea-lions. The estimated losses computed from definite loss values varied between 15 141 fish and 18 272 fish (Miller *et al.* 1982). Pacific bonito was the most frequently lost fish. Other fish lost included: Pacific mackerel, kelp bass, California barracuda, and several species of rockfish. The value of fish and gear loss in southern California varied between $37 000 and $38 800.

The gill-net and trammel-net ocean fisheries were also significantly impacted by marine mammal predation. In waters off Baja California, 12.5% of the catch was lost to sea-lion predation (Miller 1981). In southern California waters, the estimated fish loss was 2.2%; most of this loss was due to California sea-lions. Losses occurred in the following fisheries (Miller *et al.* 1982): shark drift gill-net fishery ($1400), California halibut gill-net and trammel-net fishery ($72 700; depredation rate of 10.1%), white seabass gill-net fishery ($7980; depredation rate of 10.4%), rockfish set-gill-net fishery ($18 060; depredation rate of 1.6%), white croaker gill-net fishery ($3978; depredation rate of 7.1%), and Pacific bonito gill-net fishery ($1652; depredation rate of 6.5%).

The Pacific herring fishery was difficult to monitor because nets are fished both day and night and are often left unattended. Both California sea-lions and harbour seals have been observed foraging on netted fish. In this fishery, damage to the gear (the nets) may be more significant than loss of fish. Three different types of nets are used in this fishery: gill-nets, lampara nets, and purse-seine nets. Fishermen in this fishery are more concerned with sea-lions frightening fish out of the nets than they are with the actual number of fish eaten by sea-lions that enter nets (Miller *et al.* 1982).

The dip-net squid fishery of southern California was estimated to have lost over $36 000 due to interactions with California sea-lions and short-finned pilot whales (*Globicephala macrorhynchus*) in 1980 (Miller 1981). Fish in the catch are not eaten, but the frightening of squid away from the dip-net area results in a considerably lower catch per unit effort. The squid fishery in Monterey primarily uses lampara nets, and

Table 7.2 Comparison of percentage of catch lost to marine mammal predation from interviews with fishermen and from observed trips at sea. (Figures in parentheses indicate numbers of fish.)

	Data source			
Fishery	At sea (%)		Interviews (%)	
commercial salmon (ocean)	2.4	(113)	3.2	(1506)
partyboat salmon	0.64	(72)	1.35	(157)
partyboat salmon partyboat bottomfish gill-net and trammel-net (bottomfish)	0.0	(13)	0.0	(20)
southern California	0.7	(35)	2.2	(125)
central California	0.0	(5)	2.4	(13)

interaction with marine mammals is relatively rare. The potential for frightening off fish and foraging by marine mammals in the round-haul net fishery for anchovy and mackerel was reported to be high. Data are currently not available on the value of the fish lost, but efforts are underway to determine this.

Miller (1981) provided information on fishery–marine mammal conflicts from at-sea trips and from interviews. A comparison of these techniques is currently underway. However, a preliminary comparison of these two data sets indicates that data from interviews will generally give higher estimates of fish lost to marine mammals than will data from at-sea trips (Table 7.2). Subsequent analyses will need to identify factors that may be contributing to differences between these two sampling techniques. One interpretation of these results is that fishermen overestimate the loss of fish due to marine mammal predation. An alternative hypothesis is that fishermen may be fishing differently when observers are on board. Obviously, many other hypotheses can be generated, and more information is needed to test any of them.

Marine mammal mortality in California fisheries

Miller *et al*. (1982) estimated that 300 California sea-lions were taken each year by shooting in the commercial salmon trolling fishery (Table 7.3). This was determined by interviewing fishermen. There were no reported mortalities of marine mammals associated with the commercial salmon sport-boat fishery, the recreational skiff fishery for salmon, the non-salmon commercial sport-boat fishery, or the Pacific herring fishery. In the shark drift-gill-net fishery, 49 California sea-lions were entangled in 177 at-sea days sampled (Miller *et al*. 1982). This represents a mean catch rate of 0.28 ± 0.19 California sea-lions per net-night. Other marine mammals 'taken' included two short-finned pilot whales, three grey whales (*Eschrichtius robustus*), and one baleen whale, but the interaction rates were too low to quantify. Miller *et al*. (1982) estimated that between 678 and 1227 sea-lions were drowned between September 1980 and September 1981 in shark drift gill-nets. Mortality was also reported in the shark set-gill-net fishery and the California halibut gill-net and trammel-net fishery. No mortality was observed in the white sea bass, rockfish, white croaker, California barracuda, Pacific bonito, or flyingfish fisheries (Miller *et al*. 1982), but a few entanglements were reported by fishermen.

In the Monterey Bay halibut gill-net fishery, the estimated marine mammal mortality in June 1980 was 45 California sea-lions, 15 harbour seals, and 15 harbour porpoise (*Phocoena phocoena*). These numbers were determined after 25 days of at-sea observations. No additional marine mammal mortality was reported for the rest of the year (20 observer-days reported by Miller *et al*. 1982). In June 1981, Miller *et al*. (1982) estimated mortalities of 22 harbour seals and 22 California sea-lions. The pinnipeds in 1980 and 1981 were juveniles (Miller *et al*. 1982). In May of 1982, this fishery moved north into Bolinas Bay. D. G. Ainley *et al*. (personal communication) reported that a large number of birds, 13 harbour porpoise and 15 harbour seals were found along a 40-mile stretch of coast. Of the 13 harbour porpoises found, 7 were 'fresh'; 4 had obviously been captured in nets. Historically, the number of stranded harbour porpoises averages 2.1 animals per year, a much lower rate. Additional studies are currently being planned to determine the seasonality of marine mammal mortality due to this fishery, and to assess future trends.

Miller *et al*. (1982) estimated that 10 sea-lions and as many as 30 pilot whales are

Table 7.3 The estimated marine mammal mortality in California fisheries for 1980 (data from Miller *et al.* 1982 and D. G. Ainley *et al.* personal communication).

Species	Fishery	Number
California sea-lions	commercial salmon trolling	300
	Klamath River gill-net	7[a]
	ocean gill-net + trammel-net	1209
	squid round-haul net	10
	anchovy-mackerel round haul	20
	trawl fishery	25
		1571
harbour seal	Klamath River gill-net	22[a]
	ocean gill-net	95
	in-shore gill-net	15[a]
		132
elephant seal	ocean gill-net	**25**
harbour porpoise	ocean gill-net	15
	in-shore gill-net	13[a]
		28
pilot whales	squid round-haul nets	30
	ocean gill-nets	30
		60
grey whale	ocean gill-net	**3**
baleen whale	ocean gill-net	**1**
total all fisheries		**1820**

[a] Actual count, total not estimated.

taken in the squid round-haul fishery in southern California (see Table 7.3). These estimates are based on limited information, as very few at-sea trips were made available by the fishermen. Sea-lions and pilot whales are shot at by fishermen in the squid dip-net fishery, but mortality is thought to be minimal.

In round-haul net fisheries for anchovy and mackerel, Miller *et al.* (1982) estimated that 20 California sea-lions were drowned per year. They also speculated that pilot whales may be taken in this fishery, but thought it likely that pilot whale mortality would be more common in the squid round-haul net fishery.

Finally, Miller *et al.* (1982) reported that a small number of sea-lions (see Table 7.3) are drowned by entering operating trawl nets; most have been drowned, but some lived and were returned to the water. Sea-lions are known to follow trawl nets and feed on smaller fishes passing through the webbing.

The impact of the incidental mortality presented in Table 7.3 is difficult to predict and will only be briefly discussed. Population estimates are only roughly known for some of the impacted species (Table 7.4). Relative to their maximum *per capita* growth rate, only the incidental take of California sea-lions and short-finned pilot whales is

Table 7.4 Estimated population size and percentage fishery-related mortality rate for marine mammals that occur off the coast of California.

Species	Population	Mortality from fisheries (%)	References
California sea-lion[a]	45 000–60 000	3–4	Le Boeuf and Bonnell (1980)
Pacific harbour seal			
Oregan border to Pt Conception	17 000		Miller *et al.* (1982)
Channel Islands	3 000	< 1	Stewart and Yochem (1982)[1]
	20 000		
northern elephant seal	60 000–90 000	< 1	Le Boeuf and Bonnell (1980)
harbour porpoise[b]			
short-finned pilot whales[b]	400–2 000	3–15	Dohl (1980), Stewart and Yochem (1982)
grey whale	16 000	< 1	Reilly (1981)

[a] US population only.
[b] California population.

significant. More information on the population size of harbour porpoise is needed to determine the significance of the observed level of take. In all cases where incidental take occurs, the age and sex composition of the take is unknown.

Coastal marine mammal salvage programme

Additional information on marine mammal–fisheries interactions can be collected via salvage of beached marine mammals. In 1979, the Southwest Fisheries Center (SWFC) initiated a co-operative programme among San Diego area researchers to inspect and salvage stranded marine mammals from beaches in San Diego County. Dead marine mammals are recovered routinely in this programme by staff of the Coastal Marine Mammal Project, SWFC. In addition to collecting basic data (species, sex, morphometrics, photographs) from each stranding, the staff also thoroughly inspects each carcass for external wounds or trauma which might be human related. Carcasses which are judged not excessively decomposed (usually having been dead less than approximately 48 hours) are collected intact and subsequently undergo a thorough necropsy by a marine mammal veterinarian.

Events leading to traumatic death of marine mammals may, but will not always, result in a carcass exhibiting injuries, wounds, or other obvious signs of the cause of death. Gunshot wounds are usually readily detectable even in decayed carcasses. Because of firearm restrictions on virtually all beaches in San Diego County, shooting of already beached dead animals seldom occurs, hence any bullet wound is likely to have been incurred while the animal was alive. Cetaceans which are found with severed flukes and missing terminal vertebrae can generally be assumed to have been entangled in a net, though it is not evident whether these animals died as a direct result of the injury or suffocated in a net and were subsequently cut loose. Live, 'tailless' whales, both grey whales (*Eschrichtius robustus*) and short-finned pilot whales, have been observed in southern California. Suffocation resulting from entanglement in a net results in tissue damage which is difficult to detect, and evidence for suffocation is often circumstantial. The presence of gastric contents and vomitus in the oesophagus, and froth or foam in the trachea suggests suffocation. The presence of food in the stomach generally indicates some form of sudden, untimely death, as chronically ill marine mammals which strand generally have empty stomachs.

In 1980, 16% (3 of 19) of the recovered sea-lions showed evidence of human-related mortality; all four of the salvaged pilot whales showed evidence of fishery interactions. In 1981, 34 marine mammal specimens were fresh enough to autopsy; all but four of these were sea-lions. Gunshot wounds were the most common cause of death (37%). The next most frequent cause was hypoglycemia (18%; Hansen 1981). We hope that the data collected from this type of research will provide enough information to ascertain what proportion of the total mortality is due to human activities, including commercial and recreational fisheries.

Conclusion

A financial loss of approximately $600 000 per year was found to be related to marine mammal–fishery interactions in California. Over half of this loss was from salmon fisheries. This represents damage to the catch and to gear, and does not include losses due to frightening of fish from nets or from reducing the availability of target species. The incidental mortality of marine mammals is roughly 1800 animals per year. Though not known precisely, the *per capita* mortality rate due to fishery interactions is probably only significant for California sea-lions and short-finned pilot whales. Without information on stock discreteness and the age–sex composition of the take, it is not possible to determine the impact of fishery-related mortality on any of the populations involved. Because of problems relating to placing observers on commercial fishing boats, the age–sex composition of animals caught incidental to commercial fishery activities will have to be inferred from salvaged marine mammals. Studies directed at monitoring population trends of impacted species will have to be continued to ensure that this type of human activity does not adversely affect any of the stocks of marine mammals that occur off the coast of California. Studies directed at mediating losses to fishermen are currently underway by both the California Department of Fish and Game and the National Marine Fisheries Service.

Acknowledgements

Support for the research described in this paper is through the National Marine Fisheries Service, DOC. The authors would like to thank the typing pool of the SWFC, La Jolla, and the following people for their comments: M. Brown, J. Lecky, W. F. Perrin, and J. Scholls.

References

Ainley, D. G., D. Croll and T. Keating 1981. Personal communication from Point Reyes Bird Observatory, Bolinas, California and Moss Landing Research Laboratory, Moss Landing, California.

Dohl, T. P. 1980. Final contract report AA550-CT7-36, Vol. II. Univ. of California, Santa Cruz.

Hansen, 1981. Marine mammal salvage program report for 1981. *Admin. Rep.*

Herder, M. J. 1982. *Pinniped–fishery interactions in the Klamath River system, July 1979 to October 1980.* Final contract report, No. 79-ABC-00149.

Le Boeuf, B. J. and M. L. Bonnell 1980. Pinnipeds of the California Channel Islands: abundance and distribution. In *The California Islands: proceedings of a multidisciplinary symposium,* D. Powers (ed.), 175–96. Santa Barbara, Calif.: Santa Barbara Museum of Natural History.

Miller, D. J. 1981. *Marine mammal–fisheries interaction study.* Southwest Fisheries Center Administrative Report No. LJ-81-01C.

Miller, D. J., M. J. Herder and J. P. Scholl 1982. *California marine mammal–fishery interaction study, 1979–1981.* Final contract report, No. 79-ABC-00149.

Reilly, S. B. 1981. Population assessment and population dynamics of the California grey whale (*Eschrichtius robustus*). PhD dissertation, University of Washington.

Stewart, B. and P. Yochem 1982. Final contract report 82-ABA-02069, HSWRI Tech. Report 82-143. Hubbs/Sea World Research Institute.

8 Interactions between fisheries and Cape fur seals in southern Africa

P. D. Shaughnessy

Introduction

The Cape fur seal (*Arctocephalus pusillus pusillus*) is distributed around the coasts of southern Africa, predominantly in the Benguela Current system on the west coast. In the same region several nations carry out various types of commercial fisheries. Much of the fishing is directed at species which are included in the seals' diet. This form of competition between the seals and the fishery is discussed here, as well as the more overt interactions taking the form of interference by seals with catching operations, gear damage by seals, entanglement of seals in discarded fishing gear debris and the incidental capture and deliberate shooting of seals during fishing operations. This is preceded by an outline of the biology of the Cape fur seal and an estimate of its population size, together with a resumé of the development of the fisheries and information on their catches.

Seals

Range

The Cape fur seal is the only species resident in southern Africa. It breeds in 23 colonies in South West Africa (Namibia) and South Africa from Cape Cross in the north-west to Black Rocks, near Port Elizabeth, in the south-east (Fig. 8.1). Seventeen of the colonies are on islands and six are on the mainland. In addition, there are another ten localities where seals haul-out regularly, but do not breed or do not produce a substantial number of pups. The only one of these non-breeding localities beyond the seals' breeding range is the largest, at False Cape Frio, where the maximum number recorded was 6222 seals on 3 January, 1975 (Shaughnessy 1982b).

Most of the colonies and haul-out areas are on rocky islands and coasts. Some seals also come ashore on sandy beaches, notably on the mainland at False Cape Frio, Cape Cross and Van Reenen Bay. The last two are breeding colonies, and much of the breeding activity occurs on rocky portions of them.

Cape fur seals have been reported at sea from 11°S on the west coast to 33°S on the south-east coast and up to 220 km from shore (Shaughnessy 1982a). Rand (1959) found that, close inshore, cows and bulls were relatively rare whereas most young animals occurred there, and that the number of young animals increased during spring and summer. Rand's description of the seals' distribution at sea has been supported by

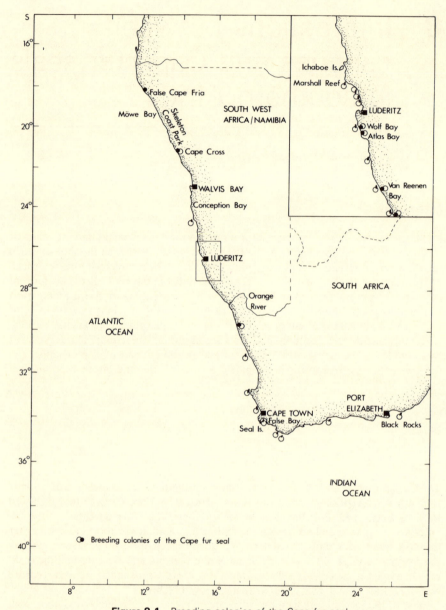

Figure 8.1   Breeding colonies of the Cape fur seal.

observations made during marine mammal collecting cruises since 1974 by personnel of the Marine Mammal Laboratory of the Sea Fisheries Research Institute.

Cape fur seals are found in three marine zones (Rand 1967, Shannon 1970). Most of the seals and most of the fisheries occur within the Benguela Current, a cold (10°C to 15°C), northward flowing stream within 185 km of the west coast of southern Africa. It is characterised by a considerable amount of upwelling of Atlantic Central

Water and by relatively high concentrations of nutrients and phytoplankton (reviewed by Newman 1977).

On the south-east coast, the Agulhas Current is a warm ($20°C$ to $25°C$), narrow, fast, southwestward-flowing stream. Inshore of it are areas with intermittent counter-currents and moderately strong upwelling which produces colder water. The two colonies of Cape fur seals on the south-east coast are within such areas.

Finally, on the south coast there is a nearshore area of mixing of Agulhas and Benguela water referred to as the Agulhas/Atlantic Mixing Area. It is variable both in extent and in hydrological conditions. Three colonies of Cape fur seals are within this region.

Life cycle

The breeding season of the Cape fur seal begins in mid-October when bulls come ashore and establish territories which they defend for about 6 weeks. Pregnant cows begin to come ashore in early November. Males are polygymous; their territories contain from 7 to 66 cows, with an average of 28 (Rand 1967).

Most pups are born in November and December. At the colony on Seal Island in False Bay, Shaughnessy and Best (1975) found that in the 1974–75 breeding season 50% of the pups were born by 1 December and that 90% of them were born during a period of 34 days.

Newborn pups weigh 4.5–6.4 kg and are 60–70 cm in length. They are born with a black pelage which is moulted between late February and April (Rand 1956). The proportion of male pups about 6 weeks old in 13 colonies averaged 0.56, with a SD of 0.003 (Shaughnessy 1982c).

Oestrus and mating occur about 1 week after the single pup is born from the previous mating (Rand 1955). Implantation of the blastocyst is delayed for about 4 months, so that the gestation period is about 8 months.

Lactation is prolonged and may continue until late September, although many pups take solid food by July (Best & Shaughnessy 1975). Solid food includes rock-lobster (*Jasus lalandii*) together with other crustaceans, cephalopods and small fish. In a few instances, pups continue nursing into their second year.

Most cows do not produce their first pup until they are 4 years old, judging from an examination of known-age (tagged) females killed at harvests (Shaughnessy 1982a, unpublished observations). An earlier report that cows produce their first pup at age three (Rand 1955) was based on the less reliable method of age determination by examination of skull sutures. Ages of sexual and social maturity of males have not yet been determined.

Cape fur seals are sexually dimorphic for size. Males are estimated to reach a maximum of 363 kg at the beginning of the breeding season (Rand 1956). Their maximum recorded 'zoological' length (measured from nose to tail over the curve of the back) is 234 cm. Maxima reported for cows are 122 kg and 179 cm, respectively.

Internal parasites

Rand (1956, 1959) briefly discussed some internal parasites of Cape fur seals, and Dailey (1975) listed them. Nematodes (*Contracaecum osculatum*) frequently occur in stomachs. The cestodes *Diphyllobothrium arctocephalum* and *D. atlanticum* are found in the intestine, as are the acanthocephalans *Corysonoma australe* and *C. villosum*.

Larval cestodes (*Phyllobothrium delphini*) are frequently embedded in the abdominal blubber. No evidence that parasites are transmitted from the seals to fish has been reported.

Population size and trends

Efforts made since 1971 to estimate the population size of Cape fur seals have been directed at pups because they are readily recognisable and they are all ashore together, unlike other age-classes. Furthermore, most of the commercial harvest is directed at this age-class. Pup numbers in colonies are estimated by two techniques, aerial survey and tag-recapture (Shaughnessy 1982b, 1982c). In the former, pups are counted on large black-and-white prints of near-vertical aerial photographs taken with hand-held cameras from fixed-wing aircraft flying at an altitude of 120–140 m. Recent aerial surveys have been timed to coincide with peak numbers in the colonies. In the second method, pups are tagged in mid-January at about 6 weeks old. An estimate of population size is made from the proportion of tagged pups in recaptures a week later. Tags are also collected from seals aged 7–10 months killed in the annual harvest, from which a third estimate of pup numbers can be made. These methods were utilised by Best and Rand (1975) to estimate the number of pups produced in the 1970–71 breeding season on Seal Island in False Bay.

Tag-recapture had been used to estimate the pup population size in 16 of the 23 colonies and the programme is continuing. Estimates range from 248 pups (SD 14) for Marshall Reef in the 1977–8 breeding season, to 64 380 with (SD 4738) at Atlas Bay in 1978–9.

Not all pups in a colony are visible on aerial photographs: some are hidden in caves, shadows or below overhangs and others are obscured by larger seals. The accuracy of the estimate of pup numbers in a colony from this method depends partly on the colony's terrain, being most reliable for sandy beaches and least reliable for steep, rocky areas. Comparison of estimates of pup numbers in 16 colonies made by aerial photography and by the potentially more accurate tag-recapture method indicated that, on average, 78% of pups were counted on aerial photographs (Shaughnessy 1982c). The whole population of pups was estimated in the 1976–7 breeding season to be 235 930 (Shaughnessy 1982b). This estimate was based on the aerial survey of the colonies made in December 1976 and on the comparison of estimates made by aerial surveys and by tag-recapture.

To estimate the total population size of the Cape fur seal from the estimate of pup numbers requires a knowledge of the population's age structure, which is unavailable at present. For both the northern fur seal (*Callorhinus ursinus*) at the Pribilof Islands and for the Antarctic fur seal (*A. gazella*) at South Georgia, the total population size has been considered to be approximately four times the number of pups. Application of that conversion factor yields an estimate of the total number of Cape fur seals of approximately 1 million animals at the end of the pupping season.

There are indications that the population size of the Cape fur seal was severely reduced by the early part of this century as a result of overharvesting (Shaughnessy & Butterworth 1981). The population has increased since then, particularly since the formation of four of the mainland colonies after 1940. These colonies are within a diamond mining area where human access is restricted. One of these is the largest colony, at Atlas Bay.

Comparison of results of aerial surveys made in the 1971–2 and 1976–7 breeding seasons indicated that the population had continued to increase, as the number of pups born increased at a rate of not more than 3.5% per annum (Shaughnessy 1982b). Results of a similar survey carried out in 1979–80 indicate that the number of pups had further increased, at a rate of 5.3% per annum (J. H. M. David, personal communication).

An attempt has been made to estimate the size of the Cape fur seal population before commercial harvesting began, using known harvest data from 1900 and a population model, together with the constraints of an estimate of pup numbers in 1940 of 100 000 and the observed increase in numbers from 1971–2 to 1976–7 (Shaughnessy & Butterworth 1981). This analysis indicates that the number of pups born annually before harvesting began was probably between 260 000 and 825 000, so that the pup production in 1976–7 was between 30% and 90% of the original, pre-harvesting, level.

Seal harvests and management

Current harvests of Cape fur seals are directed at immatures aged 7–10 months, with a small proportion of older animals, and at bulls. The former harvest takes place from July to October, the latter in the breeding season (November and December). Products include pelts, blubber oil, meat meal and bone meal. In the 5-year period 1975–9, the harvest averaged 71 859 immatures and 1051 bulls. Catches generally increased this century until 1974 when quotas were imposed.

The seal harvests are carried out by private concessionaires under government imposed controls and catch limits. Methods of killing are specified in Sealing Regulations promulgated in 1976 under the Sea Birds and Seals Protection Act 1973. All harvests are attended by sealing Inspectors.

In South Africa (including some islands off Namibia), management of seals is the responsibility of the Sea Fisheries Research Institute of the Department of Environment Affairs, and has several different objectives. In some colonies the seals are managed as a renewable natural resource to be harvested on a sustainable yield basis. Seals are also utilised as a low consumption resource for viewing by tourists in several colonies (one of which is also currently harvested). In other colonies seals are afforded total protection; these colonies are either in diamond areas of limited access or are too small for seals to be harvested economically or humanely.

For the harvest of immature seals, catch limits are set at 32% of the estimated number of pups in the colonies when they are 6 weeks old and after most of the juvenile mortality has occurred. This rate of harvesting should enable the population to reach the maximum sustainable yield level (Shaughnessy & Best 1982). In addition, the pup population size of harvested colonies is monitored frequently by aerial surveys in order to follow trends and to recommend variations in quotas where necessary. Quotas are also set for the harvest of bulls.

In Namibia, control of the harvest was the responsibility of the Sea Fisheries Research Institute until 1978, and subsequently of the SWA Department of Economic Affairs with advice still provided by the Institute biologists. As a result of pressure from the sealing and fishing industries, quotas set in Namibia have regularly exceeded the rate recommended by Institute biologists. Nevertheless, estimates of pup numbers in the harvested colonies have not decreased (Shaughnessy 1982c, unpublished observations).

Fisheries

This review of the fisheries within the range of the Cape fur seal primarily concerns the fisheries of South Africa and Namibia, and is based on annual reports of the Director of Sea Fisheries, South Africa, and on Newman (1977).

There are three major fisheries in the area: an inshore purse-seine fishery for pelagic shoaling fish, a bottom-trawl fishery for demersal fish, and a trap fishery for rock-lobster. In South African waters the fishing zone (Exclusive Economic Zone, EEZ) is 200 nautical miles (370 km) wide and in Namibian waters it is effectively 12 nautical miles (22 km) wide. Although an EEZ of 200 nautical miles was declared for Namibian waters in April 1980, it has not been recognised internationally, nor enforced.

Purse-seine fishery

The purse-seine fishery began in South Africa in 1943 and in Namibia in 1949. In South Africa it is carried out by local vessels on the west coast and south coast and is directed at six species: pilchard (*Sardinops ocellata*), anchovy (*Engraulis capensis*), mackerel (*Scomber japonicus*), horse mackerel (maasbanker, *Trachurus trachurus*), round herring (*Etrumeus teres*) and, to a lesser extent, lantern fish (*Lampanyctodes hectoris*). Horse mackerel are also taken by mid-water and bottom trawling.

In Namibian waters the purse-seine fishery is mainly carried out by local vessels working in the vicinity of and north of Walvis Bay, anchovy being the main catch. Pilchard, horse mackerel, round herring and pelagic (or bearded) goby (*Sufflogobius bibarbatus*) are also caught. Of these species, pilchard is the most desired by the fishing industry as it can be canned.

The purse-seine fishery in both South Africa and Namibia initially concentrated on the pilchard. In South Africa, catches of this species decreased markedly from 1963, after which relatively large amounts of anchovy were caught following the introduction of smaller-mesh nets. The relative proportions of the six species which now comprise the South African catches vary annually. In Namibia, pilchard catches declined steeply from 1968 to 1970; at about this time, catches of anchovy increased. Estimates of the pilchard stock increased again briefly from 1971 to 1974 after quotas were applied, but then dropped to lower levels (Cram 1977, Newman 1977).

Foreign vessels also take pelagic shoaling fish off Namibia beyond the 12-nautical-mile limit. A portion of that catch, taken by mid-water trawling, is of horse mackerel.

Bottom-trawl fishery

The bottom-trawl fishery mainly catches the two species of Cape hake, *Merluccius capensis* and *M. paradoxus*. Fishing has been carried out by vessels of several nationalities under the aegis of the International Commission for South-East Atlantic Fisheries (ICSEAF), with a minimum mesh size for nets and catch limits for hake. Since South Africa declared a 200-nautical-mile limit in 1977, the trawl fishery there has been restricted mainly to South African vessels.

Rock-lobster fishery

Most of the rock-lobster fishing occurs in the Benguela Current system, close inshore on the west coast. There, *Jasus lalandii* are caught either in baited traps or in hoop nets. Trap fishing for *Palinurus gilchristi* in deep water of the south-east coast began in 1974. A third rock-lobster fishery exists off the east coast in the Agulhas Current system beyond the range of the Cape fur seal, where *P. delagoae* is exploited by bottom trawling.

Line fishery

Another fishery employs the use of handlines from small boats, notably for snoek (*Leionura* (= *Thyrsites*) *atun.*). The fish is caught as it migrates south along the west coast and around to the south coast. Several species of tuna are also caught on lines by South African and foreign vessels.

Magnitude of the fisheries

An indication of the extent of these fisheries is provided by average annual data for the catches of selected species or groups of species from 1978 to 1980 (Table 8.1). Total catches for all the fisheries are also included. They have been summarised from FAO (1981) for landings made by South African and Namibian vessels (combined) and for FAO region 47, namely Atlantic Southeast. These two sets of data tend to under-estimate and overestimate, respectively, the extent of the fisheries in the area occupied by Cape fur seals. Thus, the former set excludes fish taken by foreign vessels from within the seals' range (although in some instances it includes small catches from the east coast which is beyond the seals' range). The latter set is an overestimate because it is for the area bounded by 6°S and 50°S latitude, 20°W and 30°E longitude, which exceeds the seals' range.

Table 8.1 Mean annual nominal catches (tonnes) from 1978 to 1980 for the major fisheries and the overall fishery from the geographic range of the Cape fur seal.[a]

Method of fishing	Major species caught	South Africa and South West Africa/Namibia	FAO fishing area 47: Atlantic, Southeast
purse-seine	Pelagic shoaling fish[b]	737 258	1 220 094
bottom-trawl	Cape hakes[c]	148 852	430 751
trap	Rock-lobster[d]	7 691	7 691
hand-line	Snoek[e]	15 557	56 481
Total catch[f]		944 020	2 647 740

[a] Data from FAO (1981). Table E-1 for catches by species for South Africa and South West Africa/Namibia. Table C47-a for catches by species of Atlantic, Southeast. Table C47-b for total catches; guano figures from Tables E-1 and C47-a.
[b] *Sardinops ocellata, Engraulis capensis, Scomber japonicus, Trachurus trachurus* (some of which are caught by trawling), *Etrumeus teres, Lampanyctodes hectoris*, and Gobiidae.
[c] *Merluccius capensis* and *M. paradoxus*.
[d] *Jasus lalandii* and *Palinurus gilchristi*.
[e] *Leionura* (= *Thyrsites*) *atun*.
[f] Data for fish, crustaceans, molluscs etc., but excluding guano.

Interactions between seals and the fisheries

Damage to fishing gear caused by seals

Interviews with skippers of purse-seine vessels in Namibia indicated that seals cause some damage to their nets (Anonymous 1972). Discussions with skippers of five vessels in 1978 revealed that fish within an encircled net that dive in response to the presence of seals sometimes cause the net to entangle in the vessel's propeller. Observations were made on purse-seine vessels on 24 occasions in 1979, but no damage of nets by seals was recorded (Shaughnessy *et al.* 1981).

Cape fur seals are reported to be frequently associated with trawling operations. Occasionally they become trapped within the net as it is surfacing, are hauled aboard and tear the net in trying to escape. This apparently does not occur often enough to be a serious matter, but problems arise on the rare occasions when seals find their way down to the factory deck (Shaughnessy & Payne 1979).

Seals attracted to boats fishing for snoek attack fish caught on the lines and, in some instances, break the lines and swim away with the fishing gear. No attempts have been made to determine the extent of this damage.

In summary, damage caused to fishing gear by Cape fur seals does not appear to be an important problem, except in the snoek line-fishery.

Interference with fish catches

Purse-seine fishery

Cape fur seals are reported to disturb and scatter fish shoals and to cause losses to catches of pelagic shoaling fish made by vessels off Namibia and, to a lesser extent, off South Africa (Director of Sea Fisheries, South Africa 1971, Anonymous 1972, Best 1973).

The effect of seals on purse-seining operations was assessed on 24 occasions during July and August 1979 in Namibian waters (Shaughnessy *et al.* 1981). Fish were caught on 23 of these occasions, and in each instance seals were observed to chase fish from the net after encirclement but before pursing, and also to consume fish. The seals moved in and out of the area encircled by the net by depressing the float line and swimming over it (illustrated in Fig. 2 of Shaughnessy *et al.* 1981). On these 23 occasions, the average number of seals in the vicinity of the vessel at various stages of the operation was as follows: net thrown, 142; net set, 196; net pursed, 209; pumping of fish commenced, 176; pumping of fish ended, 133; net aboard, 78.

Seals further interfered with operations on these 23 occasions in the following ways: one seal became lodged in the fish pump; three clambered aboard a vessel and one of them dived into the fish hold.

Interviews with fishermen indicate that seals do not always attend the setting of purse-seine nets. However, when present, seals may cause fish to dive rapidly and escape from the net before it is pursed. This results in either a reduced catch or a zero catch, so necessitating either more fishing to catch the quota or a lower overall catch. Furthermore, it raises the ire of the fishermen.

Although biologists have attended only a small number of purse-seining operations in recent years to observe interference by seals, results indicate that such interference frequently occurs. This contrasts with earlier remarks made by Rand (1959, p. 36) that the little direct competition between seals and the purse-seine fishery was 'certainly disregarded by the fishermen'. Although Rand's remarks concerned the fishery in South Africa, where less interference has been reported than in Namibia, it appears that the amount of interference caused by seals at purse-seine vessels has increased.

Bottom-trawl fishery
Cape fur seals take fish from within trawl nets as the nets are hauled to the surface, and from between the meshes until the net is hauled aboard. They also feed on offal thrown overboard from trawlers. In contrast to purse-seine operations, trawl nets are hauled aboard rapidly and the fish within a trawl net are less accessible to seals. Consequently seals cause little nuisance to trawling.

Line fishery
Cape fur seals interfere with hand-line fishing by taking fish from the line as they are being hauled to the surface and by breaking up shoals encountered by fishermen (Rand 1959). This is a particularly critical problem when the commercially valuable snoek are being caught, and forms the subject of many complaints. Seals have also been reported to take tuna from longlines (Nepgen 1970).

Seal deterrents

Attempts have been made to develop an underwater acoustic method of keeping Cape fur seals away from fishing nets (Shaughnessy *et al.* 1981). The seals responded to playback of recordings of noises made of killer whales (*Orcinus orca*) and to sweep frequency pulses, but did not flee. They did, however, move away from weighted firecrackers that exploded underwater. As a result, firecrackers were made locally and sold under the name 'Seal Deterrent'. They were used from 1973 to 1976, when the south West African Fisheries Advisory Council recommended against their use because they considered that the firecrackers disturbed fish shoals and were ineffective against seals. By then, 248 000 'Seal Deterrent' firecrackers had been sold. The firecrackers included a 10-second delay safety fuse that burnt underwater and contained 2 g of active ingredients (78% potassium chlorate and 22% aluminium dark powder).

Seals also moved away from 0.303-inch calibre rifle bullets fired into the water near the cod-end of a trawl net, but were unaffected by bullets fired over their heads.

As a consequence of the supposedly encouraging results from firecrackers and rifle bullets, an arc-discharge transducer was developed to produce underwater compression and sound levels similar to those resulting from firecrackers and 0.303-inch bullets. Its peak sound pressure level was 132 dB with reference to 1 μPa at 1 m. The transducer was effective when played at the cod-end of a trawl net lying at the surface, but had little influence on even a small number of seals within a purse-seine net.

Entanglement

Cape fur seals are occasionally seen with manmade objects around their necks. These include portions of fishing nets and lines, and plastic straps which are used (amongst other things) to bind boxes of frozen fish on trawlers. Thus the entanglement of seals in manmade objects can be partly considered as a consequence of the fishery.

The number of immature seals entangled in manmade objects was recorded during harvests from 1977 to 1979 (Shaughnessy 1980). The percentage of harvested seals recorded as entangled was 0.12%, 0.11%, and 0.12%, in the three successive years. The highest incidence (0.56–0.66%) was recorded at the Cape Cross colony, which is close to a purse-seine fishing ground.

In the hope of decreasing the incidence of this entanglement, consideration was given to encouraging fishermen not to discard fishing debris at sea. However, it was decided that publicity towards such an end could be counterproductive because of the fishermen's antipathy towards seals.

Catches of Cape fur seals during fishing operations

Trawling

The annual mortality of seals in trawling activities in South African waters has been estimated by Shaughnessy and Payne (1979) as 4210. Most of this mortality occurs as a result of drowning in nets. Less commonly, seals hauled aboard vessels in trawl nets and unable to escape overboard are killed intentionally. No data are available for the number of seals taken by foreign trawlers or by trawlers in Namibian waters; collection of such data could possibly be arranged through ICSEAF.

Purse-seining

No seals were killed on the 24 occasions when observers were aboard purse-seine vessels in July and August, 1979. However, small numbers of seals are known to have drowned in purse-seine nets. A more extensive set of observations will be required to assess the extent of this mortality.

Reports of purse-seine fishermen shooting seals in Namibian waters have been made (e.g. Anonymous 1972). Laws (1973) noted that 45 000 rounds of ammunition had been sold in one month to fishermen in Wolf Bay (*sic.*, but presumably Walvis Bay). Such killing of seals is illegal under the Sea Birds and Seals Protection Act 1973. Further, an amendment to that act in 1975 prohibited the carrying of firearms on fishing vessels. Effective enforcement of such laws is a difficult matter. Similarly, the illegal nature of this shooting makes it unlikely that pertinent data can be collected by placing observers on vessels.

Many dead seals can be seen on the beaches of Namibia. For example, 57 were counted along 70 km of coastline from a light aircraft flying at an elevation of 150 m on 3 January 1975 (Shaughnessy & Payne 1979). An indication that the Namibian purse-seine fishery is directly causing mortality in Cape fur seals has been obtained from a comparison of counts of dead seals on beaches between $18°15'S$ and $21°28'S$ near the major fishing grounds during the fishing season and the closed season, respectively. These counts were made from March 1979 to March 1980 by R. Loutit, Nature Conservator of the SWA Department of Agriculture and Nature Conservation on irregular patrols in the Skeleton Coast Park. During the fishing season from March to August 1979, patrols covered 538 km and 445 carcasses were found, averaging 0.83 carcasses per km travelled. During the closed season from September 1979 to March 1980, patrols covered 422 km and 248 carcasses were found, averaging 0.59 per km. Because of the advanced state of decay of many of the carcasses, it was not always possible to determine the cause of death. These data underestimate the number of dead seals on the beaches because some are washed back to sea, covered with sand, removed by hyaenas or eaten by jackals.

The two measures of carcasses per kilometre travelled can be compared using the binomial approximation to the normal distribution (standard normal deviate = 8.2, probability < 0.001), which indicates that the density of carcasses on beaches is significantly greater in the fishing season. This is a crude comparison because the same beaches were not necessarily patrolled in the two time periods. Nor does it take into account the possibility that natural mortality at sea could be higher in the fishing season (which includes winter) than during the summer. Despite these objections, the data suggest that there is a higher mortality rate of seals as a result of the purse-seine fishery.

Biotic interactions

Food of the seals

The feeding habits of Cape fur seals on the south-west coast of South Africa were studied from 1954 to 1956 by Rand (1959). An examination of 245 stomachs of seals collected at sea indicated that the seals preyed on a wide variety of species. The main food items were pelagic shoaling fish (horse mackerel and pilchards) and cephalopods (squid and octopus). Demersal fish (notably hake) were also recorded in the seals' stomachs, but since most of the seals were collected within the 100-fathom line, this group of fish was probably under-represented. On a volume basis, 70% of the food eaten was fish, 20% cephalopods, 2% crustaceans and 8% miscellaneous matter (stones, shells, etc.).

Exploitation of pelagic fish by purse-seine vessels commenced in southern Africa in 1943, and the composition of the catches (and presumably of the stocks) has altered appreciably since then, as already noted. Consequently, a reassessment of the food habits of the Cape fur seal was commenced in 1974 by the Marine Mammal Laboratory of the Sea Fisheries Research Institute. This survey has concentrated on Namibian waters, where the majority of the seals occur and where most complaints about competition between seals and fishermen originate.

Seals have been collected at sea on eight cruises. Data concerning stomach contents are available for four of the cruises, which occurred in Namibian waters between 1975 and 1979. These cruises took place between 3.7 and 28 km from the coast and extended for two-thirds of the length of the coast from its southern boundary (the Orange River mouth). Each cruise occurred in a different area. A total of 431 seals was collected, of which at least 39 had empty stomachs. Prey items identified by A. Batchelor of the Port Elizabeth Museum from the stomachs of 170 seals are summarised in Table 8.2. These data are preliminary because stomach contents had not been identified from all of the seals in the series when they were collated.

From these data, the following points can be made about the seals' diet in Namibian waters.

(a) They feed on a wide range of species.
(b) The most important food item is the bearded goby, particularly between Ichaboe Island and Cape Cross where 92% of stomachs with food contained this species. This accords well with information derived from hydroacoustic surveys and from an analysis of regurgitations and stomach contents of bank cormorants (*Phalacrocorax neglectus*), which indicates that in Namibian waters the bearded goby occurs primarily between Luderitz (40 km south-east of Ichaboe Island) and Walvis Bay (Cruickshank *et al.* 1980). It was the most abundant of the fish species in sound-scattering layers that were continuous for many miles. North of Walvis Bay, the bearded goby occurred less frequently, both in the surveys and in the seals' stomachs.

Table 8.2 Interim data from stomach contents of Cape fur seals in Namibian waters, 1975–9.

	Stomachs containing food		Bearded goby	Horse mackerel	Anchovy	Pilchard	Mackerel	Hake	Snoek	Jacopever	Unidentified fish remains	Loliginids	Ommastrephids	Octopods
August 1975	25	P	3	—	200	11	3	—	—	—	242	6	7	1
Orange River to														
Ichaboe Island		S	2	—	7	1	1	—	—	—	14	4	4	1
March 1977	67	P	21 554	125	12	1	—	2	2	—	53	—	1	—
Ichaboe Island to														
Conception Bay		S	64	3	2	1	—	2	2	—	3	—	1	—
October 1977	42	P	5 031	—	256	—	—	27	2	—	2	—	1	—
Conception Bay to														
Cape Cross		S	36	—	6	—	—	2	2	—	2	—	1	—
March 1979	36	P	16	933	210	13	—	8	—	2	1	—	—	5
Cape Cross to														
Möwe Bay		S	3	29	6	4	—	1	—	1	1	—	—	1

P is the number of prey individuals in the stomachs examined; S is the number of stomachs which contained that prey species.

(c) Horse mackerel (mostly juveniles) were frequently preyed on in the northern part of the seals' range between Cape Cross and Möwe Bay, where 81% of the stomachs with food included this species. Surveys by the SWA section of the Sea Fisheries Research Institute indicate that horse mackerel is most abundant in this area (Cram 1977).

(d) Of the main commercial fish species, anchovy was fairly common (12.4% of all stomachs containing food) and pilchard occurred rarely (3.5% of stomachs). The former is now the most abundant species in the catches of the Namibian fishery and the latter is the most sought after.

Three sources of bias are present in these data.

(a) Seals occur offshore to at least 220 km, but collecting was done within 28 km of the shore. As pelagic shoaling fish occur inshore, they will tend to be over-represented in the samples.

(b) No seals were collected in the vicinity of purse-seine or trawl vessels where seals frequently feed. From this point of view, the commercial species will be under-represented.

(c) Sampling was restricted to the months of March, August and October, and may not be fully representative of the seals' year-round diet.

Despite these biases, it is apparent that although the seals feed on a variety of prey in Namibian waters, they concentrate on those species which are locally abundant, e.g.

bearded goby and horse mackerel, which to date have not been of notable economic importance. They also feed on the commercially important species anchovy and pilchard, but much less frequently than on bearded goby and horse mackerel.

Horse mackerel has not featured prominently in catches of Namibian vessels, although large catches have been made by USSR vessels off Namibia (Newman 1977). The bearded goby has rarely been included in the catches of Namibian vessels (F. H. Schülein, in O'Toole 1978). Both species usually shoal deeper than the purse-seine nets. The bearded goby was first recorded in Namibian waters in catches of research vessels in the 1970–71 closed fishing season. To catch large quantities of these two species requires mid-water trawls. This fishing method is used in Namibian waters by foreign vessels and may in future be used by local vessels (Cram 1977, O'Toole 1978).

The bearded goby is the primary food of two birds endemic to southern Africa (Cruickshank *et al.* 1980, Crawford & Shelton 1983) – the jackass penguin (*Spheniscus demersus*) and the bank cormorant, as well as the Cape cormorant (*P. capensis*). An uncontrolled fishery for bearded goby could cause the seals, penguins and cormorants to seek other food. However, Newman (1977) has pointed out that as the bearded goby produces poor yields of oil, the potential of this fish resource is not as promising as some others in the area.

Changes in the composition of fish stocks of southern Africa since the advent of purse-seining have been referred to already. The seals seem to have adapted to some extent to the impact of the fishery on their food by, firstly, switching to other prey species and, secondly, associating with purse-seiners and trawlers which provide them with ready access to large quantities of food.

It should be emphasised that this information relates to the food of seals off the coast of Namibia and not necessarily of those in South African waters. A preliminary examination of the stomach contents of a limited number of seals collected from the south coast of South Africa in 1974 and 1975 indicated that seals there fed on a wider range of fish species than that indicated in Table 8.2.

Crustaceans were not represented in any of the 170 stomachs examined from Namibian waters (see Table 8.2). Fishermen have reported seals taking undersized rock-lobsters as they are discarded from fishing boats. Furthermore, claims are made by the fishing industry of substantial predation by seals on rock-lobster. These claims have probably been magnified from the above reports and from observations made by sealers that rock-lobster occurs in regurgitations of some harvested immature seals. Inspection by biologists of the contents of 1618 stomachs of immature seals harvested at several colonies showed that only 8.3% of them contained rock-lobster (J. H. M. David, unpublished observations). Thus the data from seals collected at sea and on land do not support the contention that seals prey heavily on rock-lobster.

Food consumption by seals
The amount of food consumed by the Cape fur seal population can be estimated crudely in the following manner. The amount of food (expressed as a percentage of body weight) needed daily by various species of seal to maintain a constant body weight has been the subject of several estimates and assumptions: 6–10% by Keyes (1968), 2–5% by Sergeant (1969), 3–4% by Ronald *et al.* (1975), 7% by Øritsland (1977), and 10% by Naumov and Chekunova (1980). Eight per cent will be taken as a representative figure for this calculation, although it is higher than most of the other figures. The body weight of Cape fur seals varies considerably up to an estimated maximum of 363 kg;

here, an average weight of 50 kg is taken, which is the approximate weight of a sub-adult animal. The present number of Cape fur seals is estimated as 944 000 individuals, a quarter of which are pups. Thus the estimated number of animals feeding at sea is 708 000. The amount of food eaten annually can then be calculated as

$$0.08 \times 50 \times 708\,000 \times 365 \times \frac{1}{1000} = 1.03 \times 10^6 \text{ tonnes}$$

This estimate is obviously subject to several inaccuracies, but the result is of the same order of magnitude as the amount of fish taken from within the seals' range of commercial vessels. As indicated in Table 8.1 and on p. 125, from 1978 to 1980 this amount averaged between 0.94×10^6 tonnes (the amount taken by South African and Namibian vessels) and 2.65×10^6 tonnes (the total catch in FAO area Atlantic Southeast). Furthermore, the estimate is considerably lower than those produced by the fishing industry.

Other important predators feeding in the area are species of sea birds and some cetaceans. The former consume a smaller amount of food than do Cape fur seals, most of which comprises fish. The three major species of seabird breeding in the area are the jackass penguin, Cape cormorant and Cape gannet (*Sula capensis*). Their annual food consumption has been estimated for parts of the region: for Namibian waters as 44 000 tonnes (unpublished data) and for the Saldanha Bay fishing grounds of the southern part of the Benguela Current system (in the vicinity of latitude $33°$S and many of the seabird islands off the coast of South Africa) as 16 500 tonnes (Furness & Cooper 1982). The only quantitative data that are available for cetaceans concern Bryde's whale (*Balaenoptera edeni*) which consumes pelagic shoaling fish at an estimated rate of 160 000 tonnes annually (P.B. Best, personal communication).

Control of seals in the context of fisheries management
The simple idea of managing fish populations by removing or reducing a major predator (such as a seal) is fraught with problems because of multispecies interactions. An example for the Cape fur seal is provided by its interaction with the snoek, as both have prey species in common. The snoek's diet in South African waters from 1958 to 1974 was examined by Nepgen (1970). Snoek caught on hand-lines had fed primarily on pelagic shoaling fish (notably anchovy and pilchard) and those caught in bottom trawls had fed mainly on lantern fish and juvenile hake. Each of these species is also a prey of Cape fur seals.

Although snoek occurred rarely as prey species of Cape fur seals in the survey in Namibian waters (see Table 8.2), seals are known to feed heavily on them when they encounter snoek shoals. Seals also interfere with the line fishery for snoek (see p. 127). Thus, if seal numbers were severely reduced, it is possible that the snoek population (and fishery) would benefit, but predation by snoek on other commercial fish species could also be expected to increase.

Coastal seabirds such as the jackass penguin, bank cormorant and Cape cormorant also would be likely to benefit from a reduction in seal numbers because of the overlap in their prey species and the competition for breeding space on islands.

Both the amount of food consumed by Cape fur seals and the interference they cause to fishing operations have been the subjects of many complaints and calls either for a reduction in their numbers or for eradication (e.g. Best 1973, House of Assembly debates (Hansard) for 9, 15 and 19 March 1973). The South African government has not acceded to these representations but, as indicated on p. 123 regards the seals as a renewable resource which can be harvested on a sustainable yield basis at some colonies and protected at others.

Acknowledgements

I am grateful to Dr J. H. M. David, Mr A. Batchelor and Mr R. Loutit for the use of unpublished data and to Drs P. B. Best, J. H. M. David, G. L. Shaughnessy and Mr H. G. vD. Boonstra for commenting on the manuscript; and to the Director of the British Antarctic Survey for providing office facilities for preparation of the manuscript.

References

Anonymous 1972. Crackers a deterrent for seals. *S. Afr. Shipping News Fish. Ind. Rev.* **27**(11), 47–49.

Best, P. B. 1973. Seals and sealing in South and South West Africa. *S. Afr. Shipping News Fish. Ind. Rev.* **28**(12), 49–57.

Best, P. B. and R. W. Rand 1975. Results of a pup-tagging experiment on the *Arctocephalus pusillus* rookery at Seal Island, False Bay, South Africa. *Rapp. P.-v. Réun. Cons. Int. Explor. Mer* 169, 267–73.

Best, P. B. and P. D. Shaughnessy 1975. Nursing in the Cape fur seal *Arctocephalus pusillus pusillus*. Unpublished report, Sea Fisheries Branch, South Africa.

Cram, D. L. 1977. Poor prospects for pilchards: need to diversify SWA fishery. *S. Afr. Shipping News Fish. Ind. Rev.* **32**(4), 38–9.

Crawford, R. J. M. and P. A. Shelton 1983. Population trends for some southern African seabirds related to fish availability. In *Proceedings of the symposium on birds of the sea and shore, 1979.* J. Cooper (ed.) Cape Town: African Seabird Group.

Cruickshank, R. A., J. Cooper and I. Hampton 1980. Extension to the geographical distribution of pelagic goby *Sufflogobius bibarbatus* off South West Africa and some mensural and energetic information. *Fish. Bull. S. Afr.* **13**, 77–82.

Dailey, M. D. 1975. The distribution and intra-specific variation of helminth parasites in pinnipeds. *Rapp. P.-v. Réun. Cons. Int. Explor. Mer* **169**, 338–52.

Director of Sea Fisheries, South Africa 1971. Annual report of the Director of Sea Fisheries for the calendar year 1969. *Rep. Div. Sea Fish. S. Afr.* **37**.

FAO 1981. Yearbook of fishery statistics 1980. Catches and landings. Vol. 50. *FAO Fish. Ser.* **16**.

Furness, R. W. and J. Cooper 1982. Interactions between breeding seabird and pelagic fish populations in the southern Benguela region. *Mar. Ecol. Prog. Ser.* **8**, 243–50.

Keyes, M. C. 1968. The nutrition of pinnipeds. In *The behaviour and physiology of pinnipeds*, R. J. Harrison, R. C. Hubbard, R. S. Peterson, C. E. Rice and R. J. Schusterman (eds), 359–95. New York: Appleton-Century-Crofts.

Laws, R. M. 1973. The current status of seals in the Southern Hemisphere. *In Seals: proceedings of a working meeting of seal specialists on threatened and depleted seals of the world*, 144–61. IUCN Publ. (new ser.) Suppl. Paper No. 39.

Naumov, A. G. and V. I. Chekunova 1980. Energy requirements of pinnipeds (Pinnipedia) *Oceanology* **20**, 348–50.

Nepgen, C. S. de V. 1970. Exploratory fishing for tuna off the South African west coast. *Investl Rep. Div. Sea Fish S. Afr.* **87**.

Nepgen, C. S. de V. 1979. The food of the snoek *Thyrsites atun. Fish. Bull. S. Afr.* **11**, 39–42.

Newman G. G. 1977. The living marine resources of the Southeast Atlantic Ocean. *FAO Fish. Tech. Pap.* **178**.

Øritsland, T. 1977. Food consumption of seals in the Antarctic pack ice. In *Adaptations within antarctic ecosystems*, G. A. Llano (ed.), 749–68. Washington DC: Smithsonian Instituation.

O'Toole, M. J. 1978. Development, distribution and relative abundance of the larvae and early juveniles of the pelagic goby *Sufflogobius bibarbatus* (von Bonde) off South West Africa, 1972–1974. *Investl Rep. Sea Fish. Branch S. Afr.* **116**.

Rand, R. W. 1955. Reproduction in the Female Cape fur seal, *Arctocephalus pusillus* (Schreber). *Proc. Zool. Soc. Lond.* **124**, 717–40.

Rand, R. W. 1956. The Cape fur seal *Arctocephalus pusillus* (Schreber). Its general characteristics and moult. *Investl Rep. Div. Fish. S. Afr.* **21**.

Rand, R. W. 1959. The Cape fur seal (*Arctocephalus pusillus*). Distribution, abundance and feeding habits off the south western coast of the Cape Province. *Investl. Rep. Div. Fish. S. Afr.* **34**.

Rand, R. W. 1967. The Cape fur seal (*Arctocephalus pusillus*) 3. General behaviour on land and at sea. *Investl Rep. Div. Sea Fish. S. Afr.* **60**.

Ronald, K., J. F. Uthe and H. Freeman. 1975. Effects of methylmercury on the harp seal. *ICES CM 1975/N* **9**.

Sergeant D. E. 1969. Feeding rates of Cetacea. *Fiskeridir. Skr. Ser. Havunders.* **15**, 246–58.

Shannon, L. V. 1970. Oceanic circulation off South Africa. *Fish. Bull. S. Afr.* **6**, 27–37.

Shaughnessy, P. D. 1980. Entanglement of Cape fur seals with man-made objects. *Mar. Pollut. Bull.* **11**, 332–6.

Shaughnessy, P. D. 1982a. The status of seals in South Africa and South West Africa. In *Mammals in the seas*. FAO Fish. Ser. 5.

Shaughnessy, P. D. 1982b. The population size of the Cape fur seal. *A. pusillus* 1. from aerial photography 2. from tagging and recapturing. *Investl Rep. Sea Fish. Res. Inst. S. Afr.* mimeo.

Shaughnessy, P. D. 1982c. Population size of the Cape fur seal *Arctocephalus pusillus* II. From tagging and recapturing. *Investl. Rep. Sea Fish. Res. Inst. S. Afr.*

Shaughnessy, P. D. and P. B. Best 1975. The pupping season of the Cape fur seal, *Arctocephalus pusillus pusillus*. Unpublished report, Sea Fisheries Branch, South Africa.

Shaughnessy, P. D. and P. B. Best 1982. A discrete population model for the South African fur seal, *Arctocephalus pusillus pusillus*. In *Mammals in the Seas,* Vol. 4, 103–76. FAO Fish. Ser. 5.

Shaughnessy, P. D. and D. S. Butterworth 1981. Historial trends in the population size of the Cape fur seal *Arctocephalus pusillus. p. 1305-1327. In Worldwide furbearer conference proceedings,* Vol. II, J. A. Chapman and D. Pursley (eds), 1305–27. Falls Church, Virginia: R.R. Donnelley.

Shaughnessy, P. D. and A. I. L. Payne 1979. Incidental mortality of Cape fur seals during trawl fishing activities in South African waters. *Fish. Bull. S. Afr.* **12**, 20–25.

Shaughnessy, P. D., A. Semmelink, J. Cooper and P. G. H. Frost 1981. Attempts to develop acoustic methods of keeping Cape fur seals *Arctocephalus pusillus* from fishing nets. *Biol. Conserv.* **21**, 141–58.

9 Harp seal feeding and interactions with commercial fisheries in the north-west Atlantic

W. D. Bowen

Introduction

Many fish stocks in the north-west Atlantic were overexploited, particularly during the late 1960s, and a number remain depleted today (A.T. Pinhorn, personal communication). This general pattern of overexploitation and the recent rapid development and collapse of the Newfoundland offshore capelin (*Mallotus villosus*) fishery (Carscadden *et al*. 1982) have generated concern about the possible impact of reduced prey biomass on marine mammal populations in this area. Of particular interest is the possible detrimental effect of reduced prey availability on the north-west Atlantic harp seal population (*Phoca groenlandica*) (Sergeant 1973a, 1973b).

A period of heavy hunting reduced the population size of harp seals of age one and older by perhaps 50% between 1952 and the early 1970s (Winters 1978, Lett *et al*. 1979). Since 1971, the number of harp seals killed each year has been regulated by a catch quota, and the results of several recent population studies indicate that this reduction in the number killed has resulted in some recovery of the population (Lett & Benjaminsen 1977, Winters 1978, Lett *et al*. 1979, Anonymous 1982a, Roff & Bowen 1983).

Since 1978, the policy of the Canadian Government has been to set the total allowable catch of harp seals at levels such that a slow increase in population size may be expected to occur (Anonymous 1978). Thus an important question is: to what extent might present and future levels of commercial fishing compromise this objective? Concern has been expressed also about the effect an increasing harp seal population would have on the yields of certain commercial fisheries.

This paper reviews: (a) existing knowledge of harp seal diets, (b) trends in catches and abundance of selected harp seal prey species, and (c) evidence for significant predatory interactions between harp seals and commercial fisheries in the north-west Atlantic.

Foods of harp seals

The feeding ecology of north-west Atlantic harp seals has received relatively little attention until recently. Although the major prey species are known, the relative importance, seasonal and yearly variability of foods in the diet are poorly understood. It is clear, however, that variation in harp seal diets can be large both within and between years.

Numerous authors have made passing reference to harp seal feeding habits; however, the most comprehensive treatment of this subject is by Sergeant (1973), who summarised much of the earlier literature and presented new findings on winter and spring diets of harp seals based on the contents of 421 stomachs collected between 1952 and 1971. Harp seal foods during the summer have been compiled from qualitative hunter reports in West Greenland (Kapel 1973, Kapel & Geisler 1979). Finley and Gibb (in press) investigated the summer diet and feeding behaviour of harp seals in the Canadian high Arctic, and Foy *et al.* (1981) studied the diet of spring and autumn migrants along the central Labrador coast. A recent review of the feeding habits of north-west Atlantic harp seals is given in Beddington and Williams (1980).

In discussing the foods of harp seals, it is convenient to begin with the newborn pup. Harp seal pups are nursed for approximately 9–12 days (Stewart & Lavigne 1980) on a fat-rich milk (Sivertsen 1941, van Horn & Baker 1971, Lavigne, Stewart & Fletcher 1982). At about 3 weeks of age the moulted pup acquires the juvenile pelage and is known as a beater. After an initial period of apparently voluntary fasting (Worthy *et al.* in press), most beaters begin to feed in late April. Scanty data indicate the diet consists of mainly small crustaceans. Sergeant (1973) reported that six of seven beater stomachs collected in April contained euphausiids of the genus *Thysanoessa*. Stewart and Lavigne (1980) found that 6 of 12 beater stomachs sampled in April contained shrimp (*Pandalus*), and Sergeant (1976a) reported that the stomachs of several beaters killed on the northeastern Newfoundland Shelf in early April contained shrimp (*Pandalus borealis*) and a few amphipods. Beaters migrating along the Labrador coast in June 1979 fed mainly on euphausiids, although small quantities of various gadoids, capelin and sand launce (*Ammodytes* sp.) were also identified (Foy *et al.* 1981). Euphausiids and amphipods have also been reported in the diet of beaters in the White Sea population (Sivertsen 1941).

North-west Atlantic harp seals are segregated by age during the summer. Beaters and immatures (approximately ages 1–5 years) are found mainly along the coast of West Greenland, whereas adults are generally found in the eastern Canadian Arctic (Sergeant 1965). Beaters feed heavily on small crustaceans and to a lesser extent on small fish, predominantly capelin at West Greenland (Kapel 1973). Kapel suggested that fish (capelin) account for a greater percentage of the food of immatures than of beaters. However, there are also regional and annual differences in the diet of beaters and immatures feeding at West Greenland during summer. For example, Kapel (1973) showed that in the northern and middle part of Upernavik district, crustaceans occurred in 70–100% of the stomachs examined, whereas in the southern part of this district crustaceans occurred in less than 4%, and capelin are the dominant food. Furthermore, Kapel and Geisler (1979) found that stomachs collected from Umanak district, which in the early 1970s had contained mostly 'small crustaceans', indicated that arctic cod (*Boreogadus saida*) was an extremely important food in 1978 and 1979.

Finley and Gibb (in press) analysed the stomach contents of 149 juvenile and adult harp seals collected from Grise Fiord and Pond Inlet in the Canadian Arctic during the late 1970s. In all samples, taken from August to October, arctic cod was the dominant food item (based on percentage frequency of total food items in the sample), followed by polar cod (*Arctogadus glacialis*), sea snails (Cyclopteridae), eelpouts (*Lycodes*), sculpins (Cottidae), and Greenland halibut (*Reinhardtius hippoglossoides*). Invertebrates including *Parathemisto* spp., *Mysis* spp. and various *Decapoda* were frequently consumed, but accounted for a small portion of the total food intake. Sergeant (1973) also noted the importance of *Boreogadus saida* as a dominant food of harp seals in the

Canadian Arctic, and the frequent occurrence of mysids, euphausiids and amphipods in the summer diet.

Foy *et al.* (1981) found that capelin was the dominant food of both juvenile and adult harp seals during spring migration along the coast of Labrador. Arctic cod, other gadoids, sculpins, flatfish and various invertebrates were eaten less frequently. The diet of harp seals during autumn migration along the Labrador coast was similar to that observed in spring, although arctic cod was also an important food at this time of the year.

Wintering harp seals age one and older in the Gulf of St Lawrence feed mainly on capelin, but other pelagic fish, decapod crustaceans and euphausiids are occasionally found (D. E. Sergeant, personal communication). Sergeant (1973) noted that the crustacean species *Meganyctiphanes norvegica* and *Pasiphaea tarda*, suggested pelagic feeding. In winter samples collected from the region of St Anthony, Newfoundland, Sergeant (1973) found that the diet was more variable than in the Gulf of St Lawrence, with decapod crustaceans being more frequent than fish. Recent work confirms the more variable nature of harp seal diets at northeastern Newfoundland, and indicates considerable seasonal and yearly variation in the consumption of shrimps, capelin, and arctic cod (W. D. Bowen, unpublished data).

In a spring sample (March–May. 1956) collected at the Magdalen Islands in the southern Gulf of St Lawrence, Myers (1959) found that adult harp seals fed mainly on fish, most commonly herring (*Clupea harengus*). Redfish (*Sebastes marinus*), and various flatfish (Pleuronectidae) were also found in the diet.

Lactating females in late February and March eat relatively little, but take some decapod crustaceans, especially *Pandalus* spp. (Sergeant 1973), and small gadoids (W. D. Bowen, unpublished data). In April and May, moulting juveniles and adults seem to forage intermittently. Moulting adults on ice east of Newfoundland feed on Atlantic cod (*Gadus morhua*) and flatfish in addition to capelin and shrimp (Sergeant 1973). In the Gulf of St Lawrence, Sergeant (1973) observed the rejected heads of a sea raven (*Hemitripterus americanus*) and a shorthorn sculpin (*Myoxocephalus scorpius*) on the ice near moulting harp seals.

To summarise, available data suggest that harp seals feed mainly on small pelagic fish, especially capelin and arctic cod, and a variety of invertebrates of which euphausiids and shrimps appear to be most important. Younger animals, particularly during the first year of life, feed more heavily on invertebrates, although small fish can be important. The species composition of the diet varies seasonally and from year to year. It is thought that harp seals are opportunistic feeders, but more complex foraging behaviour cannot be dismissed based upon existing information. It should be noted that, particularly in the case of capelin, large natural fluctuations in recruitment will be rapidly reflected in changes in stock biomass. Thus it is unlikely that a long-lived predator, such as the harp seal, could specialise on this type of food.

Trends in abundance of some harp seal prey species

Although available data suggest that a wide variety of foods are acceptable, in general, relatively few species constitute most of the food eaten by harp seals. Some of the species frequently consumed by harp seals are also commercially harvested. A first step then (beyond the determination of seal diets) toward determining if there are significant interactions between commercial fisheries and harp seals would be to document, in so far as is possible, the trends in abundance of those species which are taken both by harp seals and commercial fisheries. If fishing has resulted in widespread depletion of these shared resources, then it may have measurable effects on the harp seal population.

It is clearly not feasible to document trends in the abundance of all harp seal prey species. In this section, trends in the catches of major fisheries in the north-west Atlantic are given as a rough index of abundance of these species groups. Although effort data are not shown, it can be generally assumed that a decreasing trend in catches, after a peak, is the result of a decline in stock size rather than reduced fishing effort. However, increasing catches do not necessarily indicate increasing stock size. Also in this section, estimated trends in the abundance of capelin, herring, arctic cod, shrimp,

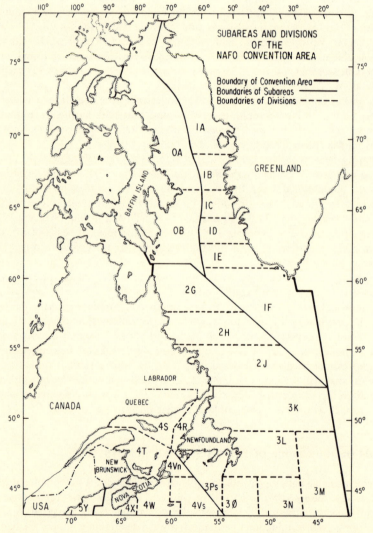

Figure 9.1 Map showing subareas and divisions of the NAFO convention area.

and Atlantic cod are considered in some detail. Capelin is stressed as an important food by almost all authors, and more recently the importance of arctic cod and shrimp has been identified. Herring is probably an important food when it is abundant (Sergeant 1973), and Atlantic cod is probably an important competitor of harp seals as well as a possible food.

Nominal catches of individual species or species complexes in Northwest Atlantic Fisheries Organization (NAFO) Subareas 0–4 (Fig. 9.1) are shown for the period 1955 to 1980 in Figures 9.2 and 9.3. Data are from the Statistical Bulletins of NAFO (formerly the International Commission of Northwest Atlantic Fisheries, ICNAF), Templeman (1966) and Pinhorn (1976).

Atlantic cod is the most important commercial fish species in NAFO Subareas 1–4, as evidenced by the high percentage of total fish catches over the period 1955–80 (Fig. 9.3). Cod landings in NAFO Subareas 1–4 increased from about 850 000 tonnes in 1955 to over 1 800 000 tonnes in 1968, and then steadily declined to about 400 000 tonnes in 1978. Catches increased to 521 000 tonnes and 536 000 tonnes in 1979 and 1980, respectively. The trend in cod landings corresponds closely to the estimated trend in the biomass of cod aged 4 years and older in several stock complexes (Fig. 9.4). Using sequential population analysis, Bishop and Gavaris (1982) estimated a decline in the 2J3KL stock from about 2.11×10^6 tonnes in 1962 to just over 300 000 tonnes in 1976. Between 1977 and 1980, the stock recovered to an estimated 4 + biomass of 1.26×10^6 tonnes. Similar changes in 4 + biomass were estimated in cod stocks in the southern

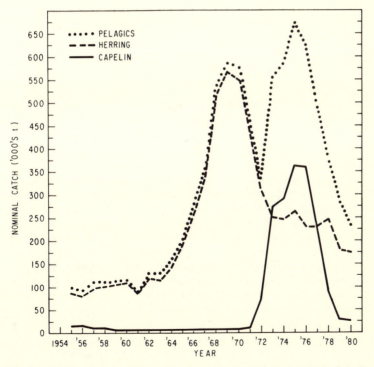

Figure 9.2 Nominal landings in thousands of metric tons of total pelagic fish (including mackerel), herring and capelin in NAFO Subareas 0–4 from 1955 to 1980.

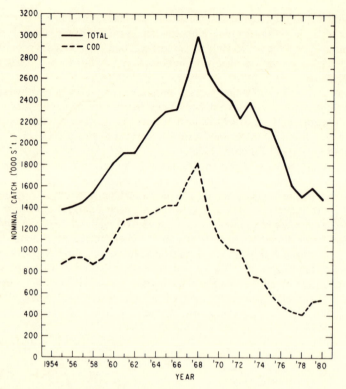

Figure 9.3 Nominal catches in thousands of tonnes of total commercial species and Atlantic cod in NAFO Subareas 0–4 from 1955 to 1980.

Gulf of St Lawrence, Divisions 4TVn, and northern Gulf of St Lawrence, Division 3Pn, 4RS (Gavaris & Bishop 1982, Maguire & Waiwood 1982). Most north-west Atlantic cod stocks have increased in abundance in recent years as a result of reduced fishing effort and good recruitment (Bishop & Gavaris 1982, Gavaris & Bishop 1982, Maguire & Waiwood 1982).

Commercial harvests of pelagic fish, especially herring, increased rapidly during the late 1960s. This resulted in overexploitation of most herring stocks and a decline in landings from a peak of 580 000 tonnes in 1969 to approximately 200 000 tonnes in 1980 (see Fig. 9.2). Estimates of 2+ biomass are available for the period 1969 to 1980 for all stock complexes in the winter range of harp seals (Fig. 9.5). Because of the uncertainties associated with estimates of vital rates for herring and other pelagic fish (e.g. capelin), the estimates of actual biomass should be interpreted with caution. However, the trends are no doubt real. All herring stocks in the Gulf of St Lawrence and along the south and east coasts of Newfoundland declined precipitously during the 1970s (Moores & Winters 1980, Cleary 1981, Moores Winters & Dalley 1981, Moores, Winters & Barbour 1981, Wheeler & Winters 1981). The greatest declines appear to have occurred in Division 4T and northeastern Newfoundland (Fig. 9.5).

Total pelagic landings (including mackerel, *Scomber scombrus*) fell rapidly to 325 000 tonnes between 1969 and 1972 and then rose to a peak of almost 675 000 tonnes by 1975, with the development of a commercial offshore capelin fishery (see Fig. 9.2).

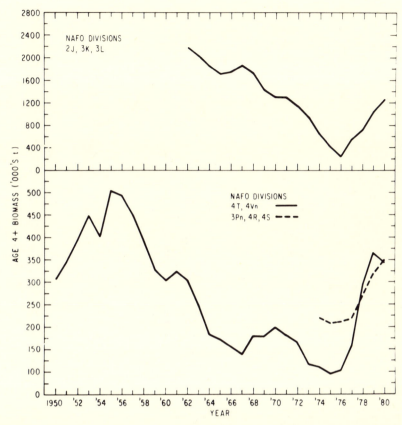

Figure 9.4 Trends in estimated 4 + biomass (thousands of tonnes) of Atlantic cod in NAFO Divisions 2J, 3K, 3L, 4T, 4Vn, 3Pn, 4R and 4S.

During the early part of this century, capelin was used extensively as a fertilizer and as a bait in the line fishery for cod (Templeman 1966). Landings during this period were as high as 25 000 tonnes. An international fishery for capelin in NAFO Subareas 2 and 3 commenced in 1972 with catches of 73 000 tonnes, and landings quickly increased to 360 000 tonnes in 1976 (see Fig. 9.2). However, just as quickly, landings had dropped to 33 000 tonnes by 1979. This led to a closure of offshore fishing in Divisions 3N and 3O in 1979 and, except for a small experimental catch, a closure of fishing in Divisions 2J and 3K in 1980 (Carscadden *et al.* 1982).

Sequential capelin abundance models presented by Carscadden and Miller (1981) and Carscadden *et al.* (1981) estimate abundance from 1972 to 1980 in NAFO Divisions 2J + 3K and 3L, respectively. These estimates of 2 + biomass on 1 January of each year were combined, and are shown in Figure 9.6. Strong year-classes in 1969 and 1973 produced high capelin abundance in the early and mid-1970s. However, biomass declined rapidly in the late 1970s, largely due to poor recruitment. It is not known to what extent commercial fishing for capelin contributed to the decline in the abundance of this fish in these areas, although fishing mortality rates, as estimated by capelin abundance models, were not substantial, being around 10% (Carscadden *et al.* 1982). Recent

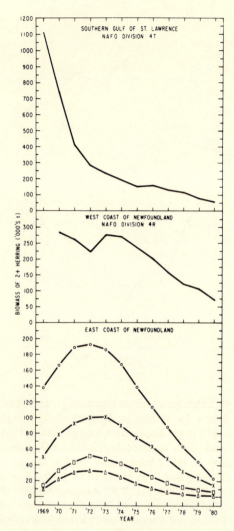

Figure 9.5 Trends in estimated 2 + biomass (thousands of tonnes) of herring in NAFO Divisions 4T, 4R and east coast Newfoundland. ○, White-Notre Dame Bay; X, Bonavista Bay; □, Trinity Bay; △, Conception Bay (southern shore) from 1969 to 1980.

assessments have indicated an increase in capelin abundance, and NAFO's Scientific Council (Anonymous 1982b) advised that by 1982 the capelin stocks in NAFO Divisions 2J and 3K – a major feeding area of harp seals during winter and spring – would have recovered to their levels of the 1960s.

In the Gulf of St Lawrence, landings from the capelin fishery have been small, ranging from 68 to 8204 tonnes. Exploitation of capelin in the Gulf has been light, and catches do not appear to have had any pronounced effects on the stock (Nakashima *et al.* 1982).

Within the range of the north-west Atlantic harp seal population, there are three areas where shrimp (*Pandalus borealis*) are commercially harvested: the Gulf of St

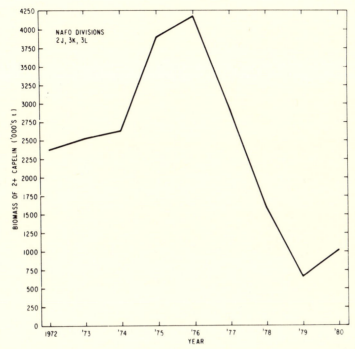

Figure 9.6 Trends in estimated 2 + biomass (thousands of tonnes) of capelin in NAFO Divisions 2J, 3K, and 3L from 1972 to 1980.

Lawrence (Subarea 4), Labrador channels (Subarea 2), and West Greenland (Subarea 0 + 1). Commercial fishing for shrimp in the Gulf of St Lawrence began in 1965 in the Sept-Iles area, in 1970 in the Esquiman Channel, and in 1974 in the area north of Anticosti Island. An area to the south of Anticosti remains lightly exploited, although catches increased sharply in 1981 (Anonymous. 1982c). Shrimp catches in the Gulf as a whole have gradually increased from about 1000–2000 tonnes prior to 1972 to 9000 tonnes annually in 1979 and 1980 (Fig. 9.7). Average annual CPUE has increased in most areas of the Gulf in recent years. The most recent exploitable biomass estimate for Sept-Iles and the Esquiman Channel from 1980 research surveys is 9490 tonnes and 19 992 tonnes respectively (Anonymous 1982c).

The West Greenland shrimp fishery began on a small scale in 1935. However, after 1950, the inshore fishery expanded rapidly, reaching a level of 9000 tonnes by 1970–71 (Carlsson & Smidt 1978). The offshore fishery in Davis Strait began on a large scale in 1972 and total landings in Subareas 0 + 1 rose to a peak of 50 000 tonnes in 1976. From 1977 to 1979, landings fell to 33 000 tonnes and then increased to 43 000 tonnes in 1980 (Fig. 9.7). In 1979, combined data from Canadian and French trawl surveys (Dupouy *et al.* 1979, Parsons 1979) led to an average trawlable biomass estimate of 45 000 tonnes of shrimp in the area of Davis Strait from 66°N to 69°N (Atkinson *et al.* 1982). Based on a trawl survey of a similar area in 1976, Horsted (1978) estimated a trawlable shrimp biomass of 55 000 tonnes which is similar to the 1979 estimate. However, because the smaller-meshed trawls used in the 1979 surveys caught relatively more small and medium-sized shrimp than in the 1976 surveys, the trawlable biomass in 1979 was probably less than in 1976.

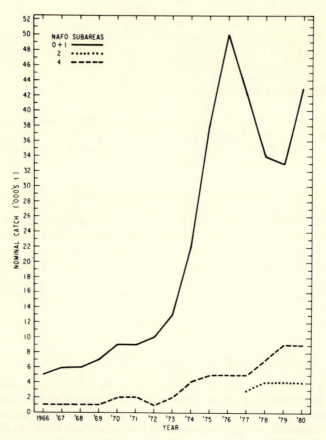

Figure 9.7 Nominal catches in thousands of tonnes of northern shrimp in NAFO Subareas 0 + 1, 2, and 4 from 1966 to 1980.

Exploitation of shrimp off Labrador began in 1977, with catches of 2617 tonnes. Landings were stable at about 4000 tonnes from 1978 to 1980 (Fig. 9.7). Parsons *et al.* (1981) estimated that minimum trawlable biomass of shrimp in this area remained relatively stable, at a level of approximately 17 000 tonnes in 1979 and 1980.

Recent studies (Finley & Gibb in press, W. D. Bowen, unpublished data) have reported arctic cod as an important food of harp seals. However, little is known of the trends in abundance of this largely non-commercial species in the north-west Atlantic, and absolute estimates are not available. However, a rough index of abundance in NAFO Divisions 2J, 3K, and 3L may be constructed of mean number caught in 30-minute tows during groundfish surveys in these areas (H. Lear, personal communication, Department of Fisheries and Oceans, St John's, Nfld). Surveys conducted by the *A. T. Cameron* from 1959 to 1970 show an increase in abundance of arctic cod in Divisions 2Jand 3K and perhaps 3L in the early to mid-1970s. Abundance appears to have decreased from 1976 to 1979 in Divisions 3K and 3L, but to have remained high in the more northern area (Division 2J), based on the results of recent surveys by the *Gadus Atlantica*. However, high catches were recorded in Division 3L during an *A. T. Cameron* survey, suggesting increased abundance in 1980. It should be noted that values from the *Gadus* surveys cannot be compared directly to those of the *Cameron* because of differences in the gear used. Therefore, recent trends in the abundance of arctic cod are difficult to interpret in relation to previous information.

Harp seal–fisheries interactions

Interactions between marine mammals and fisheries are geographically widespread and of many different kinds. These interactions often occur during fishing operations, resulting in damage to gear or to the catch. Others involve damage to the catch due to transmission of parasites, for example *Phocanema decipiens* and grey seals (*Halichoerus grypus*). In the north-west Atlantic these types of interactions between harp seals and fisheries appear to be relatively uncommon and of little practical importance (Anonymous 1981). Of greater potential significance is the predatory interaction between the harp seals and commercial fisheries. This kind of interaction is but a subset of a larger class of multispecies or community structure problems. Considerable effort has been devoted to the theoretical and experimental study of predation and competition as they affect species abundance within communities (see Paine 1980, Thiery 1982, for recent reviews). However, in dealing with specific problems we are usually constrained in our use of these results by a paucity of data on the biology of the species involved. This is currently the case concerning harp seals and their interaction with commercial fisheries in the north-west Atlantic.

Impact of fisheries on harp seals

Consider the impact of depleted fish populations on the population dynamics of harp seals. It is clear from the previous section that the abundance of many species upon which harp seals feed was reduced substantially by commercial fishing in the late 1960s and 1970s. However, we must recognise that this does not result necessarily in a decrease in the food available to harp seals. As noted earlier, harp seals are thought to be opportunistic predators exploiting a diverse array of vertebrate and invertebrate prey species. It is likely that the abundance of many non-commercial fish and invertebrate prey may have increased due to reduced predation by predators such as Atlantic cod whose populations were depleted by commercial harvesting. For example, both arctic cod and sand lance (*Ammodytes dubius*) appear to have increased in abundance during the 1970s (H. Lear, personal communication, Department of Fisheries and Oceans, St John's, Nfld, Winters 1983). Both are non-commercial pelagic or semi-pelagic species, similar in size to capelin, and both, particularly arctic cod, are harp seal foods. Thus, it is not clear that reduced abundance of capelin or other species will result in a reduction in the amount of food available to harp seals.

Another difficulty in assessing the impact of depleted fish populations on harp seals is that both harp seals and many commercial fish species eaten by them declined in abundance during the 1960s and early 1970s. The decline in harp seal abundance has been adequately explained as the result of overexploitation (Winters 1978, Lett *et al.* 1979, Roff & Bowen 1983). Furthermore, the harp seal population began to decline during the 1950s, before the intense fisheries of the 1960s had begun, and the decrease in age at maturity and the increase in fertility rate which has been reported in harp seal females argue for an increase in *per capita* consumption and hence *per capita* food availability (Bowen *et al.* 1981). This increase in *per capita* food availability may have resulted simply from the decline in seal numbers with little change in the absolute abundance of prey, or from the substantial reduction in Atlantic cod biomass during the late 1960s and early 1970s (Winters & Carscadden 1978). Cod are significant predators of various crustaceans (including *Pandalus*) and capelin (Minet & Perodu 1979, Bowering *et al.* 1982), species which are also important foods of harp seals.

The most efficient and reliable way to determine the impact of fishing on harp seal food availability would be through experimental manipulation of harp seals, their prey and/or their competitors. However, experimental study of this problem would be difficult and costly, if not impossible, and so far has not been attempted.

In the place of experimentation, other methods have been used to study the impact of fishing on harp seals. One promising approach, that taken by Stewart and Lavigne (1983) and W. D. Bowen (unpublished data), involves an analysis of trends in the condition of adult harp seal females and their pups sampled in the whelping area. It is hypothesised that changes in *per capita* food supply will be reflected in female condition and thus in the ability of the female to feed her pup; this in turn may affect pup size at birth and/or subsequent growth rate. Stewart and Lavigne collected data in the Gulf of St Lawrence in 1976 and from 1978 to 1980. They found that in 1976, females were in significantly better condition, as judged by the quantity of blubber present (stored energy), than in subsequent years. There was no significant trend, however, in female condition from 1978 to 1982. Pup weight at weaning was unaffected by annual variation in female condition.

How can we explain the decline in net energy in females from 1976 to 1978? Stewart and Lavigne correctly conclude that this change could arise through a decline in prey availability or an increase in harp seal numbers. Recent analyses have provided strong evidence for an increase in the abundance of harp seals during the 1970s (Anonymous 1982a, Roff & Bowen 1983, Bowen & Sergeant 1983). As to prey availability, Stewart and Lavigne note that capelin in the Gulf of St Lawrence, a major food of females prior to whelping (Sergeant 1976b), are thought to follow the same patterns of abundance as those in NAFO Subareas 2 and 3 (i.e. a decrease in the late 1970s, see Fig. 9.6, J. Carscadden, personal communication, Department of Fisheries and Oceans, St. John's, Nfld). However, commercial catches of capelin in the Gulf of St Lawrence were small during the 1970s, and therefore any change in capelin biomass in this area reflects natural changes in capelin recruitment and not the effect of fishing. Thus the hypothesis that increased commercial fishing for capelin was responsible for a decrease in female condition is not supported by available data. Furthermore, if recent fluctuations in capelin abundance in the Gulf of St Lawrence, and probably also in NAFO Divisions 2J and 3K, represent natural variation in the abundance of that component of the harp seal diet, there is no reason to expect them to have serious long-term effects on the harp seal population.

Having pointed out certain difficulties, the fact remains that a change in the condition of females, as judged, for example, by reduced blubber thickness at the time of parturition or lower pup weight at birth, may well be the first sign of reduced *per capita* food availability due to fishing or other causes, and for this reason such studies should be encouraged. The major drawback of this approach is that it does not address the causal mechanisms of the interactions. There is no way of knowing, without other information, whether the change in condition we observe is caused by the depletion of, say capelin, and if so, whether that depletion has been caused by the fishery or by other predators such as seabirds or Atlantic cod.

It is also possible – because of the apparent relationship between growth rate and age at maturity in phocids (Laws 1959) – to monitor mean age at sexual maturity and pregnancy rate as a means of assessing *per capita* food availability (Bowen *et al.* 1981). However, due to the time lag involved in a change in mean age at maturity, changes in the proximate condition of females or pups will probably be the most sensitive measure of competition for food (Innes *et al.* 1981).

To summarise, there is no evidence that commercial fishing in the 1960s and 1970s had a significant detrimental effect on the food available to harp seals, and hence on population growth. At present it is not possible to predict the effect of commercial fisheries on trends in the abundance of harp seals, both because of the complexity of the hypothesised relationships and because hunting has had such a strong influence on trends in the size of the harp seal population. As previously noted, both the harp seal population and various Atlantic cod stocks in the north-west Atlantic are increasing. With the available data, it is no less likely that increased abundance of a competitor such as Atlantic cod may have a greater impact on the harp seal food supply than direct catches by the fishing industry.

Impact of harp seal feeding on fisheries yields

The impact of food consumption by harp seals on yields to commercial fisheries is equally difficult to assess. The answers to several questions are required before much progress can be made. The first is, what species and age (size) classes do harp seals eat? The second is, how much of each species is eaten and when? And finally, if not eaten by harp seals, where does the excess food end up – in fishermen's nets or other predator's stomachs? These are difficult questions to answer, but it is hard to see how useful predictions can be made until answers, if only approximate, are forthcoming.

Stomach content data for harp seals summarised earlier are of limited use in estimating how much food is consumed. Generally, the results have been expressed in terms of relative frequency, volume, or the percentage of stomachs containing certain foods. Furthermore, sample sizes were often small, and sampling was not systematically carried out to assesss spatial and temporal variation in the foods taken. Measures of frequency indicate that an item was consumed, but may be misleading in terms of the actual contribution to the diet. For bioenergetic study, we need an estimate of the quantity of various prey consumed and the proximate composition of those prey species (Lavigne *et al.* 1982). At what time during the year various species are consumed by harp seals is also of considerable importance, owing to the seasonal changes in proximate composition, particularly of pelagic fishes. For example, the fat content of capelin varies from about 2–3% near spawning in spring and summer to as much as 23% in August and September (Jangaard 1974). Similar seasonal variation in fat, and hence energy content, has been measured in herring and mackerel, *Scomber scombus* (Geraci 1975, Bigg *et al.* 1978).

To calculate total food consumption of the harp seal population, we need to know age-specific energy requirements of individuals, population size and age structure. To date, no comprehensive studies have been made of food consumption of harp seals in the wild. In fact such studies are virtually impossible to conduct owing to the harp seals pelagic distribution throughout much of the year and their widespread geographical distribution marked by extensive seasonal migrations. Also their rapid digestion of food makes reliable estimation of consumption from stomach contents extremely difficult. Therefore, an assessment of food consumption by harp seals will have to rely to a considerable extent on estimates of feeding rates of seals kept in captivity and on information on the energy requirements of pinnipeds for metabolism, reproduction and growth.

Sergeant (1973) calculated that a population of 1.3×10^6 harp seals would consume about 2.0×10^6 tonnes of food per annum. In making this calculation, Sergeant assumed an average daily ration of 5% of average body weight, based on data taken from captive harp seals. This value was criticised by Boulva (1975), on the basis that most captive seals are fed to obesity, and he proposed a value of 3% of body weight daily. Ronald *et al.* (1975) maintained harp seals from 3 months to 3 years of age on an average of 3 kg of fish daily regardless of weight; this represents about 3–4% of body weight (Ronald *et al.* 1975). Reported food consumption rates of pinnipeds in captivity range from 1.75% to 10% of body weight per day (Keyes 1968, Geraci 1975, Bigg *et al.* 1978, Chuzhakina & Gudkov 1978, Gallivan & Ronald 1979). However, consumption rates in the wild may be higher due to the cost of migration and reproduction and the increased costs of foraging. This wide range of values could easily cause errors in the order of two to six times in the estimation of food requirements of a seal population.

Further research will undoubtedly refine estimates of daily energy requirements, and hence estimates of total food consumption by harp seals (see for example Ch. 19). However, it is not clear how this value, or rather range of values, could be used to assess the loss in yield to commercial fisheries. This difficulty may be illustrated by considering an extreme, and admittedly unrealistic, case. Let us assume, without any evidence to this effect, that fish eaten by seals are a direct loss to the fishing industry. The problem then is to estimate this loss from a knowledge of the consumption by seals. Further we assume that the entire seal population is eliminated, as in the case of calculations pertaining to the grey seals in the British Isles (Parrish & Shearer 1977). Using a value of 15 lb (6.8 kg) for the average daily food consumption of grey seals, Parrish and Shearer calculated the annual food consumption of the total population around the British Isles to be 168 000 tonnes. Based on available information, the proportion of the diet consisting of commercially harvested fish was estimated 'conservatively' to be not less than two-thirds, giving a total annual consumption of exploitable fish of about 112 000 tonnes by grey seals. Assuming an exploitation rate of 0.5 for all fisheries combined, then the potential loss in yield to the annual fishery is 56 000 tonnes, having an estimated market value of £13–17 million (assuming an average market price of cod as an index). Clearly this procedure would be valid only where reduction in consumption of fish by seals resulted in an increase in fish stock size of exactly that amount. H. A. Williams (York University, UK, undated manuscript) points out that two different processes have been confused here: the first concerns the competition between seals and fishermen in a single year (short-term effects), and the second is the effect on fish stocks in subsequent years of a reduction in the level of mortality (long-term effects).

The short-term effects are relatively easy to assess using the catch equation, providing one can assume that other mortality factors do not increase when seals are removed, as Parrish and Shearer also note. However, even a superficial acquaintance with the feedback mechanisms operating within natural ecosystems would indicate that this is most unlikely. For example, consider the effect of only removing a proportion of the seal population from the system. Here the remaining seals are likely to increase their feeding rate – a density-dependent response. Hence, the increased yield to the fishery is likely to be somewhat less than that estimated in the case where all seals are removed.

The long-term effects of changing harp seal abundance on fishery yields are almost certainly imponderable, for this requires knowledge of stock recruitment and interspecies predation and competition relationships. H. A. Williams (undated manuscript) notes that: 'the amount of sheer guesssswork involved in arriving at the appropriate parameters and relationships renders this a useful exercise only in qualitative terms'. In the north-west Atlantic there are several other major predators of commercial marine species, namely: whales (Sergeant 1963, 1966), seabirds (Brown *et al.* 1975), and Atlantic cod (Lilly *et al.* 1981). The existence of these other predators makes it extremely likely that compensatory, density-dependent natural mortality would occur in the various commercial fish populations, adding further to the difficulty in making quantitative predictions.

Finally, market factors should also be considered before benefits can be quantified in terms of increased or decreased revenue to the industry, due to changes in the level of predation by harp seals. Little confidence can be attached to the estimated loss in economic yield to fisheries due to grey seal predation calculated by Parrish and Shearer. Among other considerations one would, at the very least, have to consider the effect of market demand for the product on price before realistic predictions of loss due to marine mammals could be made.

Given our understanding of the interaction between harp seals, their prey and competitors and commercial fisheries, I can see no value in producing calculations of the sort produced for grey seals by Parrish and Shearer (1977). In my opinion, we simply cannot say what effect an increase or decrease in the harp seal population will have on fish catches over the long term. Future research will no doubt shed light on these problems. However, it will be difficult to obtain much of the required information, and it will be some time before useful quantitative answers to these questions are possible.

Acknowledgements

I am grateful to J. Carscadden, H. Lear, G. Lilly, J. Moores and D. Parsons for valuable discussions concerning the trends in abundance of commercial fish and invertebrate populations. G. Lilly, J. Rice, G. H. Winters, and D. M. Lavigne critically reviewed a previous draft of the manuscript. I am grateful for their comments and advice. H. Mullett drafted the figures.

References

Anonymous 1978. *1979 Seal hunt quotas announced.* News Release 11 December, 1978. Fisheries and Environment Canada. Ottawa, Canada.

Anonymous 1981. Report of Scientific Council, Special Meeting, November 1981, NAFO Sci Coun. Rep. 1981. Dartmouth, Canada.

Anonymous 1982a. *Report on the meeting of the* ad hoc *working group on assessment of harp and hooded seals in the Northwest Atlantic.* ICES C.M. 1982/N:22 Marine Mammals Committee.

Anonymous 1982b. *Provisional report of scientific council.* Dartmouth, Canada, 2–18 June 1982. NAFO SCS Doc. 82/VI/18, Ser. No. N577.

Anonymous 1982c. *Invertebrates and marine plants subcommittee.* CAFSAC Subcommittee Report 82/4.

Atkinson, D. B., W. R. Bowering, D. G. Parsons, Sv. Aa. Horsted and J. P. Minet 1982. A review of the biology and fisheries for roundnose grenadier, Greenland halibut and northern shrimp in Davis Strait. *NAFO Sci. Coun. Studies* 3, 7–27.

Beddington, J. R. and H. A. Williams 1980. *The status and management of the harp seal in the North West Atlantic.* Marine Mammal Comm. Rep MMC-79/03.

Bigg, M. A., I. B. MacAskie and G. Ellis 1978. *Studies on captive fur seals.* Progress Report No. 2. Fish. Mar. Serv. Manuscript Rep. No. 1471.

Bishop, C. A. and S. Gavaris MS 1982. *Further considerations in assessment of the cod stock in Div. 2J + 3KL.* NAFO SCR Doc. 82/IX/111, Serial No. N633.

Boulva, J. 1975. The harbour seal, *Phoca vitulina concolor,* in eastern Canada. Ph.D. Thesis, Dalhousie University, Halifax.

Bowen, W. D., C. K. Capstick and D. E. Sergeant 1981. Temporal changes in the reproductive potential of female harp seals, *Pagophilus groenlandicus. Can. J. Fish. Aquat. Sci.* **38**, 495–503.

Bowen, W. D. and D. E. Sergeant 1983. Mark-recapture estimates of harp seal pup production in the NW Atlantic. *Can. J. Fish. Aquat. Sci.* **40**(6), 728–42.

Bowering, W. R., G. R. Lilly and D. G. Parsons 1982. *Predators of shrimp (Pandalus borealis) in the Cartwright (Div. 2J) and Hopedale (Div. 2H) Channels.* CAFSAC Res. Doc. 82/9.

Brown, R. G. B., D. N. Nettleship, P. Germin, C. E. Tull and T. Davis 1975. *Atlas of eastern Canadian seabirds.* Ottawa: Queen's Printer.

Carlsson, D. M. and E. Smidt 1978. Shrimp, *Pandalus borealis* Kroyer, stocks off Greenland: Biology, exploitation and possible protective measures. *ICNAF Sel. Pap.* **4**, 7–14.

Carscadden, J. E. and D. S. Miller 1981. *Analytical assessment of the capelin stock in Subarea 2 + Div. 3K using SCAM.* NAFO SCR Doc. 81/II/4, Serial No. N268.

Carscadden, J. E., D. S. Miller and B. S. Nakashima 1982. The capelin resource. In *Regional capelin seminar, Clarenville, Nfld. January 27, 28, and 29,* 3.1–3.28. Dept. Fish. Oceans. Newfoundland Region.

Carscadden, J. E., G. H. Winters and D. S. Miller 1981. *Assessment of the Division 3L capelin stock, 1967–1980, using SCAM.* NAFO SCR Doc. 81/II/3, Serial No. N267.

Chuzhakina, Y. S. and V. M. Gudkov 1978. Feeding of the Caspian seal (*Phoca caspica*) in captivity. *Zool. Zh.* **57**, 1417–22. Transl. Series No. 4514, Fis. Mar. Serv., Dept. Environment Canada.

Cleary, L. 1981. *An assessment of the Gulf of St. Lawrence herring stock complex.* CAFSAC Res. Doc. 81/23.

Dupouy, H., J. Frechette and C. Leroy 1979. *Biomass estimate of the northern deepwater shrimp, Pandalus borealis, in NAFO Divisions IB and OB-R/V Thalassa survey, September–October 1979.* NAFO SCR Doc. 79/XI/6 (Revised), Serial No. NO17.

Finley, K. J. and E. J. Gibb. In press. Summer diet and feeding behaviour of harp seals in the Canadian High Arctic. In *The harp seal. Perspectives in vertebrate Science,* D. M. Lavigne, K. Ronald and R. E. A. Stewart (eds), The Hague: Dr W. Junk.

Foy, M. G., D. A. deGraaf and R. A. Buchanan 1981. *Harp seal feeding along the Labrador coast, 1979–1981.* LGL Limited report to Petro-Canada Exploration Limited, Calgary, Alta.

Gallivan, G. J. and K. Ronald 1979. Temperature regulation in freely diving harp seals (*Phoca groenlandica*). *Can. J. Zool.* **57**, 2256–63.

Gavaris, S. and C. A. Bishop 1982. *Assessment of the cod stock in 3Pn4RS.* CAFSAC Res. Doc. 82/37.

Geraci, J. R. 1975. Pinniped nutrition. In *Biology of the seal,* K. Ronald and A. W. Mansfield (eds), 170–87. Rapp. P.-v. Réun. Cons. Int. Explor. Mer. 169.

van Horn, D. R. and B. E. Baker 1971. Seal milk. II. Harp seal (*Pagophilus groenlandicus*) milk: effects of stage of lactation of the composition of the milk.*Can. J. Zool.* **49**, 1085–8.

Horsted, Sv. Aa. 1978. A trawl survey of the offshore shrimp grounds in ICNAF Division 1B and an estimate of the shrimp biomass. *ICNAF Sel. Pap.* **4**, 23–30.

Innes, S., R. E. A. Stewart and D. M. Lavigne 1981. Growth in Northwest Atlantic harp seals *Phoca groenlandica. J. Zool., Lond.* **194**, 11–24.

Jangaard, P. M. 1974. The capelin (*Mallotus villosus*), biology, distribution, exploration, utilization, and composition. *Bull. Fish. Res. Bd. Can.* **186**.

Kapel, F. O. 1973. *Some second-hand reports on the foods of harp seals in the West Greenland waters.* ICES C.M. 1973/N:8.

Kapel, F. O. and A. Geisler 1979. *Progress report on research on harp and hooded seals in Greenland, 1978–79.* NAFO SCR Doc. 79/XI/10, Serial No. N021.

Keyes, M. C. 1968. The nutrition of pinnipeds. In *The behaviour and physiology of pinnipeds,* R. J. Harrison, R. C. Hubbard, R. S. Petersen, C. E. Rise and R. J. Schusterman (eds), 359–95. New York: Appleton-Century-Crofts.

Lavigne, D. M., R. E. A. Stewart and F. Fletcher 1982. Changes in composition and energy content of harp seal milk during lactation. *Physiol. Zool.* **55**, 1–9.

Laws, R. M. 1959. Accelerated growth in seals, with special reference to the Phocidae. *Norsk. Hvalf.-Tid.* **48**, 425–52.

Lett, P. F. and T. Benjaminsen 1977. A stochastic model for the management of the northwestern Atlantic harp seal (*Pagophilus groenlandicus*) population. *J. Fish. Res. Bd. Can.* **34**, 1155–87.

Lett, P. F., R. K. Mohn and D. F. Gray 1979. Density-dependent processes and management strategy for the Northwestern Atlantic harp seal. *ICNAF Sel. Pap.* **5**, 61-80.

Lilly, G. R., R. Wells and J. Carscadden MS 1981. *Estimates of the possible consumption of capelin by the cod stocks in Division 2J + 3KL and 3NO.* NAFO SCR Doc. 81/II/8, Serial No. N272.

Maguire, J. J. and K. G. Waiwood 1982. *The 1982 assessment of cod in NAFO Division 4T and subdivision 4Vn (Jan.–Apr.).* CAFSAC Res. Doc. 82/22.

Minet, J. P. and J. B. Perodou 1979. Predation of cod, *Gadus morhua,* on capelin, *Mallotus villosus,* off eastern Newfoundland and in the Gulf of St. Lawrence. *ICNAF Res. Bull.* **13**, 11–20.

Moores, J. A. and G. H. Winters 1980. *An evaluation of the current status of the St. Mary's-Placentia Bay herring stock.* CAFSAC Res. Doc. 80/75.

Moores, J. A., G. H. Winters and C. I. Barbour 1981. *An examination of the status of the Newfoundland west coast herring stock.* CAFSAC Res. Doc. 81/9.

Moores, J. A., G. H. Winters and E. L. Dalley 1981. *Where have all the herring gone? The continued decline of the southeast Newfoundland herring stock.* CAFSAC Res. Doc. 81/75.

Myers, B. J. 1959. The stomach contents of harp seals (*Phoca groenlandica* Erxleben) from the Magdalen Islands, Quebec. *Can. J. Zool.* **37**, 378.

Nakashima, B. S., J. E. Carscadden and G. R. Lilly MS 1982. *Capelin (Mallotus villosus) biology and history of the fishery in the northern Gulf of St. Lawrence, Div. 4RS.* CAFSAC Res. Doc. 82/29.

Paine, R. T. 1980. Food webs: Linkage, interaction strength and community infrastructure. *J. Anim. Ecol.* **49**, 667–85.

Parrish, B. B. and W. M. Shearer 1977. *Effects of seals on fisheries.* ICES C.M. 1977/M:14. Anacat. Committee (Ref. Marine Mammal Committee).

Parsons, D. G. 1979. *Canadian research efforts for shrimp (Pandalus borealis) in Division OA and Subarea 1 in 1979.* NAFO SCR Doc. 79/XI/7 (Revised), Serial No. NO18.

Parsons, D. G., G. E. Tucker and P. J. Veitch MS 1981. *Review of abundance indices and stock assessment for shrimp (Pandalus borealis) in the Labrador Channels.* CAFSAC Res. Doc. 81/7.

Pinhorn, A. T. 1976. Living marine resources of Newfoundland-Labrador: Status and potential. *Bull. Fish. Res. Board Can.* **194**.

Roff, D. and W. D. Bowen 1983. The population dynamics and management of NW Atlantic harp seal. *Can. J. Fish. Aquat. Sci.* **40**(7), 919–32.

Ronald, K., J. F. Uthe and H. Freeman 1975. *Effects of methyl mercury on the harp seal.* ICES C.M. 1975/N:9.

Sergeant, D. E. 1963. Minke whales, *Balaenoptera acutorostrata* Lacepede, of the western North Atlantic. *J. Fish. Res. Board Can.* **20**, 1489–504.

Sergeant, D. E. 1965. Migrations of harp seal, *Pagophilus groenlandicus* (Erxleben) in the Northwest Atlantic. *J. Fish. Res. Board Can.* **22**, 433–64.

Sergeant, D. E. 1966. *Populations of large whale species in the western North Atlantic with special reference to the fin whale.* Fish. Res. Board Can. Circular No. 9.

Sergeant, D. E. 1973. Feeding, growth, and productivity of Northwest Atlantic harp seals (*Pagophilus groenlandicus*). *J. Fish. Res. Board Can.* **30**, 17–29.

Sergeant, D. E. 1976a. History and present status of populations of harp and hooded seal. *Biol. Conservation* **10**, 95–118.

Sergeant, D. E. 1976b. *The relationship between harp seals and fish populations.* ICNAF Res. Doc. 76/X/125, Serial No. 4011.

Sivertsen, E. 1941. On the biology of the harp seal *Phoca groenlandica* Erxl. investigations carried out in the White Sea 1925-1937. *Hvalradlts Skrifter* **26**.

Stewart, R. E. A. and D. M. Lavigne 1980. Neonatal growth of Northwest Atlantic harp seal, *Pagophilus groenlandicus. J. Mammal.* **61**, 670–80.

Stewart R. A. and D. M. Lavigne 1983. Energy transfer and female condition in nursing harp seals, *Phoca groenlandica.* Unpublished.

Templeman, W. 1966. Marine resources of Newfoundland. *Bull. Fish. Res. Board Can.* **154**.

Thiery, R. G. 1982. Environmental instability and community diversity. *Biol. Rev.* **57**, 691–710.

Wheeler, J. P. and G. H. Winters 1981. *An assessment of the east coast of Newfoundland herring stocks.* CAFSAC Res. Doc. 81/42.

Williams, H. A. undated. *The grey seal and British fisheries.*

Winter, G. H. 1978. Production, mortality and sustainable yield of Northwest Atlantic harp seals (*Pagophilus groenlandicus*). *J. Fish. Res. Board Can.* **35**, 1249–61.

Winters, G. H. 1983. An analysis of the biological and demographic parameters of sand launce. *A. Debies*, from the Newfoundland Grand Bank. *Can. J. Fish. Aquat. Sci.* **40**(4), 409–19.

Winters, G. H. and J. E. Carscadden 1978. Review of capelin ecology and estimation of surplus yield from predator dynamics. *ICNAF Res. Bull.* **13**, 21–30.

Worthy, G. A. J., D. M. Lavigne and W. D. Bowen in press. Post-weaning growth in the harp seal, *Pagophilus groenlandicus.* In *The harp seal. Perspectives in vertebrate science,* D. M. Lavigne, K. Ronald and R. E. A. Stewart (eds), The Hague: Dr W. Junk.

10 Competition between British grey seals and fisheries

J. Harwood and J. J. D. Greenwood

Introduction

Relations between British seals and fishermen have generally been strained, partly because both grey and common seals have been seen feeding rather ostentatiously on large salmon. The grey seal was the first wild mammal in Britain to be protected by an Act of Parliament, passed in 1914. However, fishermen have always complained of the damage to their catches caused by seals, and in 1959 a Consultative Committee on Grey Seals and Fisheries was set up to advise on a research programme on this topic and to report on the progress of that programme. Since the final report of the Committee in 1963, our understanding of grey seal biology has increased considerably, but the topic of grey seals and fisheries still causes controversy.

It may even be difficult to agree on a definition of competition. Samuel Johnson considered that competition was 'the action of endeavouring to gain what another endeavours to gain at the same time'. Most fishermen would be happy with this definition, which undoubtedly makes seals and fishermen competitors. However, ecologists' definitions are more restrictive, usually requiring that the available resource should be insufficient for all those who are attempting to gain them (Milne 1961), or that the individuals, or the population to which they belong, should be damaged by the interactions (Williamson 1972). On the other hand, the economic concept of perfect competition assumes quite the opposite: that changes in the output or pricing of individual manufacturers will not significantly affect overall demand (Lipsey 1975). Despite this potential confusion, only ecological competition can cause any real conflict between the interests of seals and fishermen, and we shall restrict ourselves to this definition.

British seals have been implicated in a variety of interactions with fisheries.

(a) Seals often remove, or attempt to remove, fish from fixed nets, drift nets, long lines or salmon farms (where salmon are kept in nets suspended in tidal waters). In doing so they may damage the gear, allowing some of the entrapped fish to escape. While the gear is being repaired, potential catches are lost. This can be a particular problem in seasonal fisheries.

(b) The presence of seals around nets may drive fish away, thus reducing the potential catch; around salmon farms they may cause 'stress' in the fish, putting them off feeding and reducing their growth rate. Fish within nets may be killed or wounded but not eaten, thus reducing their commercial value. Similarly, fish wounded at sea by seals will have a reduced value if they are later caught by fishermen.

(c)   Predation on fish by seals may reduce the number of fish available to fishermen, and vice versa.
(d)   Seals may become entangled in fishing gear either while attempting to remove fish or accidentally. Even if they do not drown as a result, they may be shot by irate fishermen.
(e)   The grey seal is an important tertiary host of the codworm (*Phocanema decipens*), a parasitic nematode whose larvae are found in the muscle tissue of many fish, but particularly the Atlantic cod (*Gadus morhua*), where their presence reduces the commercial value of the flesh.

Whereas interactions (a)–(d) involve competition in some form, the codworm problem is rather different. We shall consider this only briefly, and will concentrate on the nature and extent of the competition between grey seals (*Halichoerus grypus*) and fisheries in British waters. Although common seals (*Phoca vitulina*) are believed to cause damage, particularly to salmon fisheries, far more is known about the ecology of the grey seal, which is three times as numerous in British waters. We will make no attempt in this Chapter to assess the effects of the grey seal population on the economics of commercial fisheries, nor will we attempt to calculate the possible economic benefits or losses which may be derived from a change in the size of this population.

In 1977 a management programme to reduce the size of the Scottish grey seal population was instigated. Although this particular programme was abandoned in 1978, its effect on the grey seal population provided some valuable lessons on the way in which the effects of culls can be predicted and assessed. These lessons and the original justifications for the cull will be discussed.

The codworm problem

During the 1960s the levels of codworm in fish from certain areas increased; the size of the local seal population also increased concurrently (Rae 1972). These local populations continued to increase throughout the early 1970s, but there was no obvious change in the levels of infestation in fish during this period (Parrish & Shearer 1977), although they remained high in the sea areas adjacent to the major grey seal breeding colonies. Codworm is also claimed to be a serious problem in Canada and Norway (ICES 1977). *Phocanema* has a complex life-history, and the expected form of any relationship between seal numbers and levels of infestation in cod is not immediately obvious.

Damage to fishing gear

Some seals are undoubtedly attracted to fishing nets and will remove fish from them. In this process, the net itself may be damaged. Not only will the net need to be repaired, but captured fish may escape through the damaged section. In the past this sort of damage has been a particular problem at bag nets, which were damaged either as the seal broke into the fish court or as it tried to break out (Rae 1960). With the progressive introduction of synthetic-fibre nets in the 1960s, the number of reports of damaged nets declined markedly and very little damage was reported in the 1970s (Parrish & Shearer 1977).

Damage to individual fish and to catches

Fish scared from nets

Fishermen often report that the presence of marine mammals near their gear frightens fish and makes them more difficult to catch (e.g. Rae 1960, Mate 1980). In addition, Scottish salmon fishermen claim that they can smell when a seal has been in their nets and that this odour can deter fish from entering the net for several days (Rae 1960). Some support for this belief is provided by Alderdice *et al.* (1954), who found that the movements of Pacific salmon were influenced by the introduction of an extract from seal skin into the water. However, these effects are clearly difficult to quantify.

Fish wounded by seals

Most complaints about fish being wounded by seals refer to salmon (*Salmo salar*). Rae (1960) described the various types of injury that have been reported and considered their possible causes.

About 3% of the netsmen's catch of salmon in eastern Scotland during the 1960s and 1970s showed wounds ascribed to seals (Rae & Shearer 1965, Parrish & Shearer 1977), but the amount of damage varied considerably from place to place. Stenman (1978) found similar variation in Finland where 6–30% of netted salmon were damaged during 1974–6. In north east England, 1.4% of netted salmon were damaged (Potter & Swain 1979). The sorts of wounds recorded reduce the value of the salmon by 10–20% (Parrish & Shearer 1977), so their overall effect is relatively small, though not negligible.

Although the level of damage is variable from place to place, it shows no apparent relationship to the proximity of the netting station to known concentrations of seals. Furthermore, it remained steady in eastern Scotland during 1965–76, although the grey seal population roughly doubled in size. Parrish and Shearer (1977) suggested that the apparent independence of the level of damage and the abundance of seals was a result of most of the damage being the work of individual 'rogue' seals that haunted the fishing stations and whose numbers were independent of population numbers.

Predation at nets

The only aspect of predation around nets which has been adequately quantified is the removal by seals of fish which are already entangled. Mountford and Smith (1963) reported that fishermen drift-netting for salmon have observed seals removing fish gilled in the nets before they could be hauled in. Potter and Swain (1979) attempted to quantify this effect along the Northumbrian coast both by direct observation of seals, and by labelling the positions of enmeshed fish and then checking for their continued presence at regular intervals. They found that 3–10% of the fish caught in the nets were removed by seals, and suggested that the overall loss rate was around 5%.

Damage to fish stocks

Because competition is an indirect process, it is never easy to measure. Competitors affect each other by altering the availability of a particular resource. These changes can

be measured most easily if the total amount of resource is fixed, for example if competition is for potential breeding sites. However, in this case the resource (fish stocks) is
actually consumed by the competitors (seals and men). The rate of renewal of the
resource depends both on the number of fish which are not consumed and the
characteristics (notably the age structure) of the surviving population. Both of these are
affected by the way in which the competitors consume the resource and by a variety
of other factors. The system is both dynamic and complex; to make matters worse, it
is also scarcely amenable to experimental manipulation. Of course, these problems of
determining the extent of competition are not unique to studies of the interactions
between marine mammals and fisheries. They are common to purely academic studies
of competition and to the assessment of any fishery where more than one species is
caught.

Until recently, most fish stocks were managed on a single-species basis: each stock
was assumed to suffer a constant natural mortality. Some fisheries models now attempt
to incorporate the effects of interactions between different fish stocks (e.g. ICES 1980),
but this work is in its infancy. The problem in quantifying the impact on fisheries yield
of interactions between individual fish stocks are identical to those in assessing the impact of seals. Not only is it necessary to know how predation is distributed amongst
the different fish species and how their stocks respond to this predation, but also how
the relevant fisheries respond to changes in stock abundance.

In this section we will consider only the information which is necessary to estimate
the impact of a marine mammal on fish stocks. Although we shall concentrate on the
information which is relevant to grey seals, the same methodological and conceptual
problems will arise in the study of any other marine mammal.

There are three preliminary questions which must be answered. How many seals are
there and where are they found? What fish species do they eat? How much do they eat?

Numbers and distribution of grey seals

It is impossible to count all the grey seals in British waters directly. However, grey seals
breed colonially between September and December on a relatively small number of
sites, mostly on uninhabited offshore islands. For the first two or three weeks of life
the pups have a white, silky coat which contrasts well with the predominant
background so that they show up clearly in vertical aerial photographs. The number
of pups born each year can therefore be estimated from a series of aerial surveys of
the breeding assemblies. At each assembly, births are not perfectly synchronous so that
some pups have left the colony before the last pups are born. Therefore the maximum
count for a particular colony must be multiplied by a conversion factor to provide an
estimate of the total number of pups born (Summers 1978). There are two obvious
sources of error in this estimate: the correct conversion factor for a particular colony
may vary from year to year; and the factor used for some colonies is based on an
extrapolation from other colonies. The first source of error can be evaluated by comparing estimates of the conversion factor at the same colony in different seasons
(Greenwood 1979, Hiby & Harwood 1979). Both sources can be evaluated by examining the variance about an exponential regression of estimated pup production on time
(Hiby & Harwood 1979). The latter calculated that the 95% confidence limits for
estimates of pup production from well-studied colonies should be ±25%. Greenwood
suggested considerably wider limits, but used only three data points. The confidence
limits for less well-studied colonies will inevitably be wider – NERC (1979) suggests

±30%. Because the confidence limits for the various colonies are, in part, based on independent estimates of error, the confidence limits for the estimate of total pup production in the UK will be narrower, but not as narrow as if the estimates were completely independent: ±20–25% seems reasonable.

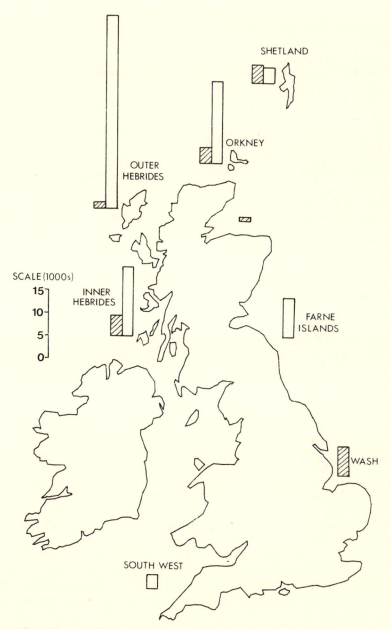

Figure 10.1 Size and distribution of major breeding concentrations of grey seals (plain bars) and common seals (shaded bars) in Great Britain.

A life table is required to estimate total population size from pup production. Harwood and Prime (1978) constructed such a table for the stock of seals breeding at the Farne Islands using the age structure of samples of seals from the breeding beaches, estimates of age-specific fecundity rates from the same animals, and estimates of population growth from 18 years of pup counts. They had to assume a fecundity rate for the fully mature animals, but recent studies (Boyd 1982) have confirmed this value. This life table has been extrapolated to the other UK seal stocks. Although studies of Orcadian and Hebridean populations have confirmed that rates of pup mortality and ages at maturity are similar to those at the Farne Islands (SMRU unpublished data), there is inevitably some imprecision in the estimation of population size from pup production. No formal estimates of the confidence regions for population size have been published, but Greenwood (1979) suggested that the conversion from pup production would add 10% to those confidence limits. This implies confidence limits of ± 30–35% for the estimate of the total British population, which was 82 500 in 1981 (NERC 1982).

The breeding distribution of British grey seals is well known. Summers (1978) used the geographical areas suggested by Hewer (1974) to divide the population into a number of stocks which show differences in the timing of the breeding season. These are: south west Britain (Scilly, Cornwall, Wales and Ireland); the Inner Hebrides and west coast of Scotland; the Outer Hebrides (including North Rona); Orkney; Shetland; and the Farne Islands (including the Isle of May and Scroby Sand). The breeding distribution and size of these stocks, and those of the common seal, are shown in Figure 10.1.

The dispersal of pups away from the breeding assemblies is also relatively well documented from tagging studies, most of which were carried out in the 1950s and early 1960s. The results are summarised in Smith (1963) and Hewer (1974). The evidence indicates that pups spread out in all directions, perhaps assisted by the prevailing wind and currents. Thus a pup tagged on North Rona was recovered in Iceland, pups tagged in Orkney and at the Farne Islands have frequently turned up in Norway, and a Welsh pup was found in northern Spain. However, very few tagged seals more than a year old have been recovered, and little is known about the distribution of adult seals outside the breeding season. Rae (1968) considered that grey seals must spend most of their time in coastal waters because they are rarely sighted by fishermen more than 20 miles from the shore. However, as Hewer (1974) points out, the bobbing head of a seal is difficult to see even under ideal conditions and fishermen at sea are usually occupied with tasks other than continuously scanning the sea for a glimpse of a seal head. Rae also suggested that grey seals are restricted to relatively shallow water because they need to use natural barriers to catch their prey and because they require regular access to haul-out sites. However, the first reason is tautological: the hunting techniques of grey seals can only be observed in shallow water, but they may use completely different techniques in deeper water. There are no data which suggest that seals *need* to haul out at all. It is therefore quite possible that grey seals are widely dispersed over a considerable area of sea outside the breeding season.

Composition of the grey seal's diet

It is difficult to determine the exact diet of any seal. The most commonly used estimation technique relies on the examination of the stomach contents of shot animals. Only rarely can these examinations provide more than qualitative information because food is digested rapidly in the seal's stomach, which usually contains a mixture of undigested and partially digested food fragments, so that it is impossible to determine how much of each food species has actually been consumed. A quantitative estimate of the size and number of certain fish species in the diet may be possible from an analysis of the otoliths and vertebrae that can be found in seal faeces (Prime 1979), but this has not been attempted on any large scale. An additional problem is that the grey seals' diet undoubtedly varies with location and time of year, and it is therefore difficult to obtain a truly representative sample.

By far the largest body of evidence on diet composition comes from stomach analyses conducted by the Marine Laboratory at Aberdeen over the last 20 years (Rae 1968, 1973; Parrish & Shearer 1977). A large proportion of these stomachs came from seals entangled in fishing gear or shot near fishing nets, and over 80% of them came from the east coast of Scotland, so that they do not represent a random sample from the population. Furthermore, the results were expressed as the percentage of stomachs containing recognisable remains of each prey species. Such figures cannot accurately reflect the true composition of the seals' diet. In particular, the sum of the individual percentages will always be greater than 100. In general, the contribution of rare species to the diet will be overestimated. Despite these drawbacks, such analyses do indicate that grey seals are probably opportunistic and catholic carnivores which eat a variety of fish species, many of which are of economic importance. Similar results have been found from the analysis of the stomach contents of Canadian grey seals (Mansfield & Beck 1977).

The problem of variability in diet is indicated by the fact that 11 of the 40 stomachs from the north and west coast of Scotland recorded by Rae (1968, 1972) contained salmon remains; but in a sample of 17 stomachs with recognisable remains from seals shot in August 1978 at haul-out sites in the Southern and Outer Hebrides, none contained any salmon remains, but four contained remains of the common mackerel (*Scomber scombrus*) which was not recorded in any of Rae's samples (SMRU unpublished data).

Quantity of food consumed by individuals

There are at least three methods which have been used to estimate the daily food requirements of seals.

A popular method is to determine how much captive animals eat. Keyes (1968) conducted a postal survey of the amount of food fed by zoo-keepers to captive seals of many different species, and found that they were fed 6–10% of their body weight each day. However, Geraci (1975) suggested that seals should be fed only 4–7% of their body weight. Harp seals, common seals and ringed seals (*Phoca hispida*) have been maintained in Canada on 3–5% per day (ICES 1979), although harp seals can be maintained on as little as 1.75% of body weight (Gallivan & Ronald 1979). Data from captive seals must be interpreted with caution because they are often fed to satiation and their activity patterns seldom correspond to those of free-living animals, so they may be eating more or less than wild animals.

An alternative approach is to use stomach content analysis. Mansfield and Beck (1977) weighed the contents of the stomachs of Canadian grey seals and found that, as long as the contents were only slightly digested, they represented between 2.9% and 5.5% of the body weight of the animal from which they came. Boulva (1973) concluded that free-living common seals probably eat only one meal per day, so Mansfield and

Beck suggested that these figures were a reasonable estimate of the grey seal's daily food intake. Havinga (1933) estimated that common seals require 5 kg of fish a day, based on the weight of fish he found in the stomach and small intestine of three seals which he shot soon after they had finished feeding and on reports of the amounts of fish fed to seals in Dutch zoos. His estimate appears to have formed the basis for Steven's calculation (quoted in Matthews 1952) that grey seals require 15 lb (6.75 kg) of fish per day. Steven's estimate was later used by Rae (1960) and Parrish and Shearer (1977).

Expressing daily food requirements as a weight of fish is, however, misleading because the calorific value of fish flesh varies greatly with time of year and from species to species. For example, cod (*Gadus morhua*) has a calorific value of 0.8 kcal/g (Altman & Dittmer 1968), while herring (*Clupea harengus*) has a value of 2.0 kcal/g (Geraci 1975). This problem can be avoided by first calculating daily energy requirements. However, realistic assumptions about patterns of activity and reproductive strategy must be made. Lavigne *et al.* (1976) assumed that harp seals spend 25% of their time swimming, 25% in pursuit of food, and 50% resting. They calculate that a 100-kg seal requires a minimum of 4770 kcal per day. Not all the calories ingested by an animal are available for activity and growth. Energy is lost in faeces, urine and during digestion, Moen (1973) estimated that for mammals these losses were approximately 20% of ingested energy. This implies that the daily food requirement of a harp seal is about 3 kg of herring or 7.5 kg of cod. This wide range indicates the problem of trying to express food consumption as a weight of fish.

Quantity of food consumed by the population

The simplest way to estimate the food consumption of a marine mammal population is to multiply an estimate of average daily food requirement by an estimate of total population size (e.g. Rae 1960). A more refined figure can be obtained by estimating food requirements as a percentage of body weight, calculating the average weight of an individual in the population, and then multiplying these two values and an estimate of population size together. This technqiue was used by the ICES Ad Hoc Working Group on the interactions between grey seal populations and fish species (ICES 1979), by Fay *et al.* (1977) for the Pacific walrus (*Odobenus rosmarus*),and by the Council for Nature (1979).

However, the problem is rather more complex than any of these calculations admit. Few marine mammal populations are in a stable state, so that their age structures and population sizes will vary from year to year. There is already some dispute in the literature about the effects of population size on the food requirements of harp seals (Winters 1975, Brodie & Påske 1980, Innes *et al.* 1981, also see Ch. 19).

Although simple population size is, of course, important in determining total food consumption, the age structure and growth characteristics of the population can have dramatic effects. Elsewhere in this volume, Hiby and Harwood analyse the effects of changes in these characteristics on the energy requirements of a hypothetical grey seal population. Although the absolute costs of reproduction, and particularly lactation, are high for seals (Lavigne *et al.* 1976, Harwood *et al.* 1979) they are a relatively small proportion of a seal's annual requirement. The most important determinant of total energy requirements is body size. Thus, if the age structure of a population changes in favour of older (and therefore heavier) animals, the average per capita food requirement will increase. The total energy (and hence food) requirements of a marine mammal population depend not only on its size, but also on its dynamics and, most importantly, on the weight structure of the population. Incorrect identification of the population parameters determining changes in abundance can lead to a gross over- or underestimation of the food requirement of the population.

Effects on fisheries yield

The available evidence suggests that commercially exploited fish make up a large proportion of the diet of grey seals. Even though it may be possible to calculate the quantity of these fish consumed annually by the British grey seal population, there is no universally agreed method for converting this figure to an estimate of the loss incurred by fisheries. The final estimate will depend critically on the assumptions made in the calculations. The most obvious way to estimate the effect of seal predation is to calculate the likely changes in fisheries yield following a change in seal numbers. It is possible to conceive of circumstances in which the removal of seals would actually decrease the stock of fish available to fishermen. However, it seems much more likely that a reduction in seal numbers would lead to some increase in the availability of fish. Nevertheless, all of this increase would not occur immediately. In fact, in the first year following such a removal, only about one-third would be available to the fishery (ICES 1979), because seal predation is spread throughout the year. A reduction in the level of natural mortality on the fish population should, however, allow each fish stock to reach a higher equilibrium level.

Where the depredations of seals exactly duplicate the size classes and species caught by the commercial fisheries, the removal of seals would be equivalent to a reduction in the number of fishing boats. Provided fishing effort did not increase after the removal of the seals, the predicted catch would rise if the fisheries effort had been above the appropriate level for maximum sustainable yield (MSY). If effort was below the level for MSY, then catches would remain constant until the fish stocks responded to the change in natural mortality levels.

Most fish stocks are managed using single-species models, in which the effects of competition and variations in food supply are not included. Such simple models have formed the basis of recent calculation of the potential loss to fisheries as a result of predation by seals (Parrish & Shearer 1977, ICES 1979). There would be little dispute about the validity of these calculations if grey seals fed on just one species of fish and if this species had an unlimited food supply and no competitors. However, grey seals undoubtedly feed on many different species and size-classes of fish and these fish are involved in a network of competitive and predatory interactions with each other. Thus, such calculations, based only on approximate estimates of the food requirements of the grey seal population and of the composition of the diet and involving simple models, should only be taken as an indication of the general scale of the problem.

If grey seals do consume between 0.6% and 2.0% of the exploitable biomass of fish in British waters (ICES 1979), then a relatively small change in seal numbers – whether because of a cull or because the population's increase is allowed to continue – will not produce an easily detectable change in fisheries yield, although the effect of this change will not necessarily be trivial economically. The exact nature of the interactions between grey seals and commercial fisheries can only be determined by careful research on the distribution, diet and energy requirements of grey seals throughout the year.

Seals and salmon

One case which has always attracted particular attention is the effect of grey seals on the stocks of Atlantic salmon. We have already mentioned the effects of seals around salmon nets, but there is also the problem of general predation by seals at sea. Because salmon stocks are not large and because salmon are frequently found in seal stomachs, it is possible that grey seals have a particularly great impact on salmon stocks. It has been suggested that they could take as many fish as the commercial fishery (ICES 1979). Research on salmon–seal interactions is particularly active at the moment, so that the comments we can make on this matter may soon need to be revised.

Figures published by the Association of Scottish District Salmon Fishery Boards (1977) show that the catch of salmon during 1952–75 and the count of salmon at fish passes during 1965–75 suffered no general decline. Although the figures show considerable annual fluctuation, so that a small downward trend would not be detectable, there can be no doubt that the increase in seal numbers over this period was not matched with a corresponding decrease in salmon stocks. The value of netted salmon in Scotland (corrected to real terms by dividing by the Retail Price Index) also showed no decline during 1960–75, though the number of men directly employed in the industry declined by one-quarter. Interestingly, the value of the catch fluctuated only slightly from year to year. This is presumably an indication of the compensatory relationship between the size of the salmon catch and the value of the fish per unit weight. However, it is likely that the availability of farmed salmon will alter this relationship, so that a decline in stocks of wild salmon may, indeed, lead to a decline in the netsmen's income.

On the evidence presently available, the salmon case is even more difficult to evaluate than the general one. On the one hand, there is greater uncertainty about the magnitude of the effect of seals on the stock. On the other hand, if there is an effect, it could be large.

Incidental catches of seals

There are no published figures for the total numbers of seals drowned in fishing nets around the British coast each year. Some indication of the magnitude of the problem might be gleaned from the fact that of 528 grey seals tagged in the UK which have since been found dead, 148 (28%) were caught in nets. However, this is certainly an overestimate of the proportion of total mortality which is due to entanglement, because tags from seals which die in nets are more likely to be returned than those from seals dying of more natural causes. Seals are also deliberately and legally killed by fishermen to prevent them damaging their gear or catch.

The management controversy

Introduction

The continuing concern of British fishermen about competition from grey seal numbers has already been referred to. In 1963, a Consultative Committee on Grey Seals and Fisheries recommended that the grey seal stocks in Orkney and the Farne Islands should be reduced to three-quarters of their current size by killing moulted pups during the breeding season. This pup cull has taken place annually in Orkney since 1962, but the operation at the Farne Islands was limited to three culls in 1963, 1964 and 1965. Nevertheless, both stocks continued to increase (Summers 1978), and in 1977 a new management scheme was instituted. Its aim was to reduce the grey seal population of the Outer Hebrides and Orkney from the 1976 level of 50 000 to 35 000 by the end of 1982. The plan required 5400 cows and 24 000 pups to be killed on breeding beaches during 1977–82.

In fact, only the first year of the plan was put into effect, because the level of public protest in 1978 was so great. Much of the protest was based on sentimental and ethical reactions to the killing of seals. It is not our purpose here to consider such reactions, though we do not dismiss them as completely irrational and certainly do not underestimate their political importance. We wish to concentrate on the arguments which led the organised conservation bodies to oppose the management plan and to mount the campaign that led to the massive public protest. The concern of these bodies stemmed mainly from the fact that the grey seal, though common enough in Scotland (where approximately 60% of the world population breeds), is not common on the world scale: its total population is about 120 000 (Summers 1979). They therefore believed that any proposal to reduce the population needed to be fully justifiable.

General competition between seals and fishermen

A major element of the fisheries case was as follows (summarised from Parrish & Shearer 1977). In 1976 there were 69 000 grey seals in British waters; each had an average daily food consumption of 6.8 kg, giving an annual consumption by the total population of 168 000 tonnes, of which about 112 000 tonnes would be commercially exploitable fish. If fishermen were able to catch half of this weight of fish, their landings would be increased by 56 000 tonnes if there were no grey seals; this is 1–2% of the commercial fish catch in British waters. Based on average value of cod landed in Scotland in 1974, this represents a loss to the fishery of £15–20 million.

As we have seen, such calculations ignore the more subtle aspects of competition. Their validity depends on whether the conclusions are robust to violations of their underlying assumptions. The conservation groups argued that because there were uncertainties at each level of the calculations, there was considerable uncertainty about what effect removing all seals would have on fish stocks. The management plan called for only a *reduction* in seal numbers and this, the groups argued, increased the uncertainty because the remaining seals, with less intraspecific competition, could be more discriminating in their diet. Thus the effect of reducing seal numbers would be greater for the less acceptable types of food than for the preferred ones.

They also pointed out that the detailed economic effects of changes in catches should be considered. We are not competent to discuss these, except to note that including imputed economic benefits adds another layer of uncertainty to the calculations. There is some evidence that value of fish per unit weight tends to decline as landings increase (Williams 1979). If this is the case, the economic benefits from a reduction in seal numbers will be proportionally less than any increase in landings.

During the early stage of the current controversy between fishery and conservation interests, there was considerable polarisation. The fisheries lobby tended to state that the evidence for significant competition between man and seals was incontrovertible. The conservationists were highly critical of the quality of the available data and tended to assert that so little was known of the interactions between fish, seals and fishermen that the effects of reducing the seal population on catches of fish were totally unpredictable. It appears to us that all parties now agree, not only about what is firmly established and what is not, but also that reducing seals is likely to increase catches. They differ in that the fisheries lobby believes that the potential increase is great enough to justify a reduction in seal numbers, while the conservation lobby believes that the uncertainty about the size of any increase in catches is so great that reducing seal numbers is not justified.

Growth of the seal population

If seals and fishermen do compete, this is likely to become more severe as the population size of each increases. The fisheries case for a cull rested not only on calculations of the amount of fish currently being removed by seals, but also on the fact that the British seal population had increased in size and that this increase was likely to continue. Therefore, it was argued, unless action was taken rapidly, the impact of seals on fisheries would inevitably increase and would become more and more difficult to control.

In 1978, when the controversy was at its height, it was widely reported that the British seal population was doubling in size every 11 years – an annual rate of increase of 7%. These reports appear to be supported by published estimates of 34 000 for the population size in the mid 1960s (Smith 1966), and 69 000 for the mid-1970s (Summers 1978). However, the true situation was, inevitably, more complex than this: different stocks have grown at different rates.

In south-west Britain and Shetland there has been no detectable change in population size. In the Inner Hebrides there was an increase of over 7% per annum between 1976 and 1981 (NERC 1982), and in the Outer Hebrides (including North Rona) total pup production increased by 6 1/2% per annum between 1969 and 1975 (Summers 1978). Conclusions about the Orkney stock depend on what use is made of estimates of pup production from the early 1960s presented by Smith (1966). Summers (1979) did not use them – apparently because they were based on a variety of not always reliable techniques, whereas all estimates after 1963 were made from aerial surveys. He concluded that pup production had increased by 6% per annum until 1969, when the effects of pup hunting became apparent, and thereafter by 3% per annum. If Smith's counts are used, the growth rate during 1960–76 was 2.5% per annum, and the introduction of pup hunting (which removed about 25% of the pup production between 1962 and 1968) had no detectable effect on this rate. At the Farne Islands, pup production increased at a rate of 7% per annum during 1951–71, and subsequently declined as a result of control measures. A recent re-interpretation of counts made during the 1930s (Coulson 1981) indicates a growth rate of about 8% between then and 1951 – not 11% as suggested earlier (Coulson & Hickling 1964).

Thus, although some undisturbed populations of grey seals have grown at rates of 6–7% per annum during recent years, others have not, and the population as a whole has been growing more slowly. Nonetheless, it is increasing. This means that the conflict with human interests is also likely to increase. Whether that increase should be prevented is another aspect of the controversy.

Another controversial matter is the extent to which the population would continue to grow in the absence of interference by man. It is tempting to suppose that growth would continue for many years, since no density-dependent factors have been identified that would limit the population, except at very high levels. This lack of knowledge may be merely a result of the difficulty of analysing the population processes in a marine animal. Nonetheless, because grey seals do not enter the breeding population until they are several years old, there is a certain momentum in their population dynamics. It is likely, therefore, that the Scottish population will continue to grow at about the present rate for 5–10 years. After that, only speculation is possible.

Implementing management

The original plan

Table 10.1 shows the original management plan. Its aim was to reduce the grey seal population of Orkney and the Outer Hebrides from 50 000 to 35 000 by 1982. The plan involved killing both pups and cows. Killing only pups is a poor management technique (Harwood 1978) because cows do not enter the breeding population until they are 6 years old; thus the effect of removing pups is not evident until at least 6 years after culling begins. The plan involved killing seals at any particular colony in alternate years only so that the effects of the cull could be monitored.

Management in practice

Table 10.2 shows the actual number of seals killed in 1977 and in subsequent years. The target was not achieved in 1977 for logistic reasons. In 1978 this was revised to a pup hunt because of widespread public concern.

Side-effects of killing adults

Recent studies have revealed three important indirect effects of killing adults at breeding colonies (Summers & Harwood 1978, 1979). First, some cows are deterred from coming ashore to breed; the exact proportion that do so is unknown, but Summers and Harwood (1979) suggested it was around 15%. Second, of the cows that do come ashore, some desert their pups if the colony is disturbed. Again, the exact magnitude of this effect is unknown, although it probably varies according to the degree of disturbance. Finally, there is strong evidence that some of the cows at disturbed colonies fail to return in subsequent years. At the colonies culled in 1977, pup production in 1978 was up to 40% lower than in 1971 (SMRU unpublished data).

Table 10.1 Culling programme for grey seals in Scotland adopted by the Department of Agriculture and Fisheries for Scotland and the Nature Conservancy Council (from Summers 1979).

| | 1977/79/81 | | 1978/80/82 | |
	Pups	Cows	Pups	Cows
Orkney	1000	0	1000	450
Gasker, Coppay, Shillay[a]	1750	450	1500	0
Monach Isles[a]	1250	450	1000	0
North Rona	0	0	500	450

[a] Sites in the Outer Hebrides.

Table 10.2 Actual numbers of grey seals killed under the management operation, and subsequently taken in the same area.

		Orkney	Outer Hebrides	North Rona
1977	Pups	841	394	0
	Cows	0	286	0
1978	Pups	1067	85	0
	Cows	0	0	0
1979	Pups	1015	0	0
	Cows	0	0	0
1980	Pups	1195	200	0
	Cows	0	0	0
1981	Pups	1200	0	0
	Cows	0	0	0

The importance of monitoring

Although some of the side-effects described above were incorporated in the original calculations for the management plan (see Summers & Harwood 1979), their total effect would probably have led initially to a greater reduction in the population than was expected. However, the planned monitoring of the population would have allowed this to be detected even during the 6-year course of the original plan, which could have been modified accordingly. Even if such side-effects were absent, the results of the management action are unlikely to have been exactly as predicted by the relatively simple population model on which the plan was based. These considerations all point to the importance of continuous monitoring of the population during any management exercise.

Future options

There now appear to be five main options available for managing the seal population.

(a) Complete protection of grey seals at all times.
(b) Pup harvesting plus shooting of adults at fishing gear, as at present.
(c) Reducing the population in a way similar to the original management proposals.
(d) Preventing the spread of the population to previously unused breeding sites. There is some evidence (SMRU data) that grey seal colonies grow very slowly when first established. By careful surveillance, it should be possible to discover new colonies. Eliminating them might involve having to kill far fewer seals than if one tries to reduce the size of the present main colonies, yet it would contain the growth of the whole population.
(e) Killing non-breeding adults. This is probably an inefficient management technique, not only in that it is physically more difficult, but also in that it is impossible to be sure which breeding colonies are being affected, so that monitoring its effects is complicated.

There will continue to be considerable argument, whichever of these options is adopted. We believe that experience since 1978 has shown that the arguments are likely to be more productive and less wasteful if:

(a) all interested parties can meet to discuss the problem;
(b) the scientific basis for such discussion is clearly established beforehand through discussions between scientists representing the various interested parties, who can thus agree on what is known;
(c) all parties recognise that there are uncertainties associated with any conclusions reached, and some attempt is made to provide a reliable estimate of the level of uncertainty.

Conclusions

Grey seals and common seals in Britain do eat commercially exploited species and size classes of fish, but it is not easy to calculate the extent to which they actually compete with commercial fisheries. Although it is possible to estimate the biomass of fish consumed by the British grey seal population, this quantity will not necessarily vary in a simple fashion with changes in population size, nor is it clear how much of this biomass will actually become available for fishing if the seal population is reduced. The British grey seal population is probably still increasing but, because fisheries catches are determined by a large number of factors in addition to predation by seals, the effect of this increase on catches over the next decade may be difficult to detect. Detailed studies, now in progress, of the distribution of seals outside the breeding season and the variations in their diet and activity patterns throughout the year, will make it easier to calculate the effects of seals on commercial fisheries.

The effects of British seals on catches of salmonids are more obvious and include scaring of fish, and removals from and damage to nets, in addition to the effects of predation at sea. However, the magnitude of these effects is not clearly related to changes in the numbers of seals; control measures aimed at particular seal breeding colonies may have little effect on the levels of damage to these fisheries.

References

Alderdice, D. F., J. R. Brett, D. R. Idler and U. Fagerland 1954. Further observations on olfactory perception in migrating adult coho and spring salmon – properties of the repellent in mammalian skin. *Fish. Res. Bd Can., Pacific Coast Station Progress Report* **98**, 10–12.

Altman, P. L. and D. S. Dittmer 1968. *Metabolism*. Bethesda, Maryland: Federation of American Societies for Experimental Biology.

Association of Scottish District Salmon Fishery Boards 1977. *Salmon fisheries of Scotland*. Farnham: Fishing News Books.

Boulva, J. 1973. The harbour seal, *Phoca vitulina concolor,* in eastern Canada. Unpublished PhD. Thesis, Dalhousie University.

Boyd, I. L. 1982. *Ovulation and pregnancy rates in grey seals from the British Coast*. ICES CM 1982/N:13 (mimeo).

Brodie, P. F. and A. J. Päsche, 1980. *Density-dependent condition and energetics of marine mammal populations in multi-species fisheries management*. NAFO DOC 80/XI/166.

Coulson, J. C. 1981. A study of factors influencing the timing of breeding in the grey seal *Halichoerus grypus*. *J. Zool.* **194**, 553–71.

Coulson, J. C. and G. Hickling 1964. The breeding biology of the grey seal *Halichoerus grypus* (Fab.) on the Farne Islands, Northumberland. *J. Anim. Ecol.* **33**, 485–512.

Council for Nature 1979. *A report to the Secretary of State for Scotland from the Council of Nature Grey Seals Group.*

Fay. F. H., H. M. Feder and S. W. Stoker 1977. *An estimation of the impact of the Pacific Walrus population on its food resources in the Bering Sea.* Report to the U.S. Marine Mammal Commission, Contracts MM4AC-006, MM5AC-024.

Gallivan, G. J. and K. Ronald 1979. Temperature regulation in freely diving harp seals (*Phoca groenlandica*). *J. Fish. Res. Bd Can.* **57**, 2256–63.

Geraci, J. R. 1975. Pinniped nutrition. In Biology of the seal. K. Ronald and A. W. Mansfield (eds) *Rapp. P-v Reun.Cons. int. Explor. Mer.* **169**, 312–23.

Greenwood, J. J. D. 1979. The British population of grey seals. In *A report to the Secretary of State for Scotland from the Council for Nature Grey Seals Group*, 22–30.

Harwood, J. 1978. The effect of management policies on the stability and resilience of British grey seal populations *J. Appl. Ecol.* **15**, 413–21.

Harwood, J., A. R. Hiby, M. A. Fedak and C. H. Lockyer 1979. *Density dependent mechanisms in Northwest Atlantic harp seal populations.* IUCN International Workshop on Biology and Management of Northwest Atlantic Harp Seals. Paper HS/WP5.

Harwood J. and J. H. Prime 1978. Some factors affecting the size of British grey seal populations. *J. Appl. Ecol.* **15**, 401–411.

Havinga, B. 1933. Der Seehund (*Phoca vitulina* L.) in den Hollandischen Gewassern. *Tijdskrift der Nederlands Dierkundige Vereeningung* **3**, 79–111.

Hewer, H. R. 1974. *British seals.* London: William Collins.

Hiby, A. R. and J. Harwood 1979. *The reliability of population estimates for British grey seals.* ICES CM 1979/N:12 (mimeo).

ICES 1977. *ICES Working group on grey seals, report of the first meeting 16–20 May, 1977, Cambridge, UK.* ICES CM 1977/N:11 (mimeo).

ICES 1979. *ICES ad hoc working group on the interactions between grey seal populations and fish species.* ICES CM 1979/N:5 (mimeo).

ICES 1980. *Report of the ad hoc working group on multi-species assessment model testing.* ICES CM 1980/G:2 (mimeo).

Innes, S., R. E. A. Stewart and D. M. Lavigne 1981. Growth in Northwest Atlantic Harp seals, *Phoca groenlandica. J. Zool., Lond.* **194**, 11–24.

Keyes, M. C. 1968. The nutrition of pinnipeds. In *The behaviour and physiology of pinnipeds.* R. J. Harrison, R. C. Hubbard, R. S. Peterson, C. E. Rice and R.J. Schusterman (eds), 359–95. New York: Appleton-Century-Crofts.

Lavigne, D. M., W. Barchard, S. Innes and N. A. Øritsland 1976. *Pinniped bioenergetics.* ACMRR/MM/SC/112. Scientific Consultation on Marine Mammals. Bergen, Norway.

Lipsey, R. G. 1975. *An introduction to positive economics.* London: Wiedenfield & Nicolson.

Mansfield, A. W. and B. B. Beck 1977. *The grey seal in eastern Canada.* Technical Report No. 704. Fisheries and Marine Service, Environment Canada.

Mate, B. R. (ed.) 1980. *Workshop on marine mammal-fishery interactions in the north eastern Pacific.* Marine Mammal Commission Report MMC-78109.

Matthews, L. H. 1952. *British mammals.* London: William Collins.

Milne, A. 1961. Definitions of competition among animals. In *Mechanisms in biological competition.* Symposium of the Society for Experimental Biology No. XV, Cambridge.

Moen, A. N. 1973. *Wildlife ecology: an analytic approach.* San Francisco: W. H. Freeman.

Mountford, M. D. and E. A. Smith 1963. Damage to fixed-net salmon fisheries. In *Grey seals and fisheries, report of the Consultative Committee on Grey Seal and Fisheries,* 33–41. London: HMSO.

NERC 1979. Annual assessment of the stocks of grey seals and common seals in Great Britain: 1979. *NERC Newsjournal* **2**(8), 56–8.

NERC 1982. Seal stocks in Great Britain: Surveys conducted in 1981. *NERC Newsjournal* **3**(1), 8–10.

Parrish, B. B. and W. M. Shearer 1977. *Effects of seals on fisheries*. ICES CM 1977/M:14 (mimeo).

Potter, E. C. C. and A. Swain 1979. *Seal predation in the north-east England coastal salmon fishery*. ICES CM 1979/N:9 (mimeo).

Prime, J. H. 1979. *Observations on the digestion of some gadoid fish otoliths by a young common seal*. ICES CM 1979/N:14 (mimeo).

Rae, B. B. 1960. *Seals and Scottish fisheries*. Marine Research 1960, No. 2. Edinburgh: HMSO.

Rae, B. B. 1968. *The food of seals in Scottish waters*. Marine Research 1968, No. 2. Edinburgh: HMSO.

Rae, B. B. 1972. *A review of the cod-worm problem in the North Sea and in western Scottish waters 1958–1970*. Marine Research 1972, No. 2. Edinburgh: HMSO.

Rae, B. B. 1973. Further observations on the food of seals. *J. Zool.* **169**, 287–97.

Rae, B. B. and W. M. Shearer 1965. *Seal damage to salmon fisheries*. Marine Research 1965, No. 2. Edinburgh: HMSO.

Smith, E. A. 1963. Results of marking-recovery experiments on grey seals 1951-1961. In *Grey seals and fisheries, report of the Consultative Committee on Grey Seals and Fisheries*, 18–22. London: HMSO.

Smith, E. A. 1966. A review of the world's grey seal population. *J. Zool.* **150**, 463–89.

Stenman, O. 1978. Damage caused by seals to salmon fisheries in Finland in 1974–1976. *Finnish Game Research (Riistatieteelisia Julkaisuja)* **37**, 48–53.

Summers, C. F. 1978. Trends in the size of British grey seal populations. *J. appl. Ecol.* **15**, 395–400.

Summers, C. F. 1979. *The scientific background to seal stock management in Great Britain*. NERC Publications Series C, No. 21.

Summers, C. F. and J. Harwood 1978. *Indirect effects of grey seal culls*. ICES CM 1978/N:4 (mimeo).

Summers, C. F. and J. Harwood 1979. The Grey seal 'problem' in the Outer Hebrides. *Proc. Roy. Soc. Edin.* **77**B, 495–503.

Williams, H. A. 1979. The grey seal and British fisheries. In *A report to the Secretary of State for Scotland from the Council for Nature Grey Seal Group*, 22–30. London: COENCO.

Williamson, M. 1972. *The analysis of biological populations*. London: Edward Arnold.

Winters, G. H. 1975. *Review of capelin ecology and estimation of surplus yield from predator dynamics*. ICNAF Res. Doc 75/2.

11 Numerical changes in the population of elephant seals (*Mirounga leonina L*) in the Kerguelen Archipelago during the past 30 years

M. Pascal

Introduction

The census results from surveys conducted in 1970 (Pascal 1979) and 1977 (Van Aarde 1980) indicated a clear decline in the population of elephant seals frequenting the Kerguelen Archipelago. Between 1958 and 1961 approximately 6000 males were removed from the population by the Societé Industrielle des Abbettoirs Parisiens (SIDAP; Table 11.1). Since that time the population has not been exploited.

Initially, in this paper, techniques are developed to quantify the abundance of the population from census data. The causes of the marked decline in the size of the population are then considered.

Material and method

The census

During the breeding period, the elephant seals gather in large numbers on certain beaches of the Kerguelen Islands, where the topography is particularly favourable to the establishment of harems (Angot 1954, Paulian 1954). The census counts have

Table 11.1 Number of elephant seals killed in the Kerguelen Islands by the SIDAP between 1958 and 1961.

	December	January	February	March	April	May	Total
1958	—	312	231	174	39	69	824
1959	124	169	131	129	—	—	553
1960	255	255	232	221	84	—	1047
1961	?	?	?	?	?	?	≠600

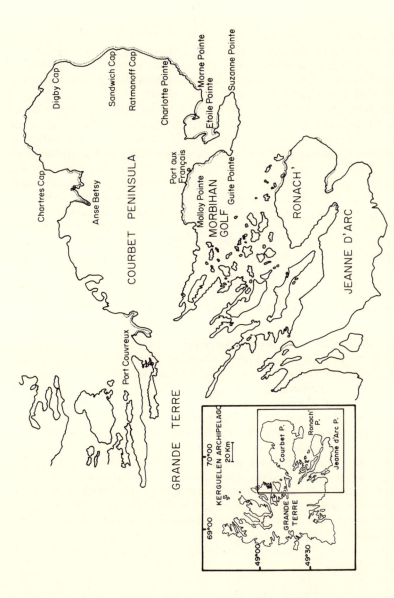

Figure 11.1 Localisation of beaches studied during the various censuses of elephant seals in the Kerguelen Islands. The portions of the beaches marked with broken lines are those which are habitually frequented by elephant seal during the breeding period.

generally been carried out on the beaches between Molloy Point and Cape Digby (Fig. 11.1) in 1951 (Paulian 1954), 1952 (Angot 1954), 1958 and 1960 (Bajard 1962), 1970 (Pascal 1979), and 1977 (Van Aarde 1980). Unfortunately the censuses carried out by these various authors are not directly comparable, because of the techniques used and, in particular, because they were conducted on different dates and along different sections of the coast. They therefore cannot be used, as they stand, for purposes of inter-year comparisons.

In an attempt to make these disparate studies comparable, additional information has been sought from the authors. The exact methodology involved in the 1958 and 1960 censuses was provided by Bajard. Pascal and Beauge have provided numerical data on the 1956 census and Langlart and Bester for 1979.

All the censuses were carried out by directly counting the number of animals present during the breeding season. In the majority of cases, only the adult males and females were counted. One or two observers worked together successively listed the beaches or parts of beaches bounded by geographical features likely to impede the mobility of the animals on land. These precautions made it possible to avoid counting the same individuals twice, and were aimed at ensuring that observers were not required to count too great a number of individuals at any one time. However, in 1956, counts were conducted simultaneously over almost the entire area under study by several teams of two observers.

Information provided by the census takers indicates (with the exception of Angot) that the census estimates will tend to fall short of the actual total by a factor of some 2–3%.

Method for evaluating the Kerguelen Islands elephant seal population

Biological factors
It is appropriate to recall briefly certain observations of the Kerguelen Islands elephant seals made by Angot (1954), Bajard (1962), Pascal (1979) and Van Aarde (1980).

Those males which are present on land during the breeding period can belong to one of three categories in the social hierarchy: harem bulls, bachelors, or juveniles. The arrival patterns, as well as the social and numerical stability of these different groups of animals, change throughout the breeding period (Angot 1954, Laws 1956, Carrick *et al* 1962). It is therefore extremely difficult to establish the size of the total population from an evaluation of the number of males alone.

In comparison, the females, who must remain with their young until they are weaned, are sedentary throughout the breeding period. A precise estimate of the total population will therefore be most easily obtained by counting the females. Laws (1960), using survival-rate tables for South Georgia, has shown that the total population dependent on a particular locality is related to the number of births in that area by a simple multiplier:

for an exploited stock

$$\text{total population} = 3.2 \times \text{annual pup production}$$

for an unexploited stock

$$\text{total population} = 3.8 \times \text{annual pup production}$$

The work of Carrick and Ingham (1960) indicated that the appropriate multiplier for Heard and Macquarie Islands was 3.5. This value was later used by Laws (1979) in estimating the total population of elephant seals in the Antarctic. The Kerguelen Islands stock of elephant seals has been exploited for part of its history. Hence a value of 3.2 has been adopted as a multiplier. It is likely that this will result in an underestimate of population size.

Since all females on land for the breeding season are pregnant, an estimation of their numbers enables us to estimate accurately the number of young, and therefore the total population dependent on the portion of coast under study.

Females start arriving on the Kerguelen Islands beaches in mid-September and have all left by mid-November. Females remain on land from 26 to 30 days and weaning is for 22–23 days. (Condy 1979, Van Aarde 1980, MacCann 1980). Hence it may be concluded that the arrival of females on the beaches is staggered (Angot 1954). In other words a census conducted at any particular time during the season will sample only a portion of the breeding females. In the next section a correction factor for this effect is derived.

Correction factor

In an earlier work (Pascal 1979), it has been shown that the Gaussian curve is a reasonable empirical representation of the percentage of females on the beach in relation to the total number of females who will be on this beach for the breeding period. In addition, it seems the maximum level date is fundamentally the same from one year to another on any one beach, and that, for any given year, this date is the same on all the beaches under consideration. Results from two censuses (1952 and 1970) show the possibility of evaluating the total female population from a census taken at a given moment during the breeding period using this model.

Van Aarde (1980), using a similar method, has attempted to formulate a parabolic equation representing, as a function of time, the percentage of the population composed of females and weaned young in relation to the total number of females and weaned young frequenting any given beach. There are two problems with Van Aarde's analysis. First, only the number of females is available and not that of their young. Second, the parabolic equation is not as good a representation of the data as, for example, is the Gaussian curve.

The model that produced the best fit to the data gave the following estimates: the date when the maximum number of females are on land is 32 days after the beginning of the breeding season (14 September), the maximum percentage of the female population observed on land is 86%. The slight difference in these estimates from those presented by Pascal (1979) is due to the method of fitting. In the former case this was by eye, in the current study a maximum likelihood technique was used. The fit to the data was good with a coefficient of determination of 0.98. Approximate 95% confidence limits on the percentage of females present on the beach are around ± 6%.

Indirect validation of the model

A female remains on land during the breeding period for an average (S) of between 26 and 30 days (Condy 1979, Vam Aarde 1980, MacCann 1980). The estimate of the date when the maximum number of females are to be observed on a beach ($V_{max} = 32.14$ days), shows that on this date a number of females have already departed and others have not yet arrived. The dates corresponding to $V_{max} \pm 2S$ are not included in the definition of the model and no female arrives before $V_{max} - 2S$, nor after

$V_{max} + S$ (Fig. 11.2). Therefore, at $V_{max} - S$, we observe all the females who arrived between V_1 (arrival date of the first female) and $V_{max} - S$. All these animals cannot be observed at V_{max} because they have left the beach at this date. At V_{max} we observe only the females who arrived between V_{max} and $V_{max} - S$, and at $V_{max} + S$ all the individuals who arrived after V_{max}. The sum of the percentages obtained for the corresponding dates should respectively be equal to 100%. If S equals 26, 27 and 28 days respectively, then the sum given above is equal to 103.50%, 100.65% and 98.15%. The model seems therefore to predict adequately the timing of arrival and departure. In reality, the average time a female stays on land can hardly vary if one takes into account the extremely rigid constraints imposed on her: she must, on the one hand, ensure the development of her young (45 kg at birth, the young will weigh 120 kg at weaning after 22 days – MacCann 1980 – and must in addition accumulate sufficient reserves so as

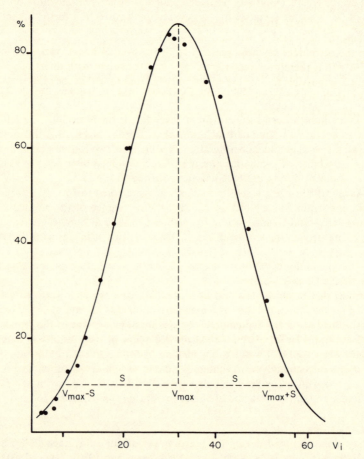

Figure 11.2 Percentage of female elephant seals present at a given moment (V_i in days, starting on the 14 September) on a given beach with respect to the total number of females who will give birth on this beach over the entire breeding season. The points correspond to the observed values. S: average time a female stays on land during the breeding period; V_{max}: moment when the maximum number of females will be observed on land.

not to have to feed for 2 to 3 weeks – Angot 1954). On the other hand, she must leave before reaching complete exhaustion, as she does not feed at all during the whole period she remains on land.

Elaboration of a strategy for enumerating the number of elephant seals in Kerguelen Islands

Analysis of the model (Fig. 11.2) enables us to determine the periods for which a census on land will give the most reliable results. For the initial or latter days of the breeding period there will be only a small number of individuals present (25% on the 27 September and 24 November). The census taken before or after one or the other of these dates will be easy to conduct, given the small number of animals present, and will therefore be very accurate. However, the correction factor to be applied will be large, and it will greatly multiply errors in counting, and will amplify the random phenomenon of the arrival and departure of the animals.

During the periods from 25 September to 11 October, and 22 October to 4 November, the daily rate of arrival or departure of the females is very high. The variation in the percentage of those present, recorded over 24 hours, varies between 3% and 4.3% and is therefore greater than the error consistent with direct counting.

Since it is impossible to time the counting operations to within the nearest hour, and since any such degree of precision would furnish little real information, these two periods should be considered as being relatively unfavourable for obtaining accurate results.

The period most favourable for taking a census of the elephant seals in the Kerguelen Islands therefore lies between 4 and 22 October.

Results

The beaches of the Gulf of Morbihan: from Molloy Pointe to Guite Pointe

The fraction of the population of elephant seal females frequenting these beaches during the breeding period increased overall by 44% between 1952 and 1958, corresponding to an average annual increase of 7.4% (Fig. 11.3). This trend was drastically reversed between 1958 and 1960, when the number dropped overall by 46.8% (average annual decrease 23.4%). This reduction was followed by a marked increase up to 1979 (total increase of 55.3%, corresponding to an average annual increase of 3.5%). The largest variation was recorded for the beaches between Port aux Francais and Guite Pointe. The results of applying this procedure to the various sites are given in Table 11.2.

The beaches of the south-east coast of Courbet Peninsula

We have divided this part of the coast into four distinct beaches, which can be grouped two by two as a function of their geographical location and of the density of elephant seals on land during the breeding period. The beaches Guite Pointe–Morne Pointe and Morne Pointe–Charlotte Pointe enclosing Norwegian Bay are sheltered from the prevailing west wind by the Isthme bas. These beaches are relatively calm, especially when compared with those on the east coast of the Courbet Peninsula, and accommodate a relatively less dense population of elephant seals during the breeding period. The

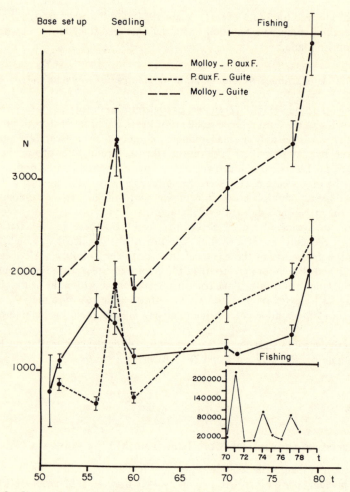

Figure 11.3 Changes in the number of elephant seal females coming to breed on the coastal sector between Molloy Pointe and Guite Pointe between 1952 and 1979. Fish catches in tonnes on the shelf of Kerguelen Islands. (From Hureau & Duhamel 1980.)

number of breeding females on Guite–Morne beach increased steadily from 1952 to 1979 (overall increase of 307.4%, or annual increase of 11.4%; Fig. 11.4). On the other hand, Morne–Charlotte beach experienced a drop in numbers on two occasions, (1956–60 and 1970–77), but the overall decrease in the population between 1952 and 1979 was 6.2%, which is relatively small.

The two beaches between Charlotte Pointe and Cap Ratmanoff, on the one hand, and between Cap Ratmanhoff and Cap Digby on the other, are the most densely populated in the archipelago. In addition, they face the open sea, and are therefore relatively rough. These two beaches underwent two falls in population, one in 1956–60 and the other in the period 1970–77. Between 1956 and 1979, the population of the two beaches decreased overall by 52.7%, or 2.3% annually.

Table 11.2 Results − raw (N) and calculated (N$_c$) − of the census of elephant seal females on land during the breeding period. Below each calculated figure are the limits of the margin of error at 95% (defined in the text). The numbers correspond respectively to the beaches: (1) Molley−Port aux Francais; (2) Port aux Francais−Guite Pointe; (3) Guite Pointe−Morne Pointe; (4) Morne Pointe−Charlotte Pointe; (5) Charlotte Pointe−Cap Ratmanoff; (6) Cap Ratmanoff−Cap Digby.

| | | Morbihan | | South and east Courbet Peninsula | | | |
		Beach 1	Beach 2	Beach 3	Beach 4	Beach 5	Beach 6
1952	Date	15−10	14−10	21−10	21−10	22−10	
	N	937	718	2680	2390	10760	
	N$_c$	1096	849	3378	3013	14062	
		1171	908	3627	3235	15135	
		1021	791	3130	2791	12989	
1956	Date	20−10	25−10	24−10	25−10	15−10	15−10
	N	1370	430	4226	3432	29580	21611
	N$_c$	1677	652	6057	5203	34599	25278
		1797	710	6564	5664	36963	27005
		1557	594	5550	4742	32236	23551
1958	Date	21−10	30−10	8−10	9−10	10−10 11−10	12−10
	N	1184	856	5350	2700	9850 10390	11640
	N$_c$	1493	1901	7788	3733	26764	14362
		1602	2148	8451	4035	28830	15397
		1383	1655	7126	3432	24696	13327
1960	Date	15−10	21−10	4−10	5−10	6−10 7−10	9−10 10−10
	N	956	564	4600	2000	7600 7900	9100 7300
	N$_c$	1153	711	8799	3537	24684	12583 9653
		1232	763	9782	3903	26980	13599 10398
		1075	659	7816	3172	22388	11567 8907
1970	Date	15−10	7−10	24−10 7−10	7−10	6−10	6−10
	N	1075	1082	1557 5480	3306	16861	14863
	N$_c$	1257	1669	2231 8456	5101	27760	24471
		1343	1820	2418 9218	5561	30430	26824
		1172	1519	2045 7694	4641	25091	22118
1977	Date	19−10	21−10	22−10 24−10	18−10 13−10	13−10	15−10 16−10
	N	1161	1500	2041 4955	1235 1245	11657	7148 7435
	N$_c$	1390	2004	2667 7101	1455 1499	13787	8361 8659
		1487	2152	2871 7696	1555 1604	14739	8932 9248
		1291	1857	2464 6507	1356 1394	12835	7790 8070
1979	Date	23−10	24−10	25−10 22−10	21−10	16−10	15−10 18−10
	N	1514	1676	3285 5079	2242	12887	5103 6207
	N$_c$	2065	2402	4980 6637	2826	15008	5969 7366
		2230	2603	5421 7144	3034	16029	6377 7876
		1901	2201	4539 6131	2618	13987	5561 6855

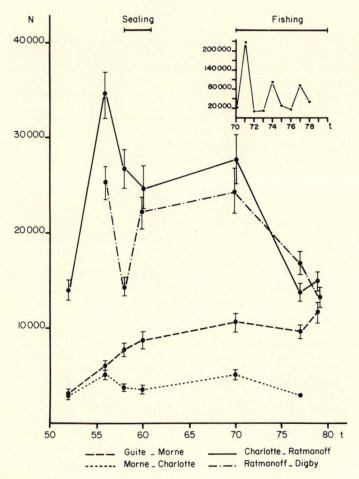

Figure 11.4 Changes in the number of elephant seal females coming to breed on the coastal sector between Pointe Guite and Cap Digby between 1952 and 1979. Fish catches in tonnes on the shelf of Kerguelen Islands. (From Hureau & Duhamel 1980.)

Inventory of total coastal sector

Between 1956 and 1979, the number of elephant seal females frequenting the coastal sector between Molloy Pointe and Cap Digby decreased by 35.7%, or by 1.6% annually (Fig. 11.5). This drop in numbers was not continuous, but occured over two distinct periods (1956–8 and 1970–77), divided by a period of relative stability and even growth (1958–70). Between 1970 and 1977, the population decrease was 33.8%, an annual average of 4.8%. The result of the 1979 census confirms the collapse of the population, but the size of error margins calculated are such that it is not possible to say if this collapse persisted from 1977 through to 1979. The analysis of data relative to all the beaches show that, overall, the population of *Mirounga leonina* in the Kerguelen Islands was in decline between 1956 and 1979. It would not appear that changes in the breeding areas of the archipelago itself are the cause.

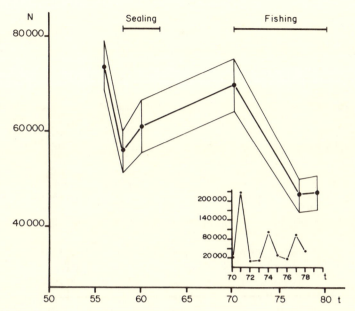

Figure 11.5 Changes in the number of elephant seal females coming to breed on the coastal sector between Molloy and Cap Digby between 1956 and 1979. Fish catches in tonnes on the shelf of Kerguelen Islands. (From Hureau & Duhamel 1980.)

Discussion

Number of elephant seals in the Kerguelen Archipelago

Laws (1960) has shown that the simple multiplication by a factor of 3.2 of the number of young animals counted on a beach provides a good estimate of the total elephant seal population of the beach under study. We have results from censuses of females on land for the breeding period. These females, it should be recalled, are all pregnant and each one gives birth to one pup; furthermore, they return faithfully to the various breeding sites. The number of females counted will therefore correspond to the number of pups, without taking account of juvenile mortality. Accordingly, we have elaborated Figure 11.5, which shows the change in the total number of elephant seals in the Kerguelen Islands between 1956 and 1979. These values are most certainly under-estimated, as only the Molloy–Digby sector is taken into account. This represents less than one-third of the total length of the Grande Terre coast. However, it should be specified that the sector under study contains the largest proportion of *Mirounga leonina* in the Kerguelen Islands.

The average of six census counts (represented in Table 11.3) enables us to establish the Kerguelen Archipelago elephant seal stock at 190 000 animals (underestimate). Laws (1960, 1979) evaluates the total elephant seal population in the South Indian Ocean at 200 000 individuals. It would seem that he has underestimated the size of this stock. Using data from the literature, we have formulated the following list, represen-

Table 11.3 Total elephant seal population in the Kerguelen, dependent on the portion of the coast between Cap Molloy and Cap Digby, calculated from the total number of females according to Laws' data. Each estimate is given with its margin of error.

	1956	1958	1960	1970	1977	1979
$N+$	78 703	60 463	66 657	77 614	50 284	50 714
	251 849	193 481	213 302	248 365	160 908	162 274
N	73 466	56 041	61 120	70 945	46 923	47 253
	235 091	179 331	195 584	227 024	150 153	151 209
$N-$	68 230	51 619	55 584	64 280	43 565	43 793
	218 336	165 181	177 869	205 696	139 408	140 137

ting the elephant seal stocks of the various South Indian Ocean Islands:

Kerguelen (present work)	190 000
Heard (Carrick & Ingham 1960)	74 000
Marion (Rand 1955 in Laws 1960)	10 000
Crozet (Barrat & Mougin 1978)	10 000
Total	284 000

The size of the South Indian Ocean stock should therefore be close to that of the South Georgia stock (315 000 − Laws 1960). The world stock of the species would therefore be as high as 700 000 individuals, and not 600 000.

Fluctuation in the numbers of elephant seals in the Kerguelen Archipelago between 1952 and 1979

Between 1952 and 1979, the number of elephant seals in the Kerguelen Islands fell on two occasions. The first decrease occurred between 1956 and 1960, the second between 1970 and 1977. The decrease in numbers from 1956 to 1960 can be attributed in part to sealing, which began in January 1958. However, this cause alone cannot fully explain the severity of the phenomenon, for:

(a) the number of animals caught is small compared with the size of the population (see Table 11.1);
(b) only the males were hunted, whereas the census also shows a drop in the number of females for the year in which sealing started;
(c) sealing was prohibited from 1 September to 1 December (Bajard 1962) which should have prevented any disruption of the harems during the breeding period;
(d) the population increased during the greater part of the sealing period;
(e) it is known, in certain cases, that sealing can cause a displacement of the populations as certain animals will not stay where there has been a cull. In the Kerguelen Islands, sealing took place mainly along the coast between Port aux Francais and Morne Pointe, whereas the most significant drop in population was located in the Charlotte Pointe–Cap Digby sector.

Sealing cannot therefore fully explain the drop in population between 1956 and 1960.

In any case it cannot be seen as the reason for the decline in population between 1970 and 1977, as all sealing ceased in 1961. In seeking the possible causes for this latter decline, we can first eliminate certain hypotheses which come immediately to mind.

Change in the physical environment
(a) No major topographical disturbance of the coastal sector under study was recorded between 1970 and 1977.
(b) No large population shift from one beach to another was noted within the area under study. We cannot explain the disappearance of nearly 20 000 seals between 1958 and 1979 in the area Guite–Digby (see Fig. 11.4) by the increase during the same time of 3000 seals in the area Molloy–Guite (see Fig. 11.3).
(c) Climatic conditions have not changed drastically over the last 20 years (Azibane *et al.* 1977).

Population movements in the South Indian Ocean
(a) In 1979 it was noted that there were still no elephant seals breeding on the Antarctic coast bordered by the South Indian Ocean. The only area where elephant seals are to be found (Vestfold Hills in the Australian sector of the Antarctic) is visited only by animals coming to land for moulting (Johnston *et al.* 1973, Tierney 1977).
(b) Heard Island is very small and could hardly support all the elephant seals which have disappeared from Kerguelen Islands.
(c) The population at Marion Island decreased between 1957 and 1975 (Condy 1977 in Van Aarde 1980a).
(d) The Crozet Islands population has been decreasing since 1935–40 (Barrat & Mougin 1978).

The explanation for the decrease in the Kerguelen Island elephant seal population is not to be found in the possible displacement of breeding sites. Furthermore, this would be contrary to what is known of the breeding habit of the species. Nicholls (1970) has shown that the animals from Macquarie Island breed at a distance of less than 30 km from where they were born.

At both Crozet and Marion, it seems that the elephant seal populations have been in continual decline for 20 years. This does not seem to be a continuous phenomenon in the Kerguelen Island. It is highly likely, therefore, that the causes are not the same in the two cases.

Finally, in the Kerguelen Islands, the trend in population size is not the same for all beaches. The relatively calm beaches of the Gulf of Morbihan and Norwegian Bay underwent relatively slight drops in numbers, and even some increases, although the populations on the other beaches were declining. On the other hand, on the much rougher east coast beaches of the Courbet Peninsula, the population is subject to much greater fluctuations. Van Aarde (1980b) defines the Kerguelen beaches by four morphological characteristics, to which the harem structure is closely related. He also demonstrates the role of population fluctuation in the organisation and size of the harems. These fluctuations seem to be locally modulated by the type of beach. This additional characteristic related to those described by Van Aarde would certainly allow for a more precise description of the beaches.

Predation
Pascal (1979) and Van Aarde (1980a) agree that predation on elephant seals in the

waters of the Kerguelen Archipelago is negligible, and cannot therefore be regarded as one of the basic causes for wide variations in population numbers.

Food supply

Laws (1979) assumed that at South Georgia and Kerguelen Island larger catches of fishes (up to 360 000 tonnes) may have had adverse effects on elephant seal populations in recent years. Van Aarde (1980a) has taken up the hypothesis, the validity of which appears to have been demonstrated for the Kerguelen Islands as a result of the simultaneous occurrence of two phenomena: the period corresponding to the decrease in the elephant seal population and the beginning of intensive fishing on the Kerguelen shelf (Table 11.4). We have investigated the possibility that the principal factor currently affecting the Kerguelen elephant seal population is the abundance of the seals' food supply.

Estimation of the food needs of the Kerguelen elephant seal population   Laws (1977) established the average weight of an elephant seal at 500 kg, and the quantity of food required annually by one animal at 20 times this weight. The preys consists of cephalopods (75%, or 7.5 tonnes/per animal per annum), and fishes (25%, or 2.5 tonnes/per animal per annum). Applying these data to the various censuses of elephant seals in the Kerguelen Islands (see Table 11.3), we obtain the biomass of fish consumed annually for these years (Table 11.5).

Estimation of the biomass of fish on the Kerguelen continental shelf   Everson (1977) estimated that the fish stocks of the Kerguelen continental shelf (estimated surface area 50 000 km^2) at 220 000 tonnes, with an annual production of 80 000 tonnes. Hureau (1979) estimated that this stock was 130 875 tonnes in 1975 (he estimated the biomass of fish at a depth of 50–100 m over a segment of continental shelf having an estimated area of 104 700 km^2), with an annual production of 20 000 tonnes. The discrepancy between these two estimates was to be expected given the difficulty of such an evaluation and the paucity of our knowledge on the subject. It is impossible, considering the degree of uncertainty attached to this type of stock estimate, to seek to use such estimates to show the existence of a predator–prey connection. However, it should be noted that the fish biomass that has theoretically been consumed by the elephant seals is substantially greater than the stock itself, regardless of which of the estimates is used.

Table 11.4 Quantity of fish (in tonnes) caught on the continental shelf, according to Fish Biology Biomass Report Series No. 3.

1970–71	1971–72	1972–73	1973–74	1974–75	1975–76	1976–77
21 000	229 500	112 800	13 100	101 600	25 000	17 400

Table 11.5 Quantity of fish (in tonnes) consumed by the Kerguelen Islands' elephant seal population.

1956	1958	1960	1970	1977	1979
587 727	448 327	488 960	567 560	375 382	378 022

This fact lends itself to three possible interpretations:

(a)   the fish stocks are heavily underestimated (very little work has been done on non-exploited species):

(b)   the food requirements of elephant seals are heavily overestimated; or

(c)   elephant seal populations take most of their food beyond the continental shelf.

These three hypotheses are not mutually exclusive.

Feeding habits   Our knowledge of the diet of the elephant seal is limited, and is based solely on the inventory established by Laws (1956) from 139 stomachs of animals killed on the South Georgian beaches. Only six of these stomachs contained food remains. We therefore have only a small sample, and in addition we have no idea of what their diet may consist of at sea. However there is every reason to believe that at sea it consists of cephalopods, and of fish on the coast.

This possibility of exploiting two types of prey should allow the elephant seal to overcome, locally and for short periods of time, a shortage in one or other of these types of prey. If there is a shortage of fish, it is possible that predation on cephalopods increases considerably. As no estimate has been made of the Antarctic and sub-Antarctic stocks of cephalopods, we have no means of directly testing this hypothesis. However, if the predation of cephalopods did in fact increase, the time spent by the elephant seal in pelagic feeding would have had to increase substantially, as would the distances they covered. If this supposition is correct, the number of elephant seals in areas such as Vestfold Hill ought to have risen, all other things being equal.

If there is a shift in the food habits of the elephant seal towards an increase in the take of cephalopods, if Laws' ideas (1979) are true (cephalopods are taken oceanically and fishes in inshore water), it is reasonable to postulate that the elephant seals remain longer offshore and travelled farther than in the past. Then it is reasonable to think that the number of animals present in the farthest localities would increase.

We have no precise knowledge of difference in feeding habits between the two sexes, and even less between the different age groups. Sexual dimorphism is particularly marked in the elephant seal (females: 400–900 kg; males: 3–4 tonnes – Laws 1979), which suggests different potentials for each sex. The difference is even more striking between a young animal, weighing 120 kg at weaning, and a harem bull, weighing 2–3 tonnes.

If the hypothesis of Laws (1979) quoted above is true, the males spend the largest part of the time required for recovering weight after breeding and moulting far from the breeding localities, and they would have to eat essentially cephalopods.

It seems that the males travel the greatest distances, and are therefore able to profit more from pelagic feeding. Laws (1956) noted that among 38 individuals observed on the Antarctic coast, only 3 were females. Carrick *et al.* (1962a), referring to individuals marked at Heard, observed two males at Vestfold Hills, one male at New Amsterdam, one male and one female at Marion Island, one male and one female at Kerguelen. Johnston *et al.* (1973) and Tierney (1977) provided some information concerning the elephant seal population frequenting the Vestfold Hills coasts: in general they were young males, the highest proportion of females ever observed being 3 females for 108 males.

If we accept the assumption of food shortage, it is highly probable that the size and composition in sex and age of the elephant seal group frequenting Vestfold Hills will undergo profound changes. Between 1975 and 1979, 12 000 elephant seal pups were marked in Kerguelen (Van Aarde & Pascal 1980). In 1980, the majority of the first individuals marked would have reached the age of their first major journey. Furthermore, since the large individuals (in particular the males) are most likely to benefit from cephalopods, the smaller animals (females and young) will be more affected by a shortage of fish. Knowing that 90% of the females above 4 years of age are to be found on the beaches during the breeding season, and that the first large catches of fish on the Kerguelen shelf were made in 1971–2, and 1974–5, it is logical that the effect on the elephant seal population should emerge in 1976–7. The repercussions on the elephant seal population of the heavy 1974–5 fish catches should have become apparent in 1979–80. This reasoning does not take into account the possibility that after such a large catch, fish stocks will only recover with difficulty. This possibility cannot be ruled out, insofar as the majority of fish species frequenting the Kerguelen shelf reach sexual maturity at the advanced age of 6–7 years (Hureau 1979, Hureau & Ozouf-Costaz 1980).

Unfortunately, the data from Vestfold Hills are largely anecdotal, and more precise data are required. The size of the moulting population of elephant seals in this locality is correlated with the fast ice. We need data on ice and elephant seal populations to compare the size of this population for the same shape of the fast ice.

It is therefore through linking observations made on the breeding sites (Kerguelen) with others made in locations far from them that one can indirectly evaluate the impact of the fish catch on the elephant seal population. These observations should benefit from the marking made between 1975 and 1979. In this way it will be possible to test the assertion of Van Aarde that the population of Kerguelen elephant seals was essentially stable but fluctuated around some unknown mean, without adult males and females fluctuating in synchrony. The fishing activities may be influencing the magnitude of these fluctuations.

Finally, there is reason to fear that the fish stocks have been depleted to the same, if not to a greater, extent than the elephant seal population (i.e. by 33%), if the major cause of the collapse of the elephant seal population in the Kerguelen Archipelago is directly linked to commercial fishing.

The technique for evaluating the elephant seal population used in this work assumes that the population structure is stable when the census is taken. In fact, on the one hand, the multiplication factor applied to the census results of the young animals assumes a well-defined population structure; on the other, the extrapolation we make in assimilating the number of females on land during the breeding period to the number of young also supposes that the sex ratio for the different age groups remains stable. We have seen that the appearance of a food shortage will, in all probability, have different consequences according to sex and age group. Consequently, if we wish to determine precisely the level of the elephant seal population in the Kerguelen Islands after 1976–7 (at which date the initial effects of commercial fishing would be felt), then we are going to have to seek to establish multiplication factors that can be applied to the raw census values for the transitional period (at least) and until such time as the population structure is once again stable. It is easy to arrive at these factors in the Kerguelen Islands by recording marked animals. But care should be taken to establish that the mortality rate for young seals on the beaches remained the same from 1952 to 1979, because in high-density years it may be assumed that the largest number of newborn pups were crushed to death as a result of fights between harem bulls. Lastly, it would be useful to define a 'condition index' for the females.

The tagging operation was undertaken on the shore between Charlotte Pointe and Ratmanoff. Of fewer than 20 000 pups born per year in this locality, more than 3000 have been tagged each year (1975, 1976, 1977, 1979), giving a total of 12 000. If we take into consideration the homing behaviour of this species (which has been indicated by the first recoveries of tags in Kerguelen and in the past literature on the subject), the tag recoveries should give us an accurate idea of the population structure.

Knowing the structure and sex ratio of the population, it will be possible to determine the future level and stability of the elephant seal population using models similar to those established by Harwood (1978) on the grey seal (*Halichoerus grypus*) of the North Atlantic. Summers (1978), Harwood (1978) and Harwood and Prime (1978) pointed out that the stability and level of the population of grey seals are particularly sensitive to adult mortality and less so to pup mortality.

Acknowledgements

I would like to thank Dr V. de Buffrenil for his suggestions and criticisms of this manuscript; Mr M. Martinez-Loscos for finalising the figures; and Mrs L. Trussell for having done the main part of the translation.

References

Angot, M. 1954. Observations sur les mammifères marins de l'Archipel de Kerguelen avec une étude détaillée de l'Eléphant de mer (*Mirounga leonina* (L)) *Mammalia* **18** (1), 1–111.

Azibane, C., B. Clavier, J. L. Dujardin, U. Touze and J. F. Rigaurd 1977. Etude sur le climat des iles Kerguelen et de la zone subantarctique de l'Ocean Indien. Climatologie de Port aus Francais. *Monographie No 99 de la meteorologie nationale.* Paris.

Bajard, P. 1962. *L'Eléphant de mer (Mirounga leonina) Biologie. Exploitation du troupeau hôte de l'archipel de Kerguelen.* Thèse de doctorat vétérinair, Lyon.

Barrat, A. and J. L. Mougin 1978. L'Eléphant de mer, *Mirounga leonina* de l'ile de la Possession, Archipel Crozet (46°25'S.; 51°45'E.). *Mammalia* **42**(2), 143–74.

Carrick, R., S. E. Csordas and S. E. Ingham 1962b. Studies on the southern elephant seal, *Mirounga leonina* (L.).IV:Breeding and development. *CSIRO Wildl. Res.* 167–97.

Carrick, R., S. E. Csordas, S. E. Ingham and K. Keith 1962a. Studies on the southern elephant seal, Mirounga leonina (L),.111: The annual cycle in relation to age and sex. CSIRO Wildl. Res. 119–60.

Carrick, R. and S. E. Ingham 1960. Ecological studies of the southern elephant seal, *Mirounga leonina* L., at Macquarie Island and Heard Island. *Mammalia* **24**, 325–42.

Carrick, R. and S. E. Ingham 1962. Studies on the southern elephant seal, *Mirounga leonina* (L.),V:Population dynamic and utilisation. *CSIRO Wildl. Res.* 198–206.

Condy, P. R. 1977. *The ecology of the southern elephant seal Mirounga leonina (Linnaeu 1758), at Marion Island.* D.Sc.Thesis, University of Pretoria, South Africa.

Condy, P. R. 1979. Annual cycle of the southern elephant seal, *Mirounga leonina* (Linn.) at Marion Island. *S. Afr. J. Zool.* **14**(2), 95–102.

Everson, I. 1977. *The living resources of the Southern Ocean.* F.A.O.GLO/SO/77/I, Rome.

Harwood, J. 1978. The effect of management policies on the stability and resilience of British grey seal populations. *J. of Appl. Ecol.* **15**, 413–21.

Harwood, J. and J. H. Prime 1978. Some factors affecting the size of British grey seal populations. *J. Appl. Ecol.* **15**, 401–411.

Hureau, J. C. 1979. La faune ichtyologique du secteur Indien de l'ocean Antarctique et estimation due stock de poisson autour des iles Kerguelen. *Mem.Mus. Natio. His. Nat.; N.S. Serie. C.* XVIII 235–47.

Hureau, J. C. and C. Ozouf-Costaz 1980. Age determination and growth of *Dissostichus elegenoides* (Smitt 1898) from Kerguelen and Crozet Islands. *Cybium. 3ème* série. **8**, 23–32.

Johnston, G. W., D. J. Lugg and D. A. Brown 1973. The biology of Vestfold Hills, Antarctica. *ANARE report.* B, **I.**

Laws, R. M. 1956. The elephant seal (*Mirounga leonina* (Linn.)) II:General, social and reproductive behaviour. *Sci. Rep. Falkland Isl. Dept. Surv.* **13**, 1–66.

Laws, R. M. 1960. The elephant seal (*Mirounga leonina* L.) at South Georgia. *Norsk Hvalfangst Tidende* **10 & 11**, 466–76 & 520–42.

Laws, R. M. 1977. Seals and whales of the Southern Ocean. *Phil. Trans. R. Soc. Lond.* B. **279**, 81–96.

Laws, R. M. 1979. Southern elephant seal. In *Mammals in the sea* Rome: FAO, Fisheries Series 5, Vol. 2.

Langlart, P. Y. and M. N. Bester 1982. Post weaning dispersion of southern elephant seal, *Mirounga leonina* (L.), underyearlings at Kerguelen. *La Terre et La Vie* **36**(2), 175–86.

MacCann, T. S. 1980. Population structure and social organisation of southern elephant seal, *Mirounga leonina* (L.). *Biol. J. of the Linnean Soc.* **14**(I), 133–50.

Nicholls, D. G. 1970. Dispersal and dispersion in relation to the birthsite of the Southern elephant seal, *Mirounga leonina* (L.), of Macquarie Island. *Mammalia* **34**(4), 598–616.

Pascal, M. 1979. Essai de denombrement de la population d'Elephant de mer (*Mirounga leonina* L.) des iles Kerguelen (49°S.; 69°E.). *Mammalia* **43**(2), 147–59.

Paulian, P. 1954. Pinnipèdes, cétacés, Oiseaux des iles Kerguelen et Amsterdam. *Mem. Inst. Sci. Madagascar.* A, **8**, 111–234.

Rand, R. W. 1955. Marion Island, home of South Africa's elephant seals. *Afr. Wildl.* **9**, 7–9.

Summers, C. F. 1978. Trends in the size of British grey seal populations. *J. of Appl. Ecol.* **15**, 395–400.

Tierney, T. J. 1977. The southern elephant seal *Mirounga leonina* (L.), in the Vestfold Hills, Antartica. *Aust. Wildl. Res.* **4**, 13–24.

Van Aarde, R. J. 1980a. Fluctuation in the population of southern elephant seal *Mirounga leonina* (L.) at Kerguelen Island. *S. Afr. J. Zool.* **15**(2), 99–106.

Van Aarde, R. J. 1980b. Harem structure of the southern elephant seal, *Mirounga leonina* L. at Kerguelen Island. *Rev. Ecol.* (Terre et Vie) **34**, 41–4.

Van Aarde, R. J. and M. Pascal 1980. Marking southern elephant seal on Iles Kerguelen. *Polar Records* **20**, 62–5.

12 Sea-otters and shellfisheries

James A. Estes and Glenn R. VanBlaricom

Introduction

Competition between humans and marine mammals for exploitation of the world's fishery resources is an issue of increasing concern. However, the consequences of these interactions remain largely undocumented from both biological and economic standpoints. This is mainly because of the immense logistical difficulties in studying the habitats where marine mammals typically feed. For example, all but a few species feed on the high seas, either in the water column or the deep benthos where their prey species are often patchily distributed, highly mobile, or both. Therefore, the prey communities of most marine mammal species are inaccessible, and their distributions unpredictable in space and time, thus making in-situ observations difficult and field experiments nearly impossible.

The sea-otter (*Enhydra lutris*) provides a notable exception to this troublesome situation. Sea-otters prey on benthic invertebrate species that inhabit shallow coastal waters of the temperate and boreal north Pacific region, most of which are sessile or weakly motile. Thus the system is accessible, observable, describable, and amenable to experimental study. These qualities have been instrumental in placing coastal marine communities among the most successfully utilised arenas of basic ecological research.

Recent historical events have added further to our understanding of how sea-otters influence benthic communities. Before the mid-1700s, otters probably occurred in most shallow habitats through the temperate and boreal north Pacific. During that time, populations of abalones, clams, crabs, and perhaps other invertebrate forms, were probably limited largely by the effective nature of sea-otter predation. Subsequently, overexploitation of sea-otters through the 18th and 19th centuries not only eliminated the otters but their ecological rôle as well, so that, by earlier standards, dense populations of their invertebrate prey developed. These high-density prey populations in turn encouraged the development of numerous commercial and recreational shellfisheries as the west coast of North America became increasingly populated and industrialised. Then, following their protection in 1911, sea-otter populations began to recover. In some areas (most notably central California) the expanding range of sea-otter populations came into direct conflict with shellfisheries. As sea-otters drove their prey populations downward toward earlier levels, certain local shellfisheries were driven to extinction.

During the past few decades, two quite different perspectives of sea-otter predation have emerged. One is purely ecological and concerns the intricate network of organisational processes whereby nearshore communities are influenced by sea otters as consumers. The other is social and economic, and has arisen through exploitation competition between sea otters and humans for shellfish resources.

This Chapter will consist of three parts. First, there is a review of the salient features of the biology of sea otters and the ecological consequences of sea-otter predation. (This section will be brief since much has already been written on the subject.) Next, a consideration of the interactions between sea-otters and shellfisheries beginning, in each instance, with a summary of the relevant biological characteristics of the species involved in the fisheries. Then follows a discussion of the current status of fisheries for the species. Where conflicts with otters have already occurred, the supporting evidence is presented and evaluated. Where they have not yet occurred because of non-overlapping distributions with sea otters, we speculate on the likelihood of future conflicts should these distributions eventually overlap one another. Last, some general conclusions are drawn concerning the interaction between sea-otters and shellfisheries deriving from comparisons across species or between geographical areas.

Biology and ecology of sea otters

Sea-otters of the genus *Enhydriodon*, not greatly dissimilar from the extant species (*Enhydra lutris*), are known from the late Miocene (Repenning 1976). These early forms were widely distributed in the Northern Hemisphere. *Enhydra* apparently arose in the North Pacific Ocean some time during the early Pleistocene. It has never ranged beyond that area.

At the time of the arrival of Europeans in the North Pacific, sea otters occurred from the northern Japanese archipelago to the central coast of Baja California (Kenyon 1969). Through most of the Pleistocene, it is likely that they were abundant wherever rocky or soft-sediment habitats offered them suitable food resources. There is evidence that aboriginal people limited otter populations, but this probably occurred only near village sites (Simenstad *et al.* 1978). More extensive exploitation began with the arrival of European fur traders, resulting in near extinction of the species by the beginning of this century. Subsequently, under the protection of an international treaty and, more recently, national and local laws, populations have grown in range and numbers.

Recovery of populations has been most complete in Alaska and the Soviet Union, where much of the aboriginal range is now reoccupied (Estes 1980, Johnson 1982). A translocated population has been established in south-eastern Alaska. Of more tenuous status are small, translocated populations in British Columbia and Washington State. A similar translocated population in southern Oregon is extinct (Jameson *et al.* 1982). The California population has grown slowly during most of the 20th century. It presently ranges from Santa Cruz to Pismo Beach and numbers about 1300 animals (J. A. Estes & R. J. Jameson, unpublished). Apparently the California population has not grown in numbers over the past decade (US Fish and Wildlife Service 1982). Because of the sensitivity of sea-otters to oil contamination, the presence of offshore petroleum development and transport in California caused the designation of the resident sea-otter population as 'threatened' (Greenwalt 1977).

Sea-otters forage in the rocky and soft-bottom benthos, from the lower littoral zones to depths of at least 55 fathoms (Newby 1975). In most areas, the majority of foraging dives seem to occur to depths less than 20 fathoms (Kenyon 1969, Estes *et al.* 1981). Many prey species are consumed, most of which are molluscs, echinoderms, and crustaceans. Fish are also important prey in some parts of the Aleutian, Commander, and Kurile islands, but not in California.

Sea-otters are effective predators and limit many of their prey populations with remarkable success, which is largely due to their great mobility compared with the sluggish or sessile nature of most of their prey. Indeed, the only ways in which most prey species can escape from otter predation are by taking refuge in cracks and crevices in rocky substrata (Lowry & Pearse 1973), or by taking advantage of their small size, deep water, or some combination thereof. This interaction appears to have numerous and far-reaching consequences to the organisation of coastal marine communities. Perhaps the most well documented of these comes from studies in Alaska where one of the principal effects of sea-otter predation is to limit the intensity of grazing of kelp by herbivorous sea urchins (Estes & Palmisano 1974, Duggins 1980). The broader consequences of these interactions to coastal food webs are less clearly understood, although they are probably both numerous and important. Most of these consequences appear to result from the physical structure or biological productivity of kelp. For example, kelps serve to nourish or protect numerous species inhabitating the coastal zone. From an energetic standpoint alone, kelp appears to be the major contributor to rocky coastal systems. The mere presence of dense beds of surface-canopy-forming kelps can have a substantial limiting influence on the intensity of wave shock which eventually reaches the shore, in turn influencing the structure and organisation of littoral communities (Palmisano & Estes 1977).

The effectiveness with which sea-otters limit grazing by sea urchins has been clearly demonstrated as far south as Point Buchon, California, in the eastern North Pacific. Interactions of the same general kind probably occur, or could occur, even further to the south. Indeed, 'urchin barrens', as Lawrence (1975) has referred to localities from which kelp has been stripped by sea urchins, are known from outside the sea-otters' range as far south as northern Baja, California. Although these barren areas are not so widespread there as they are further to the north, they could never have developed in the presence of sea-otters.

To conclude this section, we summarise two accounts of the complex ways in which sea otters may influence coastal community organisation. The first is from the western Aleutian Islands and concerns the way in which the otters' effect on their prey community influences their own behaviour (Estes *et al.* 1982). By limiting populations of sea urchins, sea-otters: (a) reduce the availability of their invertebrate prey resources, and (b) stimulate the development of kelp assemblages and associated populations of kelp bed fishes. These changes in prey resources bring about a shift in the otter's diet, from one which consists entirely of invertebrates to one which consists of invertebrates and fish. The addition of fish to their diet seems to enhance the abundance of otters to levels significantly above those which would be possible on a diet of invertebrates alone. Furthermore, it causes the otters to alter their foraging behaviour radically. That is, where their diet consists solely of invertebrates, they invest a relatively small amount of time foraging during daylight hours, and they distribute that effort uniformly over time. However, where fish are important prey items, they invest substantially more time in foraging, and distribute that effort disproportionately toward dawn and dusk to correspond with those times when fish are most vulnerable to predation.

The second account comes from central California, where the surface kelp canopy is composed mainly of two species, *Macrocystis pyrifera* (a perennial) and *Nereocystis leutkeana* (an annual). Historical reconstruction of the distribution of kelp, based on maps prepared at various times from the early part of this century, indicate a general expansion of kelp beds in various areas subsequent to the range expansion of sea-otters (VanBlaricom & Jameson 1979, VanBlaricom 1984, G. R. VanBlaricom, unpublished data). Furthermore, the overall trend has included a change in canopy composition –

from *Nereocystis* to *Macrocystis* – over these same areas and times. These changes are thought to have resulted from a reduction in the intensity of herbivory, brought about by otter predation. That is, in the absence of otters, grazing by sea urchins both limited the distribution of kelp beds and favoured *Nereocystis* as an annual species. Following the re-establishment of otters in any particular area, herbivory was essentially eliminated and the kelp beds expanded in size. Furthermore, *Macrocystis* survival was probably increased, which, in conjunction with its perennial life history, perhaps allowed it to inhibit competitively or exclude *Nereocystis* in many areas. Although anecdotal, the model makes good intuitive sense and there is now experimental evidence to support the proposed competitive mechanisms (G. R. VanBlaricom, unpublished data).

Equally intriguing stories undoubtedly will be discovered in time. Indeed, the influences of sea-otters on coastal communities are so dramatic and far reaching that ecological and evolutionary interpretations of these systems can scarcely be made without considering them.

Fishery conflicts

Sea otters are of varying importance to fisheries for each of the subsequently discussed species. In some instances, such as for abalones and Pismo clams, the problem has been acute and widely publicised. In others, such as for spiny lobsters, the problems are merely anticipated pending further range expansion of sea otters. In still others, there is neither biological evidence nor the human perception of a conflict, even though the species may co-occur with and be consumed by sea-otters. The order in which we present the following case studies is arbitrarily taxonomic, molluscs being first, crustaceans second, and echinoderms last. The detail given to each species largely reflects our perception of the severity of existing or potential fishery conflicts with sea-otters.

Dungeness crab: *Cancer magister* (Dana)

Biology and fishery

Dungeness crabs range fom around Point Conception, California, north to the Aleutian Islands (Dahlstrom & Wild 1983). Mating in California occurs from about March through June. Sperm are stored by the females until about October when the females spawn and the eggs are fertilised. One to two million fertilised eggs are carried by the females until December or January, at which time they hatch into planktonic larvae. During the early zoeal stages, the larvae migrate vertically in the water column, and although little is known of their movements at this stage, apparently they are carried seaward and northward by the Davidson Current (Reilly 1983). The larval stages last from 125 to 130 days. The megalopae (the final larval stage) become concentrated in certain areas close to shore where they settle and metamorphose to the young crab stage. The crabs molt 11 to 15 times during their 2–6-year lifespan (Program Staff 1983).

The commercial fishery for Dungeness crab began in the San Francisco area in 1848 (Dahlstrom & Wild 1983). By 1892, 1 250 000 kg of crab were landed in California (all of which were from the area near San Francisco Bay). A prohibition against the taking of female crabs was imposed in 1897, and size limits were begun in 1905. Fisheries further to the north developed with new technology and increasing market demands.

For example, significant catches in northern California began about 1935, thereafter increasing to make up the majority of the state's catch by 1945. Fishing presently occurs in waters from 4 m to 90 m in depth – most commonly between 36 m and 65 m.

In California, the major commercial fishing areas occur from Half Moon Bay to Bodega Bay, and from Cape Mendicino to the Oregon border. Smaller fisheries exist near Morro Bay, in Monterey Bay, and near Fort Bragg. Heavy fishing occurs along the entire coast of the State of Oregon, except for small areas near Cape Blanco and south of Cascade Head. In Washington, Dungeness crab fishing extends from the Columbia River to Destruction Island. The fishery is scattered in British Columbia, occurring in various bays and inlets throughout the province. The major fishery area in British Columbia is near Hecate Strait. Commercial fishing is also scattered throughout south-east and south central Alaska, extending westward along the Alaska Peninsula to near Sandman Reefs.

Dungeness crab landings undergo distinct cycles at about 10-year intervals. Since 1954, total landings have ranged between about 7 and 30 million kg/year (Table 12.1). It was recently demonstrated that fluctuations in total landings show a remarkable correlation with mean annual sunspot number (Love & Westphal 1981). In general, the cyclical fluctuations in landings appear to be most pronounced at the southern end of the fisheries' range. Temporally, cyclical patterns in crab landings in California, Oregon, and Washington are well correlated. Landings in Alaska are less distinctly cyclic and not correlated with those farther to the south. Cyclical patterns are not apparent in landings' data from British Columbia. In part, landings' fluctuations in Alaska are influenced by market conditions to the south (Kimker 1981). That is, there is increased incentive to fish in Alaska during periods when landings elsewhere are depressed.

South of Point Arena, Dungeness crab landings failed in the early 1960s, and remain depressed at present. The failure followed a change in oceanographic conditions, most notably an increased warming and intensification of the Davidson Current (Wild *et al*. 1983). Laboratory studies have shown that although elevated water temperatures of the observed range increase growth rates of fertilised crab eggs, they also cause a substantial decline in survival (Wild 1983). Intensification of the Davidson Current may also have caused crab larvae to drift further northward.

Failure of the fishery has been attributed to other causes or contributing factors as well. For example, the nemertean worm (*Carcinonemertes errans*) has been found in a high percentage of crab egg masses (Wickham 1979a). Egg parasitism, together with heavy human exploitation, are thought to produce population cycles of increasing amplitude (Botsford & Wickham 1978) which may have led to the eventual collapse of the central California crab fishery (Wickham 1979b). Increased pollution of San

Table 12.1 Ranges in reported commercial landings of Dungeness crab by state or province.

Location	Landings (kg/year)	
	Minimum	Maximum
California	0.4	9.8
Oregon	1.2	6.7
Washington	2.0	7.9
British Columbia	1.2	2.0
Alaska	0.8	5.1

Francisco Bay, the major nursery area for young crabs, has also occurred over the appropriate time period, as has increased predation by hatchery-reared salmon on the megalopae. Although the fishery probably has been intensively exploited, overexploitation does not appear to have caused its failure directly, since males only are caught, and female impregnation rates have remained high and independent of male landings (Dahlstrom & Wild 1983).

Interactions with sea-otters

A conflict between sea otters and the Dungeness crab fishery developed recently in Orca Inlet, eastern Prince William Sound, Alaska. Landings in Prince William Sound declined initially following the 1964 earthquake, due to reductions in the extent of sublittoral habitat and prey abundance which were caused by tectonic shifts in elevation (Kimker 1982a). Some recovery was expected, based on a strong recruitment of juvenile crabs in 1978. However, in 1980 the fishery was not opened due to a low preseason crab abundance. This coincided with about 180 sea-otters moving into the area in the process of their natural range expansion (Kimker 1982b). On the basis of this evidence, there may be a substantial potential for conflict between sea-otters and the Dungeness crab fishery along much of the Pacific coast of North America. At a present ex-vessel price of something more than $2.20 per kg, the economic consequences of this conflict could range into the tens of millions of dollars per year, far exceeding the potential loss from sea-otter depredation on any other shellfishery.

Rock Crabs: *Cancer* spp.

Biology and fishery

Three broadly sympatric species are known collectively as rock crabs: *Cancer antennarius* (Stimpson), *C. anthony* (Rathbun), and *C. productus* (Randall). Rock crabs range from Alaska to Baja California, Mexico, and overlap with much of the original range of sea otters (Morris *et al*. 1980). *Cancer antennarius* is the most abundant rock crab in shallow waters of the exposed rocky coast of California where sea-otters presently occur (Carroll 1982). *C. antennarius* ranges from Oregon to Baja (Morris *et al*. 1980).

The life histories of rock crabs are generally similar to that of the Dungeness crab, *Cancer magister* (see above). Major differences include a preference for a rocky substrate and, for *C. antennarius*, presence of ovigerous females in all seasons of the year (Carroll 1982).

Annual commercial landings for rock crabs in California averaged about 80 000 kg from 1950 to 1970, increasing to 545 000 kg by 1975 (Hardy *et al*. 1982). Rock crabs are also taken by recreational fishermen, primarily with baited hoop nets and traps set from piers, jetties, and skiffs. The recreational fishery seems to be fairly large, but landings data are not available. The total fishery for rock crabs is thought to be near maximum sustainable yield (Hardy *et al*. 1982).

Interaction with sea-otters

Cancer antennarius is one of the most important foods for sea-otters in California (Wild & Ames 1974, Estes *et al*. 1981). However, the impact of sea-otters on rock crab fisheries is not clear. A small (1 fisherman) commercial harvest of *C antennarius* survives in Estera Bay in spite of the presence of sea-otters in the area (Hardy *et al*.

1982). Rock crabs are regularly taken by sport fishermen at several locations within the range of sea-otters in California.

Populations of *C. antennarius* were studied near Diablo Canyon, California, from 1976 to 1981 (Carroll 1982). Sea-otters were present during the entire study and frequently ate rock crabs near sampling stations. Based on catch per unit effort in bimonthly trap samples, numbers declined gradually from 1976 (7–16 crabs/trap-day) until January 1981 (2–4 crabs/trap-day), but then increased somewhat (4–6 crabs/trap-day) until the study was terminated in April 1981. Since long-term population data are generally not available for rock crabs, it is not possible to determine if the trends described by Carroll are part of a cyclical pattern of the kind seen for *Cancer magister*, or are a result of the cumulative effects of sea-otters.

However, it seems that the effects of sea-otters on harvestable stocks of rock crabs are far less precipitous than those on abalone, sea urchins, or Pismo clams. We suggest that certain behavioural traits of rock crabs may account for the difference. Rock crabs are quite cryptic, especially during daylight hours when they generally are immobile and remain in deep crevices. The utilisation of such refuges probably reduces the efficiency of otter foraging and may contribute to the survival of harvestable stocks in the presence of sea-otters. Other explanations are plausible, however, and there is much to be learned about interactions between sea-otters and rock crabs.

California spiny lobster: *Panulirus interruptus* (Randall, 1840)

Biology and fishery
Spiny lobsters are common in the southern portion of the aboriginal range of the sea otter in North America. Lobsters typically occupy rock substrata at depths of 0–75 m along the open coast, often in association with kelp forests. Lobsters are also found in embayments, rock jetties, surf grass beds, and submarine canyons.

The life history of *Panulirus interruptus* has been summarised by Frey (1971). In California, spiny lobsters typically mate in winter or early spring. Females carry the sperm packet on the ventral surface of the abdomen. Eggs are fertilised at the time of extrusion – usually May or June. Fertilised eggs are carried by the abdominal appendages until hatching, about 10 weeks after fertilisation. Egg production increases with female size; large females may produce up to 800 000 eggs. Hatched phyllosoma larvae are capable of long-range dispersal in the plankton. The phyllosome phase is followed by a deeper-dwelling puerulus which in turn metamorphoses to the adult form.

Growth is typically slow in spiny lobsters. Females mature at age 4–5 years (Mitchell *et al.* 1969). The legal size for harvest is reached in 10–11 years (Frey 1971). Lobsters are omnivorous, feeding on sea urchins, mussels, clams, polychaetes, and various other living and dead organic matter.

Spiny lobsters range from Monterey, California, to Bahia Magdalena, Baja California Sur, Mexico, and an isolated population occurs in the northern Golfo de California (Duffy 1973). There are few recorded sightings of spiny lobsters in Monterey Bay (Schmitt 1921, Faro 1970). The northernmost populations currently known occur at Cayucos Point, Shell Beach, and Point Sal, California. These populations are known only from anecdotal information and appear to be small. Commercial harvesting of spiny lobsters presently occurs from Purisima Point, California, southward to Laguna San Ignacio, Baja California Sur (Guzman del Proo 1975, Barrera *et al.* 1976, California Department of Fish and Game 1976). In California, the best fishing grounds for spiny lobster are the offshore islands and the mainland from Point La Jolla to Point

Loma in San Diego county (Duffy 1973). The bulk of the Mexican harvest comes from the offshore islands and the central Pacific coast of the Baja California peninsula (Guzman del Proo 1975). Lobsters are taken by sport fishermen from Cayucos Point southward in California. The size of the sport harvest is poorly documented (Duffy 1973), but is apparently small relative to the commercial harvest (Hardy *et al*. 1982).

Commercial landings of spiny lobsters in California peaked in the late 1940s, then declined steadily until 1977 (Fig. 12.1a). For 1968–77, annual landings averaged about 120 000 kg/year, about one-third of the figure for 1948–57, in spite of increased fishing effort and consumer demand (Heimann & Carlisle 1970, Pinkas 1970, 1974, 1977, Bell 1971, Duffy 1973, Oliphant 1973, 1979, McAllister 1975, 1976, Hardy *et al*. 1982, California Department of Fish and Game, unpublished). Declining landings were attributed to overexploitation of lobster stocks, particularly as a result of poaching and illicit capture of animals below the minimum size limit (Duffy 1973, Duffy, personal communication, Hardy *et al*. 1982). As a result, fishery laws were changed in 1972, requiring escape ports in all lobster pots so that undersize animals could escape before

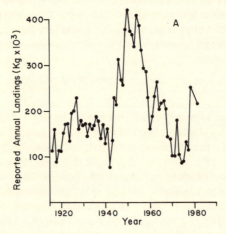

Figure 12.1a Commercial landings of spiny lobster (*Panulirus interruptus*) in California, 1916–78 and 1981 (data for 1979 and 1980 not available.) (From California Department of Fish and Game.)

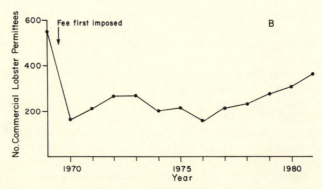

Figure 12.1b Numbers of permittees for commercial lobster harvesting in California, 1961–81 (From California Department of Fish and Game.)

the pots were pulled to the surface. Annual landings increased to 254 000 kg in 1978 and 217 000 kg in 1981 (California Department of Fish and Game, unpublished). Increased landings probably resulted from the modified pot design, although the relationship has not been unambiguously established (Duffy, personal communication). A lag of 5–6 years between the imposition of escape-port regulations and increased landings is consistent with known growth rates of spiny lobsters in California, and the size distribution of lobsters at the time regulations were changed.

The numbers of commercial fishermen with state lobster permits dropped markedly in 1970 when fees were first charged for permits. But the numbers of permits began to increase again in the late 1970s (Fig. 12.1b), apparently in response to the increased success of other fishermen (Duffy, personal communication).

In Mexico, annual landings rose from 752 000 kg in 1959 to 1.3 million kg in 1966, and have varied little since that time (Fig. 12.2).

Interaction with sea-otters
There is concern that continued southward expansion of the sea-otter population in California will damage the lobster fisheries (California Department of Fish and Game 1976, Hardy *et al.* 1982). At present, however, there is very little data on which to base predictions of interactions between spiny lobsters and sea-otters. Four captive sea-otters caught and ate 10 live spiny lobsters over a period of 5 hours (Antonelis *et al.* 1981). The extent to which such data apply to natural foraging abilities of sea-otters is unknown. In a field study of sea-otter foraging near Point Lobos, California, 3 of 455 prey items taken were reported to be spiny lobsters (Hall & Schaller 1964). Boolootian (1965) also observed occasional takes of lobsters by sea otters in the Monterey area. These observations are also difficult to interpret, in terms of potential fishery conflicts, because they occurred so far north of commercially significant populations of spiny lobsters. Faro (1970) has suggested that other prey items, such as crabs, were erroneously identified as spiny lobsters by Hall and Schaller and Boolootian.

The potential impact of sea-otters on natural lobster populations is clearly an open question. Spiny lobsters hide in crevices or caves during daylight hours. Other invertebrates which use such microhabitats are protected from consumption by sea-otters (Lowry & Pearse 1973). Lobsters emerge at night, but are capable of swimming rapidly

Figure 12.2 Commercial landing of spiny lobsters (*Panulirus interruptus*) along the Pacific coast of Baja California, Mexico, 1959–73. (From Guzman del Proo 1975.)

and forcefully when disturbed. Sea-otters appear to have limited effects on mobile or nocturnal prey. Those at Amchitka Island, Alaska, eat sluggish epibenthic fish with some regularity, primarily at dawn and dusk when the fish are inefficient at escaping predators (Estes *et al*. 1982). However, there is no evidence that fish populations have been depleted by sea-otters at Amchitka or elsewhere. Finally, spiny lobsters migrate to greater depths (> 15 m) during autumn, returning to shoaler bottoms in spring and early summer (Mitchell *et al*. 1969, Duffy 1973). The efficiency of foraging by sea otters clearly declines with increasing water depth, and preferred prey may be abundant below a depth of 15–18 m (Estes *et al*. 1978).

Spiny lobster distribution presently overlaps sea-otter range only at Cayucos Point and Shell Beach, California. Sea otters have not been seen eating lobsters at either site. Anecdotal evidence suggests recent declines in lobster numbers at both sites, but there is no quantitative basis for implicating sea-otter foraging as a cause. The use of spatial and temporal refuges may allow spiny lobster populations to coexist with sea-otters, but this possibility cannot be evaluated on the basis of existing data. It appears that overexploitation, habitual disregard for the minimum size limit, and changing fishery regulations account for at least part of the historical between-year variation in commercial landings of spiny lobsters in California. Much of the life history of spiny lobsters is poorly understood, however, and it is simply not possible to offer confident predictions regarding effects of sea-otters on lobster fisheries, should the two come into contact.

Abalone (*Haliotis* spp.)

Biology and fishery
The abalones (genus *Haliotis*) are a group of archeogastropods whose fossil record dates back to the upper Cretaceous. Modern forms are broadly distributed from subarctic to tropical seas (Cox 1962). There are eight extant species in the north-east Pacific Ocean, the geographical ranges of which are shown in Table 12.2. Commercial fisheries exist for all these species, although flat abalone and threaded abalone are rarely taken.

Abalones are broadcast spawners with planktotrophic larvae (Webber 1977). In California, spawning, although reported in all months (Boolootian *et al*. 1962, Young

Table 12.2 Geographical distribution of abalone species along the west coast of North America.

Species		Range from north	to south
pinto	(*Haliotus kamtschatkana*)	Southeast Alaska	Poiint Sur, California
flat	(*H. walallensis*)	British Columbia	La Jolla, California
red	(*H. rufescens*)	Sunset Bay, Oregon	Bahia Tortuga, Baja California
black	(*H. cracherodii*)	Coos Bay, Oregon	Cabo San Lucas, Baja California
pink	(*H. corrugata*)	Point Conception, California	Bahia Tortuga, Baja California
green	(*H. fulgens*)	Point Conception, California	Bahia Magdalena, Baja California
white	(*H. sorensenii*)	Point Conception, California	Bahia Tortuga, Baja California
threaded	(*H. assimilis*)	Point Conception, California	Bahia Tortuga, Baja California

& DiMartini 1970), occurs mainly from late spring to early fall (Cox 1962). The fertilised eggs form veliger larvae which probably remain in the plankton for a week or less
(Webber 1977). Settlement may be induced by gamma-aminobutyric acid and its
chemical analogues (Morse *et al*. 1979), substances which occur naturally in certain
species of crustose red algae. Following metamorphosis to the adult form, growth rate
seems to vary greatly among individuals (Cox 1962). Longevity is unknown; individuals
probably have the potential to live many years.

Aboriginal fisheries for abalones have existed for at least 7000 years (Orr 1960). In
California and Baja California, modern fisheries began in the mid-1800s with Chinese
pole fishermen. The early fishery was limited to the littoral and shallow sublittoral
zones by virtue of the fact that the fishermen did not dive. Abalones spotted from the
surface were dislodged and retrieved with poles and hooks. Apparently the pole fishery
depleted shallow-water populations. For that reason, the fishery was effectively
eliminated by regulations imposed by Baja California in 1880 and by the United States
in 1900. Japanese divers subsequently dominated the fishery until World War II.

Before World War II, the fishery in California was limited exclusively to red abalone.
It was centered in Monterey until about 1930, switching thereafter to Morro Bay and
expanding southward to southern California after the war. With the advent of rubber
diving suits, the fishery also moved into deeper water after the war. British Columbia
and Alaska support commercial fisheries for pinto abalones. These fisheries greatly
intensified in the mid-1970s in response to the development of a Japanese market.
There have never been commercial abalone fisheries in Oregon or Washington.

The Mexican abalone fishery occurs exclusively within the historical range of the sea-
otter. Baja California Sur currently produces about 80% of the landings (Anonymous
1978). There are four management zones for abalone in Baja California (see Luch
Belda *et al*. 1973 for map of zone boundaries), from which five species are exploited.
Landings data are available by zone from 1956 (we have been unable to obtain zone-
specific data subsequent to 1970). Overall, the fishery reached maximum production in
about 1950, at around 6 million kg per year (Luch Belda *et al*., 1973, Guzman del Proo
1975), followed by a sharp decline to about 3 million kg per year by 1955 (Fig. 12.3a).
Landings continued to decline, reaching about 2 million kg per year by 1974. Around
4 million kg were landed in 1978 (Anonymous 1978). Red abalone are common only
in Zone I (Table 12.3). White abalone also comprise a significant part of the landings
in this zone. Pink and green abalone comprise the bulk of reported landings in the other
three zones.

Landings in Zone I reached a maximum of about 450 000 kg per year in 1957,
declined to near zero in 1964, and then increased to about 150 000 kg per year in 1970.
Landings in Zone II reached a maximum of about 1.5 million kg per year in 1956, then
declined to about 900 000 kg per year by 1970. Zone III contains a younger fishery than
zones I or II. It produced maximum landings (about 2 million kg per year) in the early
1960s, followed by a moderate decline. Zone IV contains the youngest fishery. It began
at about 500 000 kg per year in 1956 and increased slowly to about 700 000 kg per year
in 1971. At that time there was no evidence of a decline in landings, although the catch
now appears to be composed mostly of small individuals.

In addition to these patterns of growth and decline in the fisheries, analyses of CPUE
and size composition of landed abalones support the view that stocks in Baja California
have been overexploited. For example, at Isla de Cedros (Zone II), landings of pink
and green abalones declined from 165 kg/diver per day in 1964 to 105 kg/diver per day
in 1975. At Punta Abreojos (Zone IV), the catch per unit effort declined from

(a)

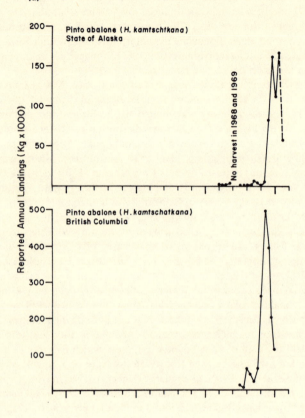

Pinto abalone (*H. kamtschtkana*)
State of Alaska

No harvest in 1968 and 1969

Pinto abalone (*H. kamtschatkana*)
British Columbia

Reported Annual Landings (Kg x 1000)

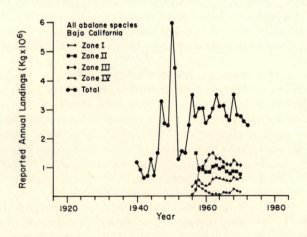

Reported Annual Landings (Kg x 10⁶)

All abalone species
Baja California

⊢—⊣ Zone I
■—■ Zone II
◆—◆ Zone III
▲—▲ Zone IV
●—● Total

Year

(b)

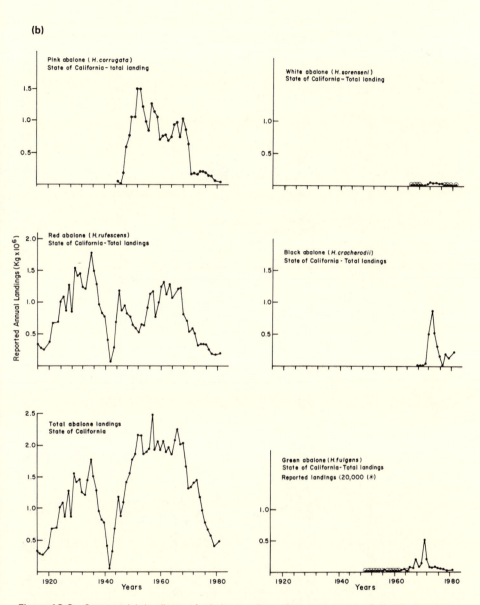

Figure 12.3 Commercial landings of abalones along the west coast of North America, 1916–81. (a) Mexico, British Columbia and Alaska; (b) California. (From: Mexico, Luch Belda *et al*. 1973; California, Cox 1962 and California Department of Fish and Game; British Columbia, Breen 1980 and Bernard 1982; Alaska, Koeneman 1982.)

Table 12.3 Size and species composition of the abalone fishery in Mexico in 1972 (after Luch Belda et al. 1973).[a]

	Species of abalone											
	H. corrugata		H. fulgens		H. rufescens		H. cracherodii		H. sorensenii		H. walallensis	
zone	% of landings	% below legal size	% of landings	% below legal size	% of landings	% below legal size	% of landings	% below legal size	% of landings	% below legal size	% of landings	% below legal size
I	19.6	38.1	4.1	41.6	36.1	25.6	0	—	39.4	25.9	0.7	0
II	53.3	64.9	41.1	52.5	0	—	11.5	0	1.8	17.2	0	—
III	68.5	73.4	18.4	62.7	0	—	2.9	0	12.1	53.4	0	—
V	91.6	94.8	8.3	74.8	0	—	0	—	0	—	0	—

[a]Original data were separated by month, but sample sizes were not indicated. Above values were obtained by averaging percentages across months.

90 kg/diver per day to 60 kg/diver per day during the same period (Doi *et al.* 1977). For all species of abalones in all areas, animals below minimum legal size make up a substantial portion of the landings (generally between 40% and 80% of the catch – (Table 12.3). In Zone IV, where annual landings had not declined by 1971, nearly the entire catch was below minimum legal size in 1972.

Landings data for abalone from California show similar patterns (Fig. 12.3b). Total landings increased gradually from the early part of this century until about 1950, except for a sharp decline during World War II. The catch subsequently levelled off at between 1.8 and 2.3 million kg per year, until the late 1960s when it began to decline to its present level of about 700 000 kg per year.

On the basis of individual species, red and pink abalones constituted the bulk of reported commercial landings (more than 90%) throughout the 1960s. Both began to decline sharply in 1967 or 1968. At about the same time, landings of less desirable species (blacks, greens, or whites) increased abruptly. Expansion of the fishery to include these species was responsible for the brief recovery in total landings between 1968 and 1973. However, in 1974 total landings again began to decline rapidly as the catch of blacks and greens peaked and fell. A decline in total landings continues to the present time.

The fishery for pinto abalone in British Columbia greatly intensified in 1976 (Fig. 12.3a). Landings reached a peak of just under 500 000 kg in 1977, then declined rapidly to about 100 000 kg by 1980 (Bernard 1982). During the same period, catch per unit effort declined from 205 kg/diver per day to 137 kg/diver per day (Bernard 1982). Consistent with these declines, Breen (1980) estimated that standing stocks of legal-sized abalones (i.e. 101 mm or greater in shell diameter) have decreased by between 60% and 75% (up to 90% in some areas) from pre-harvest levels.

The history of the Alaska fishery for pinto abalone is nearly identical to that of British Columbia (Koeneman 1982). Landings remained less than 10 000 kg per year from 1964 through 1977, increasing by 1979 to just under 160 000 kg (Fig. 12.3a). Anticipating the fisheries collapse, the State of Alaska imposed a quota of 100 000 kg in 1980; in 1981, this was further reduced to 50 000 kg (T. Koeneman, personal communication). Further restriction of take was imposed in 1982 by a season closure of just under 11 months. Koeneman (personal communication) estimates sustained yield at between 20 000 and 40 000 kg per year.

From the preceding discussions, it is evident that rapid increases, and, eventually, rapid declines in reported commercial landings are a feature common to all abalone fisheries in the eastern North Pacific. Reasons for the declines may be ascribed to one or more of the following: (a) poor fishery practices; (b) habitat degradation; (c) reduction in the intensity of fishing effort; (d) regulation changes; and (e) increased depredation by natural predators. In some instances, these causes are interdependent. Although existing data are insufficient to make definitive judgements, in each case certain causes can be eliminated, or implicated, so as to show recurrent patterns among the fisheries.

Interaction with sea-otters

Originally, the fishery for red abalone was centered in Morro Bay. Its failure has commonly been attributed to depredation by the sea-otter. The California Department of Fish and Game has maintained records of commercial abalone landings by catch block, and, theoretically, these data should show declines as sea otters expanded their range into areas occupied by the fishery. However, fishermen apparently did not adhere to accurate reporting, so that early in the period during which otters are thought to have depressed the commercial fishery, many fishermen simply worked further to the south while continuing to report landings from their original catch blocks. Later, as they became aware of the problems this was creating in data interpretation, there was a rapid shift in the location of reported landings. Consequently the data do not provide an accurate view of how sea-otters influenced the fishery. In this specific instance it is difficult to separate the effects of sea-otters from the effects of human exploitation, although it seems likely that otters contributed substantially both to the rate and to the extent of the fisheries' collapse.

Populations of black abalone in central California are also thought to have been greatly reduced by sea-otter predation. Again, unfortunately, the history of this fishery is difficult to interpret, except in a general way. There has never been a commercial fishery for black abalone in central California, and since records are not kept of sport landings, documentation of population declines following range expansion of sea otters is mainly a subjective one. There are stretches of private coast south of the Big Sur area from which the public has been largely excluded. These areas supported abundant standing stocks of black abalone before the arrival of sea-otters. Because most of the populations declined following the arrival of sea-otters, it has been inferred that otter predation was the principal cause (E. E. Ebert, personal communication).

Perhaps the most objective analysis of the sea-otter's influence on populations of red abalones comes from habitat survey data obtained by the California Department of Fish and Game in the Point Estero region. From 1965 to 1967, abalone density in this area ranged from about 0.075 to 0.085 individuals/m^2. After sea otters reoccupied the area, red abalone density declined to about 0.01 individuals/m^2 (Wild & Ames 1974).

Collectively, these data and observations leave little doubt that sea-otters have eliminated or hastened the decline of certain abalone fisheries. However, the history of abalone fisheries from outside of the sea-otters' range in California (i.e. commercial fisheries for pink, green, white, and black abalones) and elsewhere (Canada and Mexico) demonstrates that other factors have also been important. Among these, commercial exploitation was probably the most important. In retrospect, it seems unfair to place the blame for this solely on poor management practices because abalone appear to possess life history characteristics which make them especially susceptible to over-exploitation (Harrison 1969, Sainsbury 1977, Breen 1980). Initial landings were probably all composed of accumulated stocks of old individuals. Consequently, initial catch characteristics were in no way indicative of their sustainable productivity (Breen 1980).

Since abalones appear to be long-lived, slow-growing species, high initial rates of human exploitation quickly drove the fisheries to the left side of their yield–biomass curves (i.e. beyond MSY). It is not surprising, therefore, that the commercial fishery never persisted long in any given area, since it was not economically feasible for it to do so. This point is exemplified by the extremely concentrated nature of fishing effort at any specific time in the recent history of the fishery. For example, when Bissell and Hubbard (1968) reported on the status of the red abalone fishery in California, 59% of the commercial landings (composing 32% of the total statewide) were from Morro Bay. At that time, 70% of the Morro Bay landings (22% of the total state landings) came from about 9 miles of coastline between Point Estero and Cambria.

As might be expected of such fisheries, perturbations which influenced catch availability also produced immediate and dramatic effects on reported landings. The two most obvious of these perturbations were depredations by sea-otters and regulation changes. The influence of regulation changes can be clearly seen in several instances. For example, in 1959, when the minimum legal size for commercial take of red abalone was reduced from 20.3 cm to 19.7 cm (maximum shell diameter), landings increased sharply. In 1971, minimum legal size for green abalone was reduced from 18.4 cm to 17.8 cm. This resulted in a substantial increase in landings of green abalone initially, although since growth rate in this species is thought to be very low as individuals approach minimum legal size (E. E. Ebert, personal communication), landings declined again after the largest size-class was reduced. The sharp reduction in landings of pink abalone in 1971 was mainly the result of increasing the minimum size limit from 15.25 cm to 15.9 cm. If abalone populations were being exploited at levels such that they existed on the right slope of their yield–biomass curves (i.e. exploitation rate < than MSY), perturbations of these types would not be expected to have such extreme and immediate effects on the fishery.

To complicate matters, the following factors contribute to the difficulties in managing abalone fisheries at the desired level of MSY (Hardy *et al*. 1982).

(a) Although largely undocumented, there seems to be a great deal of geographical variation in growth rate and recruitment success, even within species. In fact, substantial variation of these factors frequently occurs over very short distances (E. E. Ebert, personal communication). In some areas, abalones appear to recruit infrequently. Yet, due to their long life span, large standing stocks accumulated over the years before exploitation, consequently producing high initial yields but resulting in virtually no potential for a sustained fishery. Assessment of recruitment success is complicated by the fact that small size-classes of abalones are highly cryptic in their behaviour.

(b) Beyond the effect of exploiting large adults, it is still unknown to what extent mortality at various stages in the life history of abalones is capable of limiting production. Conceivably, by increasing the abundance of larvae or the survival of recently metamorphosed juveniles, or by enhancing successful metamorphosis, one could enhance the productivity of abalone fisheries. However, it is equally conceivable that one or more of their life-history stages is not critical to potential population growth (e.g. if they show density independence at that particular stage over some range in density). Until this question is resolved, there is little reason to expect that management directed at the enhancement of any one of these stages is very likely to increase production of the fisheries.

(c) A final problem with the management of abalones stems from the fact that market values have soared with declining availability. For example, ex-vessel prices for red abalones have experienced a 200-fold increase, from \$0.50/dozen during the 1930s and 1940s to \$100/dozen at the present time (Pleschner 1982). One consequence of this is that there is little chance that abalone fisheries will become self-regulating. A more stable market, in contrast, could be expected to limit commercial exploitation once the density of legal-sized adults was reduced to some particular level (Clark 1973). Another consequence of a high market value is the development of poor fishery practices. For example, the taking of undersized specimens almost certainly has increased with the prospect of windfall profits. It also is thought that fishermen, by excessively handling and examining slightly undersized individuals, have increased the mortality of already heavily exploited populations.

(d) Information on landings by the recreational fishery is lacking, although it is speculated that their total equals or exceeds that of the commercial fishery (E. E. Ebert, personal communication).

Northern razor clam: *Siliqua patula* (Dixon, 1789)

Biology and fishery

Northern razor clams are abundant through much of the present and former ranges of sea-otters in the North Pacific. Razor clams are solenid bivalves found from Pismo Beach, California, northward through the Aleutian Islands, occurring from the low intertidal to 40 m depth (Blunt 1980, Morris *et al*. 1980), along sand beaches exposed to oceanic swell or strong tidal currents. Razor clams are suspension feeders capable of rapid burrowing in loosely consolidated sands; permanent burrows are not constructed.

The sexes are separate and fertilisation is external in northern razor clams (Morris *et al*. 1980). Spawning begins when water temperature exceeds 13°C, which occurs in May and June in Washington (Morris *et al*. 1980), and in July and August in Cook Inlet, Alaska (Nosho 1972). Larvae remain mobile for about 8 weeks. They are able to swim but spend much of the time resting on the sand (Morris *et al*. 1980, Rudy & Rudy 1983). Successful recruitments produce juvenile densities of up to $16\,000/m^2$, but juvenile mortality rates are very high, particularly during storms (Amos 1966, Rudy & Rudy 1983).

Growth rates of northern razor clams vary across latitude, and on small spatial scales as well. Sexual maturity (shell length 10 cm) is reached in 5–7 years in Alaska (Weymouth *et al*. 1931, Nickerson 1975), and in 3–4 years farther south. Minimum size for commercial harvest (11.4 cm) is reached in about 4 years in Washington and Oregon, 3–4 years in British Columbia, and 5–9 years in Alaska (Weymouth *et al*. 1931, Amos 1966, Nickerson 1975, Paul & Feder 1976, Bernard 1982).

Historically, the harvest of northern razor clams was a substantial commercial enterprise. Annual landings in Alaska exceeded 2.2 million kg in 1917, but fluctuated wildly in subsequent years as a result of localised stock depletion and variable market conditions (Orth *et al*. 1975). More recently, the Alaskan commercial harvest has been hindered by competition with north-west Atlantic clam fisheries, occasional outbreaks of paralytic shellfish poisoning, and severe habitat degradation associated with the calamitous 1964 earthquake (Baxter 1971, Orth *et al*. 1975). Annual landings averaged 134 000 kg for 1960–63, falling to 23 000 kg during 1964–74 (Fig. 12.4). Commercial

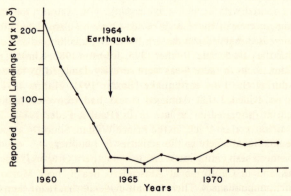

Figure 12.4 Commercial landings of northern razor clams (*Siliqua patula*) in Alaska, 1960–74. (From Orth *et al*. 1975.)

gathering of razor clams in Alaska now occurs at scattered locations on the Alaska Penninsula, Cook Inlet, Prince William Sound, and the Copper River Delta. Over 90% of the harvest is used to supply bait for the Dungeness crab fishery of the North Pacific (Orth *et al.* 1975).

In British Columbia, razor clams are abundant only at Long Beach on the west coast of Vancouver Island, and on beaches near Masset on the north-east coast of Graham Island in the Queen Charlotte Group (Bernard 1982). The commercial harvest of the Province occurs entirely at Masset. Commercial clamming began in 1924, primarily to produce canned clams for human consumption. Substantial fluctuations in landings over the years were caused by variable stock size, changing market conditions, and changing availability of labour and shipping facilities (Bernard 1982). Commercial canneries closed in the late 1960s, and the bulk of commercial landings since that time have been used as bait for the Dungeness crab fishery. Since 1970, annual landings have been variable, ranging from 18 000 kg to 100 000 kg (Bernard 1982).

Limited commercial harvesting is carried out in Washington and Oregon. The Washington fishery is located in the Willapa Spits area, producing annual landings of 3500–14 000 kg which are used primarily for Dungeness crab bait (Northup personal communication, Burge, personal communication). In Oregon, most commercial digging is done between Tillamook Head and the Columbia River. Annual landings have ranged from 18 000 kg to 55 000 kg in recent years, and most of the harvest is marketed as fresh meat for human consumption (Snow, personal communication).

Northern razor clams are collected throughout their range by sport diggers. Sport harvesting is particularly intensive in Washington and Oregon. During the period 1974–80, annual sport landings averaged 941 000 clams in Oregon (Snow, personal communication), and 10.1 million in Washington (Burge, personal communication). Recent recruitment failures in Washington and Oregon, possibly resulting from excessive harvests, have led to the imposition of foreshortened seasons and reduced daily bag limits by management agencies (Snow, personal communication). Important sport harvests also occur in California between Humboldt Bay and the Smith River (Blunt 1980), in British Columbia at Long Beach, Vancouver Island (Bernard 1982), and in Alaska in the Clam Gulch area of the Kenai Peninsula (Paul & Feder 1976).

Interaction with sea-otters

Sea-otters consume razor clams with some regularity in Alaska (Johnson 1982), but there is no documentation of the impact of sea-otters on clam populations. Sea-otter numbers have increased markedly in eastern Prince William Sound and off the Copper River Delta within the past decade (Pitcher 1975, Johnson 1982, Kimker, personal communication). Clam stocks in these areas were severely damaged by tectonic uplift and tsunami scour during the 1964 earthquake (Baxter 1971, Hanna 1971, Noerenberg 1971). There is no evidence that damaged stocks had recovered significantly when sea otters moved into the area in the late 1970s (Paul & Feder 1976). Therefore, the depressed status of razor clam stocks in the Prince William Sound–Copper River Delta areas cannot be attributed solely to the activities of sea-otters.

Sea otters have been seen eating razor clams in southern Oregon (Jameson, personal communication), and in California at Atascadero Beach, near Morro Bay (Burge, unpublished; Fitch, unpublished). There is some evidence that razor clam densities were reduced by sea-otter foraging at Atascadero Beach (California Department of Fish and Game 1976).

Pismo clam: *Tivela stultorum* (Mawe, 1823)

Biology and fishery

Pismo clams are venerid bivalves overlapping in range with the southern portion of the aboriginal distribution of sea otters in North America. Pismo clams are known from Halfmoon Bay, California, southward to Isla Socorro, Islas Revillagigedos, Mexico (Fitch 1950, 1953, Morris *et al.* 1980), occurring on surf-swept sand beaches from the intertidal zone to 25 m depth. In recent years, few Pismo clams have been seen north of Monterey Bay. Pismo clams are filter feeders. Unlike northern razor clams, which also occur on exposed beaches, Pismo clams have thick, heavy shells and are unable to burrow rapidly.

The natural history and ecology of Pismo clams have been reviewed by Fitch (1950). The sexes are separate; fertilisation is external, and spawning occurs annually in summer and autumn, generally following a rise in sea surface temperature. Spawning females may release up to 20 million eggs in a single season. Larvae apparently remain in the plankton for several weeks before settlement and metamorphosis. Major recruitments are often separated by many years, may be site specific, and do not appear to correlate with the size of breeding stock.

Growth rates of individual Pismo clams can vary substantially between years and between sites, even on a small scale (Coe 1947, Fitch 1950). Pismo clams typically become sexually mature at the age of 1 year and at a size of 3–5 cm (maximum shell length). Growth to minimum size for legal sport harvest in California (12.7 cm in Monterey Bay, 11.4 cm at Pismo Beach and Morro Bay) requires 3–9 years (Fitch 1950).

Pismo clams were harvested commercially in California from 1916 to 1947. Annual landings peaked at 302 000 kg in 1918 (Aplin 1949) and declined thereafter, except for moderately increased landings in 1923–5 and 1934–7 (Fig. 12.5). Commercial harvesting of Pismo clams still occurs in Mexico, but species-specific landings data for bivalves are not available at present. From 1935 to 1947, up to 24 million kilograms per year of fresh Pismo clams were imported from Mexico into California (Aplin 1949). Most of the commercial harvest in California was taken from beaches near Morro Bay and at Pismo Beach and Oceano (Herrington 1929). Pismo clams are harvested from

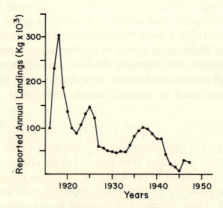

Figure 12.5 Commercial landings of Pismo clams (*Tivela stultorum*) in California 1916–47. (From California Department of Fish and Game.)

many locations in Mexico; beaches near Bahia San Quintin are perhaps the best known (Aplin 1947).

The ultimate collapse of the commercial Pismo clam harvest in California was apparently due to a combination of infrequent recruitment, poor juvenile survival, and chronic overexploitation. Management authorities expressed concern over these problems as early as 1923, and frequently thereafter (Weymouth 1923, Herrington 1926, 1929, Clark 1928, 1929, 1931, 1932, Scofield 1931, Croker 1932, Roedel 1939, 1942), calling for increased restrictions of harvesting and better enforcement of management policies. Each of the three peak periods of commercial harvest (1917–19, 1924–6 and 1935–9) was sustained largely on the strength of a few dominant year-classes. Recruitments in intervening years were not adequate to maintain commercial exploitation at high levels. Occasional pollution problems and natural disasters may have contributed to declining clam stocks (Weymouth 1919, Anonymous 1922). Pismo clams are apparently capable of concentrating the toxins of paralytic shellfish poisoning, but traditional processing techniques seem to remove toxic tissues. No cases of human poisoning from Pismo clams are known (Fitch 1950).

Pismo clams are harvested throughout their range in California by sport fishermen. Historically, the most popular sport clamming sites in central California have been the beaches in Monterey Bay, near Morro Bay, and near Pismo Beach (Miller *et al.* 1975). The best clamming locations in southern California are in Ventura, Los Angeles, and Orange counties (Knaggs *et al.* 1976, 1977).

Following the closure of the commercial fishery, the success of sport harvesting of Pismo clams in central California has been plagued by infrequent recruitment success and poor juvenile survival. Of particular concern is the chronically high mortality rate of small clams, apparently resulting from improper sport digging (Fitch 1950). Recruitment failures have occurred at all clamming beaches, but the problem is most acute at Atascadero Beach, just north of Morro Bay. Here, major recruitments have been recorded only in 1944 and 1972. Minor settlements occurred in the intervening years, but rates of juvenile survival were poor (Fitch 1952, 1954, Baxter 1962, Carlisle 1966, 1973). In a 1971 census effort, no Pismo clams of any size were found at Atascadero Beach (Carlisle 1973). However, the recruitment of 1972 produced a dense population of juveniles (Burge 1979). The above patterns are based on data from beach transect censuses traditionally used by the California Department of Fish and Game (review in Fitch 1950). In recent years, the Department has used interviews with sport clammers to develop indices of catch per unit effort as a second method of stock assessment (Miller *et al.* 1975, Burge 1979). Clammer interview data have suggested a more positive picture of the status of Pismo clam stocks in California, in some cases contradicting results of transect censuses. For example, clammer interviews at Atascadero Beach indicated relatively high success rates before 1973 (Burge 1979), in marked contrast to the dismal status reports based on transect data (Carlisle 1973).

Interaction with sea-otters

Sea otters began to re-enter Pismo clam habitat in the early 1970s. At the southern end of their range, sea-otters were first seen eating Pismo clams in February 1973 at Atascadero Beach (Wild & Ames 1974, Wade 1975). Otters foraging along the beach ate Pismo clams almost exclusively. Clam stocks appeared to be depleted at Atascadero Beach by autumn 1974, a loss attributed to foraging by sea-otters (Miller *et al.* 1975). Sea otters began eating Pismo clams at Morro spit (south of Atascadero Beach) in

February 1975 (Miller *et al.* 1975). In January 1979, sea otters moved in numbers south of Point San Luis and began feeding on Pismo clams near Pismo Beach and, later Oceano. In the following months, sea otters in the area fed primarily on Pismo clams. Clam density and sport clammer success dropped substantially during this time, suggesting significant depletion of clam stocks by foraging sea-otters (Burge 1979, Hardy *et al.* 1982).

In April 1973, sea-otters were observed eating Pismo clams near Moss Landing, as the northernmost part of the otter population moved northward across Monterey Bay (Miller *et al.* 1975, Stephenson 1977). In subsequent months, otters were seen eating these clams along beaches north of Moss Landing. In all cases, substantial reductions of Pismo clam density and sport clammer success immediately followed the onset of foraging activity by sea-otters (Miller *et al.* 1975, Stephenson 1977).

There is no question that the precipitous movement of large numbers of sea-otters into Pismo clam habitat can produce rapid local depletion of clam stocks. Indeed, this appears to be the typical pattern. However, in addition to sea-otter predation, there are other influences, in a long-term sense, on the demography of Pismo clam populations. As a specific case in point, we question the importance of sea-otter predation in the apparent failure of the 1972 clam cohort at Atascadero Beach to survive to harvestable size (Burge 1979). As noted above, juvenile survival rates of Pismo clams have been historically low at Atascadero Beach, regardless of the presence of sea otters. In 1974, high mortality rates were reported for clams of the 1972 year-class at Atascadero Beach, not because of sea-otter predation, but because of disturbance by sport clammers seeking northern razor clams (California Department of Fish and Game, unpublished). We suggest that other mortality sources may have contributed to the demise of the 1972 clam cohort, and that sea-otter predation is not the only explanation consistent with available data, both current and historical. A second case in point is the relatively recent discovery of a population of Pismo clams at Port San Luis, northwest of Pismo Beach (California Department of Fish and Game, unpublished). This area has been within the sea-otter range since 1979. Little is known about the dynamics of the population, but sea-otter predation apparently has not occurred.

An additional unresolved issue is the possible effect of motor vehicle traffic on survival rates of juvenile clams. At present, vehicular traffic is permitted on Pismo clamming beaches south of Pismo Beach. Traffic levels are often high, particularly on holiday weekends, when traffic jams and collisions are frequent. Vehicular travel extends across the intertidal zone during low tide, overlapping with tidal zones in which juvenile Pismo clams are most abundant (Baxter 1961). Vehicular disturbance may contribute to reduced survival of young clams; to date, however, there has been no documentation of the effects of motor vehicles on Pismo clams (L. Laurent, personal communication).

The recognition that sea otters can reduce Pismo clam densities to low levels raises two additional issues of a more general nature, both relevant to the development of management schemes for Pismo clams and sea-otters. The first involves the economic consequences of substantial reduction of a relatively localised sport fishery. In the mid-1970s, the prospect of 'reoccupation' of the Pismo Beach area by sea-otters caused widespread expressions of concern for the local tourist-based economy, thought to rely heavily on visitors attracted to the area by the opportunity to dig or dive for Pismo clams. A recent socioeconomic analysis suggests, however, that the economic impact of a loss of clam resources may be small, perhaps insignificant, in the Pismo Beach area (Holt 1982, Holt *et al.* in press). While these analyses are by no means the last word, they raise the intriguing hypothesis that it is the beach, not the clams, that draws people and dollars to Pismo Beach. The second issue is the extent to which depletion of Pismo clam stocks by sea-otters will persist in time. Fundamental to this question are certain aspects of the life histories of Pismo clams and sea-otters, which we will now review.

Pismo clam recruitment occurs primarily on beaches exposed at low tide, and individual clams produce identifiable annual growth rings in the shell. Thus, age structure and recruitment success can be determined more readily in Pismo clams than in most other shellfish subject to predation by sea-otters. Samples of clams were gathered annually by the California Department of Fish and Game at most major clamming beaches from 1923 to 1965 and from 1971 to the present. Data collected through 1971 have been summarised by Fitch (1952, 1954, 1955), Baxter (1961, 1962), and Carlisle (1966, 1973). These data indicate that major settlements of clams can be separated by up to 18 years on beaches south of Pismo Beach, and up to 28 years on Atascadero Beach. As noted by Tomlinson (1968), there appears to be no correlation between adult breeding stock size and annual recruitment of juvenile Pismo clams. Finally, we note that Pismo clams reach sexual maturity at an age corresponding to a shell length of 3–5 cm (Fitch 1950). For unknown reasons, sea otters are apparently unwilling or unable to eat clams smaller than about 6–7 cm in length (Miller *et al.* 1975, Stephenson 1977). Thus, some reproductive clams survive in the presence of sea-otters.

Occupation of new areas by sea-otters tends to occur in a predictable sequence of events in California. First occupants are typically dense groups of males which often congregate at range peripheries. The male groups tend to forage on a few relatively abundant prey species of high energy value when an area is first occupied. As readily available food declines in abundance, male groups move to new areas and are replaced by breeding females, territorial males, and dependent pups (Wild & Ames 1974, Estes *et al.* 1981, R. Jameson personal communication). This transition is accompanied by a drop in sea-otter density, often by a factor of ten or more. In sand beach areas, the transitional decline in density may be even greater because breeding otters seem to avoid permanent residence in open sand areas, at least in California (California Department of Fish and Game 1976).

Given the above information, we believe that the long-term influences of sea otters on Pismo clam populations remain uncertain. At present, high-density male groups occur in California in relatively close proximity to all major Pismo clam beaches. Should male groups move away from clam beaches in the course of continued expansion of the sea-otter population, predatory pressure on Pismo clams could decline substantially. As noted, clam stocks affected by foraging sea otters retain the potential to generate successful recruitments. Given sufficient time for successful recruitment (perhaps a decade or more), depleted clam stocks should increase in density, possibly to a level adequate to sustain a limited sport harvest. The time course of these events is entirely uncertain. The movement of male groups of sea otters may be related to continued growth of the population, a process very much in doubt at present (US Fish and Wildlife Service 1982). Recruitment frequency of clams cannot be predicted, nor can we predict how quickly sea otters might 're-discover' recovered clam stocks and again increase foraging effort and reduce the stocks. We offer this view as a plausible alternative to the argument of Hardy *et al.* (1982), that sea otters have irrevocably eliminated Pismo clam fisheries in central California. At present, we suggest that data are insufficient to select a model most appropriate to describe the long-term fate of the clam fishery. However, we reiterate our agreement that recent precipitous reductions in Pismo clam stocks in central California have been caused by sea otters, and we doubt that recovery of depleted stocks will occur as long as high-density groups of male otters remain near major clamming beaches.

Butter clam: *Saxidomus giganteus* (DeShayes, 1839)

Biology and fishery

The butter clam is an infaunal venerid bivalve which occupies mud, mud–sand, or mud–gravel substrata in bays or, more rarely, along semi-protected beaches from the Aleutian Islands to San Francisco (Morris *et al.* 1980, Rudy & Rudy 1983). Butter clams are found from the low intertidal to depths of 30 m, living from a few centimetres to 30 cm below the sediment surface. Butter clams are filter feeders. Mobility is limited, although siphons can be retracted when disturbed (Morris *et al.* 1980, Rudy & Rudy 1983).

The sexes are separate in butter clams. Spawning occurs in summer or autumn when water temperatures reach 12–20°C (Nosho 1972, Rudy & Rudy 1983). Fertilisation is external. Larvae are planktonic, reach veliger stage in about 2 weeks, and metamorphose and settle about 4 weeks after fertilisation. Because spawning is apparently temperature dependent, successful recruitment may be infrequent and variable between locations, particularly in more northerly populations (Nosho 1972). In some instances, significant recruitments may be separated by up to 20 years (Quayle & Bourne 1972).

Butter clams become sexually mature at shell lengths of about 40 mm (Quayle & Bourne 1972). Growth rates are typically very slow. In Alaska, maturity is reached in 5–6 years, harvestable size (64 mm) in 8–20 years (Fraser & Smith 1928, Baxter 1965, Paul & Feder 1976).

Butter clams are rare in California south of Humboldt Bay, where a small commercial harvest occurs (Morris *et al.* 1980). Commercial harvests are also small in Oregon (J. Lannon, personal communication), although they are common in coastal bays and estuaries (Rudy & Rudy 1983). Clam stocks in Puget Sound and coastal bays in Washington provide 99% of commercial landings of butter clams in the United States (Amos 1966). From 1975 through 1978, annual landings of butter clams in Puget Sound averaged 24 000 kg (Burge, personal communication).

The largest commercial fishery for butter clams is in British Columbia (Amos 1966), where annual landings averaged 600 000 kg during the 1970s (Bernard 1982). Between-year variations in landings are substantial, but no long-term trend has been apparent in Canadian landings since 1970 (Bernard 1982).

Commercial harvesting of butter clams in Alaska is largely undeveloped (Paul & Feder 1976). A small fishery developed in southeastern and south central Alaska in 1930, producing annual landings of about 10 000 kg until the mid-1940s. In 1946, changes in regulations occurred in response to problems with paralytic shellfish poisoning. The economic consequences of the regulations were such that the fishery collapsed in 1955 (Nosho 1972). At present, the Alaskan commercial harvest survives on a very small scale in a portion of Cook Inlet, where problems with paralytic shellfish poisoning occur infrequently (Orth *et al.* 1975).

Commercial exploitation of this species has been severely retarded by several factors. Butter clams concentrate the toxins of paralytic shellfish poisoning to a greater degree and for longer time periods than most other commercially harvested bivalves (Orth *et al.* 1975). Toxins are concentrated in the siphon and gills and may remain at high levels for up to 2 years after ingestion of the plankton (Quayle & Bourne 1972). In areas where blooms of *Gonyaulax* occur annually, butter clams may contain toxins continuously. Processing methods are available for removal of toxic clam tissues, but they are economically unattractive because they are labour intensive and involve considerable loss of clam meat. Since 1951, 22 cases of paralytic shellfish poisoning of people in Alaska have been attributed to consumption of butter clams; 2 of the cases were fatal (Orth *et al.* 1975). The threat of paralytic shellfish poisoning forces frequent seasonal closures of fisheries in some areas, and has led to permanent closure of some coastal areas in British Columbia (Bernard 1982).

Full development of butter clam fisheries is also restricted by techniques currently used in commercial harvests. Most commercial clamming is done with hand-operated forks or shovels, although some mechanised digging is carried out in Puget Sound (Paul and Feder 1976, Bernard 1982, Burge, personal communication). Annual landings of butter clams are apparently far below potential yields in British Columbia and Alaska, but the economic status of the clam fishery is sufficiently precarious that harvesting interests are unwilling to make the capital investments necessary to convert to more efficient and productive mechanical techniques (Orth *et al.* 1975, Bernard 1982).

Butter clam stocks are susceptible to natural catastrophic mortalities. The great earthquake of 1964 damaged most stocks of butter clams in Prince William Sound, Alaska (see below), and recovery of populations has not occurred (Paul & Feder 1976).

Butter clams are gathered by sport clammers throughout their range in California, Oregon, Washington, and British Columbia, and along the entire southern coast of Alaska. There are no published records of sport landings.

Interaction with sea-otters
The butter clam is an important prey item for sea otters in Prince William Sound, Alaska (Calkins 1978, Estes *et al.* 1981, Johnson 1982), and for the translocated population of sea-otters off Vancouver Island, British Columbia (Morris *et al.* 1981). Sea-otters translocated to Oregon also ate butter clams (Jameson 1975), but the Oregon population of sea-otters now appears to be extinct (Jameson *et al.* 1982).

Local depletion of butter clam stocks has been associated with foraging by the expanding sea-otter population in Prince William Sound (Paul & Feder 1976, Johnson 1982). However, there is no quantitative documentation of large-scale depletion of clam stocks unequivocally attributable to the activities of sea-otters. On the other hand, there is reason to suspect that long-term coexistence of sea-otters and harvestable butter clam stocks can occur on a regional scale in Prince William Sound. The most direct evidence is the observation that butter clams remain a relatively important prey item for sea-otters in areas that have been occupied by otters for many years (A. Johnson, personal communication, Estes *et al.* 1981). This notion is consistent with some novel evidence provided by the 1964 earthquake. Intertidal substrata in many parts of Prince William Sound were tectonically uplifted by several metres during the earthquake (Pflaker 1972). Infaunal bivalves in these areas were stranded well above normal tidal levels, and died in place (Baxter 1971). Sediment scour produced by tsunamis and seiches associated with the earthquake caused many stranded bivalves to be exposed or partly exposed at the sediment surface (Reimnitz & Marshall 1972). As a result, one can now find populations of 'earthquake fossil' clam shells, still positioned in the posture where they died, partly buried in the sediment in the upper intertidal throughout Prince William Sound (photographs in Hanna 1971, Harry 1973). Censusing of live butter clam populations is difficult and time consuming, but stranded shells can easily be enumerated and measured.

VanBlaricom (unpublished) has censused earthquake-stranded populations of butter clam shells at Green Island (sea otters present in 1964) and Orca Inlet (sea otters absent in 1964). At Green Island, stranded butter clam shells can be found in dense patches, typically several metres in diameter and separated by 10–20 m. Densities of large clams (>50 mm shell length) reach 25/m^2 in the patches. In Orca Inlet, stranded clams from comparable pre-earthquake tidal levels are distributed on a comparable spatial scale. Peak within-patch densities of large butter clams are somewhat higher (to 75/m^2) than at Green Island. Further study of earthquake-stranded shell populations is in progress, but available data suggest that sea-otters and significant butter clam stocks can coexist, albeit at somewhat reduced clam densities.

Several factors may contribute to the survival of butter clam stocks in the presence of sea-otters. First, the ability to excavate and consume butter clams varies markedly among sea-otters of different ages. Specifically, juvenile sea otters foraging in clam habitat are more frequently unsuccessful at obtaining prey than adults in the same habitat (Estes *et al.* 1981, A. Johnson, personal communication). Furthermore, sea otters of all ages foraging on infaunal clams make a greater proportion of unsuccessful foraging dives than those feeding on epibenthic invertebrates such as mussels (Estes *et al.* 1981). Apparently, the infaunal habits of butter clams constitute a refuge from easy capture and consumption by sea-otters. Second, butter clams in Prince William Sound are particularly abundant within beds of the eelgrass, *Zostera marina* L. (R. Rosenthal, unpublished data). Eelgrass beds are widespread in low intertidal and shallow subtidal depths in the Sound; dense networks of rhizomes in such areas almost certainly inhibit the ability of sea-otters to dig out butter clams.

It is not clear to what extent sea-otters will interfere with future development of butter clam fisheries in the north-east Pacific. Because of low rates of growth and maturation of clams, and infrequent recruitment success, significant expansion of butter clam fisheries almost certainly will run the risk of rapid overexploitation of clam stocks, much in the manner of fisheries for abalone (see above). At present, problems with paralytic shellfish poisoning and uncertain market conditions restrain the expansion of the fishery, and far outweigh any known effect of sea-otters. Should barriers to expansion of the fishery be overcome, resource depletion and conflicts with sea-otters may arise unless conservation management schemes are applied by regulatory agencies. Successful management of butter clam fisheries is complicated by site-specific differences in growth and recruitment which seem to be typical of the species (e.g. Paul & Feder 1976).

Washington clam: *Saxidomus nuttalli* (Conrad, 1837)

Biology and fishery
Washington clams occur in muddy or sandy substrata, primarily in protected bays and lagoons, from Humboldt Bay, California, southward to Isla San Geronimo, Baja California Norte, Mexico (Morris *et al.* 1980). Washington clams grow to a slightly larger maximum size than the congeneric butter clams, but life-history patterns are otherwise similar and will not be repeated here (see above discussion of *Saxidomus giganteus*).

Washington clams are particularly abundant in Morro Bay, Elkhorn Slough, Bodega Bay, Tomales Bay, and Humboldt Bay, California, and are relatively rare south of Morro Bay (Fitch 1953). Large-scale commercial harvesting of Washington clams occurred in California from 1931 to 1947. Annual landings increased to a peak value of 20 000 kg in 1935, and subsequently declined (California Bureau of Marine Fisheries

1949). To our knowledge, the only presently active commercial fishery for Washington clams occurs in Humboldt Bay, where a small annual harvest is marketed in local restaurants (C. Toole, personal communication). Washington clams are popular with sport diggers wherever they are abundant in California.

Interaction with sea-otters

Sea-otters have been seen digging and eating Washington clams in the subtidal sediments at Monterey Harbor, California (Hines & Loughlin 1980). During 1976–7, Washington clams were the dominant prey item for sea-otters foraging in the area. Densities of clams were 8–14/m² in areas regularly foraged by sea-otters. In an adjacent area thought to be free of otter foraging because of debris in the sediment, mean clam densities were 17/m² (Hines & Loughlin 1980).

The range of the California sea-otter population overlaps with the popular sport fishing grounds for Washington clams only at Morro Bay and Elkhorn Slough. There is no quantitative documentation of the impact of sea-otters in these areas on stocks of Washington clams harvested by man.

Littleneck clam: *Protothaca staminea* (Conrad 1837)

Biology and fishery

Littleneck clams (family Veneridae) range from the Aleutian Islands, Alaska, to Cabo San Lucas, Baja California Sur, Mexico, occurring in sand or sandy mud in bays and estuaries, and in gravel under cobble on open coastline (Fitch 1953, Morris *et al.* 1980). Littlenecks are filter-feeding clams which occupy shallow burrows in the lower and middle intertidal. They are virtually immobile and, because their siphons are short, live relatively close to the sediment surface (Rudy & Rudy 1983).

The sexes are separate in Littleneck clams. Individuals capable of spawning can be found throughout the year in Alaska (Paul & Feder 1976). In British Columbia, spawning occurs from April through September (Quayle 1943). Recruitment success varies from year to year (e.g. Paul & Feder 1973), but strong year-classes occur with greater frequency than in butter clams, with which Littlenecks frequently coexist.

Growth rate of Littleneck clams vary markedly among years, beaches, and tidal heights, and across latitude (Bernard 1982). Size at sexual maturity (shell length of 2–3 cm; Quayle 1943) is reached in 1–2 years in British Columbia, 3–4 years in southeastern Alaska, and 6–7 years in Prince William Sound, Alaska (Paul & Feder 1973, 1976). Harvestable size (3 cm) is reached about 1 year later in each area.

Primary commercial fisheries for Littleneck clams are located in British Columbia and Washington. Commercial landings have been influenced historically by many of the same factors which affect landings of butter clams (Bernard 1982; see above discussion), although difficulties with paralytic shellfish poisoning are somewhat less frequent. During 1970–9, annual landings of Littleneck clams in British Columbia ranged from 144 000 kg to 631 000 kg (Bernard 1982). Landings in Puget Sound, Washington, increased from 158 000 kg in 1975 to 416 000 kg in 1978 (R. Burge, personal communication). Littleneck clams were harvested commercially in southeastern Alaska until 1946, when regulatory changes forced closure of the fishery (Paul & Feder 1973; see discussion under butter clams, above). Potential harvests in Alaska appear to be large, particularly in Prince William Sound, where outbreaks of paralytic shellfish poisoning in Littleneck clams are rare (Feder & Paul 1973). This species is harvested on a small scale in Humboldt Bay, California (C. Toole, personal communication).

Littleneck clams are heavily exploited by sport clammers throughout their range. Landings data are not available for sport harvests.

Stocks of Littleneck clams in Prince William Sound, Alaska, were seriously damaged by the great earthquake of 1964. Recovery was relatively rapid, due to successful recruitments, in areas where the substratum was not severely modified (Paul *et al.* 1976). The history of Littleneck clam fisheries and the recovery of earthquake-damaged populations suggest that the clam populations may be more tolerant of exploitation than most other molluscan species examined in this review. This supposition will be tested if market conditions favour continued expansion of commercial harvesting in Washington and British Columbia.

Interaction with sea-otters

Sea-otters have been seen eating Littleneck clams in California near Cayucus Point (Wild & Ames 1974), in Oregon at Simpson Reef (Jameson 1975), and at several locations in Prince William Sound, Alaska (Calkins 1978, Estes *et al.* 1981, Johnson 1982). There are anecdotal reports that Littleneck clam stocks have been depleted locally by sea otters in California and Prince William Sound, but quantitative documentation of the interaction is lacking. Because of the relative shallowness of their burrows, Littleneck clams are probably more accessible to foraging sea-otters than butter clams, gaper clams, and other deeply buried infaunal bivalves.

However, relationships of sea-otters and Littleneck clams in Prince William Sound seem to parallel those of the butter clams (see above) in several respects. Littleneck clams remain a relatively important component of sea-otter diet in the Sound, and sport harvest can be successful in portions of the Sound occupied by sea-otters for many years (Calkins 1978, Estes *et al.* 1981, Johnson 1982, A. Johnson, personal communication). Densities of *Protothaca* shells stranded by the 1964 earthquake uplift (see detailed discussion in section on butter clams) at Green Island are locally high, approaching 60 harvestable clams/m^2 in some patches (VanBlaricom, unpublished). Sea otters had been present for a number of years at Green Island at the time of the earthquake. Although it is likely that some Littleneck populations have been reduced in size by otter foraging (Johnson 1982), it is also apparent that human exploitation of Littleneck clams can continue, at least on a recreational scale, within the range of sea otters in Prince William Sound.

Gaper clam: *Tresus nuttallii* (Conrad 1837)

Biology and fishery

Gaper clams are large, infaunal mactrid bivalves that range from the Strait of Georgia, British Columbia, to Laguna Ojo de Liebre, Baja California Sur, Mexico, overlapping with much of the aboriginal range of sea otters in North America. As adults, gaper clams live 1 m or more below the surface of sandy or mud–sand substrata in bays or along protected coastline, ranging in depth from the low intertidal to 30 m (Morris *et al.* 1980). Gaper clams are filter feeders with little mobility (Amos 1966).

The sexes are separate in gaper clams. Spawning occurs year-round in Elkhorn Slough, California; peak activity is in February–April (Clark *et al.* 1975). Larvae remain planktonic for 21–30 days before settlement and metamorphosis (Clark *et al.* 1975). The females mature sexually at 2 years of age.

Gaper clams are harvested commercially on a small scale, primarily for local marketing as fresh meat in restaurants. In recent years, commercial landings have been made in Humboldt Bay, California, and in several bays in Oregon (Amos 1966, Frey 1971). From 1950 to 1970, peak annual landings in California were 2700 kg (Frey 1971).

Gaper clams are intensively harvested in intertidal habitats by sport fishermen (Frey 1971, Clark *et al.* 1975). Sport harvest is particularly heavy in California from Morro Bay northward. Sport landings data are not available.

Interaction with sea-otters

Sea-otters have been seen eating gaper clams in California at San Simeon (Ebert 1968a, Jameson, personal communication), Cayucos Point (Wild & Ames 1974), and Morro Bay (Jameson, personal communication). Dense subtidal populations of gaper clams in Monterey Harbour were apparently depleted by foraging sea-otters (California Department of Fish and Game 1976, Hines & Loughlin 1980), although quantitative documentation is lacking. At present, sea-otter distribution overlaps important sport fishing sites for gaper clams only at Morro Bay and Elkhorn Slough. In neither area is there any evidence that sea otters have affected the success of sport harvests of this species (California Department of Fish and Game 1976).

Horse clam: *Tresus capax* (Gould, 1850)

Biology and fishery

Horse clams overlap with much of the aboriginal range of sea otters in North America, occurring from Kodiak Island, Alaska, southward to San Francisco, California (Morris *et al.* 1980, Rudy & Rudy 1983). They are most abundant in bays and estuaries; habitat selection and life history are similar to the congeneric gaper clam, discussed above.

Like gaper clams, horse clams have separate sexes and external fertilisation. Spawning occurs during winter in Humboldt Bay, California, and in early spring in Yaquina Bay, Oregon (Machell & DeMartini 1971, Rudy & Rudy 1983). Larvae apparently remain in the plankton for several weeks (Bourne & Smith 1972). Populations of horse clams in Humboldt Bay are dominated by a few year-classes, probably reflecting variable recruitment success or post-recruitment mortality (Wendell *et al.* 1976).

Small-scale commercial harvesting of horse clams occurs in Humboldt Bay, California (C. Toole, personal communication, R. Warner, personal communication). In Oregon, horse clams comprise about 60% of the annual harvests of clams from coastal estuaries (Rudy & Rudy 1983). During 1975–9, horse clam landings ranged from 7000 kg to 58 000 kg in Oregon (D. Snow, personal communication). Primary fishing grounds are Coos Bay, Netarts Bay, Tillamook Bay, and Yaquina Bay (Rudy & Rudy 1983, J. Richards, personal communication, J. Lannon, personal communication), where both intertidal and subtidal stocks are exploited. In Puget Sound, a horse clam fishery has recently developed, with annual landings of less than 1000 kg through 1978 (Burge, personal communication). The commercial fishery for this species in British Columbia is also recent, occurring primarily as a by-product of subtidal harvesting of geoducks (*Panope generose* {Gould, 1850}). Landings were 37 000 kg in 1979 and 128 000 kg in 1980, primarily from the southern strait of Georgia (Bernard 1982). Intertidal stocks in British Columbia are also harvested, primarily by hand digging; landings have been limited by low market price and handling difficulties (Bernard 1982). Horse clams are not harvested commercially in Alaska, and little is known regarding harvest potential (Paul & Feder 1976).

Interaction with sea-otters

Horse clams are gathered throughout their range by recreational fishermen. Sport landings can be substantial, as in Humboldt Bay, California (C. Toole, personal communication, R. Warner, personal communication), but landings data are unavailable. To our knowledge, sea-otters have been reported consuming horse clams only in Prince William Sound, Alaska (Johnson 1982). There are no data available with which to evaluate the impact of sea otters on horse clam populations, or on exploitation of horse clams by man.

Softshell clam: *Mya arenaria* (Linnaeus, 1758)

Biology and fishery

Mya arenaria is an infaunal myid bivalve which currently ranges from Point Barrow, Alaska, southward to Elkhorn Slough, California (Fitch 1953, Paul & Feder 1976, Morris *et al.* 1980). These clams native to the North Atlantic were introduced to San Francisco Bay in the 1870s, possibly with early transplants of the eastern oyster (Morris *et al.* 1980). They spread northward along the Pacific coast, reaching southeastern Alaska in 1956 and Prince William Sound in 1958 (Gross 1967).

Softshell clams occur in muddy substrata of quiet back-bays and estuaries, including areas of brackish water. Individual clams are relatively immobile, and live up to 30 cm below the sediment surface (Amos 1966). The sexes are separate. Spawning occurs in spring and autumn (Rudy & Rudy 1983). Sexual maturity (shells 2.5–4.5 cm long) is reached in about 3 years in Alaska (Feder & Paul 1974, Paul & Feder 1976). Harvestable size (5 cm) is reached in 6–7 years in Alaska (Feder & Paul 1974). Successful recruitment apparently occurs with some regularity; recovery was relatively rapid in clam stocks devastated by the 1964 earthquake (Paul & Feder 1976).

The softshell clam fishery is a large industry in the north-west Atlantic, but only small-scale commercial harvesting presently occurs in Pacific North America. There was a large softshell clam fishery in California from 1916 through 1947. Annual landings were large in the early years of the fishery (Fig. 12.6). Maximum annual harvest was 156 000 kg in 1922. The fishery declined steadily after 1925 (Fig. 12.6). At present, minor commercial harvests occur in Humboldt Bay, California, and in coastal

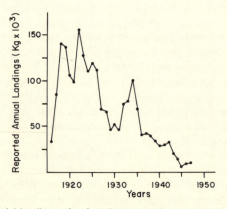

Figure 12.6 Commercial landings of softshell clams (*Mya arenaria*) in California, 1916–47. (From California Department of Fish and Game.)

bays of Oregon (C. Toole, personal communication, R. Warner, personal communication, J. Lannon, personal communication). In Puget Sound, Washington, annual landings have been as high as 150 000 kg in recent years, but the commercial take is now small (R. Burge, personal communication). Commercial landings in British Columbia are generally incidental inclusions in the harvest of other species (Bernard 1982). No commercial harvesting occurs in Alaska, although the potential harvest may be large (Feder & Paul 1973, Paul & Feder 1976).

Softshell clams are frequently harvested throughout their range by sport clammers. Non-commercial harvesting is apparently intensive in the eastern Bering Sea (Paul & Feder 1976). Sport landings data for softshell clams have not been published.

Interaction with sea-otters

Sea-otters are known to eat softshell clams in Prince William Sound, Alaska (Estes *et al.* 1981, Johnson 1982). There is no quantitative documentation of the impacts of otter foraging on populations of these clams, nor is there any firm evidence that sea otters have in any way influenced human exploitation of the species.

Basket cockle: *Clinocardium nuttallii* Conrad, 1837)

Biology and fishery

Basket cockles are filter-feeding cardiid bivalves that range from San Diego, California, northward into the Bering Sea (Fitch 1953). They live on or just below the surface of mud or sand substrate in bays, estuaries, and along semi-protected coastline, ranging in depth from the low intertidal to 200 m (Morris *et al.* 1980).

Basket cockles are simultaneously hermaphroditic (Amos 1966). Fertilisation is external and spawning occurs in spring and summer. Growth rates are apparently inversely related to latitude (Amos 1966). Basket cockles become sexually mature in 2 years (Morris *et al.* 1980). In Alaska, harvestable size (shell length 5 cm) is reached in about 4–5 years (Paul and Feder 1976).

This species was commercially harvested from 1944 to 1962 in Alaska (Nosho 1972). Annual landings ranged from zero (four different years) to 576 000 kg in 1960 (Nosho 1972). The large fluctuations in annual landings and the ultimate demise of the fishery

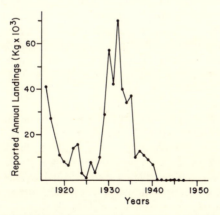

Figure 12.7 Commercial landings of cockles (*Clinocardium nuttalli*) in California, 1916–47. (From California Department of Fish and Game.)

were caused by low rates of meat recovery and intensive labour needs in processing, and by ongoing problems with paralytic shellfish poisoning (Paul & Feder 1976). No commercial harvesting occurs in British Columbia, although basket cockles are occasionally included in harvests of other bivalves (Bernard 1982). In California, a commercial fishery existed from 1916 to 1947. Landings fluctuated substantially over the years (Fig. 12.7): maximum annual harvests were 57 000 kg in 1930 and 70 000 kg in 1932. Landings declined drastically during World War II (California Bureau of Marine Fisheries 1949). Basket cockles are not presently harvested commercially in Washington, Oregon, or California, apparently because of low densities (Fitch 1953, Amos 1966).

Basket cockles are frequently taken by sport fishermen, but landings data are not available (Bernard 1982).

Interaction with sea-otters
Sea-otters have been seen consuming basket cockles in Prince William Sound (Johnson 1982) and a related species (*Clinocardium ciliatum*) has been found in sea-otter stomachs at Amchitka Island, Alaska (Kenyon 1969). There are presently no published data regarding the impact of sea-otters on cockle populations. In a 1971 study in Montague Strait, Prince William Sound, sea otters did not consume basket cockles although they were present in the area (Calkins 1978).

Rock scallop: *Hinnites giganteus* (Gray, 1825)

Biology and fishery
Rock scallops are pectinid bivalves ranging from the Queen Charlotte Islands, British Columbia, to Punta Abreojos, Baja California Sur, overlapping with a large portion of the historical range of sea-otters in North America (Fitch 1953). They occur on hard substrata from the intertidal to 50 m in depth, primarily along exposed outer coasts (Morris *et al.* 1980). The juveniles are capable of swimming to evade predators; larger individuals are attached permanently to rock surfaces. Growth rates of rock scallops are very low. Individuals may require up to 25 years to reach maximum size (5–15 cm in the intertidal, 25 cm subtidal; Morris *et al.* 1980). The sexes are separate and fertilisation external. Spawning occurs in April in central California (Morris *et al.* 1980)

Rock scallops are taken by sport fishermen throughout their range. At present there is no commercial fishery, although experimental mariculture is under development in southern California (J. Richards, personal communication). Available data suggest that rock-scallop harvesting is a minor sport fishery in California (Miller *et al.* 1972). However, excessive harvesting by sport fishermen has been implicated in apparent depletions of *Hinnites* populations in some areas (Morris *et al.* 1980).

Interaction with sea-otters
Sea-otters have been seen eating rock scallops in California and Oregon (Limbaugh 1961, Ebert 1968a, Faro 1970, Jameson 1975, Estes *et al.* 1981, Ostfeld 1982). In both areas, the rock scallops were a relatively minor portion of the sea-otter diet. In 1967, rock scallops were most abundant in portions of the California sea-otter range most recently reoccupied by otters (Ebert 1968b). Faro (1970) described rock scallop densities as low in the Point Pinos area near Monterey, California, and suggested that both sea-otters and sport fishermen were responsible. Low densities of rock scallops at Del Monte Reef, near Monterey, have been tentatively attributed to sea-otter foraging (Minter 1971). However, densities of scallops at Del Monte before the return of sea-

otters are unknown, although it is likely that sea-otter foraging does have an effect. Details of the relationship have not been documented, and the relative effects of predation on rock scallops by man and sea-otters are entirely unknown.

Oysters

Biology and fishery

In natural conditions, oysters are filter-feeding bivalves which live attached to rocks, shells, or other hard substrata on tidal flats in protected, back-bay habitats. Most commercially harvested oysters come from mariculture operations where they grow on ropes, racks, poles, or other artificial substrata more suited to efficient maintenance and harvest. Four species of oyster are now harvested in Pacific North America, three of which are non-native. All are in the family Ostreidae.

The Japanese oyster (*Crassostrea gigas* {Thunberg, 1795}) was introduced to North America early in the century. Populations capable of reproduction and successful recruitment are now established in Puget Sound, Washington, and the Strait of Georgia, British Columbia (Morris *et al*. 1980, Bernard 1982). *C. gigas* now ranges from Morro Bay, California, to British Columbia. The sexes are separate, but individuals may be sequentially hermaphroditic, changing sex over winter. In Puget Sound, spawning occurs in July or August. Larvae are free swimming for about 4 weeks. In many areas, post-larvae juvenile 'seed' oysters must be imported and planted regularly to maintain populations large enough to sustain commercial harvests (Morris *et al*. 1980).

Japanese oysters now dominate the commercial oyster harvest in the north-east Pacific. In California, Japanese oysters are cultured in Morro Bay, Elkhorn Slough, Drakes Estero, Tomales Bay, and Humboldt Bay (Conte & Dupuy 1981). Annual landings in California averaged 407 000 kg during 1970–9, primarily from Humboldt Bay (Conte & Dupuy 1981); those in Oregon during the same period averaged 103 000 kg (D. Snow, personal communication). Most oysters harvested in Oregon come from Tillamook Bay, Yaquina Bay, and Coos Bay (J. Lannon, personal communication). The annual harvest of Japanese oysters in Washington has been about 2.3 million kg in recent years (Burge, personal communication). About half the Washington harvest comes from Puget Sound, the remainder from Grays Harbour and Willapa Bay. Recent annual landings in British Columbia have been about 2 million kg, primarily from the southern part of the Strait of Georgia (Bernard 1982). *C. gigas* was cultured near Ketchikan, Alaska, with marginal success from early in the century until 1961 (Yancy 1966), when market conditions apparently forced failure of the business.

Wild populations of *C. gigas* are harvested by sport fishermen in Washington and British Columbia. Landings data are not available. Local depletion of wild oyster stocks by sport fishermen is a chronic problem, particularly in Puget Sound.

Olympia oysters (*Ostrea lurida* {Carpenter 1864}) are native to Pacific North America and ranged historically from Sitka, Alaska, to Cabo San Lucas, Baja California Sur, Mexico. They are sequentially hermaphroditic, each animal changing sex frequently during its life. Sexual phases may overlap such that some animals are simultaneously hermaphroditic for short periods (Morris *et al*. 1980). Males shed sperm clusters into the water, but females retain eggs in the mantle cavity, where fertilisation occurs. Larvae are brooded for 10–14 days, then released. The free-swimming larval period is 30–40 days, after which settlement and metamorphosis occur (Morris *et al*. 1980). *O. lurida* reaches sexual maturity 5 months after metamorphosis and produces two broods (up to 300 000 larvae per brood) per year. Growth to harvestable size (3–5 cm) requires 3–5 years in California (Morris *et al.* 1980).

Ostrea lurida was the original mainstay of the commercial oyster industry in western North America. Habitat degradation and introduction of other more marketable species have led to the virtual extinction of Olympia oysters as a commercial entity (Morris *et al.* 1980, Conte & Dupuy 1981). At present, the remnant commercial culture of *O. lurida* is centered in Puget Sound, Washington. Annual landings averaged 11 000 kg during 1970–9 (R. Burge, personal communication); the trend is one of continued decline.

The eastern oyster (*Crassostrea virginica* [Gmelin, 1971]) was introduced to San Francisco Bay in 1870, following completion of transcontinental rail lines. It quickly became the dominant commercial species in California because of its large size and better flavour than *Ostrea lurida* (Conte & Dupuy 1981). Repeated 'seeding' was necessary to maintain stocks of *C. virginica*. Annual landings peaked at 1.2 million kg of meat in 1899. Problems with pollution and habitat degradation caused a subsequent decline in production, and commercial culture of *C. virginica* in San Francisco Bay collapsed during the 1930s (Conte & Dupuy 1981). In recent years, eastern oysters have been cultured on a small scale in Elkhorn Slough, Tomales Bay, and Humboldt Bay. Annual landings in California have been less than 500 kg since 1978 (Conte & Dupuy 1981).

A fourth species, the European oyster (*Ostrea edulis* L.), was recently introduced to California. It is now cultured on a small, experimental basis at Elkhorn Slough (Conte & Dupuy 1981).

Interaction with sea-otters

Current sea-otter range now overlaps with oyster culture operations at Morro Bay and Elkhorn Slough, California. Sea-otters frequently forage on crabs and clams in the seaward portion of Morro Bay, but none has been seen near oyster beds in back-bay tidelands (L. Laurent, R. Hardy, and R. Jameson, personal communications). Although systematic observations have not been made, sea-otters apparently forage frequently within Elkhorn Slough, occasionally passing near oyster culture racks. Consumption of oysters by sea-otters has not been reported. In Coos Bay, Oregon, a sea otter from a translocated population (see Jameson *et al.* 1982) foraged on crabs but did not feed on nearby oysters (Mate, unpublished).

Sea-otters are capable of shucking and eating oysters given them by man (California Department of Fish and Game 1976), but natural foraging has not been observed anywhere. In our view, the potential for damage to the oyster industry by sea otters is limited. Sea-otters have had no rôle in the substantial variation between years in landings of oysters in the north-east Pacific. Pollution, habitat alteration, changing market conditions, episodic outbreaks of paralytic shellfish poisoning, the availability of shipping facilities, the price and availability of oyster 'seed', and problems with disease have been the principal causes of the historically variable success of the oyster industry (Paul & Feder 1976, Conte & Dupuy 1981).

Mussels

Biology and fishery

Two species of mussel (family Mytilidae) are common and ecologically important within the aboriginal range of sea otters in North America. The California sea mussel

(*Mytilus californianus* {Conrad, 1837}) dwells primarily on rocky intertidal substrata along shores exposed to oceanic swell from the Aleutian Islands to southern Baja California. Isolated subtidal populations are also known (Paine 1976). The bay mussel (*Mytilus edulis* {Linnaeus, 1758}) ranges in western North America from the Arctic Ocean to Isla de Cedros, Baja California Sur, Mexico, primarily in intertidal areas protected from heavy wave action. *M. edulis* may also be found on outer coast habitats in close association with *M. californianus* (Suchanek 1978, Morris *et al*. 1980).

The sexes are separate and fertilisation external in both species. *M. californianus* populations may include some spawning individuals throughout the year; peaks occur, for example, in July and December in California (Morris *et al*. 1980). Spawning in *M. edulis* is seasonal, the spawning season varying substantially from place to place.

Individual growth rates vary substantially over all spatial scales. For example, young *M. edulis* typically grow 7–8 cm in length in 1 year in southern California (Morris *et al*. 1980), but less than 2 cm in Prince William Sound, Alaska (VanBlaricom, unpublished data). Growth rates of this species also vary with tidal height and microhabitat type (VanBlaricom, unpublished data).

The commercial harvesting of mussels is presently a minor industry in Pacific North America. In California, small-scale mussel culturing operations are in experimental phases (J. Richards, personal communication). Minor commercial harvesting of natural populations of *M. californianus* and *M. edulis* occurs in Oregon near Cannon Beach and Newport (D. Snow, personal communication, J. Lannon, personal communication). Culturing of *M. edulis* occurs in Puget Sound, Washington, where landings reached 18 000 kg in 1980 (R. Burge, personal communication). Commercial landings of mussels in British Columbia include both natural and cultured harvests (P. Breen, personal communication, G. Jamieson, personal communication). Landings averaged 4000 kg per year in 1979 and 1980 (Bernard 1982). The potential commercial harvest of mussels in Alaska is substantial, but no such harvest now exists (Paul & Feder 1976). The commercial potential for mussel harvesting for human consumption is severely limited by the continuing threat of paralytic shellfish poisoning (PSP) along the North American Pacific coast. Mussels are notorious for their concentration and storage of PSP toxins. In 1980, for example, there were 98 cases of paralytic shellfish poisoning of people in Marin and Sonoma counties, California, including two fatalities. Most of the cases resulted from consumption of mussels by recent Asian immigrants unfamiliar with the toxic potential of Pacific coast bivalves (J. Richards, personal communication).

Both mussel species are harvested on a recreational basis wherever they occur. Sport harvests are used both for food and fishing bait.

Interaction with sea-otters

Sea-otters are known to consume both *M californianus* and *M. edulis*. Otters typically gather mussels by diving during high tide, but occasional emergent foraging occurs during low water (R. Jameson, personal communication). Mussels were apparently an important component of sea-otter diet near Monterey, California, early in the 1960s (Limbaugh 1961, Hall & Schaller 1964, Boolootian 1965, Faro 1970, Hines & Loughlin 1980). In general, however, mussels form a small portion of sea-otter diet in California (Ebert 1968a, Wild & Ames 1974, Estes *et al*. 1981, Ostfeld 1982). Mussels are occasionally taken by translocated sea-otter populations in Oregon and British Columbia (Jameson 1975, Morris *et al*. 1981). *Mytilus edulis* is an important component of sea-otter diet in Prince William Sound, Alaska (Estes *et al*. 1981, Johnson 1982).

There is no published documentation of the impact of sea-otters on commercial or sport landings of mussels anywhere within the present range of sea-otters. Otters clearly are capable of reducing mussel density on a local scale through foraging activity. For example, when sea-otters returned to the north shore of Monterey Penninsula in the 1960s, mussel biomass on rocky intertidal substrata in the area declined sharply (Faro 1970, Wilde & Ames 1974, Hines & Loughlin 1980, D. Abbott, personal communication). However, the effect of sea-otters on mussel populations is less significant elsewhere along the coast of central California, much of which is more exposed to oceanic swell than the Monterey area. Dense stands of *Mytilus californianus* are particularly common on exposed rocky headlands within the range of the California sea-otter population (Fisher 1939, Ebert 1968a,b, G. VanBlaricom, personal observations).

Since 1978, VanBlaricom has studied patches of *M. californianus* on intertidal rocks exposed to seasonally heavy surf at Point Piedras Blancas, near San Simeon, California. Sea-otters have been present at Point Piedras Blancas since 1959 (Wild & Ames 1974). From May 1978 through February 1982, virtually no mussels were taken from study plots or nearby mussel patches by sea-otters. In March 1982, sea otters removed mussels from study areas with some regularity, creating cleared patches up to 1 m^2 in size within study plots. During this period, one of three mussel patches was reduced in size by 10–20% by sea-otter foraging. A second patch received little damage, and a third was untouched. Since April 1982, sea-otter foraging on mussels has again become infrequent in the study plots.

Episodic creation of cleared patches in mussel beds is of some interest from an ecological perspective (e.g. Paine & Levin 1981). However, consumption of mussels by sea-otters in California appears to be sufficiently scattered in time and space that regional-scale depletion of harvestable stocks does not occur. The exposure of much of the central California coast to heavy surf probably provides an important refuge for mussels from foraging sea-otters. Consumption by other predators (e.g. the sea star, *Pisaster ochraceus*, and the black oystercatcher, *Haematopus bachmani*) and dislodgement by storm waves are probably at least as important as sea-otter predation in limiting the availability of mussels for human use in California.

Sea-otters are capable of reducing mussel biomass on a local scale in Alaska (Johnson 1982, VanBlaricom & Johnson, unpublished), but there is no evidence that sea-otter foraging has interfered with human harvest of mussels in Alaska.

Red sea urchins (*Strongylocentrotus franciscanus*)

Biology and fishery

The genus *Strongylocentrotus* has five extant species in the north-east Pacific. Only one of these, *S. franciscanus* (the red sea urchin), is exploited in a commercial fishery. Red urchins occur in northern Japan and along the west coast of North America from south-east Alaska to central Baja California. They range in depth from the lower littoral zones to about −90 m (Morris *et al.* 1980).

Following enlargement of the gonads during autumn and winter, most spawning occurs in April and May with the gametes being released into the water column (Bennett & Giese 1955, Giese 1959). The larvae are planktotrophic (Strathmann 1971), and, on the basis of laboratory studies, appear to remain as free-swimming forms for 61–131 days (Strathmann 1978). There appears to be no habitat selectivity by the recently metamorphosed young (Cameron & Schroeter 1980). However, settlement in the natural environment is seen only sporadically, and, in some areas at least, juveniles are found almost exclusively beneath the spine canopy of large adults (Tegner & Dayton 1977). Maximum size varies greatly among areas, occasionally reaching more than 200 mm in test diameter. Although red urchins may live to be more than 20 years old (Morris *et al*. 1980), under suitable conditions most of their growth is probably attained during the first 5–7 years (Benech 1977).

Sea urchins are among the most important of marine herbivores (see reviews by Lawrence 1975, Lubchenco & Gaines 1981). Their grazing activities often result in areas becoming entirely devoid of fleshy algae – these have been referred to by Lawrence (1975) as 'urchin barrens'. In the North Pacific, such barren areas appear to have been caused by recent population increases of red, purple (*S. purpuratus*), and green (*S. drobachiensis* and *S. polyacanthus*) sea urchins (Leighton *et al*. 1966, North & Pearse 1970, Estes & Palmisano 1974). These increases have been attributed to the following factors.

(a) *Release from predation*. Sea otters are the most commonly implicated predatory species, and indeed, the otters' range expansion has greatly reduced urchin densities in many areas (for examples, see McLean 1962, Lowry & Pearse 1973, Estes & Palmisano 1974, Benech 1977, Duggins 1980, Breen *et al*. 1982). In southern California, the exploitation in sport and commercial fisheries of other predatory species, such as sheephead (*Semicossyphus pulcher*) and spiny lobsters (*Panulirus interruptus*), is thought to have contributed to the problem (Tegner 1980, Tegner & Dayton 1981). The importance of sheephead has been corroborated by Cowen (1982, 1983), who, by experimentally removing sheephead from part of an isolated reef, demonstrated a trend of increased urchin density compared with an unmanipulated control area in which the density of urchins did not change.

(b) *Release from competition*. Since abalones and sea urchins occupy the same habitats and consume the same algal food resources, there has been speculation that they limit one another through exploitation competition (Haaker & Wilson 1975). On the basis of this proposed interaction, and because abalone populations have been reduced by the fishery, urchin population increases were perhaps facilitated by release from competition with abalones. Although intuitively appealing, there are still no data to support the proposed mechanism.

(c) *Pollution*. Kelp bed declines have been particularly dramatic near sewage effluents deriving from the large population centres in southern California (Leighton *et al*. 1966). Some of the discharged materials (e.g. dissolved amino acids) can be directly absorbed by urchins (North 1964a,b, Pearse *et al*. 1970), and at moderate concentrations these materials are thought to enhance sea-urchin growth. In addition, sewage effluents appear to cause the deterioration of kelp (North 1964a,b). Evidence in support of this explanation is mainly anecdotal, and although sewage may well have been of substantial importance in certain localised areas, it is unlikely to have been of any real consequence at many of the more remote locations throughout the North Pacific where urchin barrens also commonly occur.

Whatever their cause, the urchin barrens, once established, tend to maintain themselves through time. To some extent this appears to result from fundamental changes in the foraging behaviour of sea urchins, which cause them to switch from non-destructive to destructive grazing in the absence of a large standing biomass of kelp.

More specifically, when kelp is abundant, even moderately high densities of sea urchins tend to be largely sessile while feeding on detrital matter that falls out of the kelp canopy (Reed & Harrold 1981), and they seem to have little, if any, influence on living plants. However, where kelp is absent, urchins tend to be more highly mobile in their efforts to find food (Mattison *et al.* 1977, Reed & Harrold 1981, J. Estes unpublished data). In this active foraging mode they destructively graze the living plants that they encounter, thereby also inhibiting the successful re-establishment of newly settled plants and thus maintaining the system as a barren area.

Perturbations of this state of community organisation, in the form of disturbances which temporarily reduce the intensity of herbivory, often seem to provide the plant association an opportunity to achieve a stable refuge in size or abundance. For example, Leighton *et al.* (1966) found that by removing sea urchins from a sufficiently large area, the resulting kelp patch, once established, not only persisted but actually continued to expand its distribution into areas where urchin densities remained high. Duggins (1981) documented a similar phenomenon following an unusual accumulation of salps (*Salpa fusiformis*) and benthic diatoms (*Melosira* sp.) in the shallow coastal waters near Glacier Bay, Alaska. In this situation, the urchins preferentially fed on diatoms and salps, thereby allowing kelp plants to settle and achieve a refuge in size. The plant assemblage persisted thereafter through the summer field season. This same pattern seems to occur following numerous events that may temporarily reduce the intensity of herbivory (e.g. see Paine & Vadas 1969, Pearse & Hines 1979). Perhaps of paramount importance among these events is the depredation of sea urchins by sea otters.

In the north-east Pacific, fisheries for red sea urchins occur in British Columbia, Washington, California, and Baja California. At the present time these fisheries serve an exclusively Japanese market for urchin roe (Kato 1972). The North American fishery has developed recently. Landings data are available for the states of California and Washington, and the Province of British Columbia (Fig. 12.8). The Washington fishery is located mainly in the Strait of Juan de Fuca and the San Juan Archipelago. Reported landings increased by well over an order of magnitude between 1975 and 1978, and have remained roughly constant since that time. The urchin fishery in California began in 1971. Although a sporadic fishery has operated out of Fort Bragg in northern California, the majority of reported landings are from the northern Channel Islands. Annual landings rose from 81 kg in 1971 to 1.6 million kg in 1973 and reached 11.1 million kg in 1981. Current harvest levels are thought to be above MSY (E. E. Ebert, personal communication).

The British Columbia fishery was established in 1970; landings data are available since 1972. Initially, the fishery was concentrated near Tofino (Bernard 1982), but it collapsed after several years (Fig. 12.8), possibly as a result of competition with the then-emerging California fishery. A sporadic fishery also occurred in Georgia Strait, which increased sharply to 324 000 kg in 1980. This may have been due to an ever-increasing demand together with a stabilisation in landings by the fisheries in Washington and California. At the present time there is concern over the possibility of overexploiting the fishery in British Columbia. We have been unable to locate statistics on the Mexican fishery, although in recent years we have seen evidence of its existence at various sites from the Mexican/US border south to at least Punta Baja, Baja California Norte, Mexico.

Red sea urchin fisheries are currently undergoing rapid expansions along the Pacific coast of North America. They all are, however, too recent to allow proper interpreta-

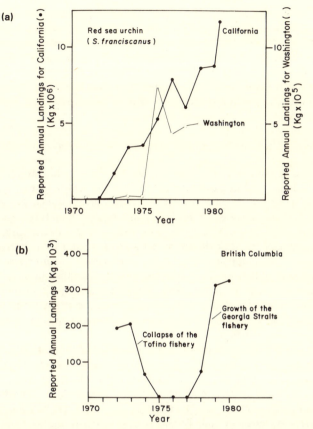

Figure 12.8 Commercial landings of red sea urchins (*Strongylocentrotus franciscanus*) along the west coast of North America. (a) California and Washington; (b) British Columbia. (From California, California Department of Fish and Game; Washington, Washington Department of Fisheries; British Columbia, Bernard 1982.)

tion of their status from landing patterns. There does seem to be the potential for overexploitation. For example, Bernard (1982) reported that areas heavily exploited in the early 1970s by the Tofino, British Columbia, fishery have been slow to recover, perhaps because there were insufficient numbers of adult-sized individuals under which the juveniles normally successfully settle.

Many areas appear suitable for urchin exploitation along the west coast of North America. Most of these are not currently being harvested because of processing and marketing problems. Nearby processing units are needed to make local fisheries feasible. Yet processing units themselves require an adequate fishery potential to operate at a profit, and this seems to be excluding the development of a fishery throughout much of the potential range.

Interaction with sea otters

Benech (1977) convincingly argued that sea-otters contributed to the failure of a developing urchin fishery in San Luis Obispo County, California. Other than this single instance, there is no overlap at the present time between sea urchin fisheries and sea-otters. Sea urchins appear to be one of the first species consumed after sea-otters expand their range into new habitats to feed, and there is abundant evidence that urchin populations are reduced both in density and mean size by otter predation (Lowry & Pearse 1973, Estes & Palmisano 1974, Gotshall *et al*. 1976, Laurent & Benech 1977, Duggins 1980, Breen *et al*. 1982). There can be little doubt that the presence of sea-otters is incompatible with red urchin fisheries.

Discussion

In reviewing these case studies, we now are faced with the task of drawing from them some sort of synthesis. Our title delineates two common themes. One of these is that invertebrate species (as distinguished from fin fishes) are exploited in each of the fisheries. However, this apparent thread of cohesiveness should be regarded with caution. Actually, the group is remarkably diverse taxonomically consisting of at least 28 species from three different phyla. In this sense, these species differ more from one another than do those comprising the whole of the world's fin fisheries. The other common theme is the actual or potential depredation of shellfish by sea-otters. This latter theme may well be unique in the sense that those same qualities that make the interaction between sea otters and shellfisheries demonstrable in some cases (see introductory remarks) also may set them apart in nature from the same kinds of interactions involving other species of marine mammals.

Based on the results of this review, we have drawn together a long list of conclusions. Not all of these explicitly concern sea otters, although in our view they are implicitly quite relevant to the problem of sea-otter–shellfishery conflicts because they help to provide a comprehensive perspective of the problems facing shellfish fisheries. We hold no illusion that the list is complete. Yet it does point out, as we have interpreted the evidence, a variety of important matters which must be drawn into any consideration of shellfish resources, and how fisheries for these resources are affected by sea-otter depredations. These conclusions follow.

(a)   In nearly all cases, the quality of evidence implicating or exonerating sea-otters in the decline or failure of various shellfisheries is poorer than one might hope for. Usually, this is because: (i) available records or data are insufficient to indicate declines, or (ii) where well-documented declines have occurred, the relative contributions of sea-otters and overfishing cannot be separated. Certainly sea-otter depredations remain an important factor in the minds of most people, but seldom has their effect been demonstrated unequivocally. Contrary to popular belief, our review suggests that some kinds of shellfisheries do survive in the presence of sea-otters (e.g. rock crabs, northern razor clams, butter clams, littleneck clams, and mussels). Others, such as commercial abalone and sea urchin fisheries, clearly do not.

(b)   Different species of shellfish seem to be of widely varying susceptibility to sea-otter predation, depending on factors such as life-history characteristics, mobility, or the use of cryptic habitats. For example, abalone and sea urchin populations have been reduced to very low levels by sea otters, especially in areas offering no habitat refuges in the form of substrate cracks and crevices. Overall, crustaceans are probably less vulnerable than are molluscs and echinoderms (sea urchins). Perhaps this is because crustaceans are, comparatively speaking, much more mobile than are most molluscan and echinoderm species, and therefore it is likely that otters must make use of visual cues to capture crustaceans. Furthermore, crustaceans are usually nocturnally active (when visual cues are apparently least effective), and some species (e.g. spiny lobsters and Dungeness crabs) spend part of the year in deep water. It also appears that estuarine shellfisheries are less severely affected (or often unaffected) by sea otter foraging compared with fisheries of the open coast.

(c) Most shellfish populations are exploited at or beyond the level of MSY. Except for those that are newly emerging, most shellfisheries have been unable to maintain a sustained level of high productivity, regardless of whether they were also subject to predation by sea otters. As a result, yields are sharply responsive to factors affecting available stock size (such as predator depredation or regulation changes).

(d) All the shellfish species discussed here have complex life histories in which their reproductive products are broadcast into the plankton where they undergo various metamorphoses before entering fishable adult populations. The larvae are planktotrophic in most instances, which greatly extends the potential time they can spend in the water column. In most species, little is known of these early life stages. In no case is it known how events acting on these various life-history stages affect the abundance of the adult populations that derive from them.

(e) Frequently, shellfish populations exhibit substantial variation between areas or over time in several aspects of their life history. For example, recruitment may occur regularly in some areas and very rarely in others; for other species it may be episodic everywhere. Similarly, growth rates and maximum sizes for a given species often vary among areas. Seldom are there sufficient data available to incorporate these sources of variation into management programmes. Consequently, following Larkin's (1977) general view of the problem, different stocks certainly have been differentially affected by exploitation, even if the intensity of exploitation was spatially uniform and low enough to be accommodated by the species as a whole.

(f) There are both commercial and recreational fisheries for most species. In some cases, landings from the recreational fisheries are though to equal or exceed commercial landings. Yet often, usually for simple practical reasons, recreational fisheries are unmonitored or effectively unregulated.

(g) Natural disasters have greatly affected a few local fisheries. For example, the earthquake of 1964, by altering coastal elevations, caused a decline in some of Alaska's clam fisheries. Similarly, paralytic shellfish poisoning precipitated the collapse of others.

(h) Economic factors often have a powerful influence on shellfisheries. These may be manifested in several ways. For example, market conditions may make it unprofitable to participate in a fishery, which would seem to be true for sea urchin fisheries along most of the coast of North America. In circumstances where price is strongly dictated by supply, it may be profitable to continue fishing even after the stock has been severely depleted (e.g. abalone).

(i) Many shellfisheries have developed rapidly. This was especially true of recent ones (e.g. the pinto abalone and red urchin fisheries). There are several consequences of this sort of rapid growth. One is that a fishery can exceed MSY while landings are still in a growth phase (e.g. Ricker 1973). Another is that the fisheries may quickly become overcapitalised or otherwise overcommitted, thus making regulations difficult to impose. Yet another consequence is that, with such rapid growth, management has neither the time nor the information to impose well-thought-out-regulations. More often than not, this results in regulations being implemented when it is too late.

We conclude that shellfisheries of the coastal north Pacific region are, in their history and behaviour, not unlike many other of the world's fisheries. Some species, due to slow growth or infrequent recruitment, seem especially susceptible to overexploitation. Indeed, the Pacific shellfisheries have to contend with a variety of pressures brought about by heavy human utilisation of the coastal environment. Of particular significance among these pressures is the prospect of predation by the sea otter, whose near extinction permitted the development of those fisheries in the first place.

Acknowledgements

We thank the following individuals for their assistance in the preparation of this paper: Dan Beck, Al Bettencourt, Ken Boettcher, Barry Brecken, Robert Brownell Jr, Paul Breen, Dick Burge, Fred Conte, Bill Donaldson, John Duffy, Marty Eaton, Earl Ebert, Dan Gotshall, Bob Hardy, Glen Jamieson, Al Kimker, Eric Knaggs, Tim Koeneman, Jim Lannon, Bud Laurent, Nick Nelson, Tom Northup, John Richards, Wink Russell, Dale Snow, Chris Toole, Ron Warner, and Paul Wild. The California Department of Fish and Game, Oregon Department of Fisheries and Wildlife, Washington Department of Fisheries, Canada Department of Fisheries and Oceans, and Alaska Department of Fish and Game provided unpublished reports and data on the history and status of various shellfisheries. Without help from these agencies and individuals, we would have been unable to complete this project.

References

Amos, M. H. 1966. Commercial clams of the North American Pacific coast. *US Dep. Int. Fish and Wildlife Service, Bureau of Commercial Fish. Circular* **237** 1–18.

Anonymous 1922. Cold weather kills Pismo clams. *Calif. Fish & Game* **8**, 124–5.

Anonymous 1978. *Anciario estadistico pesquero 1978.* Departments de Pesca de Mexico.

Antonelis, G. A. Jr, S. Leatherwood, L. H. Cornell, and J. G. Antrim 1981. Activity cycle and food selection of captive sea otters. *Murrelet* **62**, 6–9.

Aplin, J. A. 1947. Pismo clams of San Quintin, Lower California. *Calif. Fish & Game* **33**, 31–3.

Aplin, J. A. 1949. Pismo clam. *Calif. Div. Fish & Game, Fish Bull.* **74**, 165–7.

Barrera, J. P., A. J. Diaz and F. L. Salas 1976. Principales areas de pesca de langosta en la costa occidental de la peninsula de Baja California. In *Memorias del simposio sobre recursos pesqueros masivos de Mexico,* 1–72 Ensenada, B.C. del 28 al 30 de septiembre de 1976.

Baxter, J. L. 1961. Results of the 1955 to 1959 Pismo clam censuses. *Calif. Fish & Game* **47**, 153–62.

Baxter, J. L. 1962. The Pismo clam in 1960. *Calif. Fish & Game* **48**, 35–7.

Baxter, R. E. 1965. The clam resource of Alaska. In *Proceedings of joint sanitation seminar on North Pacific clams,* W. A. Felsing Jr (ed.), 3–4. Anchorage, Alaska: US Public Health Service and Alaska Department of Health and Welfare.

Baxter, R. E. 1971. Earthquake effects on clams of Prince William Sound. In *National Research Council. The great Alaska earthquake of 1964. Biology.* 238–45 Washington, DC: National Academy of Sciences.

Bell, R. R. 1971. California marine fish landings for 1970. *Calif. Depart. Fish & Game, Fish Bull.* **154**, 1–50.

Benech, S. V. 1977. Preliminary investigations of the giant red sea urchin resource of San Luis Obispo County California *Strongylocentrotus franciscanus* (Agassiz). Master's Thesis, California Polytechnic State University, San Luis Obispo.

Bennett, J. and A. C. Giese 1955. The annual reproductive and nutritional cycles in two western sea urchins. *Biol. Bull.* **109**, 226–37.

Bernard, F. R. (ed.) 1982. Assessment of invertebrate stocks off the west coast of Canada (1981). *Canad. Tech. Rep. Fish. & Aquat. Sci.* **1074**, 1–39.

Bissell, H. and F. Hubbard 1968. *Report on the sea otter, abalone and kelp resources in San Luis Obispo and Monterey Counties and proposals for reducing the conflict between the commercial abalone industry and the sea otter.* Report prepared for the California State Senate.

Blunt, C. E. Jr (coordinator) 1980. *Atlas of California coastal marine resources.* Sacramento, Calif.: California Department of Fish and Game.

Boolootian, R. A. 1965. The sea otter and its effect upon the abalone resource. In *Senate Permanent Factfinding Committee on Natural Resources. Third Progress Report to the Legislature,* 129–44, 1965 Regular Session. Sacramento, Calif.: California State Senate.

Boolootian, R. A., A. Farmanfarmaian and A. C. Giese 1962. On the reproductive cycle and breeding habits of two western species of *Haliotis. Biol. Bull.* **122**, 183–93.

Botsford, L. W. and D. E. Wickham 1978. Behaviour of age-specific, density-dependent models and the northern California Dungeness Crab *Cancer magister* Fishery. *J. Fish. Res. Bd Can.* **35**, 833–43.

Bourne, N. and D. W. Smith 1972. The effect of temperature on the larval development of the horse clam, *Tresus capax* (Gould). *Nat. Shellfish Ass. Proc.* **62**, 35–7.

Breen, P. A. 1980. *Measuring fishing intensity and annual production in the abalone fishery of British Columbia.* Can. Tech. Rep. Fisheries & Aquatic Sciences, No. 947.

Breen, P. A., T. A. Carson, J. B. Foster and E. A. Stewart 1982. Changes in subtidal community structure associated with British Columbia sea otter transplants. *Mar. Ecol. Prog. Ser.* **7**, 13–20.

Burge, R. T. 1979. *The Pismo clam fishery and resource: Before and after sea otter reoccupation.* Sea otter workshop, Santa Barbara Museum of Natural History, Santa Barbara, California.

California Bureau of Marine Fisheries 1949. The commercial fish catch of California for the year 1947 with an historical review 1916–1947. *Calif. Div. Fish & Game, Fish Bull.* **74**, 1–267.

California Department of Fish and Game 1976. *A proposal for sea otter protection and research and request for the return of management to the State of California.* Sacramento, Calif.: California Department of Fish and Game.

Calkins, D. G. 1978. Feeding behavior and major prey species of the sea otter, *Enhydra lutris,* in Montague Strait, Prince William Sound, Alaska. *Fish. Bull.* **76**, 128–31.

Cameron, R. A. and S. C. Schroeter 1980. Sea urchin recruitment: effect of substrate selection on juvenile distribution. *Mar. Ecol. Prog. Ser.* **2**, 243–7.

Carlisle, J. G. Jr 1966. Results of the 1961 to 1965 Pismo clam censuses. *Calif. Fish & Game* **52**, 157–60.

Carlisle, J. G. Jr 1973. Results of the 1971 Pismo clam census. *Calif. Fish & Game* **59**, 138–9.

Carroll, J. C. 1982. Seasonal abundance, size composition, and growth of rock crab, *Cancer antennarius* Stimpson, off central California. *J. Crustac. Biol.* **2**, 549–61.

Clark, C. W. 1973. The economics of overexploitation. *Sci.* **181**, 630–34.

Clark, F. N. 1928. Pismo clam census. *Calif. Fish & Game* **14**, 86.

Clark, F. N. 1929. Pismo clam census. *Calif. Fish & Game* **15**, 72–3.

Clark, F. N. 1931. Increasing scarcity of clams on Pismo Beach. *Calif. Fish & Game* **17**, 84.

Clark, F. N. 1932. The present status of the Pismo clam, *Tivela stultorum. Calif. Fish & Game* **18**, 170–80.

Clark, P., J. Nybakken and L. Laurent 1975. Aspects of the life history of *Tresus nuttalli* in Elkhorn Slough. *Calif. Fish & Game* **61**, 215–27.

Coe, W. R. 1947. Nutrition, growth, and sexuality of the Pismo clam (*Tivela stultorum*). *J. Exp. Zool.* **104**, 1–24.

Conte, F. S. and J. L. Dupuy 1981. The California oyster industry. *J. Wld Mar. Soc. Spec. Pub.* **1**, 1–32.

Cowen, R. K. 1982. The effect of sheephead (*Semicossyphus pulcher*) predation on the abundance and microhabitat utilization of sea urchins. In *fish food habits studies*, G. M. Caillet and C. A. Simenstad (Eds.), 268–73. Proceedings of the 3rd Pacific Workshop. Washington Sea Grant, Seattle, Washington.

Cowen, R. K. 1983. The effect of sheephead (*Semicossyphus pulcher*) predation on red sea urchin (*Strongylocentrotus franciscanus*) populations: an experimental analysis, *Oecologia* **58**, 249–55.

Cox, K. W. 1962. California abalones, family Haliotidae. *Calif. Dept Fish & Game, Fish Bull.* **118**, 1–133.

Croker, R. S. 1932. The Pismo clam in 1932. *Calif. Fish & Game* **19**, 156–7.

Dahlstrom, W. A. and P. W. Wild 1983. A history of the dungeness crab fishery in California. In *Life history, environment, and mariculture studies of the dungeness crab,* Cancer magister, *with emphasis on the central California fishery resource,* P. W. Wild and R. N. Tasto (eds.), 7–23. California Department of Fish and Game, Fish Bulletin No. 172.

Doi, T. A., S. A. Guzman del Proo, V. Marin A., M. Ortiz Q., J. Camacho A. and T. Munoz L. 1977. *Analisis de la poblacion y diagnostico de la pesqueria al abulon amarillo* (Haliotis corrugata) *en el area de Punta Abreojos e Isla de Cedros, Baja Californi.* Departmento de Pesca, Serie Cientifica No. 18.

Duffy, J. M. 1973. The status of the California spiny lobster fishery. *Calif. Dept Fish & Game, Mar. Res. Tech. Rep.* **10**, 1–15.

Duggins, D. 1980. Kelp beds and sea otters: an experimental approach. *Ecol.* **61**, 447–53.

Duggins, D. 1981. Sea urchins and kelp: the effects of short term changes in urchin diet. *Limnol. Oceanogr.* **26**, 391–4.

Ebert, E. E. 1968a. A food habits study of the southern sea otter, *Enhydra lutris nereis. Calif. Fish & Game* **54**, 33–42.

Ebert, E. E. 1968b. California sea otter – census and habitat survey. *Underwater Naturalist* **5**(3), 20–23.

Estes, J. A. 1980. *Enhydra lutris. Mammal. Spec.* **133**, 1–8.

Estes, J. A., R. J. Jameson and A. M. Johnson 1981. Food selection and some foraging tactics of sea otters. In *The Worldwide Furbearer Conference Proceedings,* J. A. Chapman and D. Pursley (eds.), 606–41 Worldwide Furbearer Conference, Inc.

Estes, J. A., R. J. Jameson and E. B. Rhode 1982. Activity and prey selection in the sea otter: influence of population status on community structure. *Am. Nat.* **120**, 242–58.

Estes, J. A. and J. F. Palmisano 1974. Sea otters: their role in structuring nearshore communities. *Sci.* **185**, 1058–60.

Estes, J. A., N. S. Smith and J. F. Palmisano 1978. Sea otter predation and community organisation in the western Aleutian Islands, Alaska. *Ecol.* **59**, 822–33.

Faro, J. B. 1970. Subtidal sea otter habitat off Pt. Pinos, California. Masters Thesis. Humboldt State College, Arcata, California.

Feder, H. M. and A. J. Paul 1973. The littleneck clam, *Protothaca staminea*, a potential fishery resource in Prince William Sound, Alaska. Proceedings of the 23rd Alaska Science Conference, College, Alaska.

Feder, H. M. and A. J. Paul. 1974. Age, growth, and size-weight relationships of the soft-shell clam, *Mya arenaria,* in Prince William Sound, Alaska. *Proc. Nat. Shellfish. Assoc.* **64**, 45–52.

Fisher, E.M. 1939. Habits of the southern sea otter. *J. Mammal.* **20**, 21–36.

Fitch, J. E. 1950. The Pismo clam. *Calif. Fish & Game* **36**, 285–312.

Fitch, J. E. 1952. The Pismo clam in 1951. *Calif. Fish & Game* **38**, 541–7.

Fitch, J. E. 1953. Common marine bivalves of California. *Calif. Dept Fish & Game, Fish Bull.* **90**, 1–102.

5

Fitch, J. E. 1954. The Pismo clam in 1952 and 1953. *Calif. Fish & Game* **40**, 199–201.

Fitch, J. E. 1955. Results of the 1954 Pismo clam census. *Calif. Fish & Game* **41**, 209–11.

Fraser, C. M. and G. M. Smith 1928. Notes on the ecology of the butter clam, *Saxidomus giganteus* De Shayes. *Trans. R. Soc. Can. Ser.* 3, **22** (Sect. V), 271–84.

Frey, H. W. (ed.) 1971. *California's living marine resources and their utilization.* Sacramento, California: California Department of Fish and Game.

Giese, A. C. 1959. Annual reproductive cycles of marine invertebrates. *Ann. Rev. Physiol.* **21**, 547–76.

Gotshall, D. W., L. L. Laurent and F. E. Wendell 1976. *Diablo Canyon power plant site ecological study annual report.* PG&E. Cooperative Research Agreement 6S-1047, Marine Resources Administrative Report No. 76-8.

Greenwalt, L. 1977. Determination that the southern sea otter is a threatened species. *Federal Register (US)* **42**, 2965–8.

Gross, J. B. 1967. Note on the northward spreading of *Mya arenaria* Linnaeus in Alaska. *Veliger* **10**, 203.

Guzman del Proo, S. A. 1975. *Sintesis de information estadistica sobre abulon y langosta en Baja California.* Instituto Nacional de Pesca. Serie Information INP/I: i31.

Haaker, P. C. and K. C. Wilson 1975. *Giant kelp.* California Department of Fish and Game, Marine Resources Leaflet No. 9.

Hall, K. R. L. and G. B. Schaller 1964. Tool-using behavior in the California sea otter. *J. Mammal.* **45**, 287–98.

Hanna, G. D. 1971. Introduction: Biological effects of the earthquake as observed in 1965. In National Research Council, *The great Alaska earthquake of 1964. Biology,* 15–34. Washington, DC: National Academy of Sciences.

Hardy, R., F. Wendell and J. D. DeMartini 1982. A status report on California shellfish fisheries. In *Social science perspectives on managing conflicts between marine mammals and fisheries,* B. Cicin-Sain, P. M. Grifman and J. B. Richards (eds), 328–40. Santa Barbara, California: University of California.

Harrison, A. J. 1969. The Australian abalone industry. *Aust. Fish.* **28**(9), 3–13.

Harry, G. Y. Jr 1973. Biology. Pages 53–60 In National Research Council. *The great Alaska earthquake of 1964. Summary and Recommendations.* Washington, DC: National Academy of Sciences.

Heimann, R. F. G. and J. Carlisle Jr 1970. The California marine fish catch for 1968 and historical review 1916–68. *Calif. Dept Fish & Game, Fish Bull.* **149**, 1–70.

Herrington, W. C. 1926. Depletion of the Pismo clam in California. *Calif. Fish & Game* **12**, 117–24.

Herrington, W. C. 1929. The Pismo clam. Further studies of its life history and depletion. *Div. Fish & Game of Calif. Fish Bull.* **18**, 1–69.

Hine, A. H. and T. R. Loughlin 1980. Observations of sea otters digging for clams at Monterey harbour, California. *Fish. Bull.* **78**, 159–63.

Holt, S. 1982. Economic impacts of sea otter migration. In *Social science perspectives on managing conflicts between marine mammals and fisheries,* Cicin-Sain, B., P. M. Grifman and J. B. Richards (eds), 136–62. Santa Barbara, California: University of California.

Holt, S., D. Fraser and J. A. Estes (in press). Some economic consequences of the depredation of pismo clams by sea otters. *Fish. Bull.*

Jameson, R. J. 1975. An evaluation of attempts to reestablish the sea otter in Oregon. MS Thesis, Oregon State University, Corvallis.

Jameson, R. J., K. W. Kenyon, A. M. Johnson and H. M. Wight 1982. History and status of translocated sea otter populations in North America. *Wildl. Soc. Bull.* **10**, 100–107.

Johnson, A. M. 1982. *Status of Alaska sea otter populations and developing conflicts with fisheries. Trans. N. Am. Wildl. Nat. Res. Conf.* Washington, DC: Wildlife Management Institute.

Kato, S. 1972. Sea urchins, a new fishery develops in California. *Mar. Fish. Rev.* **34**, 23–30.

Kenyon, K. W. 1969. The sea otter in the eastern Pacific ocean. *N. Am. Fauna* **68**, 1–352.

Kimker, A. 1981. *Shellfish report to the Alaska Board of Fisheries.* Alaska Department of Fish and Game. Commercial Fisheries. Unpublished Report.

Kimker, A. 1982a. *1982 Orca Inlet dungeness crab survey.* Unpublished report, Alaska Department of Fish and Game.

Kimker, A. 1982b. *Shellfish report to the Alaska Board of Fisheries.* Alaska Department of Fish and Game. Unpublished report.

Knaggs, E. H., E. R. Fleming and R. A. Hardy 1976. Results of the 1976 southern California Pismo clam survey. *Calif. Dept Fish & Game, Mar. Res. Admin. Rep.* **76-11**, 1–12.

Knaggs, E. H., E. R. Fleming and T. Hoban 1977. Results of the 1977 southern California Pismo clam survey. *Calif. Dept Fish & Game, Mar. Res. Admin. Rep.* **77-15**, 1–13.

Koeneman, T. 1982. *Statistical Area A (Southeast Alaska and Yakutat) Abalone.* Unpublished report to Alaska Board of Fisheries.

Laurent, L. L. and S. V. Benech 1977. *The effects of foraging by sea otter (Enhydra lutris) along their southern frontier in California from 1973 to 1977.* 58th Annual Meeting, Western Society of Naturalists, Santa Cruz, California, December 1977.

Larkin, P. A. 1977. An epitaph for the concept of maximum sustained yield. *Trans. Am. Fish. Soc.* **106**, 1–11.

Lawrence, J. 1975. On the relationships between marine plants and sea urchins. *Oceanogr. Mar. Biol., Ann. Rev.* **13**, 213–86.

Leighton, D. L., L. G. Jones and W. J. North 1966. Ecological relationships between giant kelp and sea urchins in southern California. In *Proceedings of the Fifth International Seaweed Symposium,* E. G. Young and J. L. McLachlan (eds), 141–53. New York: Pergamon.

Limbaugh, C. 1961. Observations on the California sea otter. *J. Mammal.* **42**, 271–3.

Love, M. S. and W. V. Westphal 1981. A correlation between annual catches of dungeness crab, *Cancer magister,* along the west coast of North America and mean annual sunspot number. *Fish. Bull.* **79**(4), 794–6.

Lowry, L. F. and J. S. Pearse 1973. Abalones and sea urchins in an area inhabited by sea otters. *Mar. Biol.* **23**, 213–19.

Lubchenco, J. and S. D. Gaines 1981. A unified approach to marine plant–herbivore interactions. I. Populations and communities. *Ann. Rev. Ecol. Syst.* **12**, 405–37.

Luch Belda, D., S. A. Guzman del Proo, V. Marin Aceves and M. Ortiz Q. 1973. *La pesqueria de abulon en Baja California. Un analysis de su desarollo y perspectivas futuras.* Instituto Nacional de Pesca. Serie Information INP/SI: 16.

McAllister, R. 1975. California marine fish landings for 1973. *Calif. Dept Fish Game Fish Bull.* **163**, 1–53.

McAllister, R. 1976. California marine fish landings for 1974. *Calif. Dept Fish Game Fish Bull.* **166**, 1–53.

McLean, J. H. 1962. Sublittoral ecology of kelp beds of the open coast near Carmel, California. *Biol. Bull.* **122**, 95–114.

Machell, J. R. and J. D. DeMartini 1971. An annual reproductive cycle of the gaper clam, *Tresus capax* (Gould), in south Humboldt Bay, California. *Calif. Fish Game* **57**, 274–82.

Mattison, J. E., J. D. Trent, A. L. Shanks, T. B. Adkin and J. S. Pearse 1977. Movement and feeding activity of the red sea urchin (*Strongylocentrotus franciscanus*) adjacent to a kelp forest. *Mar. Biol.* **39**, 25–30.

Miller, D. J., J. J. Geibel and J. L. Houk 1972. Results of the 1972 skindiving assessment survey. Pismo Beach to Oregon. *Calif. Dept Fish Game Mar. Resour. Tech. Rep.* **23**, 1–61.

Miller, D. J., J. E. Hardwick and W. A. Dahlstrom 1975. Pismo clams and sea otters. *Calif. Dept Fish Game Mar. Tech. Rep.* **31**, 1–49.

Minter, C. S. III 1971. Sublittoral ecology of the kelp beds off Del Monte Beach, Monterey, California. Master's thesis, Department of the Navy, Naval Postgraduate School, Monterey, California.

Mitchell, C. T., C. H. Turner and A. R. Strachan 1969. Observations on the biology and behavior of the California spiny lobster, *Panulirus interruptus* (Randall). *Calif. Fish Game* **55**, 121–31.

Morris, R. H., D. P. Abbott and E. C. Haderlie 1980. *Intertidal invertebrates of California.* Stanford: University Press.

Morris, R., D. V. Ellis and B. P. Emerson 1981. The British Columbia transplant of sea otters *Enhydra lutris. Biol. Conserv.* **20,** 291–5.

Morse, D. E., N. Hooker, H. Duncan and L. Jensen 1979. Gamma-aminobutyric acid, a neurotransmitter, induces planktonic abalone larvae to settle and begin metamorphosis. *Science* **204,** 407–10.

Newby, T. C. 1975. A sea otter (*Enhydra lutria*) food dive record. *Murrelet* **56,** 19.

Nickerson, R. B. 1975. *A critical analysis of some razor clam* Siliqua patula *(Dixon) populations in Alaska.* Anchorage, Alaska: Alaska Department of Fish and Game.

Noerenberg, W. H. 1971. Earthquake damage to Alaskan fisheries. In *National Research Council. The great Alaska earthquake of 1964. Biology,* 170–93. Washington DC: National Academy of Sciences.

North, W. J. 1964a. *An investigation of the effect of discharged wastes on kelp.* Calif. State Water Qual. Contr. Bd., Publn No. 26.

North, W. J. 1964b. Ecology of the rocky nearshore environment in southern California and possible influences of discharged wastes. *Proc. Int. Conf. Water Poll. Res.* **3,** 247–62.

North, W. J. and J. S. Pearse 1970. Sea urchin population explosion in southern California coastal waters. *Science* **167,** 209.

Nosho, T. Y. 1972. The clam fishery of the Gulf of Alaska. *A review of the oceanography and renewable resources of the northern Gulf of Alaska.* D. H. Rosenberg (ed.), 351–60. University of Alaska, Institute of Marine Science Report R72-23. Fairbanks, Alaska.

Oliphant, M. S. 1973. California marine fish landings for 1971. *Calif. Dept Fish Game Fish Bull.* **159,** 1–49.

Oliphant, M. S. 1979. California marine fish landings for 1976. *Calif. Dept Fish Game Fish Bull.* **170,** 1–56.

Orr, P. C. 1960. *Radiocarbon dates from Santa Rosa Island.* Santa Barbara Museum Nat. History, Dept. Anthropology. Bull. No. 3.

Orth, F. L., C. Smelcer, H. M. Feder and J. Williams 1975. *The Alaska clam fishery: a survey and analysis of economic potential.* University of Alaska, Institute of Marine Science Report R75-5. Fairbanks, Alaska.

Ostfeld, R. S. 1982. Foraging strategies and prey switching in the California sea otter. *Oecologia* **53,** 170–8.

Paine, R. T. 1976. Biological observation on a subtidal *Mytilus californianus* bed. *Veliger* **19,** 125–30.

Paine, R. T. and S. A. Levin 1981. Intertidal landscapes: Disturbances and the dynamics of pattern. *Ecological Monographs* **51,** 145–78.

Paine, R. T. and R. L. Vadas 1969. The effects of grazing by sea urchins, *Strongylocentrotus* spp., on benthic algal populations. *Limnol. Oceanogr.* **14,** 710–19.

Palmisano, J. F. and J. E. Estes. 1977. Ecological interactions involving the sea otter. In *The environment of Amchitka Island, Alaska,* M. L. Merritt and R. G. Fuller (eds.), 527–67. U.S. Energy Res. Devel. Adm., TID-26712, Springfield, Virginia.

Paul, A. J. and H. M. Feder 1973. Growth, recruitment, and distribution of the littleneck clam, *Protothaca staminea,* in Galena Bay, Prince William Sound, Alaska. *Fishery Bull.* **71,** 665–77.

Paul, A. J. and H. M. Feder 1976. *Clam, mussel, and oyster resources of Alaska.* University of Alaska, Institute of Marine Science Report 76-4. Fairbanks, Alaska.

Paul, A. J., J. M. Paul and H. M. Feder 1976. Recruitment and growth in the bivalve *Protothaca staminea,* at Olson Bay, Prince William Sound, Alaska, ten years after the 1964 earthquake. *Veliger* **18,** 385–92.

Pearse, J. S. and A. H. Hines 1979. Expansion of a central California kelp forest following the mass mortality of sea urchins. *Mar. Biol.* **51,** 83–91.

Pearse, J. S., M. E. Clark, D. L. Leighton, C. T. Mitchell and W. J. North 1970. *Marine waste disposal and sea urchin ecology.* Unpublished report to Federal Water Quality administration.

Pflaker, G. 1972. Tectonis. In *National Research Council. The great Alaska earthquake of 1964. Geology,* Part A. 47–122. Washington DC: National Academy of Sciences.

Pinkas, L. 1970. The California marine fish catch for 1969. *Calif. Dept Fish Game Fish Bull.* **153**, 1–47.

Pinkas, L. 1974. The California marine fish catch for 1972. *Calif. Dept Fish Game Fish Bull.* **161**, 1–53.

Pinkas, L. 1977. The California marine fish catch for 1975. *Calif. Dept Fish Game Fish Bull.* **168**, 1–55.

Pitcher, K. W. 1975. *Distribution and abundance of sea otters, Steller sea lions, and harbor seals in Prince William Sound, Alaska.* Alaska Dept. Fish and Game, Anchorage, Alaska.

Pleschner, D. B. 1982. Abalone divers: a vanishing breed. *Santa Barbara Magazine* **8**(5), 11–16, 74, 78–9.

Program Staff 1983. Summary and recommendations. In Life history, environment, and mariculture studies of the Dungeness crab, *Cancer magister,* with emphasis on the central California fishery resource, P. W. Wild and R. N. Tasto (eds.). *Calif. Dept Fish Game Fish Bull.* **172**, 319–23.

Quayle, D. B. 1943. Sex, gonad development, and seasonal gonad changes in *Paphia staminea* Conrad. *J. Fish Res. Bd. Can.* **6**, 140–51.

Quayle, D. B. and N. Bourne 1972. The clam fisheries of British Columbia. *Fish. Res. Bd. Can. Bull.* **179**, 1–70.

Reed, D. and C. Harrold 1981. The role of sea urchins (*Strongylocentrotus franciscanus*) in the formation, maintenance and persistance of barren areas in a giant kelp (*Macrocystis pyrifera*) community. Abstract, West. Soc. Nat. 62nd Ann. Meeting, Santa Barbara, CA.

Reilly, P. N. 1983. Dynamics of Dungeness crab, (*Cancer magister*) larvae off central and northern California. In Life history, environment, and mariculture studies of the Dungeness crab, *Cancer magister,* with emphasis on the central California fish resource, P. W. Wild and R. N. Tasto (eds.). *Calif. Dept Fish Game Fish Bull.* **172**, 57–84.

Reimnitz, E. and N. F. Marshall 1972. Effects of the earthquake and tsunami on recent deltaic sediments. In *National Research Council. The great Alaska earthquake of 1964. Geology,* Part A, 265–78. Washington, DC: National Academy of Sciences.

Repenning, C. A. 1976. *Enhydra* and *Endydriodon* from the Pacific coast of North America. *J. Res. US Geol. Survey* **4**, 305–15.

Ricker, W. E. 1973. Two mechanisms that make it impossible to maintain peak period yields from stocks of Pacific salmon and other fisheries. *J. Fish. Res. Bd. Can.* **30**, 1275–86.

Roedel, P. M. 1939. The Pismo clam in 1938. *Calif. Fish Game* **25**, 177–81.

Roedel, P. M. 1942. The 1941 Pismo clam census. *Calif. Fish Game* **28**, 66.

Rudy, P. Jr and L. H. Rudy 1983. Oregon estuarine invertebrates. FWS/OBS-83/16. Coastal Ecosystems Project, US Fish and Wildlife Service, Portland, Oregon.

Sainsbury, K. J. 1977. Population dynamics and fishing management of the abalone, *Haliotis iris.* Ph.D. thesis, University of Canterbury, Christchurch, New Zealand.

Schmitt, W. L. 1921. The marine decapod crustacea of California. *Univ. Calif. Publns. Zool.* **23**, 1–470.

Scofield, N. B. 1931. Increasing scarcity of clams on Pismo Beach. *Calif. Fish Game* **17**, 84.

Simenstad, C. A., J. A. Estes and K. W. Kenyon 1978. Aleuts, sea otters, and alternate stable-state communities. *Science* **200**, 403–11.

Stephenson, M. D. 1977. Sea otter predation on Pismo clams in Monterey Bay. *Calif. Fish Game* **63**, 117–20.

Strathmann, R. 1971. The feeding behavior of planktotrophic echinoderm larvae: mechanisms, regulation, and rates of suspension feeding. *J. Exp. Mar. Biol. Ecol.* **6**, 109–60.

Strathmann, R. 1978. Length of pelagic period in echinoderms with feeding larvae from the northeast Pacific. *J. Exp. Mar. Biol. Ecol.* **34**, 23–7.

Suchanek, T. H. 1978. The ecology of *Mytilus edulis* L. in exposed rocky intertidal communities. *J. Exp. Mar. Biol. Ecol.* **31**, 105–20.

Tegner, M. J. 1980. Multispecies considerations of resource management in southern California kelp beds. *Can. Tech. Rep. Fish. Aquatic Sci.* **954**, 125–43.

Tegner, M. J. and P. K. Dayton 1977. Sea urchin recruitment patterns and implications of commercial fishing. *Science* **196**, 324–6.

Tegner, M. J. and P. K. Dayton 1981. Population stucture, recruitment, and mortality of two sea urchins (*Strongylocentrotus franciscanus* and S. *purpuratus*) in a kelp forest. *Mar. Ecol. Progr. Ser.* **5**, 255–68.

Tomlinson, P. K. 1968. Mortality, growth, and yield per recruit for Pismo clams. *Calif. Fish Game* **54**, 100–7.

US Fish and Wildlife Service 1982. *Southern sea otter recovery plan.* US Department of the Interior, Washington, DC.

VanBlaricom, G. R. 1984. Relationships of sea otters and living marine resources in California: a new perspective. In *Collection of Papers Presented at the Ocean Studies Symposium, November 7–10, 1982, Asilomar, California,* 361–81. Sacramento, California. California Coastal Commission and California Department of Fish and Game.

VanBlaricom, G. R. and Jameson 1979. *Sea otter–canopy kelp relationships in central California: an historical review and a model.* Sea otter workshop Santa Barbara Museum of Natural History, Santa Barbara, California.

Wade, L. S. 1975. A sea otter possibly feeding on Pismo clams. *J. Mammal.* **56**, 720–1.

Webber, H. H. 1977. Gastropods: Prosobranchia. In A. C. Giese and J. S. Pearse (eds.). *Reproduction of marine invertebrates, Vol. IV molluscs: gastropods and cephalopods,* A. C. Guise and J. S. Pearse (eds.), 1–97. New York: Academic Press.

Wendell, F., J. D. DeMartini, P. Dinnel and J. Siecke 1976. The ecology of the gaper or horse clam, *Tresus capax* (Gould 1850) (Bivalvia: Mactridae), in Humboldt Bay, California. *Calif. Fish Game* **62**, 41–64.

Weymouth, F. W. 1919. A case of destruction of Pismo clams by oil. *Calif. Fish Game* **5**, 174–5.

Weymouth, F. W. 1923. The life-history and growth of the Pismo clam (*Tivela stultorum* Mawe). *Calif. Fish Game Commission Fish Bull.* **7**, 1–120.

Weymouth, F. W., H. C. McMillan and W. H. Rich 1931. Latitude and relative growth in the razor clam, *Siliqua patula. J. Exp. Biol.* **8**, 228–49.

Wickham, D. E. 1979a. Predation by the Nemertean *Carcinonemertes errans* on eggs of the dungeness crab *Cancer magister. Mar. Biol.* **55**, 45–53.

Wickham, D. E. 1979b. The crab-egg predator, *Carcinonemertes errans,* and cycling and collapse of dungeness crab population. Ph.D. dissertation, University of Calif., Berkeley.

Wild, P. W. 1983. The influence of seawater temperature on spawning, egg development, and hatching success of the dungeness crab, *Cancer magister.* In Life history, environment, and mariculture studies of the dungeness crab, *Cancer magister,* with emphasis on the central California fishery resource, P. W. Wild and R. N. Tasto (eds.). *Calif. Dept Fish Game Fish Bull.* **172**, 197–213.

Wild, P. W. and J. A. Ames 1974. A report on the sea otter *Enhydra lutris,* L., in California. *Calif. Dept Fish Game Mar. Res. Tech. Rep.* **20**, 1–93.

Wild, P. W., P. M. W. Law and D. R. McLain 1983. Variations in ocean climate and the Dungeness crab fishery in California. In Life history, environment and mariculture studies of the Dungeness crab, *Cancer magister,* with emphasis on the central California fishery resource, P. W. Wild and R. N. Tasto (eds.). *Calif. Dept Fish Game Fish Bull.* **172**, 175–88.

Yancy, R. M. 1966. Review of oyster culture in Alaska, 1910–1961. *Proc. Nat. Shellfisheries Assoc.* **56**, 65–6.

Young, J. S. and J. D. DiMartini 1970. The reproductive cycle, gonadal histology, and gametogenesis of the red abalone, *Haliotis refescens* (Swainson). *Calif. Fish Game* **54**, 298–309.

13 Dolphins and the purse-seine fishery for yellowfin tuna

Robin L. Allen

Introduction

In the eastern Pacific Ocean yellowfin tuna (*Thunnus albacares*) often associate with some species of dolphins (principally *Stenella* and *Delphinus* spp.). The reason for the association is not understood, but fishermen have taken advantage of it by using dolphins as a cue to find yellowfin tuna, and to assist in capturing them. When tuna were caught primarily by baitboats using the pole and line method, dolphins were not often involved and only occasionally injured. However, following the increasing use of purse-seining in the late 1950s, large numbers of dolphins were entangled in the nets and drowned in the process of catching tuna. The impact of the fishery on dolphin populations and the current management of tuna and dolphins, will be discussed in this chapter.

The fishery

The purse-seine fishery for yellowfin and other tuna species covers a large area of the eastern Pacific Ocean (shown in Fig. 13.1). Fishermen are able to catch tuna because they aggregate in schools which can be seen at the surface, or else in association with floating objects (commonly called logs), or, in the case of yellowfin tuna, with schools of dolphins. In general, unassociated schools and schools associated with logs contain smaller yellowfin (Fig. 13.2) and tend to be found closer to the shore than those which are associated with dolphin schools (Fig. 13.3). Although the amount of each type of fishing varies from year to year, on average about one-half of the total catch of yellowfin tuna is taken from schools associated with dolphins (Table 13.1).

Aggregations of yellowfin tuna and dolphins are often accompanied by birds, and it is normally either the activity of birds or splashes made by the dolphins which attract the attention of the fishermen. As well as providing a cue for the fishermen to locate a school of tuna, the dolphins serve as a target for the seiner to chase, round up, and eventually encircle with the net. During this activity the tuna remain very close to the dolphins and are also captured. Once the fish are securely encircled by the net, the fishermen attempt to release the dolphins by carrying out a manoeuvre called 'breakdown'. This involves retrieving about two-thirds of the net from the water, then moving the seiner slowly astern. The net is forced into a long channel and when the seiner reaches a certain speed, the water flowing through the seine webbing causes the end section of the net to sink, allowing the dolphins to escape over the top. In effect,

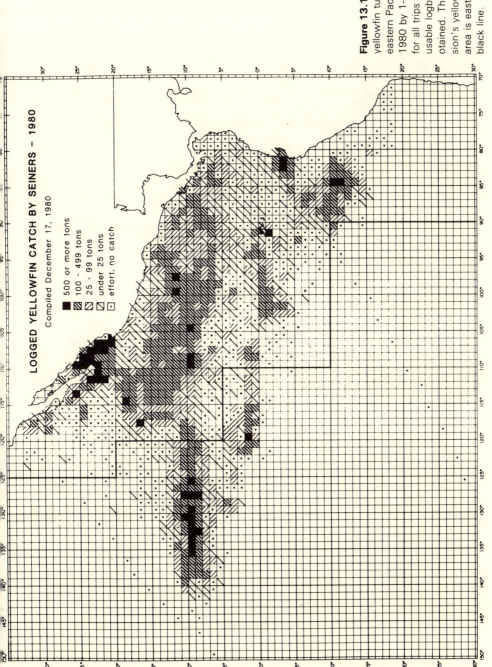

LOGGED YELLOWFIN CATCH BY SEINERS – 1980

Compiled December 17, 1980

■ 500 or more tons
▨ 100 - 499 tons
▧ 25 - 99 tons
▢ under 25 tons
⊡ effort, no catch

Figure 13.1 Catches of yellowfin tuna in the eastern Pacific Ocean in 1980 by 1-degree squares for all trips for which usable logbook data were obtained. The Commission's yellowfin regulatory area is east of the heavy black line.

PERCENT FREQUENCY

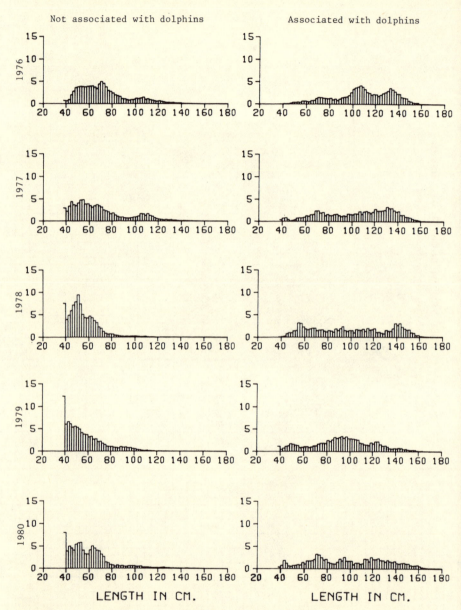

Figure 13.2 Length frequencies of yellowfin tuna from sets made in association with dolphins and sets not in association with dolphins, 1976–80.

the net is pulled out from underneath the school. During this manoeuvre it is usual for some of the crew to assist the dolphins to escape by disentangling those which get caught in the webbing, and to help others over the corkline. For this operation, one man may be in a small inflatable raft inside the net, and one or two others in speedboats which are tied to the net. Despite the efforts at ensuring that dolphins are released unharmed, there are, on average, a few killed for each set.

Dolphin species involved in the fishery

The three species most commonly involved in the fishery are spotted dolphin (*Stenella attenuata*), spinner dolphin (*Stenella longirostris*), and common dolphin (*Delphinus delphis*). In addition, several other species, including striped dolphin (*S. coeruleoalba*) and bottlenosed dolphin (*Tursiops truncatus*), are occasionally involved in the fishery. The three major species are widely distributed in the tropical waters (Rice 1977), which are also inhabited by yellowfin tuna (Cole 1981), but only in the eastern Pacific is there a large-scale fishery based on the association of yellowfin tuna and dolphins.

In the eastern tropical Pacific, several geographical forms of each of the three major species have been recognised (Evans 1975, Perrin 1975, Perrin *et al.* 1979). Based on these forms, the National Marine Fisheries Service (NMFS) has established management units for dolphins. The current boundaries of these management units for the three major species (Smith 1979) are shown, together with the distribution of sightings made by technicians aboard purse-seiners from 1977 to 1979 in Figures 13.4 to 13.6. In some cases, for example eastern and whitebelly spinners, the geographical forms are sufficiently distinct and well known to make identification in the field possible. In this case, the distributions of the stocks overlap. In other cases, either the forms cannot readily be identified in the field, or insufficient data are available to show ranges of the forms, and management units are then based on geographical areas within which a particular form appears to be most common.

Estimates of mortality

The Inter-American Tropical Tuna Commission (IATTC), the NMFS, and the Instituto Nacional de Pesca of Mexico have programmes involving the placement of biologists on a sample of the seiners which fish for tuna associated with dolphins. These biologists collect data which are used to estimate abundance and incidental mortality of dolphins, and biological samples which are used for life-history studies.

Estimates of total mortality have been made using data giving the numbers of dolphins killed during sampled trips and the total number of sets made on dolphin schools from IATTC logbook information. The estimates are made using ratio estimators and are subject to two sources of error. First, there are sampling errors in estimating average kill rate, and second, there are errors in the estimates of the total number of sets made on dolphins. From 1959 to 1972, there were only 21 observed trips on tuna seiners for which data are available, and thus sampling errors are likely to be severe. The problem is aggravated by the uncertainty as to how often the backdown procedure was used in the first few years of the fishery. This then gives rise to doubts about how well the sampled trips – all of which were made after 1963 – represent all trips during that period. The total number of sets made on dolphins is not known

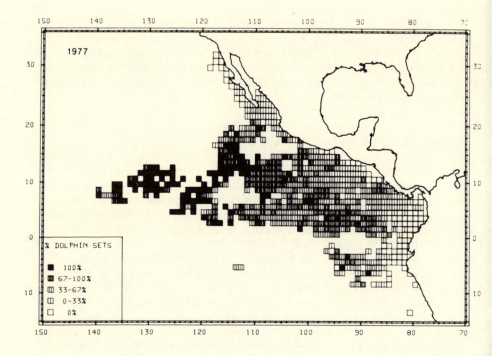

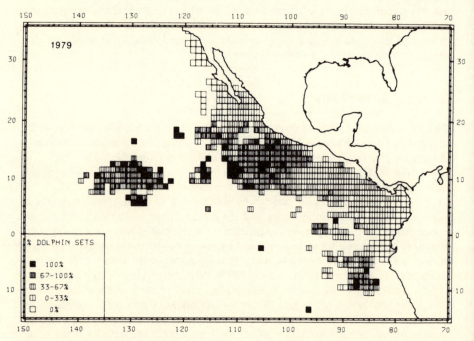

Figure 13.3 Proportion of purse-seine sets which were made on dolphin schools, 1977–80.

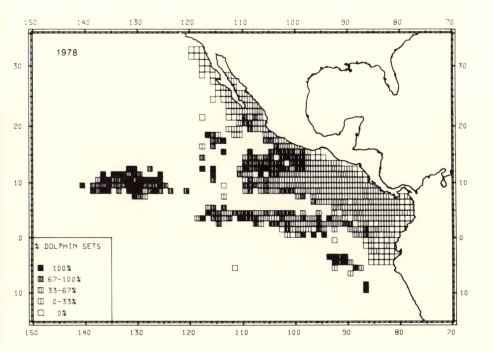

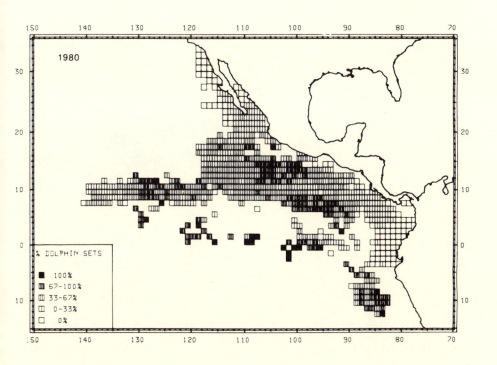

Table 13.1 Estimated purse-seine catch (thousand of tonnes) of yellowfin, eastern Pacific east of 150°W.

Year	Percentage of catch on dolphins	Total yellowfin catch
1966	59	82
1967	44	80
1968	46	103
1969	80	132
1970	68	161
1971	66	126
1972	79	186
1973	66	227
1974	52	232
1975	60	224
1976	54	261
1977	54	221
1978	34	198
1979	43	210
1980	48	176

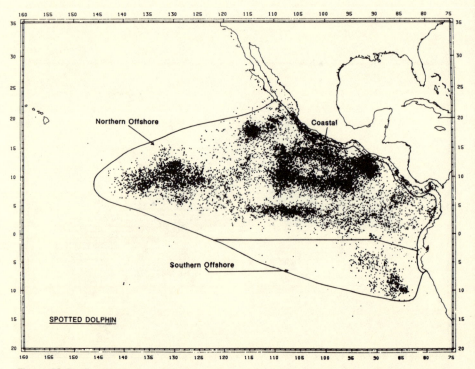

Figure 13.4 The distribution of sightings of spotted dolphins by technicians on purse-seiners, 1977–9.

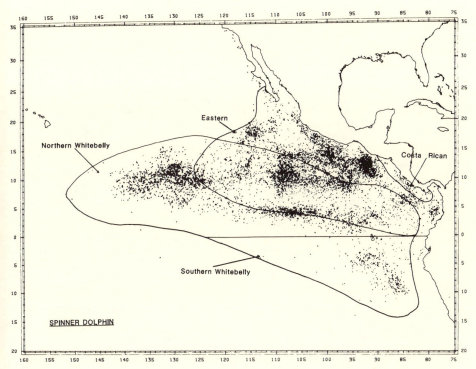

Figure 13.5 The distribution of sightings of spinner dolphins by technicians on purse-seiners, 1977–9.

exactly because fishermen do not always provide these data, and in these instances, the number is estimated. In the early years of purse-seine fishing, set type had to be estimated for slightly more than 50% of all sets on yellowfin, whereas in the years 1977–9, set type was estimated for about 18% of all sets on yellowfin.

There have been several estimates of historical kills reported in unpublished documents (e.g. Anonymous 1976, Smith 1979, Alverson 1980). These estimates have been made using different procedures and interpretations of the data and differ substantially for the years 1959–61, which are most affected by the uncertainty about whether or not backdown was used. In general terms, annual mortality was estimated to be in the range of 200 000 to 500 000 for most years in the period 1959–72. In 1973 and later years, the estimates are more reliable because of the increased number of trips sampled. Estimates of mortality by species for this period are shown in Figure 13.7. For the years 1973–8, these estimates are taken from Smith (1979), and for 1979–80 from Anonymous (1981).

Impact on populations

Estimates of the mortality in the 1960s were as high as half a million animals per year. This mortality undoubtedly had a large effect on the dolphin populations. To measure this effect it is necessary to have estimates of the size of the populations, of the net reproductive rates, and of incidental mortality.

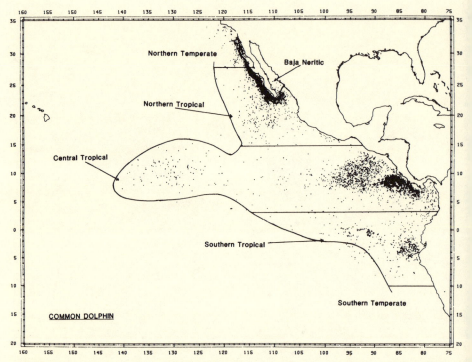

Figure 13.6 The distribution of sightings of common dolphins by technicians on purse-seiners, 1977–9.

In recent years, the NMFS has conducted several aerial and research ship surveys of the stocks. Based on these, and on data collected by observers on seiners, several estimates of population sizes have been made, using line-transect methods which depend on several assumptions. The most important of these are that all dolphin schools on the line of search are seen, that the distance to the line of search at the time of first sighting can be measured for those not directly ahead, and that the path searched is independent of population density. Without going into details, it is clear that all these assumptions might be violated (Hammond 1981), and thus estimates of the population sizes should be treated with caution. Table 13.2 shows two sets estimates of population size in 1979 based on different methods of estimating proportions of species composition for the three major species (Smith 1979). These estimates are of the order of millions, compared to kills of tens of thousands.

Attempts to measure net reproductive rates for dolphins in the eastern Pacific have not been successful. There are no direct estimates of natural mortality. Smith (1979) assumed that for unexploited stocks, the gross reproductive rate would be close to the natural mortality rate. Net reproductive rates were then estimated for exploited stocks by subtracting gross reproductive rates for unexploited stocks from those for the exploited stocks. However, the differences found were generally not significant at the 95% confidence level. Thus, estimates of the dynamics of exploited populations have had to be made using assumed values of net reproductive rates, which have most commonly been below 0.06 per annum.

The estimates of all the components (population size, mortality, reproductive rates)

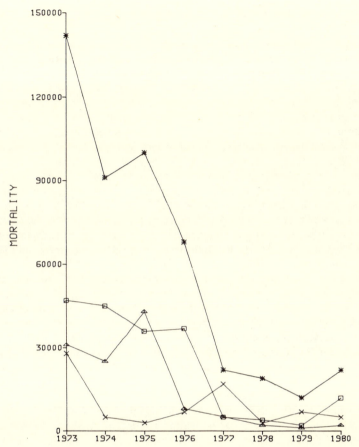

Figure 13.7 Estimates of dolphin mortality incidental to purse-seining. 1973–80.

necessary to assess the impact of incidental mortality are subject to errors which have not been fully assessed. Nevertheless, it seems clear that large kills that have been sustained in the past had a serious impact on some stocks. The most recent assessment of this impact (Smith, 1979) was that eastern spinner dolphins were at about 20% of their pre-exploitation population size, northern offshore spotted dolphins were around 40–50% of pre-exploitation size, and other stocks were about 60% of their pre-exploitation population sizes.

Table 13.2 Two sets of estimates of 1979 population size using alternative methods of calculation for offshore spotted, spinner, and common dolphins in the eastern tropical Pacific Ocean (numbers in millions).

offshore spotted dolphin	3.3	2.9
eastern spinner dolphin	0.3	0.3
whitebelly spinner dolphin	0.6	0.5
common dolphin	1.3	3.1

Management of the tuna–dolphin complex

Management responsibilities for the yellowfin tuna and dolphin populations are spread over government agencies of many of the countries involved in the fishery. However, the most important management actions have been taken by the IATTC and the NMFS.

The IATTC was established by a convention between Costa Rica and the USA, which was implemented in 1950, to carry out research and to make recommendations to member governments for the management of the tuna and associated bait fisheries of the eastern tropical Pacific Ocean. The present members of the Commission are Canada, France, Japan, Nicaragua, Panama and the USA. The IATTC management goal for tuna stocks is: '...designed to keep populations of fishes at those levels of abundance which will permit the maximum sustained catch'. In 1966, in response to IATTC recommendations, a quota management system for yellowfin tuna was instituted within the Commission's yellowfin regulatory area (CYRA), and was in effect every year from then until 1979. Although quotas were agreed to by the Commission for 1980 and 1981, member and co-operating governments have been unable to agree on means for implementing them. Thus there was no closed season within the CYRA in 1980 and 1981.

In 1976, the Commission agreed that it should concern itself with the problems arising from the involvement of dolphins in the purse-seine fishery for yellowfin. As its objectives, it was agreed that: '(1) the Commission should strive to maintain a high level of tuna production, and (2) also to maintain porpoise stocks at or above levels that assure their survival in perpetuity, (3) with every reasonable effort being made to avoid needless or careless killing of porpoise'. So far, the IATTC involvement has mainly been concerned with carrying out research. Recommendations, principally concerning fishing gear and procedures, have been made by the Commission's staff, but these have not yet resulted in any management actions.

Management of dolphins by NMFS is mandated by the Marine Mammal Protection Act of 1972. The goal of the act is that marine mammals: '... should be protected and encouraged to develop to the greatest extent feasible commensurate with sound policies of resource management...'. Management actions have been taken to place restrictions on gear and fishing techniques to reduce mortality of dolphins which have been encircled by a purse-seine, and to place quotas on some stocks and to prohibit intentional setting of nets on others. The quotas and prohibition of intentional sets on eastern spinner dolphins and other stocks of minor importance to the fishery were implemented in 1977. The NMFS regulations apply directly to seiners under the USA flag. They also apply indirectly to parts of the international fleet, through the means of import restrictions on yellowfin tuna taken in a manner prohibited for US fishermen.

Thus the management of the tuna–dolphin complex is being carried out mainly by two agencies with different goals, one to maximise the harvest of one part of the ecosystem, and the other with the goal of providing the maximum protection for another part. Furthermore, the management has been carried out so far as if the two groups of animals did not interact.

There are two types of interaction that may be considered in the management of yellowfin and dolphins. The first is that yellowfin schools associated with dolphins tend to be composed of larger fish than others. Consequently, fishing for yellowfin in association with dolphins produces a higher yield per recruit than fishing for yellowfin not associated with dolphins. The second type concerns ecological interactions between tuna and dolphins.

If only the size composition of the yellowfin catch is considered, the policies of protecting dolphins by reducing the number of sets on dolphins and the management of tuna to maintain catches at maximum levels are incompatible. Figure 13.8. shows the estimated yield per recruit as a function of fishing effort for two age-specific catchability coefficients. One set corresponds to the age composition of the 1979–80 yellowfin catches taken in association with dolphins, and the other to the age compositon of yellowfin not taken in association with dolphins in the same period. This shows that for low fishing effort, the yield per recruit behaves in much the same way for both sets of coefficients, but that for high values of fishing effort the yield per recruit of dolphin-associated fish is higher than that of fish not associated with dolphins. To complete the analysis, recruitment should also be considered. Up to now, cohort analysis has not shown any relation between stock and recruitment, but if stocks were to decline, a policy of fishing older fish is less likely to cause recruitment problems than one of

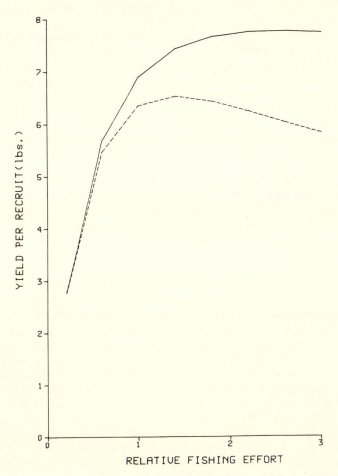

Figure 13.8 Yield per recruit of yellowfin for two age specific catchability vectors, (—) typical of fishing in association with dolphins, (– – –) typical of fishing schools not associated with dolphins.

fishing incoming year-classes. These considerations are further complicated by the fact that small yellowfin tuna are often taken in association with skipjack tuna (*Katsuwonus pelamis*), and that any attempt to direct fishing effort away from small yellowfin would to some extent reduce the catch of skipjack.

In the late 1960s, the purse-seine fleet began to fish further offshore, and apparently found previously unexploited stocks of yellowfin. To evaluate the impact of this offshore fishery on the yield, the IATTC began a policy of setting quotas that exceeded the estimated sustained yields. The rationale was that by overfishing it would be possible to observe a wide range of stock sizes, and the parameters of the models then employed could be validated. As a result of this programme, the stock is estimated to be capable of producing around 175 000 tonnes per year. Because of the difficulty in achieving agreement on management measures in 1978 and 1979, and the lack of an agreement in 1980 and 1981, yellowfin stocks have been reduced below the level at which they could produce the maximum yield. To achieve the IATTC management goals, it is thus necessary to allow the stock to recover, either by reducing the total catch or by increasing the yield per recruit.

The management implications of the ecological relation between yellowfin tuna and dolphins can only be a matter of speculation because the nature of the interactions between the two groups is largely unknown. The most obvious explanation for the association (mentioned by several authors) is the possibility that it is based on feeding, for example yellowfin tuna may be following dolphins to take advantage of their presumably superior food-finding abilities.

There have been several studies of the diet of both yellowfin tuna and dolphins based on stomach contents. Alverson (1963) examined the stomach contents of yellowfin tuna and reported the average content by volume to be fish 47%, crustaceans 45%, and cephalopods 8%. The fish Alverson examined were mostly captured by baitboats and were all taken close to the coast of Central and South America during the period 1957 to 1959. A more recent study by R. J. Olson of yellowfin tuna captured by purse-seiners in 1970 and 1971 (Anonymous 1979) showed fish making up 90% by volume of stomach contents. In particular, *Auxis* spp., which made up less than 6% in Alverson's samples, made up about 50% of the stomach contents in the latter samples. These differences may be due to the different areas sampled, as the latter study involved yellowfin from offshore areas in which dolphins and yellowfin frequently associate.

Fitch and Brownell (1968) studied feeding habits of five spinner dolphins and three spotted dolphins which had been taken in association with yellowfin tuna in the eastern Pacific. On the basis of the stomach contents, they concluded that the spinner dolphins had been feeding at 250 m or more below the surface, and that the spotted dolphins had been feeding within 30 m of the surface. Perrin *et al.* (1973) examined the stomach contents of spotted dolphins, spinner dolphins, and yellowfin tuna which had been taken in 12 purse-seine sets during the period 1968–70. The overlap of species in the stomach contents was greatest between yellowfin tuna and spotted dolphins, which both frequently contained ommastrephid squids, *Auxis* sp., and epipelagic exocetids. Ommastrephid squid were also common in the stomachs of spinner dolphins. Mesopelagic fish were frequently found in the spinner dolphin stomachs but were not frequent in the stomachs of either yellowfin tuna or spotted dolphins. Crustacea were commonly present in yellowfin stomachs but were not found in the dolphin stomachs. Among the fish species frequently found in the stomachs of spinner dolphins but rarely in spotted dolphins (Fitch & Brownell 1968, Perrin *et al.* 1973) was a mesopelagic gonostomatid, *Vinciguerria* sp., which was also at times common in yellowfin stomachs sampled in 1970 and 1971 (R. J. Olson, unpublished data). Yellowfin are taken by longliners in the eastern Pacific at depths of 100 m (Suzuki *et al.* 1968), and thus there is the potential for an overlap in consumption of mesopelagic fauna by spinner dolphins and yellowfin. The relative proportion of empty stomachs among the three species taken in the same set indicate that spinner dolphins did not feed at the same time as spotted dolphins and yellowfin tuna. This is consistent with the observations by Norris and Dohl (1980) that spinner dolphins feed at night, and by Schaefer *et al.* (1963) that yellowfin tuna feed during the day. However, apparent night-time feeding behaviour in spotted dolphins in the eastern Pacific (Leatherwood & Ljunblad 1979) and off Hawaii (Shomura & Hida 1965, Scott & Wussow 1979) has been reported.

There have been reports of dolphins eating yellowfin tuna in the Atlantic Ocean (Le Guen, unpublished data; Savini, unpublished manuscript), but this is not known for the species involved in the fishery in the eastern Pacific.

In summary, there is some overlap in the diets of yellowfin tuna and both spotted and spinner dolphins. However, because yellowfin and dolphins are opportunistic feeders, the dietary overlap could be a result of their association rather than a cause. The feeding association alone does not provide decisive evidence for either competition or facilitation among the species. Feeding competition would only be important if food were a limiting resource for one or more of the species. Furthermore, if local abundance of prey were critical, competition might be avoided by using different feeding strategies, for example feeding on different-sized prey, as noted by Perrin *et al.* (1973). Based on the results of energetic modelling of yellowfin tunas and the observed density of potential prey organisms, Sharp and Francis (1976) speculated that large yellowfin tuna (> 40 cm) are probably not food limited.

An alternative view of the relationship between yellowfin tuna and dolphins is that it is similar to that which exists between yellowfin tuna and floating objects. Floating objects such as trees, dead whales, buoys and small pieces of rope at times have schools of yellowfin and other fishes associated with them, and in fact this association is important for a substantial part of the catch of both yellowfin and skipjack tunas. Again, the reasons for the association are unknown, but in this case the potential interactions clearly would not include competition.

If there are strong ecological interactions between yellowfin tuna and dolphins, these should be considered in setting and implementing management goals for future changes in population sizes. Figure 13.9 shows the recent history of offshore spotted dolphin and yellowfin tuna population sizes as estimated by Smith (1979) and Anonymous (1981).

The yellowfin fishery was confined to within a few hundred miles of the coast prior to 1966, and subsequently expanded offshore reaching the edge of the CYRA in 1969. Thus estimates of the abundance of stocks which are currently exploited, based on catch rates or cohort analysis, cannot be made for the early years of the purse-seine fishery. The estimates of Figure 13.9 were made using cohort analysis and show biomass of large yellowfin, which form the bulk of the fish associated with dolphins, and all yellowfin. Both estimates show much the same changes, which reflect fluctuations in year-class strength and removals by the fishery. In particular, the 1974 year class was large and was followed by poor recruitment in 1976 and 1977. Overall the estimates show a decline in stock size caused by the increased catches during the period.

The population estimates for offshore spotted dolphin are inferred from estimates of 1979 population sizes and the history of mortality. In making the estimates shown here it was assumed that there was only one stock. However, very high mortalities in

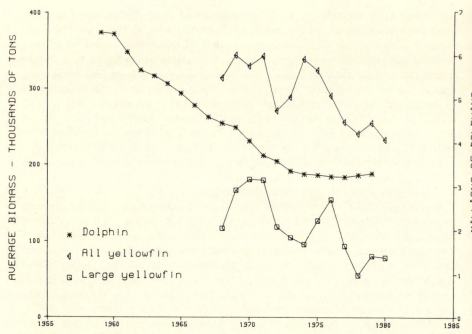

Figure 13.9 Estimated changes in population size of spotted dolphins and yellowfin tuna over the period 1959–80.

the early years only involved animals close to the coast, and consequently the pattern of decline was probably more severe in inshore water than offshore. To quantify this difference, it would be necessary to estimate the rate of mixing of dolphins from different areas.

The present management goals are to maintain dolphin populations at or above the levels which allow maximum net reproduction (NMFS), and for the yellowfin population to grow only slightly from the current size (IATTC). If the dolphin species and yellowfin are in competition, the growth of dolphin populations would be detrimental to the yellowfin stocks, whereas if dolphins assisted yellowfin to locate food, the growth of dolphin populations may be beneficial for yellowfin. Similar arguments relate the effect of yellowfin management upon the achievement of the goals of dolphin management.

What does our present knowledge about the relation between yellowfin tuna and dolphins contribute to the management of the yellowfin–dolphin complex? The issue of the relation between the yield per recruit of yellowfin and fishing yellowfin either associated with or not associated with dolphins is one of how societies value protecting dolphins compared to the industry of catching tuna. Roughly one dolphin is killed for each 3 tonnes of yellowfin taken in association with dolphins. Purse-seining on yellowfin not associated with dolphins at most produces 84% of the yield per recruit that could be taken from fishing yellowfin associated with dolphins. This latter comparison, of course, ignores two questions. Are the fisheries interchangeable and what is the contribution of skipjack to the fishery?

The question of the effect of ecological interaction on management must, because of lack of knowledge, remain open. In the absence of information about the effect of any species upon another in the complex, there seems to be no good reason to modify existing management plans to try to take account of interactions. However, this should be done recognising our ignorance, rather than by assuming that such interactions are unimportant. Research directed towards answering questions about possible effects of interactions should be actively pursued with the goal of producing more certain management.

Acknowledgements

Patrick Tomlinson and Richard Punsley provided assistance in the preparation and interpretation of much of the data used in this paper. Thanks are also due to colleagues at the Inter-American Tropical Tuna Commission and the Southwest Fisheries Center who gave helpful advice and criticism.

References

Alverson, F. G. 1963. The food of yellowfin and skipjack tunas in the eastern tropical Pacific ocean. *Inter-Am. Trop. Tuna Comm., Bull.* **7**(5), 295–396.

Alverson, F. G. 1980. Statement of Franklin G. Alverson, Vice President, Living Marine Resources, Inc. at public hearings on proposed regulations governing the take of marine mammals incidental to commercial fishing operations. MMPAH #1980–1. *Historical kills of porpoise by species/stock, 1959–1970.* March 1980.

Anonymous 1976. *Report of the workshop on stock assessment of porpoises involved in the eastern Pacific yellowfin tuna fishery.* Southwest Fisheries Center. Admin. Rep. LJ-76-29.

Anonymous 1979. *Ann. rep. of the Inter-American Trop. Tuna Comm. 1978.*

Anonymous 1981. *Ann. rep. of the Inter-American Trop. Tuna Comm. 1980.*

Cole, J. S. 1981. Synopsis of biological data on the yellowfin tuna, *Tunnus albacares* (Bonnaterre, 1788), in the Pacific Ocean. In *Synopses on the biology of eight species of Scombrids,* W. H. Bayliff (ed.), 71–150. Inter-Am. Trop. Tuna Comm. Spec. Rep. 2.

Evans, W. E. 1975. Distribution, differentiation of populations, and other aspects of the natural history of *Delphinus delphis* in the northeastern Pacific. PhD dissertation, UCLA.

Fitch, J. E. and R. L. Brownell Jr 1968. Fish otoliths in cetacean stomachs and their importance in interpreting feeding habits. *J. Fish. Res. Bd Can.* **25**, 2561–74.

Hammond, P. H. 1981. *Some problems in estimating the density of dolphin populations in the eastern tropical Pacific using data collected aboard tuna purse seiners.* Inter-A. Trop. Tuna Comm. Int. Rep. 15.

Leatherwood, S. and D. K. Ljunblad 1979. Nighttime swimming and diving behaviour of a radiotagged spotted dolphin, *Stenella attenuata. Cetalogy* **34**.

Norris, K. S. and T. P. Dohl 1980. Behaviour of the Hawaiian spinner dolphin *Stenella longirostris. Fish. Bull.* **77**, 821–49.

Perrin, W. F. 1975. Distribution and differentiation of populations of dolphins of the genus *Stenella* in the eastern tropical Pacific. *J. Fish. Res. Bd Can.* **32**, 1059–67.

Perrin, W. F., P. A. Sloan and J. R. Henderson 1979. Taxonomic status of the south-western stocks of spinner dolphin *Stenella longirostris* and spotted dolphin *S. attenuata. Rep. Int. Whal. Comm.* **29**, 175–84.

Perrin, W. F., R. R. Warner, C. H. Fiscus and D. B. Holts 1973. Stomach contents of porpoise, *Stenella* spp. and yellowfin tuna, *Thunnus albacares,* in mixed species aggregations. *Fish. Bull.* **71**, 1077–92.

Rice, D. W. 1977. *A list of marine mammals of the world.* NOAA technical report. NMFS SSRF, 711.

Savini, M. J. *Report on international and national legislation for the conservation of marine mammals. Part 2. National legislation.* FAO unpublished manuscript.

Schaefer, M. B., G. C. Broadhead and C. J. Orange 1963. Synopsis on the biology of yellowfin tuna *Thunnus (Neothunnus) albacares* (Bonnaterre) 1788 (Pacific Ocean). *FAO, Fish Rep.* **6**, 538–61.

Scott, M. D. and P. C. Wussow 1979. *The use of a sailboat for radio-tracking dolphins.* IATTC unpublished manuscript.

Sharp, G. D. and R. F. Francis 1976. An energetic model for the exploited yellowfin tuna, *Thunnus albacares,* population in the eastern Pacific Ocean. *Fish. Bull.* **74**, 36–50.

Shomura, R. S. and T. S. Hida 1965. Stomach contents of a dolphin caught in Hawaiian waters. *J. Mammalogy* **46**, 550–51.

Smith, T. 1979. *Report of the status of porpoise stocks workshop, August 27–31, 1979.* Southwest Fisheries Center Admin. Rep. LJ-79-41.

Suzuki, Z., P. K. Tomlinson and M. Honma 1968. Population structure of Pacific yellowfin tuna. *Inter-Am. Trop. Tuna Comm. Bull.* **17**, 277–441.

14 Fishery–dolphin conflict in the Iki Island area of Japan

T. Kasuya

Introduction

Iki Island is located in the Tsushima Pass, about 20 km off the northern coast of Kyushu, western Japan. It is a small island of 139 km², inhabited by about 41 000 people, whose main livelihood is derived from fisheries and agriculture. Although the conflict between dolphins and the hook-and-line fishery for yellowtails has been apparent in the area since around 1910, the two major problems only arose relatively recently.

The first problem became known to the Japanese Government in 1967. The government then set up a research team to further an understanding of the conflict and to investigate a possible solution. Although the study showed that dolphin-caused damage was common in several fisheries, it failed to suggest an effective solution.

The second problem arose when the fishermen succeeded in catching dolphin schools by the driving method and started to cull them. The government responded in 1978 to the criticism of conservationists by establishing a research team to investigate methods of driving away the dolphins without damaging them. After 3 years of unsuccessful effort, the focus of the team was shifted in 1981 to the study of the life history and population dynamics of dolphins.

The present study was started in 1979 in order to gain a better understanding of the background to the conflict and the biology of dolphins in the area. It was discontinued in 1981, when the above-mentioned research team was directed to similar objectives. Many of the biological data and samples collected in the period are still in the process of analysis, and most of the results presented here are provisional.

History of the yellowtail fishery in the Iki Island area, with special reference to the hook-and-line fishery

The following description deals mainly with the Katsumoto Fishery Co-operative Union (FCU), because this has had the greatest involvement in the dolphin–fishery conflict.

The principal fishery objectives at Katsumoto have changed over the years (Yoshida 1979). The most important fishery in the 1800s was the coastal net fishery for whales, which began between 1704 and 1710 and ended in the late 1880s, probably due to the depletion of the whale stocks. As the whale fishery ended, several kinds of net fishing for sardine began. The sardine fishery reached its peak before 1930, and finally ceased in the 1940s in the face of the substantial decline of the sardine stocks in this and other regions of Japan.

The yellowtail fishery, using line and hooks, started at Katsumoto towards the end of the last century. It began in coastal waters and, in the 1910s, expanded to include the offshore Shichirigasone (*sone* = bank), which is located about 20 km north of Katsumoto, between Iki Island and Tsushima Island. The expansion was promoted by the introduction of engine-powered fishing boats and, although the Shichirigasone ground had been traditionally (not legally) fished by the Katsumoto fishermen, it was opened in 1963 to other fishermen from Iki Island. In recent years, a few boats from other islands have been observed on the bank.

The yellowtail fishery, which operates during the winter season (Table 14.1), is one of two major fisheries in the Katsumoto area, the other being the squid fishery, which existed in the 1800s and expanded after the late 1960s. The squid fishery occurs from spring to autumn and involves larger boats than the yellowtail fishery, usually 11 or more gross tonnes. Although smaller boats do fish for squid, their involvement generally is limited to the peak of the season and to nearshore waters. The size composition of fishing vessels registered to the Katsumoto FCU (March 1979) is shown in Table 14.2.

The yellowtail stock being exploited by the Iki Island fishermen is believed to belong to the same population which is harvested in the coastal waters of the Sea of Japan and in the East China Sea. Fry (= *mojako*) as well as adult fish are taken. Although many kinds of gear are used, most fish are taken by set nets, hooks and lines, and purse-seines.

Fry are taken alive off the coast of southwestern Japan while they are drifting to the north-east from the spawning ground in the East China Sea, and are used as the seed for the culture of yellowtail. Adults are taken throughout the range during their winter migration to the south.

The set net is the method most commonly used to take yellowtail, and usually exploits larger individuals than the hook-and-line fishery, but is not used in the Katsumoto area. The purse-seine is the next most commonly used method for taking yellowtail, but fishermen of the Katsumoto FCU have refused to allow its use in the

Table 14.1 Monthly catch of yellowtail by the Katsumoto Fishery Cooperative Union, 1979 season.

Month	Weight (kg)	Value (10^3 yen)	Yen/kg
January	42 317	25 785	609
February	41 326	26 821	649
March	147 437	96 481	654
April	22 648	16 443	726
May	64 377	36 997	575
June	9 275	6 441	694
July	4 498	2 689	598
August	875	773	883
September	1 596	806	505
October	11 644	5 260	452
November	54 088	21 834	404
December	174 379	151 083	866
Total	574 460	391 413	681(av.)

Table 14.2 Size composition of fishing vessels registered to the Katsumato Fishery Cooperative Union (March 1979).

Gross tonnes	Diesel	Outboard	TotaL
below 2	78	45	123
2–4	227	0	227
4–5	101	0	101
5–7	51	0	51
7–9	48	0	48
9–11	24	0	24
11–13	29	0	29
13–15	7	0	7
15–17	11	0	11
17–19	2	0	2
19–20	55	0	55
above 20	1	0	1
Total	634	45	679

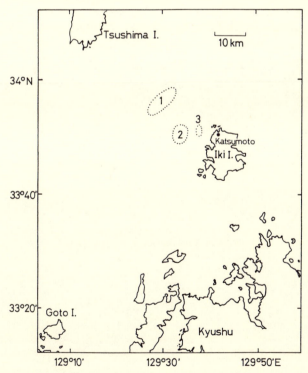

Figure 14.1 Primary grounds for yellowtail hook-and-line fishery in the Iki Island area. 1. Shichirigasone. 2. Arasone. 3. Hirasone.

area or close to the nearby banks, including the Shichirigasone. Longlines are thought to be efficient for taking yellowtail and other fish in the Shichirigasone, but their use has been prohibited, traditionally, and the tackle will be cut if found by angling (hook-and-line) fishermen.

The 'kaitsuke' (= feeding) method is the preferred method of the Katsumoto fishermen. This is a hook-and-line fishery in which the fish are fed daily, irrespective of fishing. The feeding attracts the fish and creates an artificial feeding ground for the species. This method was used in the Shichirigasone by members of the Katsumoto FCU from 1930 until the late 1940s when there was a shortage of sardine for bait. It was resumed in 1973, but abandoned after a 3-year trial period. The method currently is used only along the coast of Tsushima Island.

Angling with hook and line exploits small yellowtails under 4 years, and is the only fishing method for this species which presently is permitted in the Katsumoto area. The intention of the regulation, according to the Katsumoto FCU, is to protect the stock from overfishing and to share the profit equally among all the members of the FCU. Fishing is done from small boats and is possible only in calm weather. Each boat has one or two persons on board and each person uses one line with 1 to 80 hooks attached. The gear and bait vary according to the season. Fishing is best when the yellowtail schools surface to feed. Feeding usually occurs once or twice a day, lasts 2 hours or less, and most frequently occurs at the beginning of the tidal cycle. The fishery is open, both legally and traditionally, to any person and is regulated by the Katsumoto FCU.

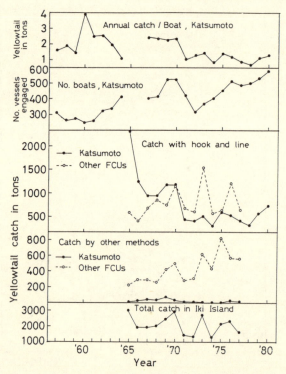

Figure 14.2 Yellowtail fishery in the Iki Island. Statistics are given for the Katsumoto Fishery Co-operative Union, for sum of other four FCUs, or for total of five FCUs in the Iki Island.

Among other things, regulations prohibit the use of anchors on the fishing grounds and the use of efficient bait such as Antarctic krill. The primary fishing grounds for yellowtail in the Katsumoto area are shown in Figure 14.1.

Figure 14.2 shows the catch of yellowtail from the vicinity of Iki Island. The total annual catch of yellowtail in the area has fluctuated between 1300 and 3000 tonnes in the last 13 years. Although the annual trend is unclear, the catch could have been either stationary or declining. The catch by the angling fishery has changed similarly. However, the proportion of that fishery in the total Iki Island catch has steadily declined from 85% in 1966 to 65% in 1977. This change has occurred in the catch of four fishery co-operative unions in the island besides the Katsumoto FCU. In these other FCUs, the catch of yellowtail has increased in both angling and other fisheries, while the catch of the Katsumoto FCU angling fishery has declined. Therefore, it is clear that the importance of the angling fishery is greater for the Katsumoto FCU than for other FCUs on the island, and that the relative importance of this fishing method has been decreasing for other FCUs. It is also clear that the proportion of the annual yellowtail catch taken by members of the Katsumoto FCU is decreasing when compared with the amount

Table 14.3 Number of fishing vessels involved in the yellowtail angling fishery, Katsumoto Fishery Cooperative Union, Iki Island.[a]

Year	Without engine	With engine 3 t	3–5 t	5–10 t	10–20 t	Total
1957	68	178	43	19	0	308
1958	21	187	43	11	0	262
1959	23	189	48	10	0	270
1960	6	166	61	12	0	245
1961	0	177	67	10	2	256
1962	5	207	78	29	2	321
1963	3	243	76	11	2	335
1964	4	303	84	22	0	413
1965	—	—	—	—	—	—
1966	—	—	—	—	—	—
1967	4	288	88	16	3	399
1968	3	305	82	18	5	413
1969	6	334	108	57	16	521
1970	6	339	108	57	13	523
1971	0	290	80	48	0	418
1972	0	233	45	25	12	315
1973	0	236	80	51	0	367
1974	0	201	86	70	41	398
1975	0	159	110	112	67	448
1976	0	170	123	115	55	463
1977	0	187	146	115	37	485
1977[b]	—	—	—	—	—	483
1078[b]	—	—	—	—	—	501
1979[b]	—	—	—	—	—	529
1980[b]	—	—	—	—	—	574

[a] If not specified, the statistics are from Nagasaki Statistics Information Office.
[b] Statistics obtained from Katsumoto FCU. The number of boats is represented by registered fishing vessels equipped with inboard engine and smaller than 11 gross tonnes.

Table 14.4 Production of yellowtail (tonnes) in Japan in 1977.

	Fishery	Culture	Total
Sea of Japan and East China Sea	21 097	39 153	60 250
other seas	5 818	75 945	81 763
total	26 915	115 098	142 013

taken by members of other FCUs, and that this decrease seems to be partly related to the policy prohibiting the use of set nets, purse-seines and other more efficient methods of catching yellowtail, and partly to the development of angling fisheries in other FCUs.

Table 14.3 shows the number and sizes of fishing vessels that were operated by members of the Katsumoto FCU from 1957 to 1980. These data indicate that both the number and sizes of the boats have been increasing. When compared with the catch data, they indicate that the average annual catch per vessel has been decreasing for the last 14 years (fig. 14.2).

The information above indicates that the availability of the yellowtail to the Iki Island fishery, including the angling fishery, has been declining over the last 14 years. This decline has been such that the fishery could not increase its catch even with an increase in the number of fishing vessels or with an improvement in fishing gear. This in turn suggests the possibility that the whole yellowtail stock may have been declining, although an analysis of the entire fishery exploiting the stock would be required for a firm conclusion on this matter. Clearly, the decline of fish availability, and hence of profit to the fishery, may decrease the tolerance of fishermen towards the presence of dolphins on the fishing grounds, and may make the dolphin–fishery competition for limited resources more serious.

No report on the status of the yellowtail population in the offshore waters of Japan has been published. The production of yellowtail in Japan in 1977 was as shown in Table 14.4. The catch from the Iki Island area is only about 10% of the total catch from the population, suggesting that the apparent decline in the size of the yellowtail population may be attributable (primarily) to yellowtail fisheries operating in other areas.

History of the fishery–dolphin conflict in the Iki Island area

Dolphins affect fisheries in a number of ways. They damage fishing gear, take caught fish, and are reported to disperse fish schools and/or to cause the fish to stop feeding. Inspection of the diary of a Katsumoto fisherman, who left a detailed record of his daily operations over the past 21 years, indicates that at the appearance of dolphins he stopped fishing and returned to port, left the area to look for other yellowtail schools, or started to fish for bottom fish which apparently are affected less by the dolphins.

Recent studies (Japanese Fisheries Agency 1968, 1969, Aoyama & Kozasa, 1971a, 1971b) have indicated that coastal fisheries for squid and yellowtail, among others, are adversely affected by dolphins. Angling fisheries are affected to the greatest extent, and longline and purse-seine fisheries to a lesser extent. Damage to the yellowtail angling fishery seems greatest because boats often operate within 30–50 m of each other when a good fish school appears. Damage to the squid fishery seems less extensive, partly, because boats are usually separated by a few kilometres or more and operate for longer periods of time.

The following is a chronology of the conflict between dolphins and the yellowtail fishery in the Iki Island area, compiled mainly from the records of the Katsumoto FCU.

1. The presence of the conflict was known in the early 1910s, when the fishery expanded to the offshore waters and dolphins were killed, sporadically, with hand harpoons.
2. Later, the Katsumoto FCU paid 1000 yen to fishermen who purchased harpoons to kill dolphins.
3. In 1956, a dolphin hunting team was established in the Katsumoto FCU. Half the cost of seven harpoon guns was paid by the town of Katsumoto. No dolphins were taken.
4. In 1957, the Katsumoto FCU began paying a bounty of 3000 yen for each dolphin killed.
5. In the early 1960s, there was an increase in the incidence of reports of dolphins taking caught fish, or otherwise interfering with fishing operations; in 1964, the Katsumoto FCU reported the presence of the conflict and the need for a solution to the Governor of the Nagasaki Prefecture.
6. In 1965, the other FCUs of Iki Island joined with the Katsumoto FCU in requesting help from the Governor. Three Iki fishermen and three Tsushima fishermen were sent to the Shizuoka Prefecture to learn dolphin hunting and ten sound emitters were purchased to drive away the dolphins.
7. In 1966, an additional 40 sound emitters were purchased and distributed to the fishing fleet. The sound emitters had minimal effect on the dolphins, especially after several periods of use.
8. In 1967, the Governor of the Nagasaki Prefecture requested the assistance of the Japanese Fisheries Agency (JFA) and the JFA set up a research team to investigate the problem.
9. In 1967, the hunting of dolphin schools by the driving method was tried with the help of dolphin hunters from the Shizuoka Prefecture. The drive was unsuccessful.
10. The reports of the research team were published by JFA in 1968 and 1969. These include studies on: (a) the fisheries disturbed by the dolphins, (b) the dolphin fauna in the Iki area, (c) the size of the dolphin population in the area, (d) feeding habits of the dolphins, (e) utilisation of dolphin meat, and (f) possible methods for driving the dolphins from the fishing ground.
11. In 1968, a dolphin hunting team, equipped with shotguns, was established by the Katsumoto FCU to scare away the dolphin schools by killing a few individuals. The hunting had little, if any, effect on dolphin behaviour or on the dolphin population.
12. In 1970, a small whaling boat (19 gross tonnes) was built to kill and scare dolphins on the yellowtail grounds. Twenty dolphins were killed in the following 6 years before the operation was stopped, probably due to the marginal results and high cost of maintaining and operating the boat. Records of dolphin sightings and of the stomach contents of the animals killed were kept by the boat.
13. In 1976, dolphin hunting with a large-mesh drift net was tried unsuccessfully.
14. In 1976, 12 *Grampus* were caught by driving by the Katsumoto FCU with the help of dolphin hunters from the Wakayama Prefecture. Later in the year, another 43 *Grampus* were caught by the Iki fishermen.
15. In 1978, the Japanese Agency of Science and Technology established and funded

a research team, for 3 years, to develop a device or devices for detecting sounds emitted by the dolphins before they arrived at the fishing grounds, and for driving them away from the fishing grounds without driving away the fish schools being fished. The team was transferred to JFA in 1979. By the end of fiscal year 1980 (March 1981): (a) the team concluded that the simulation tests of acoustic dolphin detector were successful, but appeared to be too costly for practical use, and (b) several kinds of sound emitters were tested to scare away the dolphins from fishing grounds and it was shown that further improvement was necessary for practical use (Anonymous 1981).

16. In 1981, the research team shifted its main research objectives to the study of the distribution, migration, abundance, feeding habits and life histories of the dolphins.

At present, each of the yellowtail angling boats in the Katsumoto FCU is under the control of one of 12 fishing leaders elected by the members. When a dolphin school is observed, the 12 fishing leaders decide whether it will be driven from the fishing ground or captured. If it is decided that the school is to be captured, the closest fishing vessel lights its electric lamp to indicate the position of the school. Other boats then gather in a semicircle to herd or drive the school. The fishing vessels belonging to the FCUs on Iki Island must stop operating while the 300 to 500 (rarely, 800) fishing vessels operating near the ground drive the school toward the Tatsunoshima near Katsumoto. Driving is done with the help of sound emitters (see 6 and 7 above). A sound emitter is a steel tube, about 4 cm in diameter and 3 m in length, with a steel cone (30 cm in diameter and 7 cm in depth) at the distal end. (In recent years, the Iki fishermen have also used a simple steel tube without the cone.) For use, the cone is lowered into the water and the other end of the tube is hammered to produce an underwater sound. After capture, the dolphins are kept in a net until the Dolphin Committee of the Katsumoto FCU decides how to dispose of the carcasses.

Disposal has changed from year to year: burying on land was used, but became difficult because of the shortage of suitable land; weighting with cement blocks and dumping at sea was also used, but has been prohibited since the 1979 season. Live animals have been sent to aquaria, but the demand is limited; likewise, the demand for dolphins for human consumption is limited. To permit rapid disposal of large numbers of animals, whole carcasses (until 1979) or shredded carcasses (since 1980) have been sent to a rendering plant which pays transportation costs. In the 1981 and 1982 seasons, catches were utilised either for human consumption or for aquaria, possibly because the catch was small.

The cost of the fuel for the driving boats is paid by the FCUs. Any boat violating the 'stop work' rule must surrender its catch. In 1980, several drives, with 50 selected boats, were tried, but trials were unsuccessful and the procedure using large numbers of vessels was resumed.

It is difficult to estimate how much money has been spent on efforts to try to resolve the dolphin problem. In the fiscal year 1977, when about 1000 dolphins were killed, the FCUs on Iki Island spend about 18−19 million yen on related operations. They received 10 million yen from the Nagasaki Prefecture and 5 million yen from the towns on the island. More recently, a dolphin shredder was purchased (for use in the 1980 season) and 75% of the 3.6 million yen cost of the shredder was paid by the prefecture and towns on the island. Additionally, in 1978, the Nagasaki Prefecture established a bounty on dolphins, starfish, and jellyfish to reduce damage to fisheries (Nagasaki

Prefecture Notification No. 5015). Under this arrangement 5000 yen is paid if the carcass is not sold and special processing is needed.

History of the small cetacean catch in the Iki Island area of Japan

Dolphins have occasionally been taken in some areas off northern Kyushu for human consumption. The size of the catch is not well documented, but is thought to have increased during the period from the mid 1940s to the early 1950s because of food shortages in Japan.

Table 14.5 Number of dolphins caught in the northern Kyushu and adjacent waters from 1965 to March 1980.

Year	Iki Island	Goto Island	Tsushima Island	N. Kyushu
1965	2(*Pseudorca*)	7		
1966	1	460(*Tursiops*) 14		
1967		13(*Tursiops*) 62		
1968	1(*Pseudorca*) 7(*Lagenorhynchus*) 1(*Tursiops*)	13(*Tursiops*) 12(*S. attenuata*) 51(*Delphinus*) 1(*Lagenorhynchus*)		1(*Grampus*) 4(*Pseudorca*)
1969	1(*Lagenorhynchus*) 1	1(*Tursiops*)		1(*Tursiopsa*) 1(*S. coeruleoalba*)
1970	1(*Tursiops*) 1(*Pseudorca*)		762(*Delphinus*)	
1971	5(*Pseudorca*)	22		
1972	1(*Grampus*) 2(*Pseudorca*) 5			
1973		84(*Tursiops*)		
1974		35(*Tursiops*) 105		
1975		3(*Tursiops*) 312	35(*Tursiops*) 1	
1976	a	108		
1977	a	530(*S. attenuata*)		
1978	a	6(*Grampus*) 27(*Pseudorca*)	4(*Tursiops*) 100(50 *Tursiops*) 69(*Pseudorca*)	
1979	a	14	77(*Pseudorca*) 24(*Tursiops*) 11(*Grampus*)	
1980	a	1182(*Tursiops*)		
1981	a	7(*Grampus*) 11(*Globicephala?*) 10		
1982	a	8(*S. attenuata*) 2(*Grampus*)		

[a] See Table 14.6.

Table 14.6 List of dolphins caught by driving at Katsumoto, Iki Island.

Date	Species	Number
1976 12 Apr.	*Grampus griseus*	12
1976 22 Apr.	*G. griseus*	43
1976, total		**55**
1977 27 Feb.	*Tursiops truncatus*	172
1977 14 Mar.	{ *Pseudorca crassidens*	11
	{ *T. truncatus*	566
1977 3 Apr.	*T. truncatus*	20
1977 11 Apr.	{ *P. crassidens*	24
	{ *T. truncatus*	141
1977, total		**934**
1978 22 Feb.	{ *P. crassidens*	251
	{ *T. truncatus*	759
1978 14 Mar.	*T. truncatus*	(10)[a]
1978 4 Apr.	b { *P. crassidens*	12
	{ *T. truncatus*	52
1978 12 Apr.	{ *P. crassidens*	70
	{ *T. truncatus*	97
1978 13 Apr.	*Lagenorhynchus obliquidens*	25
1978 21 Apr.	*T. truncatus*	50
1978 23 Apr.	*P. crassidens*	16
1978, total		**1332**
1979 8 Feb.	*G. griseus*	17[c]
1979 9 Feb.	*L. obliquidens*	283[d]
1979 12 Feb.	e { *G griseus*	83
	{ *T. truncatus*	10
1979 20 Feb.	*L. obliquidens*	ca. 50[f]
1979 3 Mar.	*G. griseus*	ca. 200[f]
1979 7 Mar.	*G. griseus*	ca. 100[f]
1979 8 Mar.	*P. crassidens*	ca. 20[f]
1979 8 Mar.	*G. griseus*	ca. 40[f]
1979 9 Mar.	*G. griseus*	ca. 14[f]
1979 15 Mar.	{ *P. crassidens*	138
	{ *T. truncatus*	256
1979 19 Mar.	{ *P. crassidens*	160
	{ *T. truncatus*	251
1979 16 Apr.	*T. truncatus*	24
1979, total		**1646**
1980 27 Jan.	*T. truncatus*	11
1980 22 Feb.	{ *T truncatus*	171
	{ *P. crassidens*	10
1980 27 Feb.	{ *T truncatus*	1034[g]
	{ *P. crassidens*	80[g]
1980 6 Mar.	{ *T. truncatus*	204
	{ *P. crassidens*	155
1980 14 Mar.	*T. truncatus*	154
1980, total		**1819**
1981 23 Jan.	*T. truncatus*	18
1981 15 Feb.	*L. obliquidens*	91
1981 18 Mar.	*L. obliquidens*	17

(Continued).

Table 14.6 *continued*

Date	Species	Number
1981 June	*G. griseus*	16
1981, total		**142**
1982 20 Jan.	*T. truncatus*	28
1982 24 Jan.	*P. crassidens*	6
	T. truncatus	68
1982 30 Jan.	*T. truncatus*	35
1982 11 Feb.	*T. truncatus*	26
1982, total		**163**

[a] Escaped during storm on 16 April.
[b] Excludes 66 dolphins said to have escaped in a storm after catch.
[c] Biologist recorded as 24 individuals.
[d] Biologist recorded as 247 individuals.
[e] Biologist recorded as 10 *Grampus* and 73 *Tursiops*.
[f] Mixed after driving and processed on 13 March. FCU reported that the total number was 424 individuals.
[g] 281 *T. truncatus* and 20 *P. crassidens* reported by FCU as freed by D. L. Cate (Greenpeace) not included.

The recent catch of dolphins in the islands off northern Kyushu is shown in Table 14.5. These statistics were collected by the Nagasaki Prefectural Government. The identification of the species was done by the FCU or by the fishery attaché of the prefectural branch office, using an identification manual distributed by the Nagasaki Prefecture. In cases where identification is questionable, only the size of the catch is listed. Although occasionally the name 'nezumi-iruka' appears (which literally indicates common porpoise), it is unclear which species are so denoted. In the Iki and Tsushima Islands, this name is used for *Delphinus, Tursiops, Lagenorhynchus* and occasionally for *Grampus,* simply because their voice is like that of 'nezumi' [= mouse or rat]. The distinction between *Globicephala* and *Pseudorca* was not always reliable either.

Residents of Iki Island are not accustomed to eating dolphin meat and, until recently, catches have been small. The catch of dolphins in the area, after driving began in 1976, it shown in Table 14.6. The species are believed to have been identified correctly. The estimates (counts) of the catches, made and reported by the Katsumoto FCU, are similar to independent counts or estimates made by biologists. The annual number of dolphins culled increased till 1980, when a total of 1819 dolphins were killed. It then declined to a level of about 150 individuals. The total numbers of individuals killed by the operation were 4147 *Tursiops truncatus,* 953 *Pseudorca crassidens,* 525 *Grampus griseus* and 466 *Lagenorhynchus obliquidens* (from April 1976 to January 1982). The driving of the last species was difficult, and only small parts of a school were driven. Thus the above figure may under-represent the abundance of *Lagenorhynchus* distributed in the area.

Dolphin population estimates and annual fluctuation of dolphins on the grounds

There are no reliable estimates of the size of the dolphin populations in the Iki Island area. In 1965, K. Mizue (unpublished) estimated, in a report of his survey of dolphin damage on the winter squid fishery around the Tsushima Island area, that there were approximately 300 000 dolphins in the waters off northern Kyushu, and, although the estimate is a guess and not based on any data, the figure is still quoted occasionally.

The JFA (1968) estimated (using a mathematical model developed by Doi (1974) for the sighting of large cetaceans) that there was a total of 43 000 dolphins of all species in the area (32 000 in the Iki and Tsushima area, and 11 000 around Goto Island). The estimate was based primarily upon data from sighting records kept by commercial ferry boats at the request of the Fisheries Agency. It was obtained by summing population estimates made for each 10-day interval between late November and late March. The 10-day interval was decided arbitrarily and has no apparent relationship to the migration speed of the dolphins. (If the population estimates had been made at monthly rather than 10-day intervals, the population estimates are likely to have been smaller.) The accuracy of the sighting records is questionable, and the distribution of transects was highly biased. The area covered by the transects certainly was smaller than the distributional range of the dolphins when the transects were made. Accordingly, the reliability of the estimate must be questioned.

Aoyama and Kozasa (1972) also estimated abundance using similar data collected from December 1967 through March 1969. They estimated that abundance fluctuates seasonally between 600 in September and 17 000 in April, with relatively higher values in winter and spring. A total abundance estimate of 56 000 was obtained by summing the 12 monthly estimates from 1968. This estimate has the same deficiences as the earlier one, and further study, differentiating between species and covering a larger geographical range, is needed to provide a reliable estimate of the number of dolphins, by species, in the area.

The only data indicating the annual fluctuation of dolphin abundance in the Iki Island area are the records of days when a dolphin school (or schools) was present on the yellowtail fishing grounds. They were recorded by the Katsumoto FCU, from the 1973 to 1977 season (from October of the previous year to May), and by biologists, from the 1979 to 1981 season (January to March). The latter was done by daily inquiries of several fishing leaders, who obtained information about daily operations through radio communication between the fishing vessels from Katsumoto FCU. As shown in Figure 14.3, the days when dolphins were present as a percentage of the total yellowtail fishing days increased from about 25% in the 1973 fishing season to about 79% in the 1979 season. The annual increase was about 21% ($r^2 = 0.7$). After the 1979 season, the frequency declined at an annual rate of about 26% ($r^2 = 0.997$). The increase is faster than that expected from the estimates of annual gross reproductive rate of any of the dolphin species in the area. These estimates are provisional and have been obtained from the study of culled individuals (see Table 14.8, p. 266).

All the four dolphin species confirmed on the fishing ground form relatively large schools. This suggests that if the dolphin population had really changed in such a short period, the change is likely to have affected first the school size rather than the number of schools. This implies that the changes in the number of days when the dolphins were sighted on the grounds will tend to occur less dramatically than real changes in the dolphin population. Therefore, it can be concluded that the apparent change in dolphin abundance cannot be attributed exclusively to a change in the population size. Rather, the records may be biased, or for some reason the feeding and migration patterns of the dolphins may have changed. Most probably, the dolphin schools might have concentrated on the fishing grounds or each dolphin school started to stay for a longer period in the area.

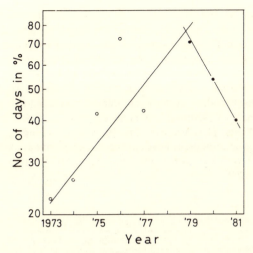

Figure 14.3 Frequency of days when dolphin school(s) was sighted by yellowtail hook-and-line fishing vessels of the Katsumoto FCU. Days are expressed as the percentage of number of days of operation, and plotted on a logarithmic scale. Open circles indicate data collected by the Katsumoto FCU, and closed circles those collected by biologists. The regressions were calculated by least squares.

A decline in the frequency of dolphin encounters accompanied the decline of culling in the 1981 and 1982 seasons. This may be explained by either the dispersion of dolphins out of the fishing grounds or the effect of the cull on the population, or a combination of the two. However, it would be unsafe to draw any firm conclusion on the decline before the prior increase of dolphin encounters is reasonably explained.

Provisional estimate of reproductive rate

The carcasses were examined randomly for species, sex, body length and reproductive status. The samples collected were reproductive tracts, teeth for age determination, and stomach contents. The reproductive status of the females was classified into immature, pregnant, lactating, pregnant and simultaneously lactating, and resting (adult females neither pregnant nor lactating). In spite of the careful examination of uteri, some of the females having corpora lutea in the ovaries showed no trace of an embryo. These individuals were classified as either lactating or resting. Male sexual maturity was provisionally identified using the presence of spermatozoa in the epididymal smear. Ages were determined only for *T. truncatus*.

Pacific white-sided dolphin, *Lagenorhynchus obliquidens*

Totals of 113 and 61 individuals were examined from one driving in 1979 and two in 1981 respectively. The maximum body lengths of adult individuals were 229 cm in females and 238 cm in males. These values are nearly the same as those for *S. attenuata* in the western North Pacific, which has a mean neonatal length of about 90 cm and a gestation period of 11.2 months (Kasuya *et al.* 1974). Therefore, an 11–12-month gestation period was assumed for the present species. A male calf of 159 cm in body length, presumably about 1 year old, had both milk and squid beaks in the stomach.

The gestation time and composition of female reproductive status give a rough estimation of annual gross reproductive rate of 3% (Table 14.7 & 14.8). However, as shown in Table 14.7, the catch in 1979 was strongly biased to males (mostly immature individuals below 210 cm in body length), and all of the few females were sexually immature, indicating that the school was an 'immature school', as observed for *Stenella coeruleoalba* (Miyazaki & Nishiwaki 1978). Accordingly, the above gross reproductive rate may not be reliable. The data from the 1981 season give higher rates of 8.1–8.9%. The accuracy of the latter figure is low, but there is no reason at present to assume that this species has the lowest gross reproductive rate among the four odontocete species involved in the conflict.

Table 14.7 Reproductive status of dolphins caught at Katsumoto, Iki Island.

Year and species	Male (%)	Female reproductive status (%) Immature	Pregnant	Pregnant and lactating	Lactating	Resting	Total (no.)
L. obliquidens							
1979	85.0	100.0	0	0	0	0	100 (17)
1981	41.1	41.7	2.8	11.1	33.3	11.1	100 (36)
total	67.7	60.4	1.9	7.5	22.6	7.5	100 (53)
T. truncatus							
1979	42.9	20.5	18.0	12.8	35.9	12.8	100 (39)
1980	42.7	43.7	21.1	1.9	27.2	6.1	100 (213)
total	42.7	40.1	20.6	3.6	28.6	7.1	100 (252)
P. crassidens							
1979	37.1	14.9	14.9	0	17.0	53.2	100 (47)
1980	41.4	34.1	7.3	0	22.0	36.6	100 (41)
total	39.0	23.9	11.4	0	19.3	45.4	100 (88)
G. griseus							
1979	56.6	43.5	13.1	4.3	13.1	26.0	100 (23)

Table 14.8 Provisional estimates of gross reproductive rate of dolphin populations around Iki Island.

Species	Sex ratio (females)	Gestation (month)	Maturity	Apparent pregnancy rate	Gross reproductive rate[a]
L. obliquidens	0.323	11–12	0.396	0.238	0.03–0.03
T. truncatus	0.573	12–14	0.599	0.404	0.12–0.14
P. crassidens	0.610	15–16	0.761	0.150	0.05–0.06
G. griseus	0.434	13–14	0.565	0.307	0.06–0.07

[a](Proportion of females) × (proportion of adult females in total females) × (apparent pregnancy rate)/(length of gestation in years).

Bottlenose dolphin, *Tursiops truncatus*

Samples were obtained from seven drivings, and 256 females and 190 males were aged using growth layers in dentine and cementum. The youngest mature and oldest immature females were aged 3.5 and 8.5 years respectively. At age 6.9 years, 50% of the females were sexually mature. The mean body length of females at this age was about 286 cm. However, since the body length increase after sexual maturity was limited, the length at which 50% of the females are sexually mature was calculated as 267 cm. (The asymptotic length was estimated at 288 cm – mean of 63 females over 20 years.) Sexual maturity was attained at lengths between 250 cm and 300 cm). Ohsumi (1966) found for Odontoceti the following relationship between the female length at 50% maturity (X in m) and mean neonatal length (Y in m):

$$Y = 0.532X^{0.916}$$

This equation and the body length at sexual maturity predict a neonatal length of 131 cm, which is close to the neonatal lengths of 126–140 cm of calves born in Japanese aquariums (Nakajima *et al.* 1963). This body length and the following equation (Perrin *et al.* 1977), give a gestation time of 13.7 months

$$\log Y = 0.4586 \log X + 0.1659$$
X = neonatal length in cm, Y = gestation length in months

Although this is slightly longer than 12 months – the gestation length of the species in the western North Atlantic (Odell 1975) – it is unclear whether the Japanese population has a longer gestation time. Thus, a gestation time of 12–14 months was assumed in the present study (Table 14.7). One female of 182 cm body length had only milk in the stomach.

The gross annual reproductive rate estimated using these figures is 12–14% (Table 14.8). The age frequency plotted on a logarithmic scale shows a steeper gradient for younger age classes and a less steep one for ages between 10 and 27 years. The slope after these age classes again becomes steeper, suggesting an increase in mortality rate in the higher ages. The apparent mortality rates calculated from the gradients combining both sexes are 13.8% (< 13 years, $r^2 = 0.77$) and 3.1% (10–27 years, $r^2 = 0.29$). The difference between the two figures could be attributable, at least partially, to a difference in natural mortality rate with age.

The gross reproductive rate estimated above is the sum of the net reproductive rate and the mortality rate of the population, and the apparent mortality rate calculated from the age frequency is the sum of the net reproductive rate and the mortality rate of the age classes. Although the 'mortality' components of the two figures are slightly different, they have to be larger than zero. Thus it can be safely concluded that the recent net reproductive rate of the population does not exceed these figures, and that it has to be below 14%.

The natural mortality rates of the spotted and striped dolphins (all age classes combined) was estimated as about 7% (Kasuya 1985). The maximum longevities of these species were 46 and 57 years respectively, which are similar to the corresponding figure for *T. truncatus* of 46 years, obtained from a smaller sample (446 individuals). If this natural mortality rate is accepted for the present population of the bottlenose dolphin, and if a simple subtraction is done, its net reproductive rate may not exceed

7%. However, since the fishing mortality rate of the population might have been significant in that area (see Table 14.5), the upper limit of the net reproductive rate could be less than 7%.

False killer whale, *Pseudorca crassidens*

A total of 158 samples was collected from six drivings. The apparent pregnancy rate was low in this species. Two of the largest fetuses and two of the smallest neonates were found in the body length interval of 170–179 cm. One female of 212 cm in body length had only milk in the stomach. Thus the mean neonatal length was estimated as about 175 cm. This and the equation of Perrin *et al.* (1977) give an estimation of gestation time as 15.7 months. Assuming a gestation time of 15–16 months, the gross annual reproductive rate of the population is calculated at 5–6%. This figure is close to the mortality rate of some well-analysed delphinids (Kasuya 1985, Kasuya & Marsh 1984), and it is impossible to conclude from the present data that the species has been increasing significantly in recent years.

Risso's dolphin, *Grampus griseus*

Only 23 females and 20 males were collected from the catch of six drivings. The scanty data suggest the mean female length at attainment of sexual maturity to be about 265 cm. Using the same method as above, the gestation time is estimated as 13–14 months, and the gross reproductive rate as 6–7%. Although the accuracy of these results is questionable, it was not possible to conclude from the present study that the species has increased considerably in recent years.

Food of dolphins on the yellowtail grounds

During the three fishing seasons, dolphin stomachs were collected from individuals dead on the day of driving or on the next day (Table 14.9). The interim result of the analysis was published by Miyazaki (1981). This can be compared with the previous work of the JFA (1968).

Pacific white-sided dolphin, *Lagenorhynchus obliquidens*

Only three of seven samples had food in the stomach. One individual had yellowtail remains, but no squid beaks nor fish otoliths. Another had squid beaks representing a minimum of three squids, seven fish otoliths and, almost intact, three black mullet, *Mugil cephalus* L. (standard length 37.4–37.7 cm). The third individual had no identifiable food remains.

The JFA (1968) reported food of six *L. obliquidens* killed in the winter season in the Iki or Goto Island area. Two of them had remains of both fish and several kinds of squid. Three had only squid remains, and one individual had only fishes. None of these individuals (or two others in the same study) gave any indication that yellowtail is a food of this species.

Although the data were obtained from only 11 individuals, they suggest that yellowtail is uncommon as a food of *L. obliquidens*. The total length of one yellowtail found in one dolphin stomach was estimated from the skull length as about 37 cm

Table 14.9 Stomach contents analysis of dolphins taken at the yellowtail ground off Iki Island[a].

	T. truncatus	*P. crassidens*	*L. obliquidens*[d]	*G. griseus*
Number of samples	6	5	3	1
Body length(cm)	238–287	382–503	194–222	244
weight of stomach contents (g)				
range	65–570	1585–9750	48–2400	–
mean	185	4391	1224	–
number of squid beaks[b]				
range	2–47	0–7	0–3	+
mean	16	2	1	+
number of fish otoliths				
range	0–10	0–5	0–7	0
mean	6	1	2	0
number of yellowtail bodies				
range	0	0–4	0–1	0
mean	0	2	0.3	0

[a]After Miyazaki (1981). [b]Larger number of either lower or upper jaws.
[c]Contralateral distinction was not done. [d]In addition, one of the individuals had three black mullets, *Mugil cephalus*.

(Table 14.10). This was much smaller than the size of the same species eaten by the false killer whale.

Bottlenose dolphin, *Tursiops truncatus*

Although 14 stomachs were collected in the expeditions, seven were empty or contained only milk. All the other seven stomachs had squid beaks, and six individuals also had fish otoliths. No yellowtail remains were found in any. One should not expect to find

Table 14.10 Total lengths of yellowtail found in the stomach of *P. crassidens* and *L. obliquidens* (after Miyazaki 1981). Length was estimated from the skull length.

Dolphin species	Sample no.	Yellowtail	
		No.	Total length(mm)
P. crassidens	1	3	760–765
	2	4	600–725
	3	2	693–751
	4	1	874
L. obliquidens	5	1	373

evidence of predation of yellowtail using the fish otoliths, because the species has no otolith recognisable in the dolphin stomach.

The JFA (1968) listed the stomach contents of 11 individuals, none of which was obtained in the yellowtail fishing ground. All of them had fish remains (minimum of 10 teleostomi species ranging from 15 cm to 46 cm in length) and, in addition, two other dolphins had small amounts of squid remains, but no indication of yellowtail.

Although *T. truncatus* seems to live on various kinds of fish and squids, there is no direct indication that this species feeds on yellowtail. Indeed, the consumption of yellowtail might be uncommon even on the yellowtail fishing grounds. It is worth noting for future analyses that *T. truncatus* are often found with *P. crassidens*, which are known to eat yellowtail. In catches the two species are found together regularly, and from a total of 22 drives, both species were present in 11.

False killer whale, *Pseudorca crassidens*

Data were obtained from five weaned individuals. The stomachs of four of them contained the remains of yellowtails, ranging in number from one to four. The body lengths were estimated from the skulls as from 60 cm to 87 cm (Table 14.10). The stomachs of two of these dolphins contained a small number of squid beaks, that represented a minimum of two to seven squids. The last individual had only two squid beaks and five fish otoliths in the stomach.

The JFA (1968) reported stomach contents of one false killer whale shot on a yellowtail ground (Shichirigasone). It contained a yellowtail skull. Another three individuals caught in another area by set net had perch, *Lateolabrax japonicus* (Cuvier), and squids in their stomachs.

The above information indicates that the false killer whales on the yellowtail fishing grounds feed mainly on yellowtail, although they may eat other kinds of large fish when these are available. The average body size of yellowtails found in their stomachs was larger than that found in the one Pacific white-sided dolphin.

Risso's dolphin, *Grampus griseus*

One stomach investigated by Miyazaki (1981) contained only squid beaks, but the number was not given. The JFA (1968) reported a Risso's dolphin caught in a set net on the coast of northern Kyushu, which contained the beaks of 10 squids. These data suggest that the Risso's dolphin lives exclusively on squids in the area.

Conclusions and recommendations

1. There is no doubt that the presence of certain dolphin species affects the operation of the squid and yellowtail angling fisheries and, perhaps, other fisheries in the Iki Island area. The apparent decline in availability of yellowtail and the apparent increase in dolphins on the fishing grounds might have contributed, in some degree, to the present serious dolphin–fishery conflict.
2. From available information on the feeding habits of dolphin species and from information provided by the Iki fishermen, it seems likely that the squid fishery is affected primarily by *Grampus* and, to a lesser extent, by the other dolphin species. However, it is also clear that all of the four dolphin species caught by the Iki

fishermen may not interact in the same way with the yellowtail angling fishery. More information on the feeding habits of the dolphins and more observation of the behaviour of the dolphin and yellowtail schools are needed.

3. The available information is insufficient to determine why there apparently has been an increase and, very recently, a decline in the number of dolphin schools on the fishing ground, or how this apparent change has affected the yellowtail angling fishery. Additional data must be collected to determine the nature and extent of the problem.

4. The problem of dolphin interference with fishing operations and direct dolphin-caused fish loss and gear damage can be solved by: exterminating the dolphins in the area; developing a device or system to expel the dolphins from the fishing ground; or developing a fishing method which is not affected by the presence of dolphins. The first alternative cannot be recommended. The second, if successful and used widely, could deprive the dolphins of important habitat and result in a population decline. In the last case, the fishing method should not be so efficient as to overfish the yellowtail or to deprive the fishermen of jobs.

5. Another problem is the possible competition between fishermen and dolphins for the same fish resources. At least some species of dolphins eat squid or yellowtail. However, available data are insufficient to determine whether the yellowtail population might increase if the dolphin populations are reduced. Available information is also insufficient to determine how other components of the marine ecosystem might respond to a reduction of the dolphin populations. Intensive study of the food web and the interactions among the species comprising the food web is needed to make these determinations.

6. If it is deduced from the on-going study that the exploitable fish resources might be increased by reducing the dolphin populations, it may be appropriate to start an experimental operation to reduce the dolphin populations. Such an experiment should be preceded by a careful evaluation of the welfare of the people dependent upon the fish resources, and should be accompanied by careful monitoring of the populations and the ecosystems of which they are a part. The goal of maximum sustainable yield (MSY) is not appropriate in this case because the dolphins are not being killed for use. A more appropriate objective may be to keep the populations above the lowest level at which survival can be assured.

7. The approach outlined in 6 above is ideal, but may not be practical. The 'dolphin war' is in progress and, at present, there is no legal or biological basis for ending the killing. It is likely that the killing will continue and, although the present capture techniques and catch levels seem inadequate to eliminate any of the populations, they may well result in significant change in abundance and/or population structure. Consequently, there is a critical need for studies to determine: (a) the nature and extent of gear and fish damage caused by the dolphins; (b) the species, number, ages, sexes, physical condition, and reproductive condition of the dolphins being killed; (c) the status of the dolphin populations (i.e. present distribution, size, and productivity), and how the distribution, size and productivity of the populations are being affected by the take; and (d) how the apparent conflict between the fishermen and dolphins can be resolved.

8. Until harvest levels can be established on biological grounds, the bounty or other financial support given to the Fishery Co-operative Unions should be set at a level which does not provide the FCUs with a profit for the operation. This may help to safeguard the dolphin populations.

Acknowledgements

I wish to express my sincere thanks to all who helped me in the present study. The field work was done with the assistance of several volunteers: Mr Yasuharu Izumizawa, Mr Satoshi Shiraga, Mr Chihiro Tominaga, Mr. Kazuhiro Okamoto, Mr Yoshibumi Komyo, Miss Chieko Osaka and Mr Motoi Yoshioka. The Katsumoto Fishery Co-operative Union provided me with the opportunity to study the dolphin carcasses and records of fishery operations. The Nagasaki Statistics Information Office offered the statistical information. Miss Toshie Shirai assisted in data analyses, typewriting and drawing. This study was financially supported by World Wildlife Fund Japan (1979), US Marine Mammal Commission (1980), Toyota Foundation (1980/81) and Japanese Ministry of Education (1980/81).

References

Anonymous 1981. *Report of study in search of countermeasure of biological obstacles on fisheries in the fiscal year 1979 and 1980.* Shimizu, Japan: Tokai University. (In Japanese with English summary.)

Aoyama, T. and E. Kozasa 1971a. The damage to coastal fishery by dolphins and porpoises in the western and northern sea areas of Kyushu-I. The aspect of damage derived from a questionnaire survey. *Bull. Seikai Reg. Fish. Res. Lab.* **41**, 1–9. (In Japanese with English summary).

Aoyama, T. and E. Kozasa 1971b. The damage to coastal fishery by dolphins and porpoises in the western and northern sea areas of Kyushu-II. The actual state of damage derived from operation report. *Bull. Seikai Reg. Fish. Res. Lab.* **41**, 11–20. (In Japanese with English summary).

Aoyama, T. and E. Kozasa 1972. The stock assessment of dolphins and porpoises migrated in the western sea area of Kyushu by sighting observation. *Bull. Seikai Reg. Fish. Res. Lab.* **42**, 1–12. (In Japanese with English summary.)

Doi, T. 1974. Further development of whale sighting theory. In *The whale problem, a status report,* W. F. Schevill (ed.), 359–68. Cambridge Mass: Harvard University Press.

Japanese Fisheries Agency (ed.) 1968. *Report of the basic survey in search of countermeasures of the damage by dolphins on the fisheries in western Japan.* Tokyo. (In Japanese).

Japanese Fisheries Agency (ed.) 1969. *Final report of the basic survey in search of countermeasures of the damage by dolphins on the fisheries in western Japan.* Tokyo. (In Japanese.)

Kasuya, T. 1985. Effect of exploitation on the reproductive parameters of the spotted and striped dolphins off the Pacific coast of Japan. *Sci. Rep. Whales Res. Inst. (Tokyo),* **36**: 107–38.

Kasuya, T. and H. Marsh 1984. Life history and reproductive biology of the short-finned pilot whale *Globicephala macrorhynchus* off the Pacific coast of Japan. *Rep. Int. Whal. Commun.* (Spec. Iss. 6): 259–310.

Kasuya, T., N. Miyazaki and W. H. Dawbin 1974. Growth and reproduction of *Stenella attenuata* in the Pacific coast of Japan. *Sci. Rep. Whales Res. Inst. (Tokyo)* **26**, 157–226.

Miyazaki, N. 1981. Food habit. p. 33-35. In Dolphin and fishery–dolphin conflict in the Iki Island area, T. Kasuya and N. Miyazaki, (eds), 33–35. *Geiken Tsushin (Tokyo),* **340**, 25–36. (In Japanese.)

Miyazaki, N. and M. Nishiwaki 1978. School structure of the striped dolphin off the Pacific coast of Japan. *Sci. Rep. Whales Res. Inst. (Tokyo),* **30**, 65–115.

Nakajima, M., K. Takahashi, M. Ogura and K. Sawaura 1963. On the growth of infants of the small size toothed whales. *J. Zool. Gardens. Aquariums* **5**(1), 16–22. (In Japanese.)

Odell, D. K. 1975. Status and aspects of life history of the bottlenose dolphins, *Tursiops truncatus,* in Florida. *J. Fish. Res. Bd Can.* **32**(7), 1055–8.

Ohsumi, S. 1966. Allomorphosis between body length at sexual maturity and body length at birth in the cetacea. *J. Mamm. Soc. Japan* **3**(1), 3–7.

Perrin, W. F., D. B. Holts and R. B. Miller 1977. Growth and reproduction of the eastern spinner dolphin, a geographical form of *Stenella longirostris* in the eastern tropical Pacific. *Fish. Bull.* **75**(4), 725–50.

Yoshida, T. (ed.) 1979. *A social anthropological study of a Japanese fishing village.* Tokyo: University of Tokyo Press.

Problems in estimating food consumption

In order to assess the potential interactions among marine mammal predators, commercial fisheries, and their common prey species, it is necessary to know, in quantitative terms, precisely what prey species are consumed by marine mammal populations in relation to those caught by commercial fisheries, what size/age categories of prey are removed by both, and when and where such 'consumption' occurs.

The case studies in the previous section identify deficiences in available information and some of the assumptions which are necessary in current studies because of methodological limitations. These studies also emphasise the need for improved techniques for describing and quantifying interactions between marine mammals and fisheries. The final section of this book addresses some of the current difficulties associated with the estimation of food consumption by marine mammal populations.

There are essentially two approaches to the study of feeding habits and energy requirements of marine mammal populations. The traditional approach involves the examination of stomach contents to provide a direct description of food items consumed. Although superficially straightforward and simple, this approach is fraught with difficulties. Data are often recorded only in terms of frequency of occurrence or per cent volume (or weight) for each identifiable prey species. However, as noted years ago, neither measure in isolation is a satisfactory index of the relative contribution of various prey to the diet of a marine mammal population (see Lowry & Frost 1981, Lavigne *et al.* 1982).

In Chapter 15, Bigg and Perez introduce an approach to stomach content analysis, called 'modified volume', which proposes an analytical procedure to overcome some of the limitations and biases which have characterised earlier studies. The approach is particularly applicable to those marine mammals which consume a mixed diet of squid and fish. The accuracy and precision of the modified volume method for estimating food consumption of marine mammals from stomach contents now awaits experimental confirmation.

There are numerous other problems associated with the analysis of stomach contents. For example, stomachs will be sampled at various times after the consumption of a meal and a sample of stomachs from any population, or indeed the stomach of an individual seal, may consequently contain food items in various stages of digestion. This problem is further complicated by the fact that not all the food in a stomach may have been consumed at one time. Estimates of the amount of food consumed will also vary depending on whether the quantity of prey items is measured in terms of numbers (or frequency), biomass (or volume), some combination of frequency and volume (e.g. modified volume, Chapter 15), or energy (e.g. kcal per day). Chapters 16 and 17 begin to address some of these problems.

In Chapter 16, Bigg and Fawcett present the results of a feeding experiment involving northern fur seals (*Callorhinus ursinus*). They note that stomach and scat contents may not represent the actual proportions of various prey items consumed, an assumption which underlies many diet determination studies for marine mammals. Methods for dealing with some of the biases inherent in such studies are presented.

A second experiment, designed to assess the problems and assumptions associated with the use of otoliths of prey species to analyse stomach contents, is described by Murie and Lavigne in Chapter 17. For seals consuming a fish diet, they note that a large percentage of otoliths are completely digested in the stomach. Use of otolith analyses may thus underestimate the actual consumption of small teleost fishes by marine mammals.

The magnitude of the problems facing scientists attempting to quantify feeding habits of some marine mammal populations are self-evident, as shown in Chapter 18. Kajimura notes that more than 50 species of fish and 10 species of squid have been identified in stomach contents of northern fur seals in the eastern Pacific between 1958 and 1974. He concludes that the determination of the relationship between northern fur seals and other living marine resources represents an enormously complex problem, one which may not be completely understood within our lifetime.

At the present stage of research development, it is clear that stomach content analyses can provide only a crude measure of the prey species consumed by a marine mammal in a particular place at a particular time. Measures of the size categories of prey, the relative volumes of prey, and the relative caloric contributions of various prey in the meal or meals represented in each stomach sampled are still infrequently assessed. Without adequate documentation of annual variation in location and frequency of feeding, average meal size, and caloric density of prey, including a knowledge of fasting periods when little or no food is consumed, the stomach contents approach will not provide absolute estimates of the annual food intake of a marine mammal population in terms of biomass of various prey species consumed. Nor will it provide a measure of their annual caloric requirements.

As an alternative to the analysis of stomach contents, food consumption may be estimated by reconstructing the energy budget from a knowledge of metabolic energy requirements, taking into account energy losses associated with faeces, urine, heat increment of feeding, etc. Although this approach does not answer specific questions about the absolute consumption of individual prey species, it does provide a framework for addressing several problems relevant to the assessment of marine mammal–fishery interactions. In Chapter 19, for example, Lavigne, Innes, Stewart and Worthy reconstruct an annual energy budget for North-west Atlantic harp seals. This analysis suggests that average daily energy requirements of harp seals are in line with those of other mammals. In addition, because harp seals are highly migratory animals with catholic feeding habits, many of their prey are non-commercial species of invertebrates and fish, or they are consumed in areas where traditional commercial fisheries do not operate. Further, biomass estimates of food consumption are shown to be misleading because of large differences in caloric density and digestibility of invertebrate and vertebrate prey. It is concluded that the consumption of commercial fish species (and thus the perception of competition between seals and fisheries) by North-west Atlantic harp seals has been vastly overestimated in recent years.

In the final chapter, Hiby and Harwood generalise this approach, using a hypothetical grey seal population, to investigate the effects of variation in population parameters on population energy requirements. One important result of this analysis is that changes in *per capita* consumption of prey·by seal populations, in relation to changes in population density, appear much smaller than previously thought.

As the workshop report indicated, there remain many problems associated with the accurate estimation of food consumption by marine mammals, and ultimately, the assessment of marine mammal–fishery interactions. Some of the problems will be overcome through the design of carefully controlled feeding experiments using captive animals. Other questions will be answered through the development of models to identify general principles related to food consumption and predator–prey interactions in marine ecosystems. At this time, we can only reiterate the priority, identified by the pinniped working group at the FAO Consultation on marine mammal management in Bergen, Norway, in 1976, for additional studies of energy flow through marine mammal populations so that the dynamic interactions among components of marine ecosystems may be better understood.

References

Lavigne, D. M., W. W. Barchard, S. Innes and N. A. Øritsland 1982. Pinniped bioenergetics. In *Mammals in the seas, Vol. IV Small cetaceans, seals, sirenians and otters,* 191–235. FAO Fisheries Ser. 5.

Lowry, L. F. and K. J. Frost 1981. Feeding and trophic relationships of phocid seals and walruses in the eastern Bering Sea. In *The eastern Bering Sea shelf: oceanography and resources*, Vol. 2 D. W. Hood and J. A. Calder (eds.), 813–24. Seattle, WA: University of Washington Press.

15 Modified volume: a frequency–volume method to assess marine mammal food habits

Michael A. Bigg and Michael A. Perez

Introduction

The main difficulty in describing the food habits of marine mammals is the uncertainty as to which method best measures the relative importance of each food type. Traditional methods in wildlife food habits studies are volume, frequency of occurrence, and counts of individual prey items (Hynes 1950, Pillay 1952, Windell & Bowen 1978, Berg 1979, Hyslop 1980, Korschgen 1980). Recently techniques have been developed which incorporate one or more of the above into a single procedure (e.g. the index of relative importance – Pinkas *et al.* 1971). From the same data, each technique tends to produce a different value of relative rank for food species. This is due partly to inherent differences in what each method measures. Unfortunately, none of the procedures can be tested for accuracy as no experimentally known set of rank values for food species exists for comparison. Thus, the decision of which method to use must be based, to some extent, on a subjective evaluation of numerous potential biases.

An example of the difference in results obtainable from different techniques can be seen in studies on northern fur seal (*Callorhinus ursinus*) food habits. Wilke and Kenyon (1957) and Spalding (1964) pointed out that a marked difference exists between volume and frequency measures when calculating the ratio of fish to squid. Perez and Bigg (1980) discussed different methods and their limitations in ranking food types eaten by northern fur seals.

In the current report, we consider biases in the available procedures for measuring diet proportions, using the northern fur seal as an example for marine mammal diet analysis. We propose a new method, called modified volume, which incorporates measures of volume and frequency of occurrence of prey species identified in stomach contents.

Measurement limitations

The following is a discussion of the likely biases in available methods. To illustrate how each procedure gives different measurement values, we use the proportion of fish to squid in the total diet of northern fur seals. The data base consisted of 10 699 non-empty stomachs collected by the US and Canada during 1958–74. Figure 15.1 compares the proportions of fish and squid by each method.

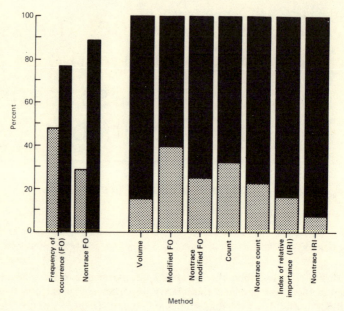

Figure 15.1 The proportion of fish (solid) to squid (stippled) in the diet of northern fur seals as measured by nine percentage methods of stomach contents assessment.

Volume

The percentage volume or mass of the total stomach contents which a food species makes up provides the most direct measure of its importance. It quantifies the biomass of each prey species consumed, automatically accounting indirectly for the number and size of prey individuals. Its main potential bias is the effect of progressive digestion, which is assumed in this method to be similar for all prey. Food types which digest more quickly or are eaten earlier than others will be under-represented. Of relevance here is that market squid seem to be digested at about twice the rate of Pacific herring (see Chapter 16). Thus, squid in the diet of northern fur seals are substantially under-represented by the volumetric procedure. It seems best, when using volume, to compare only species which are taxonomically similar.

Frequency of occurrence

Percentage frequency of occurrence of a prey species is the proportion of stomachs which contain that species. It measures the proportion of seals feeding on a particular food type, exclusive of the volume (or mass) and number of prey. The main bias is that unimportant species, which are consumed incidentally, are given exaggerated importance. However, unlike volume, stage of digestion has little effect on ranking. For this reason, Spalding (1964) suggested that with small numbers of stomachs, where digestion could be important, frequency of occurrence is less biased than volume.

A long-suspected bias in the frequency method, as applied to squid and fish proportions in fur seals, is that squid beaks remain in the stomach longer than fish bones, with a resulting exaggeration in importance of squid. This has now been shown experimentally to be true (see Ch. 16). Beaks apparently remain because they are indigestible and their irregular shapes tend to result in entrapment in stomach rugae. To eliminate this bias, we have previously excluded prey species of both squid and fish which were represented in the stomach only by beaks or other trace evidence. We call this revised procedure non-trace frequency of occurrence (Perez & Bigg 1980). This method substantially reduces the importance of squid to approximate more closely that of volume. However, compared to volume measurement, non-trace frequency probably still exaggerates the number of important foods through the familiar bias of incidental feeding. Based on all 1958–74 data pooled, non-trace frequency produced 21 important species compared to 15 by volume.

Unlike volume, the percentages by frequency of occurrence will sum to more than 100%, because some stomachs contain more than one food type. An alternative approach, discussed by Hynes (1950) and used by Spalding (1964) and by us in this report, is to adjust the proportion of each prey item to total 100%. This we call modified frequency of occurrence.

Count

Percentage count or number is the proportion of individuals of a food species to the total number of individuals from all species eaten. No consideration is given to prey volume. Biases exist in that the numbers of individuals of a more rapidly digested species will be under-represented, and the retention of squid beaks will overestimate the importance of squid. When trace data were eliminated, a method we now call non-trace count, the proportion of squid decreased markedly.

Index of relative importance (IRI)

In this method, the percentage frequency of occurrence of each prey species is multiplied by the sum of the percentage volume and percentage count to yield an index for comparison among prey species. The rationale for this procedure seems to be that the formulation would tend to cancel various biases of each component. One remaining bias is that food types comprising <1% by the component methods will be under-represented due to the multiplicative effect of fractions.

When proportions of fish and squid are calculated by this index, using normal frequency, volume, and count as the component methods, the values are similar to that found by volume alone. This similarity is more coincidental than meaningful because the component methods of normal frequency and count are biased by the retention of squid beaks. When non-trace frequency and non-trace count data are substituted, the non-trace IRI method gives a seemingly low proportion of squid. Perez (1979) and Perez and Bigg (1980) utilised the IRI in preliminary analyses of the 1958–74 pelagic fur seal data. Crawford (1980) used it in an examination of the feeding habits of the Dall's porpoise (*Phocoenoides dalli*), and Pitcher (1980) used a modified version (no count data) to study harbour seal (*Phoca vitulina richardsi*) feeding. Pitcher (1981) used a similar integrative technique, the combination rank index to analyse the food habits of northern sea-lions (*Eumetopias jubatus*); in this procedure ranks, but not percentages, by volume and frequency were multiplied and ordered.

Modified volume procedure

Of the existing methods, non-trace frequency of occurrence appears to be the best measure for estimating the ratio of fish to squid consumed by seals, while the ratio of prey species within fish and squid is best determined by volume. We pooled the two procedures to give relative percentages for prey species. First, the proportion of total fish and total squid in the diet is determined by non-trace frequency of occurrence. Second, the ratio of each species within only fish and within only squid is determined by volume. Next, these volumetric ratios for squid and for fish species are adjusted to sum, respectively, to the total proportion of squid and fish in the diet. Finally, all values are readjusted to total 100%. We term this two-step method, modified volume.

The technique of preparing the raw food data for modified volume was as follows. The taxonomic categories recorded in the laboratory which overlap were either pooled with higher taxa (e.g. *Oncorhynchus* spp. with Salmonidae), or were proportionally divided among component species (e.g. Clupeidae vs. *Clupea harengus pallasi* and *Alosa sapidissima*), depending on which level of taxon had the most data. This prevented food categories from being compared against themselves. A detailed listing of these regroupings of prey taxa is found in Perez and Bigg (1981). The categories of unidentified fish and unidentified squid were used to establish the ratio of fish to squid in modified volume, but were omitted to compare individual prey species within fish and within squid, except when these were the only food items in a sample. We excluded all food types which comprised ≤1% of the total volume of fish or squid. Such food types increase the variance of statistical tests which compare rank because their irregular occurrences change the lower ranking orders in a non-meaningful way. The remaining prey values were adjusted to sum to 100%.

The values derived by modified volume appear reasonable when compared to those obtained by other methods. Comparisons were made on the same taxa for 117 combinations of the 1958–74 data by region, subregion, and month, where the sample size

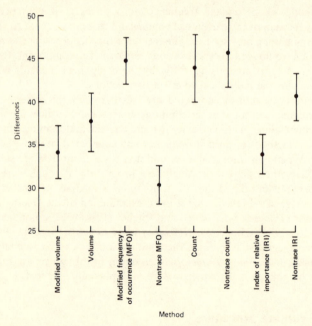

Figure 15.2 The sum of the absolute differences (mean and 95% CI) between percentage ranking values assigned by each of eight methods versus the average value among all methods with the same prey in 117 combinations of region and month.

was ≥ 20 stomachs containing fleshy remains. The above techniques used to obtain data in modified volume were also used in each of seven other methods to calculate the importance of prey, and percentage values for food categories were adjusted to sum to 100%. The Kendall coefficient of concordance (Siegel 1956) showed significant (p < 0.05) agreement in rank orders among the methods. This indicated that each procedure assigned essentially the same order of importance for food types. It does not imply that the absolute percentages for each taxon were the same among methods. Figure 15.2 compares the mean and 95% confidence interval (CI) for the sum of the absolute differences in the percentage values assigned by each method against the average of all methods. The food types were the same in all eight procedures. The binomial approximation for proportions (Fleiss 1981) was used to calculate 95% CI values. Non-trace modified frequency, modified volume, and the IRI were closest to the overall average. While methods with values closest to the overall average are not necessarily the most accurate, they are probably representative of the true diet. This was suggested by Hynes (1950), who found that any of the commonly accepted techniques used to assess the composition of an animals's diet yielded essentially similar results for large numbers of stomachs when the results were reduced to comparable percentage compositions of diet.

Figure 15.3 relates percentage similarity (Goodall 1973) values derived by comparing each food percentage from modified volume with that obtained by each of the seven other methods. The standard arc sine transformation (Zar 1974) was used to normalise percentage similarity values to compute the mean and 95% CI. The modified volume method assigned percentage values which were closest to those given by volume (90%), with non-trace modified frequency second (82%).

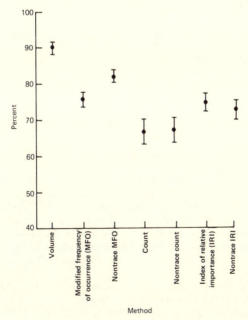

Figure 15.3 The average percentage similarity (with 95% CI) between percentage ranking values assigned by both modified volume and each of seven other methods with the same prey in 117 combinations of region and month.

Implications

The modified volume method has two advantages for estimating the proportion of each prey found in northern fur seal stomachs. First, it removes the effect of trace remains (e.g. accumulated squid beaks) in stomachs by using fleshy remains as evidence of diet. Without this procedure, squid are given exaggerated importance. Second, it reduces the effect of faster digestion rates of squid relative to fish. It does this by comparing the relative proportions of species only within fish or within squid groups, rather than comparing all species against each other. Without this consideration squid would be underestimated.

Recently Perez and Mooney (1984) have used this technique to assess the relative significance of northern fur seal prey, and also extended its use to consider the importance of energy in the diet. Since many species of pinnipeds and cetaceans are known to feed on both squid and fish (Fiscus 1979, 1982), the modified volume method has wider application in food studies of marine mammals.

References

Berg, J. 1979. Discussion of methods of investigating the food of fishes, with reference to a preliminary study of the prey of *Gobiusculus flavescens* (Gobiidae). *Mar. Biol.* **50**, 263–73.

Crawford, T. W. 1980. Vertebrate prey of *Phocoenoides dalli*, (Dall's porpoise), associated with the Japanese high seas salmon fishery in the North Pacific Ocean. MS Thesis, University of Washington, Seattle, Washington.

Fiscus, C. H. 1979. Interactions of marine mammals and Pacific hake. *Mar. Fish. Rev.* **41**(10), 1–9.

Fiscus, C. H. 1982. Predation by marine mammals on squids of the eastern North Pacific Ocean and the Bering Sea. *Mar. Fish. Rev.* **44**(2), 1–10.

Fleiss, J. L. 1981. *Statistical methods for rates and proportions,* 2nd Edn. New York: Wiley.

Goodall, D. W. 1973. Sample similarity and species correlation. In *Handbook of vegetation science,* R. Tuxen (ed.), 105–156. Part 5: Ordination and classification of communities, R. H. Whittaker (ed.). The Hague, Netherlands: W. Junk.

Hynes, H. B. N. 1950. The food of fresh-water sticklebacks (*Gasterosteus aculeatus* and *Pygosteus pungitius*), with a review of methods used in studies of the food of fishes. *J. Anim. Ecol.* **19**, 36–58.

Hyslop, E. J. 1980. Stomach contents analysis – a review of methods and their application. *J. Fish. Biol.* **17**, 411–29.

Korschgen, L. J. 1980. Procedures for food-habits analyses, p. 113-127. In *Wildlife management techniques manual,* 4th edn, S. D. Schemnitz (ed.), 113–27. Washington, DC.: Wildlife Society.

Perez, M. A. 1979. Preliminary analysis of feeding habits of the northern fur seal in the eastern North Pacific and Bering Sea. In *Preliminary analysis of pelagic fur seal data collected by the United States and Canada during 1958–74,* H. Kajimura, R. H. Lander, M. A. Perez, A. E. York and M. A. Bigg, 180–245. Unpublished report of 22nd meeting of the North Pacific Fur Seal Commission, Washington, DC. Seattle, Washington: National Marine Mammal Laboratory, NOAA.

Perez, M. A. and M. A. Bigg 1980. Interim report on the feeding habits of the northern fur seal in the eastern North Pacific Ocean and eastern Bering Sea. In *Further analysis of pelagic fur seal data collected by the United States and Canada during 1958–74,* Part 2, H. Kajimura, R. H. Lander, M. A. Perez, A. E. York and M. A. Bigg, 4–172. Unpublished Report of 23rd meeting of the North Pacific Fur Seal Commission, Moscow. Seattle, Washington: National Marine Mammal Laboratory, National Marine Fisheries Service, NOAA.

Perez, M. A. and M. A. Bigg 1981. *Modified volume: a two-step frequency–volume method for ranking food types found in stomachs of northern fur seals.* Unpublished Report of the 24th meeting of the North Pacific Fur Seal Commission, Tokyo. Seattle, Washington: National Marine Mammal Laboratory, NOAA.

Perez, M. A. and E. E. Mooney 1984. Energetics and food consumption of lactating northern fur seals, *Callorhinus ursinus.* Unpublished manuscript. Seattle, Washington: National Marine Mammal Laboratory, NOAA.

Pillay, T. V. R. 1952. A critique of the methods of study of food of fishes. *J. Zool. Soc. India* **4**, 185–200.

Pinkas, L., M. S. Oliphant and I. L. K. Iverson 1971. Food habits of albacore, bluefin tuna, and bonito in California waters. *Calif. Dept. Fish Game, Fish. Bull.* **152**.

Pitcher, K. W. 1980. Food of the harbor seal, *Phoca vitulina richardsi,* in the Gulf of Alaska. *US Natl Mar. Fish. Serv., Fish. Bull.* **78**, 544–9.

Pitcher, K. W. 1981. Prey of the Steller sea lion, *Eumetopias jubatus,* in the Gulf of Alaska. *US Natl Mar. Fish. Serv., Fish. Bull.* **79**, 467–72.

Siegel, S. 1956. *Nonparametric statistics for the behavioral sciences.* New York: McGraw-Hill.

Spalding, D. J. 1964. Comparative feeding habits of the fur seal, sea lion, and harbour seal on the British Columbia coast. *Bull. Fish. Res. B. Can.* **146**.

Wilke, F. and K. W. Kenyon 1957. The food of fur seals in the eastern Bering Sea. *J. Wildl. Manag.* **21**, 237–8.

Windell, J. T. and S. H. Bowen 1978. Methods for study of fish diets based on analysis of stomach contents. In *Methods for assessment of fish production in fresh waters,* T. Bagenal (ed.), 219–26. IBP Handbook No. 3, 3rd edn. Oxford: Blackwell Scientific.

Zar, J. H. 1974. *Biostatistical analysis.* Englewood Cliffs, NJ: Prentice-Hall.

16 Two biases in diet determination of northern fur seals (*Callorhinus ursinus*)

Michael A. Bigg and Ian Fawcett

Introduction

Studies of the diets of marine mammals are usually based on an examination of either stomach or scat (faeces) contents. The hard and fleshy remains of prey eaten provide good information on the range of prey species. However, the relative importance of each food is more difficult to establish because of two assumptions underlying frequency of occurrence and volume analyses. In frequency of occurrence measurements, the hard remains, such as cephalopod beaks and fish bones, are assumed to remain in the stomach for the same duration for each prey species. In volumetric ranking, the fleshy parts are assumed to digest at about the same rate for all food species. Thus, stomach and scat contents are assumed to represent the true proportions of various foods consumed at the same time.

In this report we examine experimentally the validity of these two assumptions, using captive northern fur seals (*Callorhinus ursinus*). We determine the passage rate through the digestive tract for two important foods of this seal – herring (*Clupea harengus pallasi*) and squid (*Loligo opalescens*) – and their rates of artificial and natural digestion. The results are discussed with respect to the interpretation of stomach and scat contents in northern fur seals and the implications for diet studies involving other marine mammals which feed on fish and cephalopods.

Methods

For the experiment we used five northern fur seals held at the Pacific Biological Station, Nanaimo. All were mature, non-pregnant females which had been kept in captivity for 2–4 years and used in other studies on caloric requirements and reproduction for the North Pacific Fur Seal Commission. Each was kept outdoors, individually, in circular wooden tanks, 3.7 m in diameter, with circulating salt water 0.9 m deep. During captivity, their diet was exclusively herring fed twice a day, each meal averaging about 1200 g. Seals typically spent most of the day swimming rapidly around the tanks, resting at night for several hours.

For studies on passage and digestion times, each seal was first fasted for 24–48 h to empty the digestive tract. Known weights of herring and squid were then offered and the amount consumed within 15 min was recorded. To determine the passage time of denser, larger bone than that found in herring, we put otoliths from sockeye salmon (*Oncorhynchus nerka*) into gelatin capsules and inserted these into the abdominal cavity of the herring. The otoliths measured 4–5 mm in length. Whole herring measured about 20 cm (standard length) and squid 10 cm (dorsal mantel length). Herring were always eaten immediately, although in variable amounts, ranging from a small to average-sized meal (see Table 16.2). Squid were eaten voluntarily only by seal No. 12. Other seals were tube fed, mainly on squid buccal masses containing beaks. The weight of such squid tissue was too small to be considered in digestion time comparisons, and thus the weights were ignored. The tube-feeding procedure required about 10 min. After feeding, seals were left to swim in their tanks. Seal No. 12 was fed herring and squid three times over a 2-day period, which allowed comparison of the digestion rates. To distinguish between the last two feedings, which were 4 h and 2 h before death, herring and squid of the last feeding were fin clipped. All other seals were fed only once during the experiment. On several occasions prior to this experiment some were fasted and given whole herring and squid to determine whether otoliths, statoliths and eye lenses passed intact through the digestive tract and were defecated.

At 2–33 h after feeding, all seals were euthanised with an intraperitoneal injection of T-61 (Euthanasia solution, Hoechst, Montreal). Weights and occurrences of digested food in the stomach, small intestine and large intestine were determined. The time until first defecation following the meal was also recorded by inspecting the tank each hour, using a fine-mesh net for evidence of beaks or salmon otoliths.

Rates for artificial digestion of herring and squid were determined because so few seals were available to determine natural digestion rates, and because of the difficulty in feeding equal amounts of squid and fish to seals. The digestive solution used was 10 l of 1% HCl and 1% pepsin. Together, these two naturally occurring gastric components make an active proteolytic enzyme system (Bard 1956, p. 505). The temperature of the solution was kept at $38°-40°C$. Five similar-sized squid totalling 311 g and five similar-sized herring weighing 303 g were put individually in mesh containers and suspended in the digestive solution. At 1 h intervals, each individual was weighed in its container. The container weight was subtracted to establish the weight of individuals. Only male squid were used because the artificial digestion solution was unable to digest the female nidamental gland, oviductal gland and external glandular oviduct, and only digested the ovary slowly. These organs are apparently digested easily by the seal, as they are not found in stomachs of wild northern fur seals. The reproductive organs of female herring were digested in the laboratory as quickly as those of the male.

Results

Passage time

Table 16.1 gives the percentage of squid beaks and fish otoliths found in each part of the gut at various times after feeding. Squid beaks were found in all five stomachs and remained up to 33 h after feeding. Usually they clustered near the pyloric sphincter, and often appeared entrapped in the stomach rugae. The passage rate of squid from the stomach to the intestine was variable, as indicated by the low proportion present at 12 h in seal No. 7 and the high proportion at 33 h in seal No. 5. Salmon otoliths and other hard tissues, such as vertebrae and scales, were present in the stomach only up to 9 h. Thus, squid beaks can remain in the stomach for at least a day longer than fish bones.

Table 16.1 Percentage of squid beaks and fish otoliths (in parentheses) found in the stomach, small intestine, and large intestine of captive northern fur seals euthanised at 2–33 h after feeding, and time for the first defecation containing otoliths (OT) or squid beaks (B).

Time (h)	Seal no.	No. of beaks and (otoliths) fed	Percentage beaks and (otoliths) found in			First defecation (h)
			Stomach	Small intestine	Large intestine	
2	12[a]	12(12)[b]	100(100)	0(0)	0(0)	>2
4	12[a]	12(12)[b]	100(58+)	0(17)	0(0)	>4
6	2	100(100)	100(50+)	0(4)	0(22)	>6
9	15	78(96)	100(21)	0(1)	0(18)	>9
12	7	96(100)	3(0)	1(2)	0(16)	7(B & OT)
25	12[a]	66(−)	8(−)	0(−)	3(−)	22(B & OT)
33	5	82(100)	95(0)	1(0)	2(27)	6(OT)

[a]Seal no. 12 was fed three times with squid and herring over a 25-h period. The remains of the three feedings were identified in a single examination of the digestive tract after euthanasia.
[b]Herring otoliths; for other seals only salmon otoliths were used.

Few remains of squid or fish were found in the small intestine, presumably because the passage rate here was relatively rapid. The first otoliths were seen at 4 h after feeding. The largest numbers of otoliths were found in the large intestine near the colon, the first appearing at 6 h. Although squid beaks were first recorded here at 25 h, they can arrive much earlier, as indicated by the presence of squid beaks in faeces of seal No. 7 at 7 h. The time of first defecation was variable, ranging from 6 h to 22 h after feeding.

Passage through the digestive system had no visible effect on the appearance of squid beaks. However, squid pens appeared partly digested in that they were often shredded when found in the intestines and scats. This may also have been due to mechanical action in passage. Some squid statoliths and eye lenses passed into the faeces. Most herring vertebrae were completely digested, with only a few recognisable in the intestines and scats. The salmon otoliths exhibited little sign of digestion along the edges. Some herring otoliths and eye lenses were found in the faeces.

Digestion time

The fleshy parts of all meals probably digest within about 12 h. Table 16.2 gives the percentage weight of food remaining in the stomach at various times after feeding. It shows that average-sized meals of herring consumed by seals No. 2 and No. 15 were mostly digested by 6–9 h. They would have probably been completely digested before 12 h, assuming a digestion pattern similar to that discussed later for artificial digestion. By 12 h after a small meal, seal No. 7 had digested all herring. A comparison of the time required to reach similar proportions of digestion in seals No. 12 and No. 15 suggests that evidence of smaller meals would leave the stomach more rapidly than larger meals. Such would be expected for the larger surface area to volume ratio on which digestion would act.

An examination of a large meal consumed by seal No. 2 showed the state of digestion of 17 herring in the stomach by 6 h after feeding. The outer fish were completely digested, with gross evidence of six fish having disappeared completely. One herring located in the inner core was only slightly digested, with loss only of the skin, head and

Table 16.2 Percentage digestion for squid and fish (in parentheses) in the stomachs of captive northern fur seals euthanised at 2–33 h after feeding.

Time (h)	Seal no.	weight eaten (g)	Percentage remaining in stomach
2	12[a]	225 (407)	66 (66)
4	12[a]	225 (407)	0 (18)
6	2	− (1770)	− (25)
9	15	− (1243)	− (13)
12	7	− (425)	− (0)
33	5	− (904)	− (0)

[a]See Table 16.1.

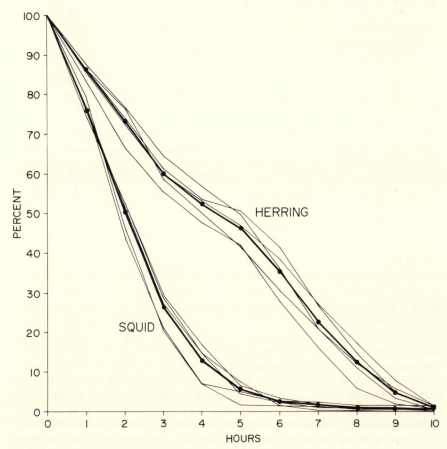

Figure 16.1 Individual and average percentage weight remaining, by hour, of five herring and five market squid kept in an artificial digestive solution.

Table 16.3 Sequence of artificial digestion for squid and herring.

Time (h)	Squid	Herring
1	skin, eye sockets gone	fins, most skin gone
2	suction cups gone, pen showing	
		skin, most of head gone
3	pen free, body collapsed	head, half of gut gone
4	body is pulp	less muscle but firm
5	part of head and tentacles left	gut gone, muscle reduced
6	mainly buccal mass remains	muscle bands splitting but firm
7–10	beaks and pen remain	muscle bands digest

fins. Other herring were in various stages of digestion, with broken muscle and cleaned vertebral columns. Clearly, digestion of the inner fish occurred later than the outer.

A comparison of the digestion rates for herring and squid was possible only in seal No. 12. Here, a small meal of squid and herring was digested to the same extent by 2 h. However, by 4 h, all squid were digested except for traces of buccal mass flesh attached to beaks, while 18% of herring remained, suggesting a greater digestion rate for squid.

Figure 16.1 shows the decrease in weight of individual and average squid and herring remaining after each hour of artificial digestion. Squid digested more quickly than herring. An average of 90% digestion of squid occurred by 4.4 h, while 90% of fish was digested within 8.3 h. For the 10% intervals between 10% and 90% digested, squid digested at an average rate of 2.0 times (1.9–2.3) faster than herring. Beaks and pens showed no signs of digestion.

Table 16.3 compares the artificial digestion sequences for squid and herring. The soft body of squid was rapidly digested and had collapsed by 4 h. The head, which contained the buccal mass and tentacle bases, was of relatively dense tissue and was slow to digest. This is reflected in the shallow slope of the squid digestion curve after 5 h in Figure 16.1. Herring digested differently, mainly through the loss of the extremities and gut. The muscle bands were the last to be digested. The rate of digestion within the seal would no doubt be increased by mechanical action of the stomach but, based on an examination of stomach contents, the sequence of digestion *in vivo* did not appear to differ substantially.

Discussion

Researchers studying the diet of northern fur seals have long suspected that squid beaks accumulate in the stomach. The circumstantial evidence cited is that squid beaks are indigestible and often occur in stomachs without the presence of squid flesh (Scheffer 1950, p. 7, Fiscus & Kajimura 1967, p. 12). Such is not generally the case with fish remains. Results from the present study confirm the indigestibility and retention of beaks. Retention in the stomach is probably caused by the irregular shape of the chitinous beaks. The upper and lower beaks have sharp projections, called wings, walls, hoods, crest and rostrum (Clarke 1962, p. 428). These projections point in different directions to form an anchor among the stomach rugae. The beaks also seem to tangle with one another to form a bolus near the pyloric sphincter which impedes the passage of some beaks into the intestine. Pitcher (1981) found 'wads' of cephalopod beaks packed at the pyloric end of the stomach of harbour seals. Such a bolus might occasionally block the escape of stomach contents and cause spewings, such as those seen on rookeries by Wilke and Kenyon (1952, p. 397). Miller (1978, p. 15) noted that spewings occurred at about 2-day intervals in captive northern fur seals fed squid, whereas we have never observed such spewings in northern fur seals kept at Nanaimo on a diet of only herring.

The fact that no fish bones remained in the stomach was no doubt due to the digestibility of most small bones and their easy passage into the intestine. However, as pointed out by Fiscus and Baines (1966, p. 198) in studies on the diet of Steller sea-lion (*Eumetopias jubatus*) and California sea-lions (*Zalophus californianus*), bones of large fish may persist in the stomach for a longer time than those of small fish. Thus, for example, the otoliths of rockfish (*Sebastes* sp.), whiting (*Merluccius productus*), and walleye pollock (*Theragra chalcogramma*), which are relatively large and dense, might be retained.

Our results have implications for determining the relative importance of various foods, by frequency of occurrence, from the gut and scat of marine mammals which feed on fish and cephalopods. Retention of beaks in stomachs will exaggerate the importance of cephalopods in stomachs, and perhaps also in intestines and scats. Beaks from a single feeding could still be present in the stomach after several subsequent days of feeding, and only gradually enter the intestines and scats. It is possible that this bias exists to some extent for large-boned species of fish. The retention bias can be eliminated when ranking stomach contents by using only the fleshy remains of a species eaten as evidence of a recent meal. The study indicates that flesh is digested in 12 h. The expected bias effect on the ranking of squid can be seen in a study in which beaks, pens and trace remains (< 10 m^3) of each fish and squid species were removed from 10 699 food stomachs of northern fur seals collected by the US and Canada for the North Pacific Fur Seal Commission (see Perez & Bigg 1980, pp. 134–5). The percentage squid by frequency of occurrence decreased from 38.7% (fish 61.3%), when beaks, pens and trace remains were included, to 24.6% (fish 75.4%) when these were excluded. The bias is more difficult to eliminate when ranking diet by the contents of the intestines and scats because no fleshy parts are present. The only parts of cephalopods which probably pass out of the stomach quickly, and thus can be used as an index of diet, are statoliths and eye lenses.

The most commonly identified fish parts in scats are the otoliths (Pitcher 1981). Except perhaps for large otoliths, these structures are likely to pass out of pinniped stomachs rapidly. Some uncertainty exists about whether otoliths pass rapidly out of the multiple stomachs of cetaceans (Fitch & Brownell 1968). Other biases occur when the heads of fish, and thus otoliths, are not eaten and when elasmobranchs, which are cartilaginous, are eaten. The biases in using scats can be minimised if a variety of dietary evidence is used, such as statoliths, eye lenses, vertebrae, scales and perhaps other bones.

Passage times for consumption to defecation are likely to be highly variable, depending on the amount and type of food consumed, the feeding frequency and individual physiology. Gilmartin (North Pacific Fur Seal Commission 1980, p. 14), in a summary note, reported that passage times of small resin beads fed to northern fur seals ranged from 2.3 h to 7 h. An abstract from Helm and Morejohn (1979, p. 27) reports that for 22 individual harbour seals (*Phoca vitulina*), California sea-lions and northern elephant seals (*Mirounga leonina*), the average first defecation time was about 5 h. We found, from observations of captive fur seals at Nanaimo, that one cause of variability is the time of the subsequent feeding. Feeding usually stimulates defecation of an earlier meal within about 2 h. Other causes include temperament and activity. With first defecations at less than 6 h, and complete removal of a large meal from the stomach requiring close to 12 h, the present study indicates that part of a meal can be defecated while remains are still digesting in the stomach.

Another long-suspected bias in studies of northern fur seals is the larger rate of squid digestibility compared to fish. Evidence cited for this is the relatively soft body of the squid, the tendency for squid to appear more digested than other foods in the stomach, and the fact that the proportion of squid in the diet is relatively high when ranked by frequency of occurrence and low by volume (Marine Mammal Biological Laboratory 1970, p. 44, Wada 1971). The present study confirms the faster rate of digestion for squid. The reason for a faster digestion rate, in addition to the soft squid body, may also be the larger surface area to volume ratio and less muscle in squid than in fish. The body form of squid is basically tubular, with little muscle, soft inner organs and long tentacles, compared to the solid muscular form of the fish.

The significance of a faster digestion rate for squid is that squid will be under-represented by measure of volume when compared to fish. The under-representation will increase with time after feeding. The effect of rapid squid digestion is seen when the proportion of squid measured by volume, in the sample of 10 699 food stomachs of northern fur seals, is compared to that measured by frequency, with beaks, pens and trace evidence removed. By volume, squid comprised only 14.6%, while by frequency they comprised 24.6% (Perez & Bigg 1980, p. 134). It is well known that all food-ranking measures should give about the same values for large samples. Such is shown to be the case when the proportions of squid and fish are compared by volume and frequency in a sample of fur seal stomachs where no digestion had occurred. In 100 stomachs collected in Canada, the proportion of squid was 28.0% (compared with 72.0% for fish) by frequency of occurrence and a similar 23.5% by volume (Bigg unpublished data).

The digestion rate bias can be eliminated to some extent by ranking squid only against other squid, and fish only against fish, rather than fish against squid. This procedure assumes that the differences in digestion rates are greater between fish and squid than among individual fish species or squid species. However, differences among a group probably also exist. For example, Fiscus *et al.* (1965, p. 16) reported that the squid *Gonatus fabrisii* are very soft bodied and may be digested more rapidly than the other squids, *Gonatus magister* and *Gonatopsis*. Also, Wada (1971) suggested that the flesh and skin of the fish *Engraulis*, *Scomber*, *Cololabis* and *Hemiramphus* were firm and probably difficult to digest, whereas those of *Diaphus*, *Notoscopelus*, *Theragra* and *Laemonema* were softer and more easily digested. Details of how the two biases – retention of beaks and rapid squid digestion – are treated to determine relative importance of stomach contents of northern fur seals are given in Chapter 15 using a new ranking method called modified volume.

Some studies record the stage of digestion to compare digestion rates or eventually to recalculate the original volume consumed (see Wada 1971). Our results suggest that recalculated original volumes are of limited value. In partially digested meals of small prey, some individuals may be digested completely and thus not be included in the recalculated amount of prey consumed. An exception may be the bony remains of large prey which probably require many hours to digest.

References

Bard, P. 1956. *Medical physiology*. St. Louis: C. V. Mosby.

Clarke, M. R. 1962. The identification of cephalopod 'beaks' and the relationship between beak size and total body weight. *Bull. Brit. Mus. (Nat. Hist.), Zoology* **8**(10), 426–80.

Fiscus, C. H. and G. A. Baines 1966. Food and feeding behavior of Steller and California sea lions. *J. Mammal.* **47**, 195–200.

Fiscus, C. H., G. A. Baines and H. Kajimura 1965. *Pelagic fur seal investigations, Alaska, 1963*. US Fish and Wildl. Serv. Spec. Sci. Rep. – Fisheries No. 489.

Fiscus, C. H. and H. Kajimura 1967. *Pelagic fur seal investigations, 1965*. US Fish. Wildl. Serv. Spec. Sci. Rep. – Fisheries No. 537.

Fitch, J. E. and R. L. Brownell 1968. Fish otoliths in cetacean stomachs and their importance in interpreting feeding habits. *J. Fish. Res. Bd Can.* **25**(12), 2561–74.

Helm, R. C. and G. V. Morejohn 1979. Initial defecation time and intestinal length of three species of pinnipeds: *Phoca vitulina, Zalophus californianus* and *Mirounga angustirostris*. In *Third biennial conference of the biology of marine mammals*, Abst. p. 27. Sponsored by the National Marine Mammal Laboratory, National Marine Fisheries Service, Seattle, Washington 98115.

Marine Mammal Biological Laboratory 1970. *Fur seal investigations, 1967*. US Fish and Wildl. Serv. Spec. Sci. Rep. – Fisheries No. 597.

Miller, L. K. 1978. *Energetics of the northern fur seal in relation to climate and food resources of the Bering Sea*. Mar. Mam. Comm., Wash. D.C. Rep. No. MMC-75/08.

North Pacific Fur Seal Commission 1980. *North Pacific Fur Seal Commission report on investigations during 1973–76*. Washington, DC.

Perez, M. A. and M. A. Bigg 1980. Interim report on the feeding habits of the northern fur seal in the eastern North Pacific Ocean and eastern Bering Sea. In *Further analysis of pelagic fur seal data collected by the United States and Canada during 1958–74*, H. Kajimura *et al.* (eds), 4–174. Unpub. Rep. Part 2. March 1980. Seattle, Washington: National Marine Mammal Laboratory, NWAFC.

Pitcher, K. W. 1981. Stomach contents and faeces as indicators of harbor seal, *Phoca vitulina*, foods in the Gulf of Alaska. *Fish. Bull.* **78**, 797–8.

Scheffer, V. B. 1950. *The food of the Alaska fur seal*. US Dept. Interior, Fish and Wildl. Serv., Wildl. Leafl. 329.

Wada, K. 1971. *Food and feeding habits of northern fur seals along the coast of Sanriku*. Bull. Tokai Reg. Fish. Res. Lab. No. 64, p. 1–37. (Transl. Mar. Mamm. Div. NMFS: Seattle.)

Wilke, F. and K. W. Kenyon 1952. Notes on the food of fur seal, sea-lion and harbor porpoise. *J. Wildl. Manag.* **16**, 396–7.

17 Digestion and retention of Atlantic herring otoliths in the stomachs of grey seals

D. J. Murie and D. M. Lavigne

Introduction

Anlayses of teleost otoliths found in gastrointestinal tracts are often used to identify prey species of fishes consumed by piscivorous marine mammals. Intact otoliths, and allometric relationships involving fish length and weight, and sagittal otolith length, are also used to determine number and size (length and weight) of fish ingested.

When using otoliths to estimate the size and quantity of fish consumed by a marine mammal, it is usually assumed that the marine mammal does not ingest selected parts of its prey, that the otoliths do not shrink significantly due to digestion in the stomach (Bailey & Ainley 1982), and that otoliths are not retained in the stomach over several periods of feeding (Fitch & Brownell 1968). The present study addressed the problems of otolith digestion retention implicit in the latter two assumptions, using Atlantic herring (*Clupea harengus*) as an experimental diet for grey seals (*Halichoerus grypus*). In addition, the state of digestion of the fish in the seal stomachs and absolute stomach clearance rates were determined in relation to the elapsed time after feeding.

Methods

Five mature female grey seals (*Halichoerus grypus*) were used in the study. The seals were held in outdoor tanks ($6 \times 7 \times 1$ m) located at the University of Guelph, Guelph, Ontario. The seals were maintained on two feedings of herring (*Clupea harengus*) per day, a 1000-g meal in the morning followed by 3000 g in the afternoon. The animals were 7.5 or more years old and ranged between 132 kg and 204 kg total weight ($\bar{x} = 158$ kg $\pm$ 28 (SD)).

Each seal was fasted for 36 h prior to receiving a meal of herring. The time difference between a seal's consumption of fish and collection of the stomach was defined as the elapsed time after feeding. For two seals (seal Nos. 82-6 and 82-5), this elapsed time was approximately 3 h (2.80 h and 2.83 h respectively). For seal Nos. 82-4 and 81-2, the elapsed time was approximately 6 h (5.71 h and 5.67 h respectively), for the fifth seal (seal No. 80-2), it was 18.23 h.

One of the 3−h seals (seal No. 82-6) and one of the 6-h seals (seal No. 82-4) were fed herring with the head (and hence the otoliths) removed for 7 days prior to the fast. The other three seals were fed intact herring for 7 days prior to the fast.

The herring used in the experimental feedings had an average standard length of 251 mm ($\pm$15 mm (SD), $n = 119$) and weight of 214.1 g ($\pm$50.0 (SD), $n = 119$). Herring of this size had corresponding sagittal otolith lengths ranging from 4.4 mm to 5.2 mm.

The experimental meal for each seal consisted of approximately 6000 g of intact herring (individually recorded for each seal, Table 17.1). Seal No. 82-6 became agitated when brought into indoor holding facilities a day prior to the experiment, and consumed only 2000 g of the offered meal. Subsequent seals were left in the outdoor tanks throughout the fast and the experimental feeding. The entire experimental meal was consumed by each of the latter four seals in 15 min or less.

The seals were euthanised using 50 cm^3 of sodium phenobarbitol. No regurgitation of stomach contents occurred. A ventrosagittal incision exposed the viscera of the animal. The stomach was then tied off and excised at the oesophageal and pyloric sphincters and removed from the body cavity within 13 min after death. Stomach and contents were weighed using a suspended-pan scale ($\pm$5 g). The stomach was opened longitudinally along the lesser curvature, and the condition of the fish contents was recorded. The stomach contents were then washed into a large bucket using a minimum amount of water. The stomach was separately scrubbed and washed to dislodge any otoliths caught in the stomach rugae. The empty stomach was then weighed.

The contents of the stomach were washed through a series of five brass sieves (4.75, 2.36, 1.40, 0.850, and 0.425 mm mesh) and water-displacement baths. Otoliths were collected and recorded as either having been found within an intact fish head or skull case, or loose in the stomach contents. The wash-water from the scrubbed stomach was poured over a 0.425-mm sieve, and any otoliths present were collected.

The complete intestinal tract of each seal was also excised, weighed, and measured. Each metre (starting at the duodenum) of the intestine was excised, slit longitudinally, and its contents washed over a 0.425-mm sieve. The position of otoliths recovered within the tract was noted.

Absolute stomach clearance rates were determined by subtracting the wet weight of the stomach contents (g) from the wet weight of the experimental meal (g), with the difference being divided by the elapsed time after feeding (h).

Table 17.1 Recovery of herring otoliths (*Clupea harengus*) from stomachs and intestines of grey seals (*Halichoerus grypus*) at 3, 6, and 18 h of elapsed time after feeding.

Seal no.	Herring diet 7 days prior	Elapsed time (h)	Total no. otoliths ingested[a]	Otoliths recovered in stomach (%)	Otoliths recovered in intestines (%)	Recovered otoliths found in skulls (%)	loose	Recovered loose otoliths showing digestion (%)
82–6	headless	2.80	16	100	0	13	87	21
82–5	intact	2.83	56	100	0	93	7	0
82–4	headless	5.71	54	69	2	51	49	33
81–2	intact	5.67	48	71	2	24	76	46
80–2	intact	18.23	64	0	39[b]	0	100	44

[a]Total no. of otoliths ingested = no. of fish ingested $\times$ 2 (two sagittal otoliths per fish).
[b]May be an underestimation because of potentially unobserved defecation prior to death.

Results

Digestion and retention of otoliths

One hundred per cent of ingested otoliths were recovered in the stomachs 2.80 h and 2.83 h after feeding (seal Nos. 82-6 and 82-5; Table 17.1). However, after 5.67 h and 5.71 h, only 71% and 69% of the ingested otoliths were found in the stomachs of seal Nos. 81-2 and 82-4 respectively. Two per cent of ingested otoliths were recovered in the upper reaches of the intestinal tract (0–600 cm from the pyloric sphincter). The remaining 27% and 29% of ingested otoliths were not recovered. After 18 h (seal No. 80-2), no ingested otoliths were present in the stomach (Table 17.1); 39% were recovered in the small and large intestines, with the majority (31%) found in the latter.

Three hours after feeding, 13% and 93% (seal Nos. 82-6 and 82-5 respectively) of recovered otoliths were present in skull cases, with the remaining 87% and 7% subsequently found loose in the stomach (Table 17.1). After 6 h, 24% and 51% of recovered otoliths for seal Nos. 81-2 and 82-4 respectively were found in skull cases (76% and 49% found loose in the stomach contents). Recovered skull cases contained either one or two sagittal otoliths. Otoliths retained in skulls did not show any evidence of degradation, although those found loose in the stomach contents did. Digested otoliths were characterised by having rounded and smoothed edges with a loss of surface topography (fluting), and in some cases, holes appeared in the thinned areas of the otolith. The percentage of loose otoliths showing obvious digestion was estimated as 0% and 21% for 3-h stomachs (seal Nos. 82-5 and 82-6) and 33% and 46% for 6-h stomachs (seal Nos. 82-4 and 81-2) – see Table 17.1. Approximately 44% of the otoliths recovered in the intestine of seal No. 80-2 were considerably degraded.

It was apparent, through pairwise comparisons of seal Nos. 82-6 and 82-5, and seal Nos. 82-4 and 81-2, that the percentage of otoliths recovered in the stomachs for each of the pairs of seals did not differ markedly, regardless of whether they were fed headless or intact herring before the fast (Table 17.1). No otoliths were recovered in the stomach of seal No. 80-2, which was fed intact herring prior to the fast. Furthermore, no otoliths were recovered in the wash-water from the scrubbed stomach of each seal.

Description of stomach contents

Qualitative assessment of stomach contents showed little digestion after 3 h of elapsed time. Fish in the main body of the stomach were either whole or in halves (as they were ingested by the seal). Scales were absent on fish but were found loose in the stomach. The skin, and sometimes the skin coloration, remained on the sides of the fish. The heads of the fish were either recognisably whole (as in seal No. 82-5) or broken up (as in seal No. 82-6). Viscera of the fish were intact. In the pyloric region of the stomach, the skin of the fish was absent, the flesh was broken into pieces, and the skeletal elements were fragmented.

After 6 h, the fish flesh was either loosely adherent to vertebral columns or free and fragmented. Scales were absent. Skin, when present, was only on the sides of fish which were in direct contact with other fish. Some skull cases and heads were still recognisable, although they fragmented when handled. Some vertebral columns were entire, with caudal fin rays attached. Viscera of the fish were digested. In the pyloric

Table 17.2 Absolute stomach clearance rates of grey seals (*Halichoerus grypus*) at 3, 6, and 18 h of elapsed time after feeding. (See text for definition of terms.)

Seal no.	Elapsed time (h)	Wet weight of final meal (g)	Wet weight of stomach contents (g)	Stomach clearance rate (g/h)
82–6	2.80	1930	1805	45
82–5	2.83	5880	5080	280
82–4	5.7	6160	4710	255
81–2	5.67	5790	4710	190
80–2	18.23	5975	0	≥330

region of the seal's stomach, the vertebral columns, flesh, operculae, and superficial head bones were fragmented.

By 18 h, the stomach contents consisted solely of gastric fluid and a minute amount of identifiable fish flesh. No hard skeletal parts of fish remained, either in the main body or the pyloric region of the stomach. The stomach was considered to be essentially empty of fish contents.

Absolute stomach clearance rates

Seals ate either by taking a whole fish head-first or by ripping the fish in roughly equal halves and consuming the parts individually, head-first or tail-first. For seals which ate the complete 6-kg meal, stomach clearance rates ranged from 190 g to 280 g herring per hour ($\bar{x} = 240$ g/h ± 45 (SD), $n = 3$) – see Table 17.2. In addition to these three animals, the stomach clearance rate for seal No. 80-2 was estimated as greater than or equal to 330 g/h based on its empty stomach. The stomach clearance rate for seal N. 82-6, which ate only 2 kg of the offered meal, was 45 g/h.

Discussion

The assumption that a marine animal consumes all parts of its prey is implicit in the use of otolith analysis to assess stomach contents. Bailey and Ainley (1982) considered the assumption valid for California sea lions (*Zalophus californianus*), based on the knowledge that a smaller otariid, the northern fur seal (*Callorhinus ursinus*), eats all parts of large fish after breaking them up (Stroud *et al.* 1979, cited in Bailey & Ainley 1982). This assumption, however, is questionable for a small cetacean such as the harbour porpoise (*Phocoena phocoena*) which appears to capture relatively large prey from behind, biting through them in the gill region, and not ingesting the heads of the fish (Smith & Gaskin 1974). Harbour seals (*Phoca vitulina*) may also fragment large fish such as salmon (*Oncorhynchus* spp.), usually discarding the head (Pitcher 1980), and probably seldom eat heads of their fish prey (Boulva 1973). It would thus appear that stomach-content analyses employing otoliths as an indicator of diet are of limited use for marine mammals which disproportionately reject the heads of fish when feeding. Although it may be possible to produce a correction factor for the diet analysis of such species, consideration should be given to alternative methods of analysis (see Ch. 16).

To date, the importance of observations of degraded otoliths in stomach contents has been considered insignificant. Fitch and Brownell (1968) noted that teleost otoliths are slow to digest, and Finley and Gibb (in press) stated that otoliths encased in skulls of fish tend to be the last remnants of digestion. Treacy and Crawford (1981) reported that otoliths are the densest structures in the body of teleost fishes, and are the most resistant to digestion. In every published account of stomach-content analysis, however, digested otoliths are mentioned, either directly or indirectly, without any comment on the significance of the observation in the interpretation of results (with the exception of Prime 1979).

Since otoliths are composed of calcium cabonate (Lagler *et al.* 1962), their degradation when exposed to the gastric acids of mammals would normally be expected. McMahon and Tash (1979) partially addressed this matter by recording the serial changes that occurred in otoliths when exposed to 0.01 M hydrochloric acid, used to simulate gastric fluids. These tests indicated that green sunfish (*Lepomis cyanellus*) otoliths remained identifiable to species after 12 h, but dissolved completely within 24 h at 25° C. Pastukhov (1971) found that there was a statistically significant difference in the average dimensions of otoliths in a control series (before ingestion) and an experimental series (from faeces) recovered from Baikal seals (*Phoca sibirica*). Nevertheless, he evaluated the digestion of the otoliths as insignificant because those which had been in the digestive system of the seals did not differ superficially from those which were removed from whole fish. However, Prime (1979), in his faecal analysis of a young common seal (*P. vitulina*), also reported a reduction in otolith width during passage through the gastrointestinal tract. In addition, he noted that 14% of gadoid (*Gadus morhua, Melanogrammus aeglefinus, Pollachius virens, Merlangius merlangus*) otoliths ingested did not reappear in the faeces of the seal, suggesting that the otoliths had been completely digested while in the gastrointestinal tract. Faecal samples examined in his study only occasionally contained traces of the thin, fragile otoliths from the herring used to carry the experimental gadoid otoliths. Prime therefore speculated that faecal samples collected at seal haul-outs (as in scat analyses) would tend to underestimate that part of a seal's diet consisting of small fish.

From the present observations of grey seals consuming herring, it is apparent that by 3 – 6 h post-feeding, 30% or more of the initially ingested otoliths have already been completely digested (see Table 17.1). Not taking this factor into account would lead to a significant underestimation of the number of fish consumed. In addition, since up to 46% of the remaining loose otoliths are considerably degraded, and therefore smaller (see Table 17.1), back-calculation of weights of fish initially ingested, based on otolith dimensions, would also underestimate the size and total biomass of fish consumed. Frost and Lowry (1980) avoided this latter bias (in dealing with more durable otolith types) by only using measurements of intact and non-degraded otoliths for the back-calculation of weight and length of fish initially ingested by ribbon seals (*Phoca fasciata*). For small fragile otoliths, like those found in herring, this approach may present sample size problems (i.e. if 46% of the 76% of the recovered loose otoliths cannot be used in the back-calculations).

Regarding the assumption that otoliths are not retained in the stomach over several feeding bouts, Fitch and Brownell (1968) suggested that not even the 15 191 otoliths (representing more than 7596 fish) reported by Schmidt (1923, cited in Fitch and Brownell 1968) represented a 'full' meal for the *Delphinus* from which they were removed. However, Finley and Gibb (in press), in their analysis of stomach contents of harp seals (*Phoca groenlandica*), found that for one seal the estimated intake of fish (25.4 kg) greatly exceeded the stomach capacity. Thus they concluded that in this one case, at least, otoliths had been retained during repeated feedings. Such retention of herring otoliths in the stomachs of grey seals was not found in the present study. Otoliths were not retained over repeated feedings prior to the fast, nor through the 18 h after feeding for one seal (see Table 17.1). Herring otoliths were not observed to become physically trapped in rugae of the stomach, although this could vary among seal species and be affected by the size and quantity of fish species ingested (see Ch. 16).

A partial solution to the biases of otolith digestion is to evaluate the stomach contents qualitatively into time categories. With grey seals eating herring, for example, stomach contents which qualitatively resemble the description given for 3 h after feeding need not have an otolith correction factor applied, since 100% were recovered; although a correction factor for partial otolith degradation may be in order (0% and 21% degraded for seal Nos. 82-5 and 82-6 respectively). However, contents which could be described as being taken from a stomach 3–6 h after feeding would require a correction factor in the order of 30% to compensate for lost otoliths, plus an additional factor for the partial digestion of otoliths if they are to be used in back-calculations. That such a method may be practicable is supported by the study of Bigg and Fawcett (see Ch. 16). Their description of the state of digestion of 17 herring in the stomach of a northern fur seal (seal No. 2) 6 h after feeding is strikingly similar to the description given for the stomach contents of the two 6-h grey seals in the present study. In addition, the sequence of artificial digestion for herring given in Table 16.3 (p. 288) is compatible with our results.

Since recovered skull cases sometimes only contained one otolith instead of the usual two, it is apparent that otoliths can be released from a skull case before the skull itself fragments, and that both otoliths may not be released at the same time. Differential degradation of the otoliths within the same fish, as well as between different fish of the same species, is therefore possible. Added to this, differential dissolution of otoliths from different species of fish is highly plausible. The shape, size, and durability of otoliths vary considerably between fish species. Hence, the otoliths of pollock (*Theragra chalcogramma*), arctic cod (*Boreogadus saida*), saffron cod (*Eleginus gracilis*), and eelpouts (*Lycodes* spp.) are classified as being large and durable in relation to the smaller fragile otoliths of capelin (*Mallotus villosus*), pricklebacks (*Lumpenus* spp.), Greenland halibut (*Reinhardtius hippoglossoides*), sculpins (family Cottidae), poachers (family Agonidae), and snailfish (family Cyclopteridae) (Frost & Lowry 1980). Moreover, when a marine mammal is known to consume cartilaginous fish or cephalopods in addition to teleost fish, the differential digestion of the hard skeletal parts (otoliths, pens, beaks) in relation to the flesh of the animals becomes increasingly confounding (see Ch. 16).

Clearance rates of pinnipeds have primarily been studied through manipulation of live animals, and as such constitute apparent gastrointestinal clearance rates, rather than the absolute stomach clearance rates calculated for the seals of the present study. From Table 16.2 (p. 287), it is possible to calculate absolute stomach clearance rates for two of the five northern fur seals used in the study. For Bigg and Fawcett's seal No. 2 (6 h after feeding) and seal No. 15 (9 h after feeding), absolute stomach clearance rates were 220 g/h and 120 g/h respectively. For the two 6-h grey seals (seal Nos. 82-4 and 81-2), the average stomach clearance rate was 220 g/h $\pm$ 45 (SD), $n = 2$ (see Table 17.2). With acknowledgement that the two studies differ in seal species, body weights, and weight of fish consumed, it is interesting that in addition to the similar states of digestion noted previously, stomach clearance rates over 6 h were also similar in the two species, one a phocid seal, the other an otariid.

Studies employing marked fish to determine gastrointestional or otolith clearance rates may also require some reconsideration. The practice of placing chromium oxide (Cr_2O_3) tablets, or otoliths of test fish species, in the gut region of a carrier fish may be inappropriate, since the viscera of the fish are differentially digested with respect to the main muscle and skeletal mass of the fish.

Evaluation of feeding habits of many piscivorous marine mammals is based on stomach contents, disregarding the qualitative state of digestion of the contents, or on faecal analyses. Accordingly, if the marine mammal in question is known to feed on teleost fish with small sagittal otoliths, the potential for considerable bias in the results is clear. Of major concern is the total digestion of a substantial proportion of small otoliths ingested. To our knowledge, this bias has not been taken into account in any stomach-content or faecal analyses reported to date. Fish consumption by marine mammals which feed on small teleosts may have been seriously underestimated in such analyses. This has important implications for the construction of energy budgets and in the evaluation of marine mammal–fishery interactions, especially when species such as herring or capelin – both of which constitute a substantial portion of the diets of various marine mammals (Sergeant 1973) – are involved.

The grey seals used in the present study were fasted prior to receiving an experimental 6-kg meal of herring. Further studies are necessary to clarify the effect of repeated (or continuous) feeding on otolith dissolution, which may better simulate natural foraging conditions. Also, work on other species of marine mammals and fish is needed in order to develop a general model to correct for otolith retention and digestion in studies where specific data are not available.

Acknowledgements

We thank Professor K. Ronald, Dean of the College of Biological Science, University of Guelph, for the opportunity to carry out the feeding study in tandem with a project in his laboratory. Support and co-operation provided throughout the study by S. Innes, H. Pedersen, R. Frank, J. Kay, C. Matthews, and J. Moir were greatly appreciated. We thank G. Worthy, B. Webb, R. Stewart, O. Schmitz, T. D. Nudds, K. Kovacs, and J. Hickie for reviews of the draft manuscript.

References

Bailey, K. M. and D. G. Ainley 1982. The dynamics of California sea lion predation on Pacific hake. *Fish. Res.* **1**, 163–76.

Boulva, J. 1973. The harbour seal, *Phoca vitulina concolor*, in eastern Canada. PhD Thesis, Dalhousie University, Halifax.

Finley, K. J. and E. J. Gibb in press. Summer diet and feeding behaviour of harp seals in the Canadian high Arctic. In *The harp seal. Perspectives in vertebrate science*, D. M. Lavigne, K. Ronald and R. E. A. Stewart (eds), The Hague: W. Junk.

Fitch, J. E. and R. L. Brownell 1968. Fish otoliths in cetacean stomachs and their importance in interpreting feeding habits. *J. Fish. Res. Bd Can.* **25**(12), 2561–74.

Frost, K. J. and L. F. Lowry 1980. Feeding of ribbon seals (*Phoca fasciata*) in the Bering Sea in spring. *Can. J. Zool.* **58**, 1601–07.

Lagler, K. F., J. E. Bardach and R. R. Miller 1962 *Ichthyology*. New York: Wiley.

McMahon, T. E. and J. C. Tash 1979. Effects of formalin (buffered and unbuffered) and hydrochloric acid on fish otoliths. *Copeia*, (1) 155–6.

Pastukhov, V. D. 1971. The feeding of the Baikal seal under experimental conditions. *Fish. Res. Bd Can. Transl. Ser.* **3185**, 451–60 (1974).

Pitcher, K. W. 1980. Stomach contents and faeces as indicators of harbor seal, *Phoca vitulina*, foods in the Gulf of Alaska. *Fish. Bull.* **78** (3), 797–8.

Prime, J. H. 1979. *Observations on the digestion of some gadoid fish otoliths by a young common seal*. Marine Mammal Committee, I.C.E.S., CM 1979/N:14.

Sergeant, D. E. 1973. Feeding, growth, and productivity of northwest Atlantic harp seals (*Pagophilus groenlandicus*). *J Fish. Res. Bd Can.* **30**, 17–29.

Smith, G. J. D. and D. E. Gaskin 1974. The diet of harbor porpoises (*Phocoena phocoena* (L.)) in coastal waters of Eastern Canada, with special reference to the Bay of Fundy. *Can. J. Zool.* **52**, 777–82.

Treacey, S. D. and T. W. Crawford 1981. Retrieval of otoliths and statoliths from gastrointestinal contents and scats of marine mammals. *J. Wildl. Manag.* **45**(4), 990–93.

18 Opportunistic feeding by the northern fur seal, (*Callorhinus ursinus*)

Hiroshi Kajimura

Introduction

The purpose of this study is to improve our understanding of the fur seal species in order better to address the questions posed by the Interim Convention on Conservation of North Pacific Fur Seals (signed February 1957 by Japan, Canada, the USSR, and the USA). The two broad objectives of the Convention are: (a) to achieve and sustain maximum productivity of the northern fur seal (*Callorhinus ursinus*) resource, and (b) to determine the relationship between northern fur seals and other living marine resources. The latter is an enormous and complex problem and may not be completely understood in our lifetime. However, we can increase our knowledge of the subject and advance towards achieving this goal by identifying the fur seals' feeding habits, their major prey species, and the relative importance of each prey item throughout the seals' feeding range, particularly in areas of intense commercial fishing. Knowledge of the abundance and distribution of fish/squid stocks utilised by fur seals is also important in studying this relationship between fur seals and other living resources.

In order to answer some of these questions, the fur seal feeding data collected by Canada and the USA during 1958–74 were examined and a comparison made between the principal forage species of fur seals and the relative abundance of fishery resources available to fur seals in the area. The conclusion that feeding of northern fur seals in the eastern North Pacific is opportunistic in nature was obtained primarily for the eastern Bering Sea and off California, focusing on the principal forage species based on stomach content volume and the relative abundance of fishery resources available in the area. The principal forage species of fur seals for other areas between California and the Bering Sea are also briefly discussed.

Following the purchase of Alaska by the USA in 1867, the most critical period for the survival of the northern fur seal occurred between 1879 and 1909, when no effective international conservation agreement existed. During that period, almost 1 million fur seals (mostly pregnant females) were taken at sea. Because of the unrestricted harvest of females at sea, the Pribilof Island fur seal population declined from about 2 million in 1880 to approximately 300 000 animals in 1909. Under international management since 1911, the Pribilof Island fur seal population recovered to about 2 million during the early 1950s. The population now numbers about 1 million animals (approximately 80% of the world population) and appears to be declining (Fowler 1982).

Northern fur seal distribution at sea

Northern fur seals occupy the subarctic waters of the North Pacific Ocean and Bering

Sea, extending southward to the California/Mexican border (latitude $32°$ N) in the eastern Pacific to about the middle of Honshu Island, Japan, (latitude $36°$ N) in the western Pacific (Fig. 18.1). Most fur seals found in the eastern North Pacific Ocean are from the Pribilof Islands (principally St Paul and St George Islands in the eastern Bering Sea), which are the main breeding grounds of the northern fur seal. Two additional rookeries in the eastern North Pacific Ocean are off southern California on San Miguel Island and nearby Castle Rock near the southern limit of the fur seals' range. The San Miguel colony was discovered in 1968 with about 100 fur seals (Castle Rock colony was discovered in 1972). By 1979, this San Miguel–Castle Rock colony had grown to more than 3000 animals.

The USSR manages rookeries on the Commander Islands (Medney and Bering Island) in the western Bering Sea, Robben (Tulyeniy) Island off Sakhalin Island in the Okhotsk Sea, and on a few of the Kurile Islands. The Robben Island population (like the Pribilof Island seals) appears to be declining (Yoshida & Baba 1982). Recoveries of tagged animals have shown that seals from both the eastern and western Pacific Ocean breeding islands do intermix to a small extent at sea and on the breeding islands.

Some northern fur seals are found throughout their eastern Pacific Ocean range during all months of the year, with periods of peak abundance varying by time and area. Many immature seals of both sexes remain at sea during the first year of life and do not return to their island of birth until aged 2 or 3 years. Most fur seals spend about half the year at sea (November through May–June), and the remainder on and around their home islands during the breeding season. Fur seals congregate in tight social groups on land, but at sea they are usually solitary. They are most frequently seen from about 70 km to 130 km offshore, and usually occur in greatest numbers along the continental shelf and slope throughout their range, primarily because of abundant food resources in that area.

From January to March, fur seals are found along the continental shelf and slope, entering coastal waters in pursuit of prey, from the Gulf of Alaska south to California. Fur seals continue to increase in abundance during December and January off Washington and California. In February and March, fur seals are most abundant from California to Sitka, Alaska. The numbers of fur seals wintering off California reach a peak during late January through March, and decrease as they begin their northward migration, starting in late March. Most fur seals have left this area by early June, with the exception of those from the San Miguel–Castle Rock colony, which remain in California waters.

In April, fur seals are widely dispersed from Kodiak Island, Alaska, to California, with the population reaching its peak in the Gulf of Alaska during May. Bigg (1982) suggests that the northbound adult females off California travel further offshore directly to the Aleutian Islands, missing the coastal areas of Washington and British Columbia. In June, fur seals are scattered throughout the North Pacific Ocean. Fur seals are in the eastern Bering Sea and on or near the breeding islands of St Paul. St George, and Sea Lion Rock (Pribilof Islands) in greatest numbers during July, August, and September (most age groups of both sexes).

Northern fur seal feeding at sea

Fur seals feed on a variety of fishes and squids throughout their range. As a general rule, small schooling fishes and neritic squids are usually the principal forage species over the continental shelf region, and oceanic squids are the important forage species

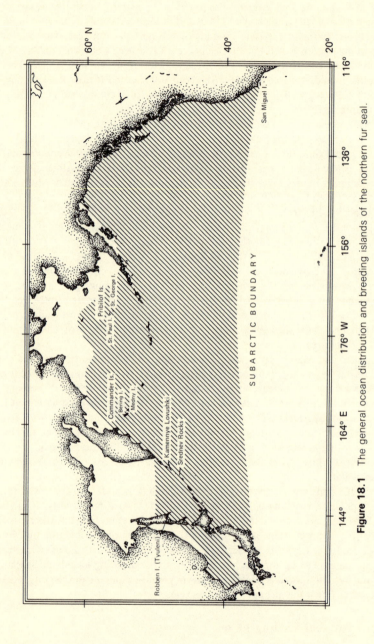

Figure 18.1 The general ocean distribution and breeding islands of the northern fur seal.

over deepwater areas seaward of the continental shelf and slope. Fur seals feed primarily at night, perhaps influenced by the fact that many forage species rise toward the surface after dark and become readily available to fur seals and other predators which feed primarily in the epipelagic and mosepelagic zones. Fur seals generally swallow small prey whole below the surface, and bring larger prey to the surface where they bite them into smaller pieces before swallowing. However, fur seals are not necessarily limited to eating small fish or limited to prey that are found near the surface. Time–depth recorders placed on fur seals in the wild recorded depths of dives to 190 m (570 ft) which lasted for 5.6 min (Kooyman *et al*. 1976).

Materials and methods

Figure 18.2 illustrates the seven areas into which the eastern North Pacific region was divided for the purpose of conducting the dietary studies reported here. For the areas shown in Figure 18.2, the boundaries (in parentheses) are as follows: California (latitude $32°–42°$ N); Oregon (latitude $42°–46°$ N); Washington (latitude $46°–49°$ N); British Columbia (latitude $49°–54°30'$ N and longitude $146°$ W); Gulf of Alaska (latitude $54°30'$ N to coast and longitude $158°$W, and $49°–54°30'$ N between $146°$ and $158°$ W); western Alaska (west of longitude $158°$ W and north of latitude $49°$ N, and

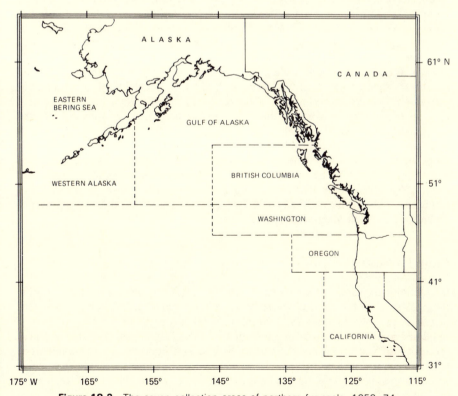

Figure 18.2 The seven collection areas of northern fur seals, 1958–74.

north to the Alaska Peninsula and Aleutian Islands); and eastern Bering Sea (north of the Alaska Peninsula and Aleutian Islands).

Field procedures

Fur seals were shot with 12-gauge shotguns using magnum loads of 00 buckshot. Pertinent biological data were recorded from each seal before the abdominal cavity was opened. The stomach was then tied off below the intestine and at the junction of the oesophagus (pyloric and cardiac sphincters, respectively), then removed and injected with 10% formalin to stop digestive action, and stored in a barrel containing formalin for later laboratory examination.

Laboratory procedure

The stomach was cut open by slicing the entire length of the stomach lining, cutting with care so food organisms would not be damaged. When the stomach contained whole fish or squids, the contents were placed directly into a weighing pan. If the contents were largely liquid, they were placed into a sieve to drain, and then transferred into the weighing pan. The stomach lining was rinsed to obtain all food particles, since otoliths and squid beaks often adhered to the stomach wall. Excess fluid was drained from the weighing pan prior to each weighing.

Stomach contents weighing less than 10 g (or digested fish, squid remains, otoliths, squid beaks and pens, or vertebrae fragments) were recorded as 'trace' amounts unless a whole specimen or body parts was present. For contents with a weight of 100 g or less, the volume was not measured but was assigned a value as though the contents had the same density as water (for example, if weight equals 55 g, the volume equals 55 cm^3). Weight and volume < 100 g were checked early in the programme and found not to vary significantly. Non-food items such as rocks, pebbles, shells, etc. were not entered on food data sheets as part of the total weight and volume. Stomach content volumes (cm^3) were obtained by the water-displacement method in large graduated beakers capable of holding 2000 cm^3.

When two or more species could not be easily separated, the examiner estimated their proportionate volume to the nearest 5%. The weight and volume of each individual species were calculated by multiplying estimated percentage times total weight and volume. Specimens were identified by comparing them to known preserved whole specimens or known skeletal material in the laboratory collection, and by using various cephalopod and fish identification keys.

Fishery resources significant to northern fur seals

In examining the variety of prey consumed by fur seals throughout their eastern Pacific range, 53 species of fish and 10 species of squid have been identified from the stomachs of fur seals (Tables 18.1 and 18.2). From this total, 14 species of fish and 6 species of squid are considered the principal prey of fur seals (Table 18.3). The principal prey species of fur seals in each of these areas, as based on stomach content volume (four largest by month and area), generally do not change even though the ranking by volume within this list may change for each area. Further information on fur seal feeding can be found in Chapter 15.

Table 18.1 Fishes eaten by northern fur seals in the eastern North Pacific Ocean and eastern Bering Sea, 1958–74, by area.

Food items	California	Oregon	Washington	British Columbia	Gulf of Alaska	Western Alaska	Bering Sea
Lampetra tridentata	+	+	+	+	+	+	+
Squalus acanthias	+	−	−	−	−	−	−
Hydrolagus colliei	−	−	+	+	−	−	−
Clupeidae	+	−	+	+	+	−	−
Alosa sapidissima	+	+	+	−	−	−	−
Clupea harengus pallasi	+	+	+	+	+	+	+
Engraulis mordax	+	+	+	−	−	−	−
Salmonidae	−	−	+	−	−	+	+
Oncorhynchus spp.	+	+	+	+	+	+	+
O. gorbuscha	−	−	+	−	+	+	+
O. keta	−	−	+	+	+	+	+
O. kisutch	−	−	+	−	+	+	−
O. nerka	−	−	+	−	−	+	+
O. tshawytscha	−	−	+	−	+	+	−
Salmo gairdneri	−	−	+	−	−	−	−
Osmeridae	−	−	+	+	+	+	+
Hypomesus pretiosus	+	−	+	+	−	−	−
Mallotus villosus	−	−	+	−	+	+	+
Thaleichthys pacificus	+	−	+	+	+	−	+
Bathylagidae	−	−	+	−	−	−	+
Tactostoma macropus	+	−	−	−	−	−	−
Scopelosaurus sp.	−	+	−	−	−	−	−
Paralepis atlantica	+	−	+	−	−	−	−
Myctophidae	+	+	+	−	+	−	+
Tarletonbeania crenularis	+	+	+	−	−	−	−
Symbolophorus californiensis	+	−	−	−	−	−	−
Lampanyctus sp.	−	−	−	−	−	−	+
Anotopterus pharao	−	−	−	−	+	−	−
Cololabis saira	+	+	+	+	+	−	−
Gadidae	−	−	+	+	+	+	+
Gadus macrocephalus	−	−	−	+	+	+	+
Merluccius productus	+	+	+	+	−	−	−
Microgadus proximus	−	−	+	−	+	−	−
Theragra chalcogramma	−	−	+	+	+	+	+
Gasterosteus aculeatus	−	−	+	+	+	−	−
Trachipteridae	+	−	+	−	−	−	−
Trachipterus altivelis	+	+	+	−	−	−	−
Trachurus symmetricus	+	+	+	−	−	−	−
Sciaenidae	+	−	−	−	−	−	−
Brama japonica	+	−	+	−	−	−	−
Medialunma californiensis	+	−	−	−	−	−	−
Scomber japonicus	+	−	−	−	−	−	−
Sebastes spp.	+	+	+	+	+	+	+
S. alutus	−	−	−	−	+	−	−
S. entomelas	−	−	+	−	−	−	−

(continued)

Table 18.1 *Continued.*

Food items	California	Oregon	Washington	British Columbia	Gulf of Alaka	Western Alaska	Bering Sea
S. jordani	+	+	–	–	–	–	–
Anoplopoma fimbria	+	–	+	+	+	+	+
Hexagrammidae	–	–	+	–	–	–	+
Pleurogrammus monopterygius	–	–	–	–	–	+	+
Cottidae	–	–	–	–	–	+	+
Cyclopteridae	–	–	–	–	+	+	+
Aptocyclus ventricosus	–	–	–	–	–	–	+
Trichodontidae	–	–	–	–	–	–	+
Trichodon trichodon	–	–	–	–	+	+	+
Ammodytes hexapterus	–	–	+	+	+	+	+
Bathymasteridae	–	–	–	–	–	–	+
Bathymaster signatus	–	–	–	–	–	+	–
Anarhichadidae	–	–	–	–	–	–	+
Anarhichas orientalis	–	–	–	–	–	–	+
Zoarcidae	–	–	+	–	–	–	–
Tetragonurus cuvieri	–	–	+	–	–	–	–
Atherinopsis californiensis	+	–	–	–	–	–	–
Pleuronectiformes	–	–	+	–	–	–	–
Citharichthys sp.	+	–	–	–	–	–	–
Pleuronectidae	+	–	+	+	+	–	+
Atheresthes stomias	–	–	–	–	+	+	–
Hippoglossus stenolepis	–	–	–	–	–	–	+
Lyopsetta exilis	+	+	–	–	–	–	–
Reinhardtius hippoglossoides	–	–	–	–	–	–	+
Porichthys notatus	+	–	–	–	–	–	–
Unidentified	+	+	+	+	+	+	+

California

The leading four prey species consumed by fur seals during the six collection years (January through June, 1958–66) off California contributed 82–99% of the total stomach content volume. From a total of 26 species of fish and 8 species of squid identified in stomachs of fur seals taken off California, only 6 species of fish (1 unidentified in the genus *Sebastes* spp.) and 2 species of squid are considered the principal prey of fur seals in this area (based on percentage of total stomach content volume). These principal forage species included northern anchovy (*Engraulis mordax*), Pacific whiting (*Merluccius productus*), the market squid (*Loligo opalescens*), Pacific saury (*Cololabis saira*), jack mackerel (*Trachurus symmetricus*), rockfishes (*Sebastes* spp.), sablefish (*Anoplopoma fimbria*), and the oceanic squid (*Onychoteuthis* sp.). The first three species were among the four leading forage species during every monthly collection off California.

The relative abundance of fishery resources available in the California Current System has been determined from egg and larvae surveys conducted by the California

Table 18.2 Squids eaten by northern fur seals in the eastern North Pacific Ocean and Bering Sea, 1958–74, by area.

Area and year	Loligo opalescens	Onychoteuthis sp.	Onychoteuthis borealijaponicus	Moroteuthis robusta	Abraliopsis spp.	Octopoteuthis sp.	Gonatidae	Gonatus spp.[a]	Berryteuthis magister	Gonatopsis borealis	Chiroteuthidae	Chiroteuthis sp.	Unidentified squid
California													
1958	+	+	+	−	−	−	−	+	−	−	−	−	+
1959	+	+	−	−	−	−	−	+	−	−	−	−	+
1961	+	+	−	−	+	−	+	−	−	+	−	−	+
1964	+	−	+	−	−	−	+	+	−	−	−	−	+
1965	+	−	+	+	+	−	+	+	+	+	−	−	+
1966	+	−	+	+	+	−	+	+	−	−	−	−	+
Oregon													
1958	+	+	−	−	−	−	−	−	−	−	−	−	+
1959	+	+	−	−	−	−	−	+	−	−	−	−	+
1961	+	−	−	−	−	−	+	−	−	−	−	−	+
1964	+	−	+	−	−	−	+	+	−	−	−	−	+
1965	−	−	+	−	+	−	−	−	+	−	+	−	+
Washington													
1958	−	−	−	−	−	−	−	−	−	−	−	−	+
1959	+	+	−	−	−	−	−	+	−	−	−	−	+
1960	+	−	−	−	−	−	−	−	−	−	−	−	+
1961	+	+	−	−	−	−	+	−	−	+	−	−	+
1962	+	−	−	−	−	−	−	−	−	−	−	−	+
1963	−	−	−	−	−	−	−	−	−	−	−	−	+
1964	+	−	+	−	−	−	+	+	+	+	−	−	+
1965	+	−	−	−	−	−	+	+	−	−	−	−	+
1966	−	−	+	−	+	+	−	+	+	−	−	−	+
1967	+	+	+	−	−	−	+	+	+	−	−	−	+
1968	+	+	+	−	−	−	+	+	+	−	−	+	+
1969	+	+	+	−	+	−	+	+	−	−	−	+	+
1970	+	+	+	+	+	+	+	+	+	+	+	+	+
1971	+	+	+	−	+	+	+	+	+	+	+	+	+
1972	+	+	−	+	+	+	+	+	+	+	−	+	+
1973	+	−	−	−	−	−	−	−	−	−	−	−	−
1974	+	−	−	−	−	−	−	−	−	−	−	−	−
British Columbia													
1958	−	−	−	−	−	−	−	−	−	−	−	−	+
1959	+	−	−	−	−	−	−	−	−	−	−	−	+

(continued)

Table 18.2 *Continued.*

Area and year	Loligo opalescens	Onychoteuthis sp.	Onychoteuthis borealijaponicus	Moroteuthis robusta	Abraliopsis spp.	Octopoteuthis sp.	Gonatidae	Gonatus spp.[a]	Berryteuthis magister	Gonatopsis borealis	Chiroteuthidae	Chiroteuthis sp.	Unidentified squid
1960	−	−	−	−	−	−	−	−	−	−	−	−	+
1961	+	−	−	−	−	−	+	−	+	−	−	−	+
1962	+	−	−	−	−	−	−	−	+	−	−	−	+
1963	−	−	−	−	−	−	−	−	−	−	−	−	+
1964	−	−	+	−	−	−	−	−	+	−	−	−	+
1965	−	−	+	−	−	−	−	−	+	−	−	−	+
1966	−	−	+	−	−	−	−	−	+	−	−	−	+
1967	−	−	+	−	−	−	−	−	+	−	−	−	−
1968	−	−	+	−	−	−	−	+	+	−	−	−	+
1969	+	−	−	−	−	−	−	−	−	−	−	−	−
Gulf of Alaska													
1958	+	−	−	−	−	−	−	−	−	−	−	−	+
1959	−	−	−	−	−	−	−	−	−	−	−	−	+
1960	−	+	−	−	−	−	−	+	−	−	−	−	+
1961	−	−	−	−	−	−	−	−	−	−	−	−	+
1962	+	−	−	−	−	−	−	−	+	−	−	−	+
1963	−	−	−	−	−	−	−	−	−	−	−	−	+
1968	−	−	−	−	−	−	+	+	+	+	−	−	+
Western Alaska													
1958	−	−	−	−	−	−	−	−	−	−	−	−	+
1960	−	−	−	−	−	−	−	−	−	−	−	−	+
1962	−	−	−	−	−	−	+	−	+	+	−	−	+
1968	−	−	−	−	−	−	+	+	+	+	−	−	+
Bering Sea													
1960	−	−	−	−	−	−	−	−	−	−	−	−	+
1962	−	−	−	−	−	−	+	+	+	+	−	−	+
1963	−	−	−	−	−	−	+	+	+	+	−	−	+
1964	−	−	−	−	−	−	+	+	+	+	−	−	+
1966	−	−	−	−	−	−	+	−	−	−	−	−	−
1968	−	−	−	−	−	−	+	+	+	+	−	−	+
1973	−	−	−	−	−	−	+	+	+	+	−	−	+
1974	−	−	−	−	−	−	+	+	+	+	−	−	+

[a]Squids identified as *Gonatus fabricii* in earlier reports have been listed as *Gonatus* spp.

Table 18.3 Principal forage species utilised by northern fur seals in the eastern North Pacific Ocean and the eastern Bering Sea, 1958–74, by area.

Forage species	California	Oregon	Washington	British Columbia	Gulf of Alaska	Western Alaska	Bering Sea
fish							
Clupea harengus pallasi	−	−	+	+	+	+	+
Engraulis mordax	+	+	+	−	−	−	−
Oncorhynchus spp.	−	−	+	+	+	+	−
Mallotus villosus	−	−	+	−	+	+	+
Thaleichthys pacificus	−	−	+	+	−	−	−
Cololabis saira	+	+	−	+	−	−	−
Gadidae	−	−	−	−	−	−	+
Gadus macrocephalus	−	−	−	+	−	−	−
Merluccius productus	+	+	+	+	−	−	−
Theragra chalcogramma	−	−	−	+	+	+	+
Trachurus symmetricus	+	−	−	−	−	−	−
Sebastes spp.	+	+	+	+	+	−	−
Anoplopoma fimbria	+	−	+	+	−	+	−
Pleurogrammus monopterygius	−	−	−	−	+	+	+
Ammodytes hexapterus	−	−	−	−	+	+	−
cephalopods							
Loligo opalescens	+	+	−	+	−	−	−
Onychoteuthis sp.	+	+	+	−	−	−	−
Onychoteuthis borealijaponicus	−	−	−	−	+	−	−
Gonatus sp.	−	−	−	−	+	−	−
Berryteuthis magister	−	−	−	−	+	+	+
Gonatopsis borealis	−	−	−	−	−	−	+
unidentified squid	−	−	−	−	+	−	−

Cooperative Oceanic Fisheries Investigations (CalCOFI). Based on surveys conducted by CalCOFI, the major fishery resources (arranged in order of their relative abundance) were determined to be: (1) northern anchovy, (2) Pacific whiting, (3) rockfishes, (4) jack mackerel, (5) Pacific saury, and (6) the market squid.

The California marine fish fauna consists of about 554 species, of which 439 are found in coastal waters (to 120-m depth), 48 are mesopelagic or bathypelagic species, and 67 are deepwater fishes (Miller & Lea 1972). In addition, 40 species of pelagic cephalopods are known to inhabit the waters off southern California and Baja California, Mexico (Young 1972).

Northern anchovy (Engraulis mordax)
The northern anchovy is one of the major forage species utilised by fur seals wintering off California, and has been among the top four forages species consumed by fur seals

during every monthly collection (January through June) off California. The northern anchovy is also the most abundant and largest fishery resource in the California Current System based on CalCOFI surveys and on acoustic–midwater surveys (Ahlstrom 1968, Frey 1971, Mais 1974). The anchovy is also one of the principal forage species of fur seals occurring off Washington during February, March and April. The extensive use of anchovy as bait in commercial and sport fisheries also shows its acceptance as food for a variety of fishes. The general distribution of this species is from the Queen Charlotte Islands, British Columbia, south to Cape San Lucas, Baja California, Mexico.

Pacific whiting (Merluccius productus)

Pacific whiting is among the principal forage species consumed by fur seals off California during April and May and second in importance during January, February and March. All months combined, Pacific whiting was second only to northern anchovy as the leading forage species consumed by fur seals off California. Egg and larval studies by CalCOFI also indicate that whiting is consistently ranked second to anchovy in annual estimates of relative abundance in the survey area (Ahlstrom 1968). Off Washington, whiting becomes one of the principal forage species during spring, when it migrates into the area and becomes available to fur seals. This fish is distributed over the continental shelf and slope from the Gulf of California to the Gulf of Alaska where whiting undertakes an annual migration northward in the spring and summer and southward beginning in autumn.

Market squid (Loligo opalescens)

The market squid is one of the leading forage species of fur seals off California, as evidenced in collections made during January, March, April, and June. A schooling species generally found over continental shelf and in coastal waters, it is an important forage food of many fishes, seabirds, and marine mammals and is an important link between zooplankton and the higher trophic levels in the pelagic environment of the California Current System. Young (1972) reported that the market squid is probably the most abundant squid off the California coast. Based on CalCOFI surveys, the market squid ranked third among cephalopods in abundance (Okutani & McGowan 1969). Although a few occurrences of this species have been identified in stomachs of fur seals taken in the Gulf of Alaska, the known geographical range of the market squid is from Hecate Strait, British Columbia, into Puget Sound, Washington, and south to Guadalupe Island and Turtle Bay, Mexico (Berry 1912, Okutani & McGowan 1969).

Pacific saury (Cololabis saira)

Pacific saury is one of the leading forage foods of fur seals off California during February and March. Typically oceanic, the Pacific saury ranges across the entire North Pacific Ocean from Japan to North America; the eastern Pacific saury stock is principally located in waters from northern Baja California, Mexico, to Washington. The saury population is considered to be large (fifth most abundant species) as determined from CalCOFI surveys (Ahlstrom 1968). Pacific saury, in common with the northern anchovy and market squid, form an important link between lower and higher trophic levels as they provide forage for a large variety of fishes and marine mammals in the eastern North Pacific Ocean.

Rockfishes (Sebastes spp.)

Rockfishes ranked fourth in both volume and frequency as forage food of fur seals off California in 1965. Rockfishes of the family Scorpaenidae form one of the important and largest fish families in this area, with at least 55 species of *Sebastes* spp., a single species of *Scorpaena*, and 2 of *Sebastolobus* (Phillips 1964, Frey 1971). The larvae of *Sebastes* spp. have consistently ranked third or fourth in abundance in the CalCOFI survey area (Ahlstrom 1968). Rockfishes are a highly desirable food resource, subjected to both commercial and sport fishing pressure. They are also considered a large but under-utilised fishery resource off California in terms of abundance (Frey 1971). In the eastern Pacific, rockfishes are generally distributed from Baja California to the Bering Sea.

Jack mackerel (Trachurus symmetricus)

Jack mackerel is among the leading forage species of fur seals collected during April and June off California. This fish was second only to the northern anchovy in frequency of occurrence in midwater trawl catches conducted by CalCOFI scientists, with the highest catch rates and largest catches made in the southern and northern California regions (Mais 1974). Jack mackerel exhibit both coastal (north–south) and inshore–offshore movements. The larger and older fish are found offshore in deeper waters, whereas the younger fish are generally found over rocky banks and shallow coastal areas (MacCall *et al.* 1980). Juvenile jack mackerel stay inshore (0–90 km) for the first 3–6 years of their lives, gradually moving farther offshore with increasing age and size. MacCall *et al.* (1980) estimated the current jack mackerel spawning biomass to be 1–2 million tonnes, with 1.5 million tonnes as the working estimate.

Bering Sea

The Bering Sea marine fish fauna is made up of about 300 species of fish representing about 40 families (Quast & Hall 1972, Wilimovsky 1974). From this group, fur seals are known to prey on fish species from 17 families. Oceanic squids representing three genera from the family Gonatidae have also been identified in stomachs of fur seals from the eastern Bering Sea. Other species of pelagic cephalopods known to inhabit the Bering Sea are deep-water species which, therefore, are probably not available to fur seals.

The principal prey species of fur seals comprised 75–99% of the total stomach content volume during the 7 collection years (1960, 1962, 1963, 1964, 1968, 1973, and 1974). The majority of the samples were collected during July, August, and September, and some were taken in June and October. From a total of 23 species of fish and 3 species of squid identified in stomachs of fur seals taken from this area, only 4 species of fish and 2 species of squid were considered the principal prey of fur seals. These principal forage species included walleye pollock (*Theragra chalcogramma*), capelin (*Mallotus villosus*), Atka mackerel (*Pleurogrammus monopterygius*), oceanic squids (*Berryteuthis magister* and *Gonatopsis borealis*), and Pacific herring (*Clupea harengus pallasi*). Deepsea smelt of the family Bathylagidae and salmon *Oncorhynchus* spp. were among the principal forage species during annual collections, but not when data from the entire period were combined by month for the Bering Sea. Salmon occurred among the principal forage food of fur seals in 1960, and deepsea smelt in 1963, 1968, 1973, and 1974. Greenland turbot (*Reinhardtius hippoglossoides*) was an important forage food in 1973.

The rank order by percentage frequency of occurrence of the 20 most common fish species in the eastern Bering Sea (based on 1975 bottom-trawl surveys) includes four of the principal forage species of fur seals. These are: first, walleye pollock (occurred in 91% of the stations fished); second, Greenland turbot (occurred in 78% of the stations fished), eleventh, Pacific herring (occurred in 37% of the stations fished); and capelin, at seventeenth place, occurred in 22% of the stations fished.

Although we know that trawls are selective (due to the inability to sample all substrates and incomplete sampling of the water column), and that estimates of standing stocks are representative only for those species which are accessible to the trawl, the total fish biomass for the Bering Sea was estimated at 4.4 million tonnes (Pereyra *et al.* 1976). Fishes of the families Gadidae and Pleuronectidae accounted for over 90% of the Bering Sea fish catch.

Walleye pollock (Theragra chalcogramma)

Walleye pollock has been among the principal prey species throughout the 7 years that fur seals were collected in the eastern Bering Sea. This species occurs as the principal prey when fur seals are collected on the shelf or near the shelf edge. Walleye pollock is the most important and abundant demersal fish population in the eastern Bering Sea in terms of biomass and landings in the fishery. Its biomass from the 1975 survey was estimated at 2.4 million tonnes. Total biomass for all species was estimated at 5.9 million tonnes (Pereyra *et al.* 1976).

Walleye pollock are widely distributed over the continental shelf in the eastern Bering Sea, forming schools near bottom during daylight and then dispersing into the water column at night (Smith 1981). Smith also reported that the walleye pollock move to the spawning area along the outer shelf west and north-west of Unimak Island in the spring, and to the outer and central shelf in summer. The general distribution of walleye pollock extends from off central California northward through the Bering Sea and the Sea of Okhotsk and the Sea of Japan (Hart 1973).

Oceanic squids (Berryteuthis magister)

Oceanic squids comprise some of the principal forage foods of fur seals, not only in the eastern Bering Sea but throughout their range whenever seals are taken seaward of the continental shelf over deep water. Oceanic squids of the family Gonatidae are found in the subarctic waters of the North Pacific Ocean and Bering Sea, and include about 12 species representing three genera: *Gonatus*, *Berryteuthis*, and *Gonatopsis* (Young 1972, Okutani 1973, Naito *et al.* 1977, Anderson, 1978, Bublitz 1981). In the Bering Sea, squid representing each genera have been identified in fur seal stomachs. These are *Gonatus* spp., *Berryteuthis magister*, and *Gonatopsis borealis*. The latter two species have been among the principal forage species of fur seals collected from June to October in the Bering Sea. Although only gonatid squids have been found in stomachs of fur seals, 8 other families of squid, which include 15 additional species, have been identified from stomachs of sperm whales (*Physeter macrocephalus*) taken in the Bering Sea–Aleutian Islands area (Okutani & Nemoto 1964, Kodolov 1970).

The oceanic squid fauna of the North Pacific Ocean and the Bering Sea is poorly known, but the population of some pelagic squids can probably be considered to be largely based on information obtained from the stomach contents of marine mammals and seabirds. Sanger estimated that the consumption of squids by seabirds during the summer in Alaska was at least 53 000 tonnes (Mercer 1981). Kawakami (1980), in reviewing sperm whale feeding, reported that the frequency of squids found in sperm whale stomachs was between 71% and 94% of total stomach contents in sperm whales taken in the Bering Sea–Aleutian Islands area, and 32% for the Gulf of Alaska.

Capelin (Mallotus villosus)
Capelin, a member of the smelt family Osmeridae, is one of the principal forage species of fur seals in the eastern Bering Sea. The occurrences of capelin were primarily near the Aleutian Islands (Unimak Pass). This fish is considered an arctic species, with its centre of abundance in the Bering Sea (along the Aleutian Islands) or Arctic Ocean (Hart & McHugh 1944). Capelin are bathypelagic fish during most of the year and are located near the bottom, moving inshore as the spawning period approaches (Andriyashev 1954, Trumble 1973, Macy *et al.* 1978).

Capelin ranked 17th by percentage frequency of occurrence of the 20 most common taxa in the eastern Bering Sea survey conducted in 1975 (Pereyra *et al.* 1976). Little is known about the relative abundance of capelin in the Bering Sea, but the species was observed in large numbers along the Alaska coast in shallow water at about the same time as spawning Pacific herring (Barton & Steinhoff 1980). Based on an ecosystem model, Laevastu and Favorite (1980) estimated the pelagic fish species – consisting primarily of capelin and Pacific sand lance (*Ammodytes hexapterus*) – biomass to be 4.3 million tonnes. Based on feeding studies, capelin is an important link in the food chains of the North Pacific and Bering Sea for many fishes, marine mammals, and seabirds, and it is probably a large and important resource in the North Pacific Ocean and associated seas. During an ichthyoplankton survey of the Bering Sea in 1977, the larvea of capelin were the sixth most abundant species taken (Waldron & Vinter 1978).

Pacific herring (Clupea harengus pallasi)
Pacific herring is important in the food web throughout its range as it is one of the primary forage foods of many animals in the marine environment, including fishes, marine mammals, and seabirds. In the Bering Sea, Pacific herring was one of the principal foods consumed by fur seals taken during August north-east of St Paul Island. The migration of herring in the Bering Sea is such that, in August, herring migrate back to their major wintering grounds located north-west of the Pribilof Islands; in late March, they leave the wintering grounds and migrate towards the coast, where they spawn on intertidal vegetation during spring and early summer (Wespestad & Barton 1981). Pacific herring has also been among the principal forage foods of fur seals in southeastern Alaska (Sitka Sound), and is especially important to fur seals off Washington & off British Columbia (Vancouver Island), Canada. The importance of Pacific herring in this area can be attributed to an abundant adult herring population and feeding grounds for juvenile and immature herring located off the Strait of Juan de Fuca. Pacific herring is distributed in coastal waters from Baja California, Mexico, northward along the North American coast into the Arctic Ocean, and southward along coastal waters to Korea, Japan, and the Sea of Okhotsk (Hart 1973).

Atka mackerel (Pleurogrammus monopterygius)
Atka mackerel was second only to capelin as the principal forage species based on percentage of total stomach content volume for seals collected in Unimak Pass and beyond the shelf area between the Aleutian and Pribilof Islands during 1962 (Fiscus *et al.* 1964). During the breeding season, Atka mackerel is concentrated in waters off the Aleutian Island chain from Attu Island to Unimak Island, the Alaska Peninsula, the Shumagin Islands, and Kodiak Island, and is widespread in the open ocean at other

times. Larkins (1964) reported Atka mackerel catches incidental to high seas salmon gill-net sampling as the fourth most abundant species caught. To take advantage of the Atka mackerel's breeding habits, the commercial fishery for this species is centered near the Aleutian Islands, Shumagin Islands, and Kodiak Island. Atka mackerel and Pacific saury are the most commonly found fish prey of humpback (*Megaptera novaengliae*) and sei (*Balaenoptera borealis*) whales in the eastern North Pacific Ocean. The former is considered one of the favourite foods of humpback whales in waters off the western Aleutians and south of Amchitka Island (Nemoto 1957). Based on fur seal studies, it appears that fur seals collected in the Aleutian Island passes during the summer months (June through October) prey principally on Atka mackerel.

Oregon

Among the remaining five designated collection areas (from south northward), the collection of fur seals off Oregon was made while the chartered research vessel was enroute between Washington and California during 1959, 1961, 1964, and 1965. Although the sample sizes were small, a total of 14 species of fish and 7 species of squid were identified in the stomachs of fur seals (see Tables 18.1 and 18.2). The principal prey species included northern anchovy, Pacific whiting, rockfish, and squid (see Table 18.3).

Washington

The ocean area off Washington has the most extensive time coverage as well as the greatest variety of prey species eaten by fur seals (33 species of fish and 10 species of squid) than in any of the other six areas (see Tables 18.1 and 18.2). Surveys and collections were conducted from late November through early June, with March, April, and May receiving the most time coverage. April was the only month in which collections were made during every collection year from 1958 through 1974. The principal prey species utilised by fur seals off Washington (see Table 18.3) included the Pacific herring, capelin, eulachon (*Thaleichthys pacificus*), northern anchovy, rockfish, salmon, Pacific whiting, sablefish and the oceanic squid (*Onychoteuthis* sp.). These principal prey species contributed from 64% to 99% of the total food volume.

British Columbia

Surveys and collections in British Columbia waters occurred from January through June, 1958–68, with extensive time coverage primarily during April and May. The principal prey species of fur seals taken off British Columbia (see Table 18.3) included the Pacific herring, eulachon, salmon, sablefish, rockfish, walleye pollock, Pacific cod, (*Gadus macrocephalus*), Pacific whiting, Pacific saury, and squid (*L. opalescens* and *Onychoteuthis borealijaponicus*). These principal prey species contributed from 66% to 95% of the total food volume.

Gulf of Alaska

The Gulf of Alaska collections occurred primarily from 1958 through 1968, with surveys and collections taken during May and June when fur seals were expected in this area in greater numbers enroute to the Pribilof Islands. The principal prey species utilised by fur seals in the Gulf of Alaska (see Table 18.3) included Pacific herring, capelin, salmon, walleye pollock, Pacific sand lance, rockfish, Atka mackerel, and oceanic squids (*Gonatus* spp. and *B. magister*). These species contributed from 89% to 99% of the total food volume based on percentage of the total stomach content volume of seals taken in this area.

Western Alaska

Surveys and collections in the western Alaska region were made primarily during June, 1958, 1960, 1962, 1968, and 1974. The principal prey species utilised by fur seals in this region (see Table 18.3) included Pacific herring, capelin, salmon, walleye pollock, sablefish, Atka mackerel, and Pacific sand lance as well as the oceanic squid (*B. magister*). These species contributed from 77% to 99% of the total stomach content volume of seals taken in this area.

Discussion and summary

Evidence presented on the abundance and distribution of the principal forage species known to be consumed by northern fur seals suggests that fur seals are opportunistic in their feeding, preying on those species that are most available in the area. The predominance of single food items in the stomachs of fur seals may reflect the availability and abundance of species of fish and squid more than it reflects the selection or preference of one particular species over another. Other factors such as taste probably play some rôle, although these factors can only be studied through experimentation.

Northern fur seals are known to feed on a variety of fishes and squids throughout their range, and they certainly restrict their diet to certain species based on size. As a general rule, small schooling fishes and neritic squid are the principal forage species over the continental shelf region, and oceanic squids are important over deep water, seaward of the continental shelf and slope. Location is important in considering the diet of fur seals as prey species, and fur seal abundance generally, differs from area to area (north–south; inshore–offshore) and seasonally. The migratory patterns of forage species must be considered as well, since they may be available to fur seals only at certain times of the year. Local movement and distribution of fur seals is probably simply a result of the abundance of the forage species in the area. Fur seals seem to move to and feed in areas where food is abundant, and depart in search of other areas of concentrated prey when it becomes scarce. An indication that food is probably not a major factor in the migration of fur seals can be attributed to: (a) the intermingling (both on land and at sea) between the eastern and western Pacific population of fur seals, and (b) the absence of male fur seals in the southern portion of their eastern Pacific range where the majority of the female fur seals migrate.

Although fur seals are usually solitary at sea, they tend to congregate loosely in areas near submarine canyons, seamounts, and along the continental shelf and slope, where abrupt changes occur in depths and where upwellings of nutrient-rich water occur which influence the concentration of food for most marine life. For the seven study areas, 14 species of fish and 6 species of squid were considered the principal prey species of fur seals based on the percentage of total stomach content volume. This list, in each of these areas, generally does not change over time, even though the ranking by volume within it may change. Some species are important in more than one area. Some are commercially fished, while others are not of commercial importance but are important forage food for many other predators including fishes, seabirds, and other marine mammals. For those species fished commercially or sampled in surveys, there tends to be a correspondence between indices of abundance and indices of importance in fur seal diets.

Based on the relative abundance of the resources of fish and squid off California (northern anchovy) and the eastern Bering Sea (walleye pollock), the data suggest that fur seals are opportunistic feeders, foraging on the most abundant species of fish and squid available in an area. This type of feeding prevails throughout their range in the eastern North Pacific Ocean and eastern Bering Sea.

Acknowledgements

I am particularly grateful to Charles Fowler, National Marine Mammal Laboratory, Seattle, Washington, for suggesting that I contribute a chapter in this volume. Thomas Loughlin and Charles Fowler also provided helpful comments on this chapter.

References

Ahlstrom, E. H. 1968. An evaluation of the fishery resources available to California fishermen. In *The future of the fishing industry of the United States*, D. W. Gilbert (ed.), 65–80. Univ. Wash., Seattle, Publ. Fish., New Ser. 4.

Anderson, M. E. 1978. Notes on cephalopods of Monterey Bay, California, with new records for the area. *Veliger* 21, 255–62.

Andriyashev, A. P. 1954. *Ryby severnykh morei SSR* (fishes of the northern seas of the USSR). Akad. Nauk SSSR, Opredeliteli po Faune SSSR 53. Izd. Akad. Nauk SSSR, Moscow-Leningrad. In Russian. (Transl. by Israel Program Sci. Transl., 1964, avail. US Dept Comm., Nat. Tech. Inf. Serv., Springfield, VA, as OTS 63-11160.)

Barton, L. H. and D. L. Steinhoff, 1980. Assessment of spawning herring (*Clupea harengus pallasi*) stocks at selected coastal areas in the eastern Bering Sea. *Alaska Dep. Fish Game, Inf. Leafl.* 187.

Berry, S. S. 1912. A review of the cephalopods of western North America. *Bull. U.S. Bur. Fish.* 30, 267–36.

Bigg, M. A. 1982. *Migration of northern fur seals in the eastern North Pacific and eastern Bering Sea: an analysis using effort and population composition data.* Paper submitted to the 25th Annual Meeting of the Standing Scientific Committee, North Pacific Fur Seal Commission.

Bublitz, C. 1981. Systematics of the cephalopod family Gonatidae from the southeastern Bering Sea. MSc Thesis, University of Alaska, Fairbanks.

Fiscus, C. H., G. A. Baines and F. Wilke 1964. Pelagic fur seal investigations, Alaska waters, 1962. *US Fish. Wildl. Serv., Spec. Sci. Rep. Fish.* 475.

Fowler, C. W. 1982. Interactions of northern fur seals and commercial fisheries. *Trans. 47th N. Am. Wildl. Nat. Resour. Conf.*, 278–92.

Frey, H. W. 1971. *California's living marine resources and their utilization.* Calif. Dept. Fish Game., Sacramento.

Hart, J. J. 1973. Pacific fishes of Canada. *Bull. Fish. Res. Bd Can.* 180.

Hart, J. L. and J. L. McHugh 1944. The smelts (Osmeridae) of British Columbia. *Bull. Fish. Res. Bd Can.* 64.

Kawakami, T. 1980. A review of sperm whale food. *Sci. Rep. Whales Res. Inst. Tokyo* 32 199–218.

Kodolov, L. S. 1970. O. kalmarakh v Beringovom more (Squids of the Bering Sea). *Tr. Vses. Nauchno-issled. Inst. Morsk. Ryhn. Khoz. Okeanogr.* **70** (*Izv. Tikhookean. Naucho-issled. Rybn. Khoz. Okeanogr.* **72**, 162–5. In Russian. (Transl. by Israel Prog. Sci. Transl., 1972, In *Soviet fisheries investigations in the northeastern Pacific*, part 5, P. A. Moiseev (ed.), 157–60. avail. US Dept Comm., Nat. Tech. Inf. Serv., Springfield VA, as TT71-50127.)

Kooyman, G. L., R. L. Gentry and D. L. Urquhart 1976. Northern fur seal diving behavior: a new approach to its study. *Science* **193**, 411–12.

Laevastu, T. and F. Favorite 1980. Fluctuations in Pacific herring stocks in the eastern Bering Sea as revealed by an ecosystem model (DYNUMES III). *Rapp. P.-V. Reun. Cons. Int. Explor. Mer* **177**, 455–9.

Larkins, H. A. 1964. Some epipelagic fishes of the North Pacific Ocean, Bering Sea, and Gulf of Alaska. *Trans. Am. Fish. Soc.* **93**, 286–90.

MacCall, A. D., H. W. Frey, D. D. Huppert, E. H. Knaggs, J. A. McMillan and G. D. Stauffer 1980. *Biology and economics of the fishery for jack mackerel in the northeastern Pacific.* US Dept Commer., NOAA Tech. Memo NMFS SWFC-4.

Macy, P. T., J. M. Wall, N. D. Lampasakis and J. E. Mason 1978. Resources of non-salmonid pelagic fishes of the Gulf of Alaska and eastern Bering Sea, Part 1. Unpublished manuscript. Seattle, Washington: Northwest and Alaska Fish. Cent., Natl. Mar. Fish. Serv., NOAA.

Mais, K. F. 1974. Pelagic fish surveys in the California Current. *Calif. Dep. Fish Game, Fish. Bull.* **162**.

Mercer, R. W. (ed.) 1981. *Proceedings of the squid workshop.* NWAFC Processed Rep. 81-11. Seattle, Washington: Northwest and Alaska Fish. Cent., Natl. Mar. Fish. Serv., NOAA.

Millert, D. J. and R. N. Lea 1972. Guide to the coastal marine fishes of California. *Calif. Dep. Fish Game, Fish. Bull.* **157**.

Naito, M., K. Murakami, T. Kobayashi, N. Nakayama and J. Osgawara 1977. Distribution and migration of oceanic squids (*Ommastrephes bartrami*, *Onychoteuthis borealijaponicus*, *Berryteuthis magister* and *Gonatopsis borealis*) in the western Pacific Region. In *Fisheries biological production in the subarctic Pacific region*, 321–37. Hokkaido Univ., Hakodate, Jpn, Res. Inst. North Pac. Fish. Spec. Vol.

Nemoto, T. 1957. Foods of baleen whales. *Sic. Rep. Whales Res. Inst. Tokyo* **12**, 83–9.

Okutani, T. 1973. Guide and keys to squid in Japan. *Bull. Tokai Reg. Fish. Res. Lab.* **74**, 83–111.

Okutani, T. and J. A. McGowan 1969. Systematics, distribution, and abundance of the epiplanktonic squid (Cephalopoda, Decapoda) larvae of the California Current, April, 1954–March, 1957 *Bull. Scripps Inst. Oceanogr. Univ. Calif.* **14**, 1-90.

Okutani, T. and T. Nemoto 1964. Squids as the food of sperm whales in the Bering Sea and Alaskan Gulf. *Sci. Rep. Whales Res. Inst. Tokyo* **18**, 111–22.

Péreyra, W. T., J. E. Reeves and R. G. Bakkala 1976. *Demersal fish and shellfish resources of the eastern Bering Sea in the baseline year 1975.* Processed Rep. Seattle, Washington: Northwest and Alaska Fish. Cent., Natl. Mar. Fish. Serv., NOAA.

Phillips, J. B. 1964. Life history studies on the species of rockfish (Genus *Sebastodes*). *Calif. Dep. Fish Game, Fish. Bull.* **126**.

Quast, J. C. and E. L. Hall 1972. *List of fishes of Alaska and adjacent waters with a guide to some of their literature.* US Dept. Commer., NOAA Tech. Rep. NMFS SSRF-658.

Smith, G. B. 1981. The biology of walleye pollock. In *The eastern Bering Sea shelf: oceanography and resources*, Vol. 1, D. W. Hood and J. A. Calder (eds), 527–51. Washington, DC: US Government Printing Office.

Trumble, R. J. 1973. Distribution, relative abundance, and general biology of selected under-utilized fishery resources of the eastern North Pacific Ocean. MS Thesis, University of Washington, Seattle.

Waldron, K. D. and B. M. Vinter 1978. *Ichthyoplankton of the eastern Bering Sea.* Processed Rep. Seattle, Washington: Northwest and Alaska Fish. Cent., Natl. Mar. Fish. Serv., NOAA.

Wespestad, V. G. and L. H. Barton 1981. Distribution, migration, and status of Pacific herring. In *The eastern Bering Sea shelf: oceanography and resources*, D. W. Hood and J. A. Calder (eds), 509–25. Washington, DC: US Government Printing Office.

Wilimovsky, N. J. 1974. Fishes of the Bering Sea: the state of existing knowledge and requirements for future effective effort. In *Oceanography of the Bering Sea with emphasis on renewable resources*, D. W. Hood and E. J. Kelley (eds), 243–56. University of Alaska, Fairbanks, Inst. Mar. Sci., Occas. Publ. 2.

Yoshida, K. and N. Baba 1982. *Trend analysis of fur seal pups population of Robben Island origin*. Paper submitted to the 25th Annual Meeting of the Standing Scientific Committee, North Pacific Fur Seal Commission.

Young, R. E. 1972. The systematics and areal distribution of pelagic cephalopods from the seas off southern California. *Smithson. Contrib. Zool.* **97**, 1–159.

19 An annual energy budget for north-west Atlantic harp seals

*D. M. Lavigne, S. Innes, R. E. A. Stewart and
G. A. J. Worthy*

Introduction

Prior to the Scientific Consultation on Marine Mammals sponsored by the Food and Agriculture Organization (FAO) of the United Nations in Bergen, Norway, in 1976, a review was prepared outlining what was then known about feeding relationships and energetic requirements of pinniped populations (Lavigne *et al*. 1982a). During the consultation, studies of energy flow through seal populations were identified as a priority for future research (FAO 1978), and the review itself provided the framework for several subsequent studies of seal energetics (e.g. Ashwell-Erickson & Elsner 1981, Fedak *et al*. 1981), including additional research on harp seals (e.g. Gallivan & Ronald 1979, 1981, Lavigne & Stewart 1979, Stewart & Lavigne 1980, Innes & Ronald 1981, Innes *et al*. 1981, Keiver 1982, Lavigne *et al*. 1982b, Stewart *et al*. 1983, Worthy & Lavigne 1983a, 1983b).

The present study updates earlier estimates of food consumption by north-west Atlantic harp seals (Sergeant 1973a, 1976, Lavigne *et al*. 1982a) in relation to potential interactions with commercial fisheries. Estimation of food consumption by harp seals (and other pinnipeds) from a knowledge of prey species ingested is extremely difficult (Lavigne *et al*. 1982a). Direct observations of feeding animals are not usually possible, and stomach content data alone are of limited use in estimating the total amount of food consumed (see Ch. 9). The problem can, however, be approached from the opposite direction (Lavigne *et al*. 1982a). Energy requirements of individual seals, as a function of age, size, sex, and population density, can be estimated and projected to various population sizes and age structures to predict annual food consumption by an entire population. Although this approach does not overcome all the difficulties of estimating the biomass of prey species consumed, it does provide a method for addressing some important biological questions related to the problem of marine mammal–fishery interactions. These include questions about density-dependent changes in *per capita* food consumption (Winters 1975, Innes *et al*. 1981) and the relative amounts of prey consumed in different parts of the species' range. Such an approach also provides a mechanism for testing certain hypotheses, such as Sergeant's (1973a) conclusion that seals (and perhaps other marine mammals) are less efficient than terrestrial mammals in converting food into usable energy.

Generalised bioenergetic scheme

The generalised bioenergetic scheme or pattern of energy flow through higher vertebrates is illustrated in Figure 19.1. This scheme is similar to that used in our 1976 review (Lavigne *et al.* 1982a), but it incorporates later modifications proposed by the National Research Council, USA (1981). Most notably, the category 'net energy' has been deleted in favour of partitioning metabolisable energy into the heat increment of

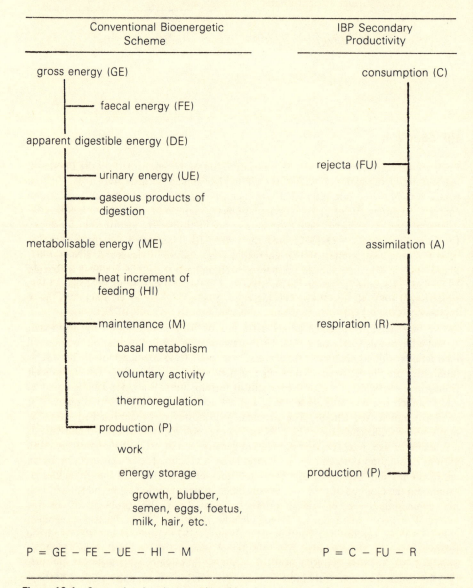

Figure 19.1 Conventional schemes describing components of animal energy budgets. (Adapted and modified from Kendeigh *et al.* 1977, NRC 1981, Lavigne *et al.* 1982a.)

feeding (or specific dynamic action, SDA), production and maintenance. Coincidentally, this change facilitates comparisons with the scheme commonly employed by the International Biological Programme (IBP) and many ecologists (e.g. Humphreys 1979, Lavigne 1982a, see also Fig. 19.1).

The schemes outlined in Figure 19.1 may be used to describe energy flow through an individual animal of known sex, age, size, and reproductive condition. They may also be used to describe energy flow through an entire population, given additional information on sex ratio, age structure, and population size.

In order to describe an annual energy budget specifically for north-west Atlantic harp seals, a population model was developed as a book-keeping device to record the partitioning of energy flow throughout one year. (The model was written in 'A Progamming Language' (APL) and a listing is available from the authors on request.) The model's structure follows the annual life cycle of the population, and is briefly described below.

The model

The fiscal year for our harp seal population begins on 1 March, with a presumed age structure (numbers-at-age) including the number of pups produced that year. The sex ratio of the population is 1 : 1. For the sake of simplicity, all pups are assumed to be born on 1 March, whereas, in reality, pup production begins in late February and extends into early March (Stewart 1983).

For the purposes of book-keeping, the year was then divided into 26 2-week periods. Total mortality, partitioned either as natural mortality or hunting mortality, occurs throughout the year, thereby reducing the numbers-at-age from one biweekly period to the next. Hunting mortality for harp seals occurs at discrete times of the year. In the model, catch statistics (as a function of age) for coastal (including net) 'fisheries', from December through February, for the annual seal hunt in the Gulf of St Lawrence and Front area off Newfoundland and Labrador, and the eastern Canadian arctic and West Greenland summer hunts, were subtracted from appropriate biweekly periods. Natural mortality, assumed to operate continuously throughout the year, was then applied to the numbers of animals alive in each biweekly period to give the numbers dying, and thus the age structure of the population at the end of each biweekly period.

The energy budget of an imaginary harp seal was then constructed over its entire lifetime, i.e. from birth to the age of 30. The energy budget varied with age, depending on whether the animal was mature or immature. For mature animals, the energy budget also varied with sex and reproductive state. Energy required for growth-at-age was also tabulated.

Starting at age 0, growth due solely to energy contained in milk produced by the female was calculated. At weaning, about 9 days post-partum, the pup begins a fast which lasts for about 5 weeks, during which it relies on body reserves laid down during nursing. During the 6th week it begins to feed and to regain body weight, and growth is then assumed to continue until the animal reaches sexual maturity. After the onset of sexual maturity, the lean body mass and skin continue to grow (harp seals, like most mammals reach sexual maturity prior to achieving final body size), whereas blubber mass was assumed to follow the observed pattern determined by season and reproductive condition.

Energy costs of basal metabolism and activity were estimated from body mass over each biweekly period. Costs of reproduction, growth of the fetus plus the heat increment of gestation, were estimated for fertile, mature females. Specific dynamic action (SDA), or heat increment of feeding, was calculated as 20% of metabolisable energy for all animals.

Energy requirements of individual, known-age harp seals were multiplied by stable age distributions, or by age structures from the literature, to generate the annual energy budget for an entire population. Energy requirements for specific periods within a year were used to compute the amount of energy required at various geographical locations throughout the annual migration.

Input parameters

The sources of information which provided input into the model are briefly described below. Additional information can be found in the literature cited.

Age structures

Initially, stable age distributions were calculated by applying natural mortality and fecundity schedules to an arbitrary starting population. Three constant, average, annual mortality rates were used (0.08, 0.10, and 0.12), approximating the range of natural mortality estimates for North-west Atlantic harp seals found in the literature. Since it is unlikely that natural mortality remains constant for all age-classes over all years, a more typical 'U-shaped' mammalian mortality schedule (Caughley 1966) was also employed (Capstick et al. 1976). Following Lavigne et al. (1982a), natural mortality of pups was given as 0.20, declining exponentially to a constant value of 0.095 from ages 6 through 21, and increasing to 0.95 by the terminal age of 30. Such a mortality schedule provides an average annual mortality of about 10%. Fecundity schedules were estimated from Bowen et al. 1981 (see 'Mean age of maturity and fertility' below).

The resulting age structures were used to investigate the effects of changing natural mortality (M), mean age of maturity (MAM – Bowen et al. 1981), and fertility (f – Bowen et al. 1981) on the energy budget of a harp seal population.

Age structures for exploited populations were obtained from assessments of stock abundance and trends (Lett & Benjaminsen, 1977, Winters 1978, Beddington & Williams 1980). These provided a range of population sizes from about 1.0 million to in excess of 3.0 million seals, and age structures for both decreasing and increasing populations.

Catch statistics (hunting mortality)

These have recently been assembled by Bowen (1982). Samples of the catch were pro-rated to the total catch and expressed in terms of catch-at-age. The approximate time frame for each hunt is also known. Catches were distributed on a biweekly basis in the present analyses.

Mean age of maturity and fertility

Mean age of maturity of north-west Atlantic harp seals has apparently declined from more than 6 years in the early 1950s to less than 4 years in the late 1970s (Sergeant 1966, 1973b, Bowen et al. 1981). For our analyses, estimates of 4.5, 5.1 and 5.5 years, corresponding to representative populations from the 1970s, 1960s, and 1950s respectively, were used.

Concomitant with the decline in mean age of maturity, fertility rates of north-west Atlantic harp seals appear to have increased from about 80% to more than 94% between 1950 and the late 1970s (Bowen *et al.* 1981). Estimates of fertility, corresponding to those of mean age of maturity given above, were 94.3%, 86.3%, and 81.8%. In our calculations with stable age distributions, fertilities of 75% and 100% were used.

Sex ratio

The sex ratio of harp seals at birth is not significantly different from 1 : 1 (Stewart & Lavigne 1980). For 1 + harp seals, there have been suggestions that exploitation on moulting patches may have biased the catch in favour of males, and that this has resulted in a shift in the sex ratio in favour of females (Lett & Benjaminsen 1977). This hypothesis was not, however, supported by a subsequent sample of the catch of moulting seals (Lett & Benjaminsen 1977). Since harp seals do not exhibit marked sexual dimorphism in body size of adults (Innes *et al.* 1981), and sexual dimorphism is frequently correlated with a biased sex ratio (Bartholomew 1970, Krebs & Davies 1981, Stirling 1983), we assumed, in the absence of contradictory evidence, a 1 : 1 sex ratio for the entire population.

Growth

Growth of harp seals from birth to adult body size has been described in detail by Innes *et al.* (1981), Stewart and Lavigne (1980), Worthy (1982), and Worthy and Lavigne (1983a, 1983b). Changes in body weight were converted to energy units using estimates of the caloric density of entire harp seals in relation to age (Worthy 1982, Worthy & Lavigne 1983a, 1983b), and, in some cases, of specific components (skin, blubber, and lean body mass) of known-age animals (Worthy 1982).

Stored energy (blubber)

A large percentage of the total weight of a harp seal is comprised of stored energy in the form of blubber (Innes *et al.* 1981). This energy reserve fluctuates in a rather regular way throughout any given year (Sergeant 1973a, Lavigne *et al.* 1982a).

Generally, blubber stores increase during the first years of life, but fluctuate seasonally. In particular, blubber stores are used by young animals during the post-weaning fast (Worthy 1982, Worthy & Lavigne 1983a). Similarly, blubber stores decrease in both adult males and females during the breeding season (Sergeant 1973a). An average 'reproductive' weight loss was computed for females (Stewart 1983, Stewart & Lavigne 1984). Males also fast at this time and presumably have increased metabolic demands associated with courtship and mating. Lacking adequate empirical data, it was assumed that males expended energy at three times basal metabolic requirements for 4 weeks, beginning 1 March, and that this energy was derived from blubber reserves. Additional blubber losses occur during the annual moult. In the model, blubber levels were reprovisioned at a constant rate between whelping and the moult, and after the moult, until they reached pre-whelping levels (Stewart & Lavigne 1984).

Although relatively large variations in stored energy occur from year to year (Stewart & Lavigne in press), we restricted consideration to average animals observed in the North-west Atlantic since 1978 (Innes *et al.* 1981, Stewart & Lavigne 1984).

Metabolism

Basal metabolic rates (BMR) of adult harp seals (Gallivan in press, Innes, unpublished data) do not differ significantly from Kleiber's (1975) relationship for terrestrial mammals. For younger, growing animals, a relationship between BMR and body size was generated from empirical data (Gallivan in press).

Empirical estimates of the energy cost of locomotion (activity) in relation to body size and swimming speed were also available (Innes & Ronald 1981a, 1981b, Innes, unpublished data). Lacking any information on time–activity budgets, we assumed that the daily cost of activity was equivalent to swimming at 1 m/sec for 18 h.

Faecal and urinary energy losses
Few studies have been attempted to quantify the proportion of gross energy which is actually available to a seal as metabolisable energy (Keiver & Ronald 1981, Keiver 1982, Lavigne *et al.* 1982a). Faecal and urinary energy losses vary with the amount of food consumed, the proximate composition of the diet, and, therefore, with prey species and season (Keiver 1982). In our earlier calculations, we estimated that, for an average fish meal, between 82.7% and 84.7% of gross energy was realised as metabolisable energy (Lavigne *et al.* 1982a). Later, empirical determinations for harp seals eating herring (*Clupea harengus*) showed that metabolisable energy represented between 86.1% and 89.0% of gross energy consumed (Keiver 1982). In contrast, only about 60.9% of gross energy was realised as metabolisable energy when the diet consisted only of shrimp (*Pandalus borealis* – Keiver 1982).

Since harp seals eat a number of prey species of variable caloric density, and in varying amounts, we generally assumed that, for harp seals consuming a mixed diet, 80% of gross energy was realised as metabolisable energy. In addition, we used a range of values for the metabolisable energy coefficient, in conjunction with appropriate caloric densities of food, to demonstrate their influence on estimates of prey biomass.

Heat increment of feeding
The heat increment of feeding for harp seals has been estimated at about 17% of gross energy ingested (Gallivan & Ronald 1981, Gallivan in press).

Results

Changes in natural mortality, fertility, and mean age of maturity produced small changes in *per capita* energy requirements of unexploited populations with a stable age distribution (Table 19.1). *Per capita* requirements ranged from 2.63×10^6 to 2.76×10^6 kcal per year. Estimates of metabolisable energy (ME) and gross energy (GE) requirements for populations of varying age structures and sizes (Lett & Benjaminsen 1978, Winters 1978, Beddington & Williams 1980), and corresponding estimates of *per capita* requirements are given in Table 19.2. *Per capita* consumption for these populations varied between 2.3×10^6 and 2.6×10^6 kcal per year.

Estimates of population energy requirements were sensitive to changes in population size, basal metabolism, and the energy cost of locomotion (activity). For entire populations, a 10% change in population size resulted in a 10% change in population energy requirements (as would be expected) when all other variables were held constant. In comparison, a 19% change in basal metabolism, or a 23% change in activity was necessary to produce a $\simeq 10\%$ change in energy requirements. A change in natural mortality from 0.08 to 0.12 (an increase of 50%) caused a decrease of 2.6% in population energy requirements, whereas a decrease in fertility from 100% to 75% resulted in a 1.3% increase in population requirements.

Table 19.1 Estimates of energy requirements (kcal per year) for a hypothetical, unexploited harp seal population of 1 million animals with a stable age distribution (see text for details).

M	MAM	f	ME	Per capita GE[a]
1. 0.08	4.5	100	2.16×10^{12}	2.70×10^{6}
2. 0.08	4.5	75	2.19×10^{12}	2.74×10^{6}
3. 0.08	5.1	100	2.18×10^{12}	2.73×10^{6}
4. 0.08	5.1	75	2.20×10^{12}	2.75×10^{6}
5. 0.08	5.5	100	2.18×10^{12}	2.73×10^{6}
6. 0.08	5.5	75	2.21×10^{12}	2.76×10^{6}
7. 0.10	4.5	100	2.14×10^{12}	2.68×10^{6}
8. 0.10	4.5	75	2.17×10^{12}	2.71×10^{6}
9. 0.10	5.1	100	2.15×10^{12}	2.69×10^{6}
10. 0.10	5.1	75	2.17×10^{12}	2.71×10^{6}
11. 0.10	5.5	100	2.15×10^{12}	2.69×10^{6}
12. 0.10	5.5	75	2.18×10^{12}	2.73×10^{6}
13. 0.12	4.5	100	2.11×10^{12}	2.64×10^{6}
14. 0.12	4.5	75	2.14×10^{12}	2.68×10^{6}
15. 0.12	5.1	100	2.12×10^{12}	2.65×10^{6}
16. 0.12	5.1	75	2.15×10^{12}	2.69×10^{6}
17. 0.12	5.5	100	2.13×10^{12}	2.66×10^{6}
18. 0.12	5.5	75	2.15×10^{12}	2.69×10^{6}
19. var	4.5	100	2.10×10^{12}	2.63×10^{6}
20. var	4.5	75	2.14×10^{12}	2.68×10^{6}
21. var	5.1	100	2.11×10^{12}	2.64×10^{6}
22. var	5.1	75	2.14×10^{12}	2.68×10^{6}
23. var	5.5	100	2.12×10^{12}	2.65×10^{6}
24. var	5.5	75	2.15×10^{12}	2.69×10^{6}

[a]Assuming ME = 0.80 GE.

Production efficiency 100P/P + R estimates for unexploited harp seal populations with stable age distributions ranged from 4.0% to 4.4% (Table 19.3), increasing to between 5.4% and 6.0% for exploited populations (Table 19.4). Gross efficiency 100P/I estimates for unexploited populations ranged from 3.2% to 3.5% (Table 19.3), whereas for exploited populations they ranged from 4.6% to 5.2% (Table 19.4).

Of the total energy required by exploited populations throughout the year, approximately 54% was needed north of Hamilton Inlet (Figs. 19.2 & 19.3), i.e. during the late spring, summer, and autumn, whereas the remaining 46% was required south of Hamilton Inlet, before, during and shortly after whelping and breeding, from December to May.

Discussion

Any discussion of possible competition between harp seals and commercial fisheries for common prey species usually centres around the quantity of food consumed annually

Table 19.2 Estimates of energy requirements (kcal per year) by various age structures and population sizes of north-west Atlantic harp seals.

Year	Population size	ME	GE[a]	Per capita GE
Winters (1978)				
1952	3 021 000	6.1×10^{12}	7.0×10^{12}	2.3×10^{6}
1962	2 144 000	4.1×10^{12}	5.1×10^{12}	2.4×10^{6}
1972	1 390 000	2.8×10^{12}	3.5×10^{12}	2.5×10^{6}
1975	1 571 000	3.2×10^{12}	4.0×10^{12}	2.5×10^{6}
1977	1 637 000	3.4×10^{12}	4.3×10^{12}	2.6×10^{6}
Lett and Benjaminsen (1977)				
1952	2 754 367	5.6×10^{12}	7.0×10^{12}	2.5×10^{6}
1962	1 976 799	3.7×10^{12}	4.6×10^{12}	2.3×10^{6}
1972	1 426 261	2.8×10^{12}	3.5×10^{12}	2.5×10^{6}
1975	1 582 025	3.2×10^{12}	4.0×10^{12}	2.5×10^{6}
Beddington and Williams (1980)				
1952	3 750 001	7.9×10^{12}	9.9×10^{12}	2.6×10^{6}
1962	2 255 803	4.5×10^{12}	5.6×10^{12}	2.5×10^{6}
1972	1 183 175	2.5×10^{12}	3.1×10^{12}	2.6×10^{6}
1978	1 146 548	2.5×10^{12}	3.0×10^{12}	2.6×10^{6}

[a]Assuming ME = 0.80 GE.

Table 19.3 Production and gross efficiency estimates (%) for hypothetical, unexploited harp seal populations of 1 million animals with stable age distributions, various mean ages at maturity and two mortality schedules.

	Production	Respiration	Production efficiency	Gross efficiency
1.	8.8×10^{10}	2.1×10^{12}	4.1	3.3
2.	8.7×10^{10}	2.1×10^{12}	4.1	3.3
3.	8.7×10^{10}	2.1×10^{12}	4.0	3.2
4.	9.2×10^{10}	2.0×10^{12}	4.4	3.5
5.	9.1×10^{10}	2.0×10^{10}	4.3	3.4
6.	9.0×10^{10}	2.0×10^{10}	4.3	3.4

1. $M = 0.10$; MAM = 4.5 years; $f = 100\%$ (population 7, Table 19.1).
2. $M = 0.10$; MAM = 5.1 years; $f = 100\%$ (population 9, Table 19.1).
3. $M = 0.10$; MAM = 5.5 years; $f = 100\%$ (population 11, Table 19.1).

4. $M = $ var; MAM = 4.5 years; $f = 100\%$ (population 19, Table 19.1).
5. $M = $ var; MAM = 5.1 years; $f = 100\%$ (population 21, Table 19.1).
6. $M = $ var; MAM = 5.5 years; $f = 100\%$ (population 23, Table 19.1).

Table 19.4 Estimates of production efficiencies and gross efficiencies for exploited harp seal stocks of varying sizes given in Winters (1978).

	Production	Respiration	Production efficiency	Gross efficiency[a]
1.	3.7×10^{11}	5.9×10^{12}	5.9	5.2
2.	2.5×10^{11}	4.0×10^{12}	6.9	4.9
3.	1.6×10^{11}	2.7×10^{12}	5.4	4.6
4.	1.9×10^{11}	3.1×10^{12}	5.7	4.8
5.	2.0×10^{11}	3.3×10^{12}	5.7	4.7

[a]Gross energy for each population given in Table 19.2.

by the seal population (e.g. Anonymous 1976, 1979, 1982a, Cowley 1982, Lavigne 1982b). The present analysis suggests that *per capita* energy requirements for exploited populations range from about 2.3×10^6 to 2.6×10^6 kcal per year (see Table 19.2). If it is assumed that harp seal food has the average caloric density of biological tissues (2 kcal/g, Odum 1971), the range of energy requirements translates into 1.2–1.3 tonnes of food per average seal per year. Such calculations should not, however, be taken very seriously. The caloric density of food depends on the prey species consumed, and since caloric density of prey may vary with location and season (Lavigne *et al.* 1982a), it is also necessary to know when and where a particular prey item was consumed.

Harp seals are generally considered to be opportunistic feeders, consuming a variety of fish and invertebrate species (Sergeant 1973a, 1976, Beddington & Williams 1980, Lavigne *et al.* 1982a; see also Ch. 9). Species composition of the diet changes with age, season, and geographical location, and is not well documented in quantitative terms (Lavigne *et al.* 1982a, see also Ch. 9).

Therefore, in the absence of good data, we can only begin to establish possible limits for total biomass of food consumed by north-west Atlantic harp seals. Assume, for example, that harp seals consume a diet of fish with a caloric density as high as 2.6 kcal/g (Table 19.5), where approximately 88% of GE is realised as ME (Keiver 1982) – rather than the 80% used throughout our previous calculations. Under these circumstances, annual *per capita* energy requirements would translate into 0.80–0.91 tonnes of food per year. If, at the other extreme, harp seals consumed a diet of invertebrates with a caloric density of 1.2 kcal/g (Table 19.6), where approximately 60% of GE is realised as ME (Keiver 1982), then *per capita* requirements would increase to between 2.6 and 2.9 tonnes of food. Mixed diets involving both fish and invertebrates of varying caloric densities and digestibilities would yield intermediate estimates of the biomass of food consumed (Table 19.7).

Most statements about food consumption by north-west Atlantic harp seals can be traced to Sergeant's (1973a) initial (and, admittedly, 'crude') estimate. He assumed that immature and adult harp seals required 5 kg of food per day (caloric density not specified), and, allowing for fasting periods, estimated annual *per capita* consumption at 1.5 tonnes – well within our limits. By simple multiplication, Sergeant went on to estimate that a population of 1.33 million harp seals would consume about 2 million tonnes of food per year.

The close correspondence between Sergeant's (1973) estimate and our own range of estimates may, however, be quite coincidental. Indeed, Sergeant later (1976) revised his initial estimate in light of Boulva's (1973) observation that seals in captivity had a daily

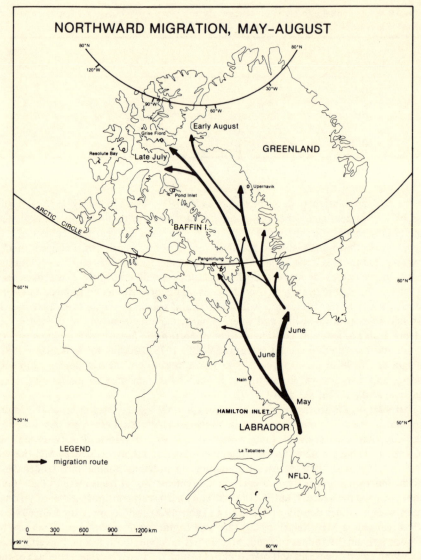

Figure 19.2 Approximate timing and location of northward migration of north-west Atlantic harp seals. (After Sergeant 1965, Beddington & Williams 1980.)

feeding rate of about 3% of body weight per day, in contrast to the 5% estimated previously. Changing this one assumption reduced the estimate of annual population food consumption by a population of 1.33 million animals to 1.2 million tonnes, an average *per capita* rate of 0.90 tonnes per year, or near the lower limit of our range of estimates.

Sergeant (1973a) took the analysis one step further, and attempted to partition annual food consumption into various types of prey. He used frequency of occurrence of different food items in harp seal stomachs to suggest that fish constituted about 60%

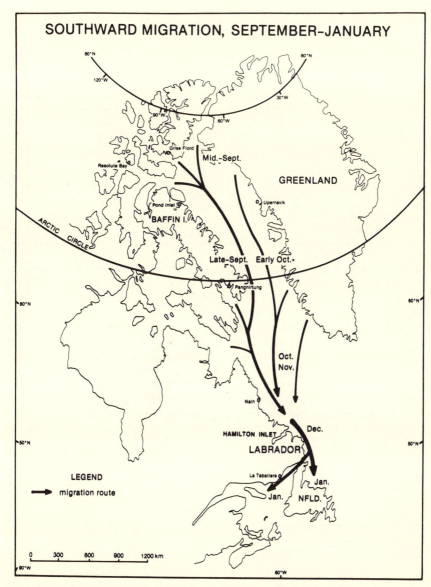

Figure 19.3 Approximate timing and location of southward migration of north-west Atlantic harp seals. (After Sergeant 1965, Beddington & Williams 1980.)

of the diet (25% of the diet was considered to be capelin); the remaining 40% was comprised of various invertebrates. Again, by simple multiplication, these figures suggest that a harp seal population of 1.33 million animals would consume 500 000 tonnes (Sergeant 1973a) or 300 000 tonnes (Sergeant 1976) of capelin annually. Such estimates may be erroneous for a variety of reasons. Most importantly, measurements of frequency of occurrence only indicate that a food item was consumed, but provide little information on its relative contribution to the diet in energy terms (Lavigne *et al.*

Table 19.5 Seasonal changes in caloric density and proximate compostions in capelin (*Mallotus villosus*), assuming 9.4 kcal/g for fat and 4.5 kcal/g for fat-free solids (from Jangaard 1974).

Month	Fat (%)	Fat-free solids (%)	Water (%)	Caloric density kcal/g
January	20	16	64	2.60
February	16	16	68	2.22
March	12	16	72	1.85
April	8	16	76	1.47
May	6	16	78	1.28
June/July	2	16	82	0.91
August	10	16	74	1.66
September	18	16	66	2.41
October–December	22	16	62	2.79

1982a). In the absence of adequate data to partition food consumed throughout the year among various prey species (Lavigne *et al*. 1982a, see also Ch. 9), it is not feasible to produce estimates of capelin (or any other prey species) consumption by north-west Atlantic harp seals.

As an alternative approach to the question of interactions between harp seals and commercial fisheries, it is possible to estimate the amount of food required by harp seals to meet their energetic requirements in different parts of their range. For convenience, we used Hamilton Inlet (Figs. 19.2 & 19.3) to divide the harp seal year temporally, geographically, and in relation to major commercial fisheries. Harp seals are usually found north of Hamilton Inlet from June to November; they migrate south in the autumn and spend the months of December to May in the Gulf of St Lawrence and off Newfoundland–Labrador (Sergeant 1965), where most traditional commercial fisheries in the north-west Atlantic occur (Scarratt 1982).

Table 19.6 Caloric densities for a variety of fish and invertebrate prey species of harp seals.

Species	Caloric density		References
fish			
Herring (*Clupea harengus*)	April	0.9	1,2
	December	2.9	
arctic cod (*Boreogadus saida*)	August	1.3	3
polar cod (*Arctogadus glacialis*)	August	1.1	3
Atlantic cod (*Gadus morhua*)	0.8–1.1		4,5
invertebrates			
Parathemisto	August	1.2	3
Mysis	August	1.1	3,6,7
Pandalus	All year	1.3	6,7

References: 1. Stoddard (1968). 2. Hodder *et al*. (1973). 3. Finley and Gibb in press. 4. Altman and Dittmer (1968). 5. Geraci (1975). 6. Tyler (1973). 7. Cummins and Wuycheck (1971).

Table 19.7 Changes in *per capita* food consumption (biomass in tonnes) of harp seal populations with changes in the proportion of the diet (i.e. energy requirements) comprising fish (caloric density, 2.6 kcal/g; ME = 0.88 GE) and invertebrates (caloric density, 1.2 kcal/g; ME = 0.60 GE). These calculations are based on a *per capita* ME requirement of 2.0×10^6 kcal per year.[a]

| Fish : Invertebrate | Biomass (tonnes) consumed per year | | |
	Fish	Invertebrates	Total
100 : 0	0.9	0	0.9
75 : 25	0.7	0.7	1.4
60 : 40	0.5	1.1	1.6
50 : 50	0.4	1.4	1.8
40 : 60	0.3	1.7	2.0
25 : 75	0.2	2.1	2.3
0 : 100	0	2.8	2.8

[a]Back-calculated from estimated *per capita* GE requirements of 2.5×10^6 kcal per year (Table 19.2), i.e. $0.80 \times (2.5 \times 10^6) = 2.0 \times 10^6$ kcal per year.

Our model suggests that exploited harp seal populations require 54% of their energy north of Hamilton Inlet and 46% in the south. Most of this difference can be attributed to the fact that harp seals do not eat continuously during the spring (Sergeant 1973a). Adult harp seals generally fast during the nursing season and the annual moult (Sergeant 1973a, Stewart & Lavigne 1984), and pups rely on stored energy for as long as 6 weeks after weaning (Worthy & Lavigne 1983a).

Based on the above estimates of *per capita* energy requirements, this suggests that an average harp seal requires between $1.1 \times 10^6 \times 1.2 \times 10^6$ kcal from the southern end of the annual migration or between 0.55 and 0.60 tonnes of food (again assuming an average caloric density of food of 2 kcal/g and ME = 0.80 GE). Since harp seals consume a variety of prey species in these waters (Sergeant 1973a, Lavigne *et a.* 1982a, see also Ch. 9), it seems that Sergeant (1973a, 1976) may have overestimated the amount of capelin consumed by north-west Atlantic harp seals.

In northern waters, harp seals appear to depend to a large extent on arctic cod, and to a lesser extent on largely unexploited capelin off West Greenland (Kapel 1973, Finley & Gibb in press, see also Ch. 9). In addition, they consume a variety of invertebrates, most of which are also unexploited. Consequently, competition between harp seals and man in these arctic and subarctic waters is not generally perceived to be a problem. However, if the pattern of commercial fisheries in the north-west Atlantic proceeds along current trends, shifting from one species to another and percolating downwards through the trophic web (Horwood 1981), numerous areas exist for conflict in the future. For example, the development of shrimp fisheries throughout the north-west Atlantic, including West Greenland, Hudson Strait, and the Gulf of St Lawrence (Stewart 1979, Dupuoy *et al.* 1981, Kanneworff 1981, Atkinson *et al*, 1982, Parsons *et al.* 1982), adds another prey species of the harp seal to the list of potential conflicts (Lavigne *et al.* 1982a).

In most discussions of harp seal–fishery conflicts it is usually assumed that the feeding behaviour of the seals is having an adverse effect on fishery yields. At present, however, there is no evidence that harp seals are affecting fishery yields or that a reduction in their numbers would result in increased yields (Anonymous 1981a, 1981b). On the other hand, some concern has been expressed that over-fishing prey species may adversely affect harp seal populations (FAO 1979, Lavigne 1979, 1982b). Indeed, harp seals in the north-west Atlantic have been characterised by reduced energy (blubber) stores and decreased condition since 1978, a change initially observed between 1976 and 1978 which was correlated with the precipitous decline in capelin catches (Lavigne 1979, 1982b, Stewart & Lavigne 1984, see also Ch. 9).

Another perception that colours discussions of harp seal–fishery interactions originates from Sergeant's (1973a) conclusion that: 'Harp seals (as perhaps other sea mammals) are ... inefficient converters of fish flesh.' His estimate of the ratio of production to ingestion (often called gross efficiency of yield to ingestion – Wiegert 1964, Lavigne *et al*. 1982a) was 0.5%. Parsons (1977) later revised this figure upwards to 1.76% by using energy values rather than biomass estimates in the calculation. In our subsequent analysis (Lavigne *et al*. 1982a), we obtained estimates of gross efficiency ranging from 1.92% to 4.94%, with a mean of 3.9%. Our current estimates, based on considerably more empirical data, produced revised figures of 3.2–5.2% (see Tables 19.3 & 19.4). All estimates, except Sergeant's (1973a), are consistent with published results for other seals (Parsons 1977, Lavigne *et al*. 1982a), other mammals (Steele 1974) and homoiotherms generally (Turner 1970).

To investigate ecological efficiencies of harp seals further, we also calculated production efficiencies (production/assimilation) from the outputs of our model. These ranged from 4.0% to 4.4% for unexploited populations (see Table 19.3), increasing to 5.4–6.0% in a variety of exploited populations (see Table 19.4), as might be expected in a population with density-dependent feedback responses. Again, these values are entirely consistent with results from other homoiotherms (Humphreys 1979, May 1979). In conclusion, there is no evidence or justification for viewing harp seals (and, indeed, other sea mammals) as being less efficient than other mammals in converting food into usable energy.

The present analysis also suggests that the effects on *per capita* food consumption of density-dependent changes in population parameters have been grossly over-estimated. Winters (1975) estimated that an increase in harp seal numbers from approximately 1.3 million animals to 3.0 million (i.e. an increase of more than 100%) would result in an increase in population food consumption of less than 50%, implying a marked change in *per capita* consumption. In contrast, we found that changes in growth rates of individual animals (Innes *et al*. 1981), mean age of maturity, and fertility, associated with changes in population size over the last 30 years (Bowen *et al*. 1981), had only minor effects on *per capita* consumption. For example, a change in population size from 1.4 million to 3.0 million animals (see Table 19.2, Winters' 1972 and 1952 populations) resulted in a decline in *per capita* consumption of ≈8%. Such changes in *per capita* consumption depend very much on the age structure of the population, e.g. a change in population size from 1.4 million to 2.8 million animals (see Table 19.2, Lett and Benjaminsen's 1972 and 1952 populations) resulted in a change in *per capita* consumption of only approximately 1%. In retrospect, this result is consistent with analyses presented by Innes *et al*. (1981). Only small changes in *per capita* food consumption were necessary to account for changes in growth rates which would correspond to a 2-year decline in mean age at maturity.

Just as there are serious limitations in available stomach content data required to estimate directly food consumption by north-west Atlantic harp seals, there are also numerous deficiencies in available data for estimating population food consumption indirectly from a knowledge of individual energy requirements. In particular, estimates of population energy requirements, using the approach outlined here, will only be as accurate as the estimates of population size and numbers-at-age. Even today, estimates of abundance for the well-studied north-west Atlantic harp seal population are plagued with considerable uncertainty (Anonymous 1982b, 1982c).

Another parameter which is not well known, and to which the output of the model is particularly sensitive, is the time–activity budget of harp seals of different sex, age, and size, in relation to season and location. We assumed that harp seals remain active for 18 h per day, swimming at an average speed of 1 m/s. It would seem that only detailed telemetry studies of harp seals at various locations throughout the year, particularly in arctic waters, will yield the necessary data to improve this aspect of our calculations. Similarly, more data are required on weight loss of male harp seals during the fasts preceding mating and during the annual moult, and on the percentage of gross energy ingested which is realised as metabolisable energy for the range of prey species (and associated caloric densities) which are consumed by harp seals.

On the positive side, our first attempt to construct an energy budget for north-west Atlantic harp seals (Lavigne *et al.* 1982a) required many more assumptions and extrapolations, in the absence of empirical data, than the analysis presented here. Many new data have been collected in the intervening years, and, in many cases, our first approximations (in some cases 'educated guesses') were vindicated. In view of the similarities in energy budgets which exist among mammals (Lavigne 1982a), such an approach may be the only way we can even begin to answer questions and to generate testable hypotheses about food consumption of marine mammals and how these may relate to the entire question of marine mammal–fishery interactions.

Acknowledgements

Financial support for this analysis was provided by the International Fund for Animal Welfare and the Natural Sciences and Engineering Research Council, Ottawa. We particularly thank S. Best for his interest and support. J. Harwood asked appropriate questions about the magnitude of density-dependent changes in food consumption discussed in Innes *et al.* (1981); the answers to his questions are reflected in the present discussion. B. E. Webb produced the figures. We thank J. Harwood, K. M. Kovacs, D. J. Murie, E. G. Nancekivell and O. J. Schmitz for critically reviewing the MS.

References

Altman, P. L. and D. S. Dittmer 1968. *Metabolism*. Biological Handbook. Bethesda, Maryland: Federation of American Societies for Experimental Biology.

Anonymous 1976. *Report of scientific advisors to Panel A (seals)*. ICNAF Summ. Doc. 76/XII/47.

Anonymous 1979. *Growing seal population seen as threat to world fish supply*. Press Release. Government of Newfoundland and Labrador. New York City, 9 January 1979.

Anonymous 1981a. *Report of IUCN workshop on marine mammal/fishery interactions, La Jolla, California, 30 March–2 April 1981*. Gland, Switzerland: International Union for the Conservation of Nature and Natural Resources.

Anonymous 1981b. *Report of special meeting of Scientific Council, Northwest Atlantic Fisheries Organization, 23–26 November 1981, Dartmouth, Canada*. NAFO SCS Doc. 81/XI/29.

Anonymous 1982a. [Canadian Government comments on] *Proposal of Committee on the Environment, Public Health, and Consumer Protection for a ban on trade in sealskins*. Ottawa: Canadian Government.

Anonymous 1982b. *Recommendations and status reports on harp and hooded seals – revision of the 1981 report EUR 7317 EN*. London: Nature Conservancy Council of Great Britain.

Anonymous 1982c. *Report on the meeting of the ad hoc working group on assessment of harp and hooded seals in the Northwest Atlantic*. ICES C.M. 1982/N:22.

Ashwell-Erikson, S. and R. Elsner 1981. The energy cost of free existence for Bering Sea harbor and spotted seals. In *The eastern Bering Sea shelf: oceanography and resources*, Vol. 2, D. W. Hood and J. A. Calder (eds), 869–99. Seattle, Washington: Office of Marine Pollution Assessment, NOAA, University of Washington Press.

Atkinson, D. B., W. R. Bowering, D. G. Parsons, S. A. Horsted and J. P. Minet 1982. A review of the biology and fisheries for roundnose grenadier, Greenland halibut and northern shrimp in Davis Strait. *NAFO Sci. Coun. Studies* **3**, 7–27.

Bartholomew, G. A. 1970. A model for the evolution of pinniped polygyny. *Evolution* **24** 546–59.

Beddington, J. R. and H. A. Williams 1980. *The status and management of the harp seal in the North-west Atlantic. A review and evaluation*. US Marine Mammal Commission Report No. MMC-79/03. Springfield, VA: National Technical Information Service.

Boulva, J. 1973. The harbour seal, *Phoca vitulina concolon*, in eastern Canada. PhD Thesis. Dalhousie University, Halifax, Nova Scotia.

Bowen, W. D. 1982. Age structure of Northwest Atlantic harp seal catches, 1952–1980. *NAFO Sci. Coun. Studies* **3**, 53–65.

Bowen, W. D., C. K. Capstick and D. E. Sergeant 1981. Temporal changes in the reproductive potential of female harp seals (*Pagophilus groenlandicus*). *Can. J. Fish. Aquat. Sci.* **38**, 495–503.

Capstick, C. K., D. M. Lavigne and K. Ronald 1976. *Population forecasts for Northwest Atlantic harp seals, Pagophilus groenlandicus*. ICNAF Res. Doc. 76/X/132.

Caughley, G. 1966. Mortality patterns in mammals. *Ecology* **47**, 906–18.

Cowley, G. 1982. Information. Public Affairs Information, Canadian High Commission, Canada House, UK. 25 March 1982.

Cummins, K. W. and J. C. Wuycheck 1971. Caloric equivalents for investigations in ecological energetics. *Commun. Inst. Assoc. Theor. Appl. Limnol.* **18**.

Dupuoy, H., J. P. Minet and P. Derible 1981. *Catch, effort and biological characteristics of shrimp (Pandalus borealis) in the French fishery off West Greenland, 1981*. NAFO SCR Doc. 81/XI/147.

FAO (Food and Agriculture Organization). 1978. Mammals in the sea, Vol. I. *Report of the FAO ACMRR working party on marine mammals*. FAO Fisheries Ser. 5.

FAO (Food and Agriculture Organization). 1979. Mammals in the sea, Vol. II. *Pinniped species summaries and report on sirenians*. FAO Fisheries Ser. 5, 153 p.

Fedak, M. A., S. S. Anderson and J. Harwood 1981. *The energetics of the grey seal (Halichoerus grypus) in European waters: energy flow and management implications*. Final Rep. to the European Communities on contract ENV 405-80-UK (B).

Finley, K. J. and E. J. Gibb in press. Summer diet and feeding behaviour of harp seals in the Canadian high arctic. In *The harp seal. Perspectives in vertebrate science*, D. M. Lavigne, K. Ronald and R. E. A. Stewart (eds.). The Hague: W. Junk.

Gallivan, G. J. in press. Metabolism. In *The harp seal. Perspectives in vertebrate science*, D. M. Lavigne, K. Ronald and R. E. A. Stewart (eds.), The Hague: W. Junk.

Gallivan, G. J. and K. Ronald 1979. Temperature regulation in freely diving harp seals (*Phoca groenlandica*). *Can. J. Zool.* **57**, 2256–63.

Gallivan, G. J. and K. Ronald 1981. Apparent specific dynamic action in the harp seal (*Phoca groenlandica*). *Comp. Biochem. Physiol.* **69A**, 579–81.

Geraci, J. R. 1975. Pinniped nutrition. *Rapp. P.-v. Reun. Cons. Int. Explor. Mer.* **169**, 312–23.

Hodder, V. M., L. S. Parsons, G. H. Winters and K. Spencer 1973. Fat and water content of herring in Newfoundland and adjacent waters, 1966–1971. *Fish. Res. Bd Can. Tech. Rep.* **365**.

Horwood, J. W. 1981. Management models of marine multispecies complexes. In *Dynamics of large mammal populations*, C. W. Fowler and T. D. Smith (eds), 339–60. New York: Wiley.

Humphreys, W. F. 1979. Production and respiration in animal populations. *J. Anim. Ecol.* **48**, 427–53.

Innes, S. and K. Ronald 1981a. *Preliminary estimates of the cost of locomotion in phocid seals.* ICES C.M. 1981/N:13.

Innes, S. and K. Ronald 1981b. *Preliminary estimates of the cost of swimming in three species of phocid seal.* 4th Biennial Conference on the Biology of Marine Mammals, 14–18 December, 1981, San Francisco, California.

Innes, S., R. E. A. Stewart and D. M. Lavigne 1981. Growth in Northwest Atlantic harp seals *Phoca groenlandica. J. Zool., Lond.* **194**, 11–24.

Jangaard, P. M. 1974. The capelin (*Mallotus villosus*). Biology, exploitation, utilization and composition. *Fish. Res. Bd Can. Bull.* **186**, 1–70.

Kanneworff, P. 1981. *Biomass of shrimp (Pandalus borealis) in NAFO subarea 1 in 1978–81 estimated by means of bottom photography.* NAFO SCR Doc. 81/XI/155.

Kapel, F. O. 1973. *Some second hand reports on the food of harp seals in West Greenland waters.* ICES C.M. 1973/N:8.

Keiver, K. M. 1982. Apparent digestible and metabolizable energy in harp seals (*Phoca groenlandica.* MSc Thesis. The University of Guelph, Guelph, Ontario.

Keiver, K. M. and K. Ronald 1981. *Digestible energy in harp seals.* ICES C.M. 1981/N:4

Kendeigh, S. C., V. R. Dol'nik and V. M. Gavrilov 1977. Avian energetics. In *Granivorous birds in ecosystems*, J. Pinowski and S. C. Kendeigh (eds), Cambridge: 127–204: Cambridge University Press.

Kleiber, M. 1975. *The fire of life*, 2nd edn. New York: Wiley.

Krebs, J. R. and N. B. Davies 1981. *An introduction to behavioural ecology.* Sunderland, Mass: Sinauer.

Lavigne, D. M. 1979. Management of seals in the Northwest Altantic Ocean. *Trans. N. Am. Wildl. and Natural Resource Conf.* **44**, 488–97.

Lavigne, D. M. 1982a. Similarity of energy budgets of animal populations. *J. Anim. Ecol.* **51**, 195–206.

Lavigne, D. M. 1982b. Marine mammal/fishery interactions: A report from an IUCN workshop. *Trans. N. Am. Wildl. and Natural Resource Conf.* **47**, 312–21.

Lavigne, D. M., W. W. Barchard, S. Innes and N. A. Øritsland 1982a. Pinniped bioenergetics. In Mammals in the seas. Vol. IV. *Small cetaceans, seals, sirenians and otters*, 191–235. FAO Fisheries Ser. 5. Rome.

Lavigne, D. M. and R. E. A. Stewart, 1979. Energy content of harp seal placentas. *J. Mammal.* **60**, 854–6.

Lavigne, D. M., R. E. A. Stewart and F. Fletcher 1982b. Changes in composition and energy content of harp seal milk during lactation. *Physiol. Zool.* **55**, 1–9.

Lett, P. F. and T. Benjaminsen 1977. A stochastic model for the management of the Northwest Atlantic harp seal (*Pagophilus groenlandicus*) population. *Can. J. Zool.* **34**, 1155–87.

May, R. M. 1979. Production and respiration in animal communities. *Nature (Lond.)* **282**, 443–44.

National Research Council 1981. *Nutritional energetics of domestic animals and glossary of energy terms.* Washington, DC: National Academy Press.

Odum, E. P. 1971. *Fundamentals of ecology.* Philadelphia: W. B. Saunders.

Parsons, D. G., G. E. Tucker and P. J. Veitch 1982. *An update of the assessment of shrimp (Pandalus borealis) stocks off Labrador.* CAFSAC Res. Doc. 82/10.

Parsons, J. L. 1977. Metabolic studies on ringed seals (*Phoca hispida*). MSc Thesis, The University of Guelph, Guelph, Ontario.

Scarratt, D. J. (ed.) 1982. *Canadian Atlantic offshore fishery atlas.* Can. Spec. Publn Fish. Aquat. Sci. 47.

Sergeant, D. E. 1965. Migrations of harp seals, *Pagophilus groenlandicus* (Erxleben) in the Northwest Atlantic. *J. Fish. Res. Bd Can.* **22**, 433–64.

Sergeant, D. E. 1966. Reproductive rates of harp seals *Pagophilus groenlandicus* (Erxleben). *J. Fish. Res. Bd Can.* **23**, 757–66.

Sergeant, D. E. 1973a. Feeding, growth, and productivity of Northwest Atlantic harp seals (*Pagophilus groenlandicus*). *J. Fish. Res. Bd Can.* **30**, 17–29.

Sergeant, D. E. 1973b. Environment and reproduction in seals. *J. Reprod. Fert.*, Suppl. **19**, 555–61.

Sergeant, D. E. 1976. *The relationship between harp seals and fish populations*. ICNAF Res. Doc. 76/X/125.

Steele, J. H. 1974. *The structure of marine ecosystems*. Oxford: Blackwell Scientific.

Stewart, K. 1979. Exploratory shrimp survey off Northern Labrador. *Fish. & Oceans News* **4**, 7–8.

Stewart, R. E. A. 1983. Behavioural and energetic aspects of reproductive effort in female harp seals, *Phoca groenlandica*. PhD Thesis, The University of Guelph, Guelph, Ontario.

Stewart, R. E. A. and D. M. Lavigne 1980. Neonatal growth in Northwest Atlantic harp seals *Pagophilus groenlandicus*. *J. Mammal.* **61**, 670–80.

Stewart, R. E. A. and D. M. Lavigne 1984. Energy transfer and female condition in nursing harp seals *Phoca groenlandica*. *Holarctic Ecol.* **7**, 182–94.

Stewart, R. E. A., B. E. Webb, D. M. Lavigne and F. Fletcher 1983. Determining lactose content in harp seal milk. *Can. J. Zool.* **61**, 1094–1100.

Stirling, I. 1983. The evolution of mating systems in pinnipeds. In Advances in the study of mammalian behavior, J. F. Eisenberg and D. Kleiman (eds). *Spec. Publ. Amer. Soc. Mamm.* **7**, 489–527.

Stoddard, J. H. 1968. Fat contents of Canadian Atlantic herring. *Fish. Res. Bd Can. Tech. Rep.* **79**.

Turner, F. B. 1970. The ecological efficiency of consumer populations. *Ecology* **51**, 741–2.

Tyler, A. V. 1973. Caloric values of some North Atlantic invertebrates. *Mar. Biol.* **19**, 258–61.

Wiegert, R. G. 1964. Population energetics of meadow spittlebugs (*Philaenus spumarius* L.) as affected by migration and habitat. *Ecol. Monogr.* **34**, 217–41.

Winters, G. H. 1975. *Review of capelin ecology and estimation of surplus yield from predator dynamics*. ICNAF Res. Doc. 75/2.

Winters, G. H. 1978. Production, mortality, and sustainable yield of Northwest Atlantic harp seals (*Pagophilus groenlandicus*). *J. Fish. Res. Bd Can.* **35**, 1249–61.

Worthy, G. A. J. 1982. Energy sources of harp seals, *Phoca groenlandica*, during the post-weaning period. MSc Thesis, The University of Guelph, Guelph, Ontario.

Worthy, G. A. J. and D. M. Lavigne 1983a. Energetics of fasting and subsequent growth in weaned harp seal pups, *Phoca groenlandica*. *Can. J. Zool.* **61**, 447–56.

Worthy, G. A. J. and D. M. Lavigne 1983b. Changes in energy stores during neonatal development in the harp seal, *Phoca groenlandica*. J. Mammal. **64**, 89–96.

20 The effects of variation in population parameters on the energy requirements of a hypothetical grey seal population

A. R. Hiby and J. Harwood

Introduction

There has been some dispute in the literature over the effects of changes in the size of a marine mammal population on its *per capita* food or energy requirements. While Winters (1975) and Innes *et al*. (1981) predict that a large harp seal population will have a lower *per capita* requirement than a small one, Brodie and Påsche (1980) predict the opposite. All of these authors acknowledge the importance of age structure, *per capita* food availability, growth rate, size-dependent energy requirements, and the energy costs of locomotion, but the relative importance of these factors has never been evaluated. We have attempted to do so, using information on the population dynamics and energetics of British grey seals.

Population model

We have modelled only the female section of the population, because the costs of reproduction for male seals are relatively low (Fedak *et al*. 1981), and because females are likely to show more dramatic changes in reproductive rate and survival with variations in population size. The initial population model and parameter values used were those described by Harwood and Prime (1978) for a population increasing by 7% each year. We have made two important additions. Harwood and Prime (1978) grouped together all females over the age of 5 years because fecundity appeared to be constant above this age. However, females may continue to grow until they are at least 10 years old, and we extended the number of age-classes in the model to 17. Although Harwood and Prime (1978) found no evidence for a change in average age at maturity with increasing population size, such a relationship has been demonstrated for at least two other seal species. We have therefore derived, and incorporated in the model, a theoretical relationship between age at sexual maturity and individual growth rate (which will presumably be related to food availability – see Harwood *et al*. 1979), and this is described below.

Individual growth and energy requirements

We have analysed the relationship between age and total body length for 645 female grey seals shot in management culls or killed at fishing nets around the British coast over the last 20 years (SMRU unpublished data). A variety of growth curves provides an equally good fit to these data using non-linear least squares techniques. For convenience, we have chosen to use the Bertalanffy relationship:

$$l_t = L_\infty - (L_\infty - l_0)\exp(-Kt) \tag{20.1}$$

where l_t represents the length of an animal of age t. Although normally l_0 is the length of animal at birth, the Bertalanffy equation provides a poor description of growth during the first months of a grey seal's life, and in this case, it is simply a fitting parameter. l_∞, l_0 and K were estimated to be 1.83, 1.08 and 0.239 respectively. Laws (1959) suggested that the weight of a seal should be proportional to l^3, and this is known to be a good approximation for harp seals (Innes *et al.* 1981), and for ringed seals (Usher & Church 1969).

Measurements of the resting metabolic requirements of captive adult grey seals and pups (Fedak *et al.* 1981) indicate that pups have a rather higher requirement than adults (39.2 kcal/kg per day for pups compared with 34.6 kcal/kg per day for adults), and we have assumed that this difference represents the extra energy expenditure of a growing animal. The resting energy requirement (E_t) of an animal age t is thus made up of two components: a maintenance cost which is directly proportional to its weight (and therefore to l^3), and a growth cost which we assume to be proportional to the rate of change in body weight (i.e. to dl^3/dt). Thus:

$$E_t = a(l^3 + bdl^3/dt) \tag{20.2}$$

We are concerned here only with the relative energy requirements of animals of different ages, and the value of a is not needed. The value of b can be determined from the ratio of the energy requirements of pups to those of adults.

Using these relationships, it is possible to calculate the resting metabolic requirements of a female of any age. Energy requirements for all other activities are expressed as a simple multiple of this.

Annual energy budgets

There seems to be some measure of agreement that the average daily energy requirements for many mammals are about twice the resting requirement (see, for example, Table 8 of Lavigne *et al.* 1976), and we have taken this value as an estimate of the requirement for all seals for most of the year. However, grey seals spend about 2 weeks of every year moulting, when they feed little. Fedak *et al.* (1981) guess that their energy requirement at this time is only 20% higher than resting, and we have followed their example.

Direct measurements have indicated that the energy expenditure of a lactating female is about six times her resting requirement (Fedak *et al.* 1981). In addition, breeding females have to move considerable distances to reach their chosen breeding sites. We have assumed that the additional cost of this activity is equivalent to twice the resting requirement for the 2 weeks prior to the breeding season.

These measurements and assumptions can be combined to provide an estimate of the average daily energy requirements of non-breeding and breeding females over the course of a year. Breeding animals require 17% more energy than non-breeders.

Age at sexual maturity

The average age at first pupping, and hence the average age at sexual maturity, of harp seals and crabeater seals (*Lobodon carcinophagus*) is known to have varied with population size. Traditionally, these changes have been attributed to a change in growth rate as a result of a change in food availability. This follows from Laws' (1959) hypothesis that seals become sexually mature when they reach a fixed proportion of their final body length, which is itself a constant for a particular species.

According to this hypothesis, the variation in age at sexual maturity is due to variation in individual growth rate. We have chosen to model this variation by replacing the constant K in Equation (20.1) by a random variable k, normally distributed with mean $\mu(\tilde{k})$ and variance $\sigma^2(\tilde{k})$ and thus we maintain the same initial and asymptotic lengths for all animals despite their differences in growth. The value of k necessary for an animal to become sexually mature at a particular age t', say k' is given by:

$$k' = \frac{1}{t'} \ln \frac{L_\infty - l_{mat}}{l_0 - l_{mat}} \tag{20.3}$$

where l_{mat} is the critical length for sexual maturity. Thus, the proportion of animals actually mature at t' is:

$$\int_{k'}^\infty N(\mu(\tilde{k}), \sigma^2(\tilde{k})) \, dk \tag{20.4}$$

The best fit to the available data on age at maturity for British grey seals, using the parameter values already estimated for Equation 20.1, occurs when l_{mat} is 1.59 m and the coefficient of variation for $\tilde{k}$ is 18.9%. The effects of variation in $\mu(\tilde{k})$ on the maturity ogive and on the mean age at sexual maturity are shown in Figures 20.1 and 20.2. We have assumed that once a female becomes sexually mature, she will exhibit a constant fecundity.

Calculation of energy requirements

The following standard population parameters were chosen: mean Bertalanffy growth parameter $\mu(\tilde{k}) = 0.239$, fecundity = 0.9, adult survival = 0.935, juvenile survival (from weaning to age 1) = 0.60. These give a population with a net rate of increase of 7% per annum. Each parameter was varied independently, holding all the other parameters at their standard values. For each combination of population parameters, the rate of increase of the population, its stable age structure immediately after the breeding season, the number of pregnant animals, and the weight distribution for each age-class were calculated. These values were then used to calculate the average *per capita* and per kilogram energy requirements of the population at that instant, and these were expressed as a percentage of the requirements of the standard population. Because the

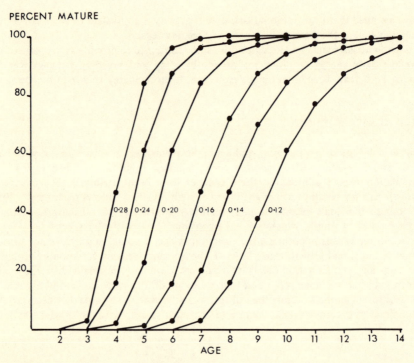

Figure 20.1 The effect of varying the Bertalanffy growth parameter K on the maturity ogive for a hypothetical grey seal population. The appropriate values of K are shown to the right of each curve.

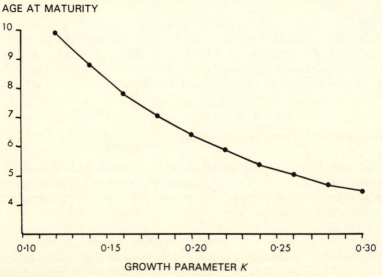

Figure 20.2 The relationship between mean age at sexual maturity and the mean value of the Bertalanffy growth parameter K for a hypothetical grey seal population.

survival rates for the different age-classes are very similar, the instantaneous energy requirement is a realistic approximation to the energy requirements of the population over the entire year.

Results

The effects of changes in individual population parameters on average *per capita* energy requirements and population rate of increase are shown in Figure 20.3. As survival

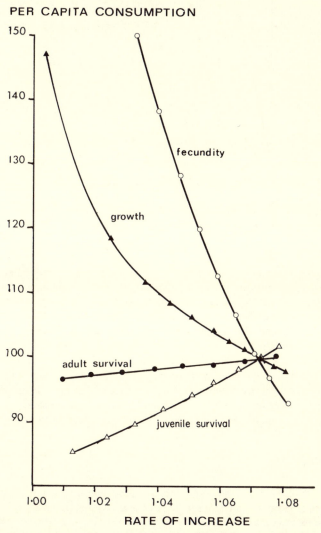

Figure 20.3 The effects of variation in individual population parameters on the rate of increase of the population and on average *per capita* energy requirements for a hypothetical grey seal population. Values are expressed as a percentage of the requirements of a population increasing by 7% per annum.

PER KILO CONSUMPTION

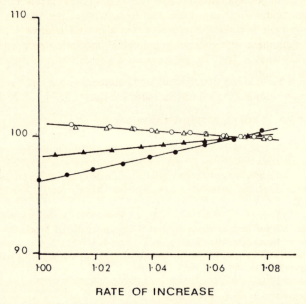

Figure 20.4 The affects of variation in individual population parameters on the per kilogram energy requirements of a hypothetical grey seal population. Values have been expressed as a percentage of the requirements for a population increasing by 7% per annum. (The symbols used are the same as in Figure 20.3.)

decreases from the standard value, the rate of increase of the population and the average energy requirement of its individuals, both decrease, though only slowly. On the other hand, although a decrease in fecundity or in the growth parameters (which is also equivalent to a decrease in the average fecundity of the population) also results in a decrease in the population's rate of increase, there is a considerable increase in *per capita* energy requirements.

These changes are almost entirely due to variations in the age and weight structure of the population. This can be seen from Figure 20.4, which shows the equivalent changes in the energy requirement per kilogram of seal and provides an indication of the effect of the costs of growth and reproduction on the overall energy requirements. Their effect is very small over the range of population parameters considered.

Conclusions

For a population with a stable age structure, food consumption is proportional to population size. However, a change in any of the individual parameters – whether for natural reasons or because of a cull – will change the age structure, and therefore the *per capita* consumption, of the population. In general, therefore, a knowledge of changes in population size alone is not sufficient for the reliable prediction of changes in food consumption.

The absolute levels of *per capita* requirement shown in Figure 20.3 should be interpreted with caution. They are derived for a population which has attained a stable age structure. Real populations of marine mammals may never reach this blessèd state because the individuals are long lived and because many populations are subject to erratic management policies. Nevertheless, the sign and relative magnitude of the changes in requirement with changes in individual population parameters do provide an indication of what is likely to happen when a population is in transition from one age structure to another.

References

Brodie, P. F. and A. J. Påshe 1980. *Density-dependent condition and energetics of marine mammals populations in multi-species fisheries management.* NAFO DOC 80/XI/166.

Fedak, M. A., S. S. Anderson and J. Harwood 1981. *The energetics of the grey seal in European waters: Energy flow and management implications.* Report to the EEC, Contract ENV 405-80-UK(B).

Harwood, J., A. Hiby, M. A. Fedak and C. H. Lockyer 1979. *Density dependent mechanisms in Northwest Atlantic harp seal populations.* IUCN International Workshop in Biology and Management of Northwest Atlantic harp seals. Paper HS/WP5.

Harwood, J. and J. H. Prime 1978. Some factors affecting the size of British grey seal populations. *J. appl. Ecol.* **15**, 401–11.

Innes, S., R. E. A. Stewart and D. M. Lavigne 1981. Growth in Northwest Atlantic harp seals, *Phoca groenlandica. J. Zool., Lond.* **194**, 11–24.

Lavigne, D. M., W. Barchard, S. Innes and N. A. Øritsland 1976. *Pinniped bioenergetics.* ACMRR/MM/SC/112. Scientific Consultation on Marine Mammals, Bergen, Norway.

Laws, R. M. 1959. Accelerated growth in seals with special reference to the Phocidae. *Norsk Hvalfangstitid* **48**, 42–55.

Usher, P. J. and M. Church 1969. On the relationship of weight, length, and girth of the ringed seal (*Pusa hispida*) of the Canadian Arctic. *Arctic* **22**, 120–29.

Winters, G. H. 1975. *Review of capelin ecology and estimation of surplus yield from predator dynamics.* ICNAF Res. Doc. 75/2.

Index

m.m. = marine mammals